Sociology of Death and the American Indian

Sociology of Death and the American Indian

Gerry R. Cox

Foreword by Neil Thompson

LEXINGTON BOOKS
Lanham • Boulder • New York • London

Published by Lexington Books
An imprint of The Rowman & Littlefield Publishing Group, Inc.
4501 Forbes Boulevard, Suite 200, Lanham, Maryland 20706
www.rowman.com

86-90 Paul Street, London EC2A 4NE

Parts of this manuscript appeared previously in Cox, Gerry R. 2015. *Sociology of the American Indian*. Lewiston, New York: Edwin Mellen Press. Used with permission. Parts of this manuscript appeared previously in Cox, Gerry R., and Ronald J. Fundis. 1993. "Native American Burial Practices." In *Personal Care in an Impersonal World: A Multidimensional Look at Bereavement*, edited by John D. Morgan, 191–203. Abingdon, Oxfordshire: Routledge. Used with permission.

British Library Cataloguing in Publication Information Available

Library of Congress Cataloging-in-Publication Data Available

Names: Cox, Gerry R., author.
Title: Sociology of death and the American Indian / Gerry R. Cox.
Description: Lanham : Lexington Books, [2022] | Includes bibliographical references
    and index. | Summary: "This book presents a sociological analysis of death and
    bereavement practices of American Indians with oral histories from select tribes
    describing their practices"—Provided by publisher.
Identifiers: LCCN 2022021670 (print) | LCCN 2022021671 (ebook) |
    ISBN 9781666908503 (cloth) | ISBN 9781666908527 (paperback) |
    ISBN 9781666908510 (epub)
Subjects: LCSH: Funeral rites and ceremonies—United States. | Indians of North
    America—Death. | Bereavement—United States. | Mourning customs—United States. |
    Indians of North America—Social life and customs.
Classification: LCC GT3203 .C69 2022 (print) | LCC GT3203 (ebook) |
    DDC 306.9—dc23/eng/20220527
LC record available at https://lccn.loc.gov/2022021670
LC ebook record available at https://lccn.loc.gov/2022021671

Raymond Pierson
Robert Duquaine
Don "Grubby" Daudelin
Rabbi Earl Grollman

Contents

Foreword by Neil Thompson ix

Preface xi

Acknowledgments xv

Introduction 1

**PART I: SOCIOLOGY OF DYING, DEATH,
AND THE AMERICAN INDIAN** **21**

  1 Sociology of Dying and Death 25

  2 Why a Sociology of Dying and Death? 35

  3 Sociology of the American Indian 45

  4 Burial and Mortuary Customs of American Indians 55

  5 Culture of American Indians 63

  6 American Indian Cultural Denigration 71

  7 Problems in Understanding Other Cultures 91

**PART II: SOCIOLOGY OF THE AMERICAN INDIAN
SPIRITUALITY, DYING, AND DEATH** **99**

  8 Sociology of American Indian Religion 101

  9 American Indian Religion and Death 113

  10 The Sacred Way and Loss: American Indian Spirituality 123

11 Death and Intimacy Impairment Later in Life   131

12 American Indian Grief: The Healing Path   149

**PART III: TRIBAL PRACTICES IN DYING, DEATH,
DISPOSAL, AND BEREAVEMENT**   **165**

13 Anasazi Disposal and Bereavement Practices   167

14 Aztec Disposal and Bereavement Practices   175

15 Maya Disposal and Bereavement Practices   181

16 Mounds Builders Disposal and Bereavement Practices   187

17 The Dine (Navajo) Disposal and Bereavement Practices   193

18 The Inde (Apache) and Tohono O'odham Disposal
        and Bereavement Practices   205

19 Hopi Disposal and Bereavement Practices   235

20 Lakota and Blackfeet Disposal and Bereavement Practices   243

21 Cheyenne, Shawnee, and the Potawatomi Disposal
        and Bereavement Practices   271

22 Ojibwe/Anishinabe/Chippewa, Shoshone, and
        Stockbridge-Munsee Disposal and Bereavement Practices   285

**PART IV: UNDERSTANDING THE SOCIOLOGY OF
DYING, DEATH, AND THE AMERICAN INDIAN**   **321**

23 Dying: What We Can Learn from American Indians   323

Conclusion   335

References   351

Index   365

About the Author   377

Foreword

by Neil Thompson

Issues relating to death, dying, and grief are generally examined in predominantly psychological terms, with a focus on the experience of the individual. Important though these psychological factors are, they tell only part of the story. This is because death, dying, and grief arise in a social context and that context will be highly significant in shaping how such phenomena are experienced by individuals, groups, and whole communities. Psychological perspectives therefore need to be counterbalanced by sociological understandings.

Dr. Gerry Cox has played an important role in putting a sociological perspective on death on the agenda for scholars, policy makers, and health and human services practitioners through his teaching and publications. This book is a very welcome addition to his impressive list of contributions.

What this book also offers more specifically, though, is a helpful analysis of death and related matters within a particular cultural and geopolitical context, namely, that of the American Indian. Combining a lifetime of academic study with insights from his own personal ancestry, Dr. Cox provides a rich and fascinating account of death in the world of American Indians.

History teaches us that the "discovery" of the "New World" led to explorations by Europeans that quickly became exploitations. The story of the treatment of the indigenous people of the Americas by the European settlers is not a happy one in many ways. There is clearly much to be regretted in terms of discriminatory exclusion, marginalization, dispossession, and worse.

However, as Dr. Cox admirably illustrates, it is also a story of survival, resilience, and, in some respects, flourishing. Grossly misleading stereotypical images and narratives of American Indians (and, indeed, aboriginal groups, more broadly) are, of course, part of the popular consciousness. This book helps to challenge some of these by providing a fuller, more accurate and more realistic characterization of American Indian life and, particularly, American Indian death.

Part of the history of European settlement in the Americas is a discourse of "civilizing the savages," but, of course, a closer look at that history and the atrocities involved leads us to wonder who were the civilized ones and who were the savages. This reflects a common theme in the study of racism, where cultural differences are translated into cultural deficits. "My culture is different from yours" readily becomes "my culture is superior to yours." Replacing my culture with yours then comes to be seen as the way forward, as was tragically the case here.

Survival and resilience are therefore key themes in the study of the American Indian world, and these are well captured in this book. Its focus on death and dying helps to paint a very human picture, one that shows how loss and grief can bring people together as well as set us apart. It offers a sound foundation for understanding complex issues, and, in doing so, enlightens us all about an important group of people who are so often marginalized and an important topic that is also prone to being marginalized much of the time.

There is much to be learned from what this book has to offer. Dr. Cox deserves considerable credit for providing such a helpful account of this intriguing field of study. It will no doubt be of value to people involved in the death, dying, and bereavement field who want to know about American Indian perspectives and, likewise, people studying American Indian life who want to learn about how death is understood and managed within that context. Both groups will find much of interest within these pages.

Preface

Like all people, death has been a presence in my life. Because I had aunts and uncles who had children who were older than my parents, in my youth, I attended many funerals for cousins, aunts, uncles, grandparents, and friends of my older relatives. Every year of my life someone that I cared about has died. From relatives, close friends, classmates, teammates, teachers, coaches, heroes, people who touched my life, Cheryl (Cox) Manlove, Paul Desotelle, Carl Green, Carl Anderson, James Dean, Ray Nitschke, Reggie White, Jim Clark, Bill Hammer and other friends who died in Viet Nam, Gus Grissom, John Kennedy and later Bobby Kennedy, Leo Mench, Dean Wright, Don Green, Doug Strong, Christopher O'Shea, Christopher Taylor, Don Taylor, Don Douglas, Father David Douglas, Father Robert Gerth, Father Joseph Kelly, William Osborn, Father George Loner, Monsignor Emile A. Schweier, Ron Barrett, Phyllis Schmidt, Matthew Stewart, Stephen Gay, Dave Autry, Kenny Burke, Don "Grubby" Daudelin, Rabbi Earl Grollman, Robert Fulton, Jack Morgan, all the members of my family, and many others in accidents, illness, or natural causes who were close to me who have died. I apologize for listing many who will not be known to the readers, but I specifically wanted to acknowledge the impact of their death upon me.

As a first-year teacher in 1965–1966, I had to tell a fifth-grader that his thirty-nine-year-old father had died. His father was also a friend and role model for me, and it was a major loss for his wife and ten children including one child under age one. I struggled to know how to tell him that his father had died and with how to attend to his grief during the rest of the school year. In my helplessness, I searched for better ways to help my students. This lack of knowledge led to me writing my master's thesis in 1966 and later my PhD dissertation in 1975 on attitudes toward dying and death. I have spent my career trying to learn about death, grief, and bereavement. Teaching the

Sociology of Death and Dying since 1970, I have dealt with my own grief while sharing my knowledge with students. Many of my American Indian students and so many from other cultures have shared with me about their views on dying, grief, and bereavement. It has been a great honor to share what I have learned from my students, my mentors, the dying, and the grieving that I have had the pleasure to serve during my career. This book is an attempt to share some of what I have learned over the years.

There are many paths to knowledge and understanding. I would like to share some of my understanding of American Indian practices regarding dying and death. We can learn from other cultures. While I will not share specific rituals and practices that are sacred and are not to be shared with those who are not members of the clan or group that practices them, I will share a view of dying and death that might allow people of other faiths, practices, and cultures to enrich their own view of dying and death. I am not encouraging non-American Indians to adopt cultural practices that are not their own. Wannabe American Indians have done enough damage. Anglo-Europeans can benefit and learn from the traditions of American Indians, but they can never truly understand or know those traditions.

The traditions are complex, deep, rich, and based on rigor filled with hope. The traditions lead to sacrifice rather than escape from life. I also am not doing an archaeological or anthropological analysis. As learning a foreign language gives one greater appreciation and better understanding of one's own language, learning about the practices of other groups should help one's understanding of one's own practices. My hope is to show that while the Anglo-European culture basically tried to destroy the American Indian way of life, that had they not be so quick to destroy the rich cultures and way of life that they might have learned the beauty and growth that comes from a positive way of life that cultural sharing would have enriched both cultures. American Indians have experienced loss of way of life, land, language, culture, and been oppressed, but in spite of all of the losses, American Indians have adapted and survived. The considerable loss and grief that American Indians have experienced over the centuries make them a rich source of resilience and survival in the face of dying, death, and bereavement. The history of injustice makes many American Indians wary of sharing with researchers.

While many would view the ideas of American Indians as not being equal to Western and Eastern ideas of the world, my hope is that the reader will come to understand what can be gained from studying American Indian ideas and philosophies. Given the oppression, the disadvantaged status, and the exploitation, the fact that American Indians and their philosophy have survived should make them worth studying. I apologize to any elders that might be offended by what I say. I have asked some to read and correct my writings and to eliminate anything that should not be shared.

It is my hope that my inaccuracies, incomplete descriptions, and ineptitude will inspire those with more knowledge to preserve what will surely be lost if they do not respond and explain what I have not been able to explain. The wisdom of the elders will be lost if it is left entirely to the oral traditions. I have forgotten most of what I have been told. I only wish that I had spent my years recording and remembering what I was taught with more zeal and concern for the children of the future. As the transcriptions of oral histories that I have included will show, many regretted not listening more closely to their elders as well.

Acknowledgments

I cannot separate my yesterday from today. Long before I began to put together this book, I began asking people questions, learning their ways, their histories, and their way of life. For many years, people have shared with me their experiences, their inner thoughts, and their spirituality. All research and writing are the result of sharing with others who serve as sources of inspiration, support, guidance, and assistance. In writing this book, I have relied upon the community that has sustained me throughout my life.

First and foremost, I would like to thank my family, my wife, Linda Diane Cox; my parents, Alva and Thelma Gene Cox; my children Christopher Cox, Andrea Sullivan, Kelly Huggins, Gregory Cox, and Theresa Motes; their spouses Patricia Mendosa Cox, James Sullivan, Jason Huggins, and Dustin Motes; and their children Isaac Motes, John Sullivan, Elanor Sullivan, Olivia Motes, Finley Huggins, Alaina Motes, Eamon Sullivan, Declan Huggins, Conner Sullivan, and Gaston Mendosa Cox; my sisters Terry Desotelle, Tonia Armstrong, Cheryl Manlove, and Melissa Wilmoth; and my brother Thomas Cox and their spouses, Paul Desotelle, Gary Wilmoth, and Sheri Cox. I have many wonderful aunts and uncles, cousins, in-laws, and relatives including many that I never met who have impacted my life. I thank all of my ancestors who helped mold me.

I would like to acknowledge the support and help in preparing this book to my mentors and friends Rabbi Earl Grollman, John D. Morgan, Bill Lamers, Carl Goreman, Everett Ferrill, Lionel Nieman, Lester Schmidt, Herbert Hamilton; George Henry, Robert Fulton, Whitney Gordon, Robert Bendiksen, Rob Stevenson, Neil Thompson, Dan Festa, Peter Ford, Robert Howell, Reverend Dr. Richard Gilbert, Mitchell Stone, Jac Bulk, Max Douglas, Greg Williams, Phillip Hulse, Brian Settles, and the many people on the over forty reservations that I visited who allowed me to learn from them. I want to apologize to the many who gave me oral histories that I did not include in this book. I also want to acknowledge those who allowed me to learn about their sacred ways but asked me to not share in writing what I learned from them. I have honored that request by not including their oral histories. All of the people I have mentioned and many others have given me profound knowledge and insights.

I would also like to acknowledge Courtney Morales, Megan Murray, Emma Ebert and Rajeswari Azayecoche of Lexington Books and the reviewers who helped with this project! Their work and suggestions were greatly appreciated! I would also like to thank Edwin Mellen Press for allowing me to use the oral histories and other materials from the *Sociology of the American Indian*.

Introduction

SOCIOLOGY OF DEATH AND THE AMERICAN INDIAN

Sociology of Death and the American Indian is a sociological analysis of the culture, dying, and death practices of American Indians. It is written from a sociological perspective based upon a lifetime of experience with and the study of the American Indian, oral histories gathered from visiting over forty reservations, the work of many scholars, and with contributions of many friends and kind strangers who provided knowledge that would have otherwise not been available. It is my hope that it will offer a perspective that will allow others to appreciate and better understand the plight, hope, and practices of some American Indian groups, and that it will allow those who study the material to better face their own dying and deaths as well as those of others that they care about.

The very term "Indian" has no definite referent. It does not point to any particular type of individual or group of people. If nothing else, it causes statistical problems. Census figures count Indians, but who are Indians? Not only in the United States, but also in Canada, Central and South America, the term Indian generally refers to a group of bands or enclaves that are culturally unique and socially isolated. This would suggest that Indians are a distinct ethnic group or more accurately, became Indians as a result of the multiple invasions by Europeans of the American continents. Has there been no invasion, there would have been no Indians, but rather there would have been Incas, Mayas, Dine, Inde, Hopi, and many others. There are many communities of those who are now known as Indians.

Life is larger than language. Any discussion or writing should be prefaced with this warning. The topic of death and the American Indian cannot be discussed without attention to the broader social context of secondary others or community reacting to significant others in the dying and death situations. The community of the secondary other is the culture-creating and culture-perpetuating group. At the same time, human behavior while being social behavior is also individual and unique. In every instance, there is some variation on the theme of cultural patterning. While we are culturally programmed to behave in an accepted manner, we vary from those expectations, making generalizations about behavior that much more difficult to study. Yet, we are able to discern general patterns that will be presented in this discussion of applying sociology to the study of dying, death, and the American Indian.

Death as a sociological subject has a short history. As sociology is a relatively new area of study, so, too, is the study of death as a sociological subject. Thomas Eliot wrote about the need for the analysis and study of grief in the early 1930s (1930, 1932). Anthropologists had already begun the study and analysis of exotic burial sites and funeral practices on the Egyptian pyramids, for example, but they did not use a similar effort or analysis on those of ordinary people. Robert Habenstein and William Lamers published *Funeral Customs the World Over* in 1960 which was written from a sociological perspective. The work of Robert Fulton, John Morgan, Herman Feifel, Glen Vernon, and others emerged in the 1950s and 1960s. Fulton developed the Center for Death Education in 1969 at the University of Minnesota which was the impetus for training many in the field of thanatology with a sociological emphasis. Fulton also taught the first college course on death and dying in 1963. The center was later moved to the University of Wisconsin—La Crosse where it continues today. John Morgan developed a similar research and service center, the King's College Centre for Education about Death and Bereavement at King's College in London, Ontario. Morgan also created the International Death, Grief, and Bereavement Conference which has also been moved to the University of Wisconsin—La Crosse to continue the tradition started by Dr. Morgan.

There is little doubt that people are fascinated with the behavior of other people. Sociologists are paid to do what people do for free, to study the behavior of other people. People-watching happens in airports, concerts, restaurants, schools, and virtually anywhere people congregate. Sociology is the scientific study of social behavior. Social behavior is the subjective meaning that is assigned by the actor or actors in assessing the behavior of themselves and others. Sociology attempts to develop causal principles and explanations and ultimately understanding of social behavior. Basically, sociology attempts to discover and explain social behavior and then by understanding how things work, make predictions about future behavior. Thanatology is the study of dying, death, and bereavement.

Since everyone will eventually die, all humans are in the process of dying while they are still living. Dying itself happens while one is still alive. This book will examine the very complex processes of dying and death-related behavior by humans. Sociology is one of many disciplines to study dying and death-related behavior. Philosophy, literature, psychology, history, and other disciplines also examine death-related behavior. Sociology uses the "social" aspect of such behavior as its starting point. Rather than examining from the psychological or philosophical perspective, sociologists look at the impact that other people, whether real or imagined, have on an individual or groups' dying and death-related behavior.

When a significant other dies, the rituals that take place amid the death process are an attempt by others to say that it is okay, you are not alone. This is why they bring food to the home, send flowers and cards, and attend the rituals. Sadly, most will do little other than attend to the rituals and period immediately after the death. The alone period after the services is the time when even more support is needed. Because most relationships are based upon the sociological concept of reciprocity or interdependence, when we can no longer do our "share" for the significant other, we are left with a feeling of unfinished business or guilt about failing to do our part. It is typically more intense in the cases of untimely or unexpected deaths. Our general understandings of grief and bereavement will be combined with a sociological approach to examine the approach of various American Indian groups.

Sociology is the study of human social activity from a scientific perspective. The social life of human activity is what sociologists study. Sociology is the study of choice making. The sociology of dying and death offers the opportunity: to learn about the process of decision-making; to learn why some make choices that cause them to live life as they choose, why others live the life chosen by others, or why some choose to give up on life and turn to drug or alcohol, or to learn about those who raise their families in obscurity, and those who retire and continue to live their dreams. Sociology focuses upon society which it views as a living, continuously developing social organism, as a functioning system that develops in accordance with changing institutions, social norms and values, economic systems, environmental and climatic changes, and interactions with other societies. As individuals are interdependent upon each other, so, too, are social organisms interdependent upon each other. Interdependent communities make up interdependent societies. Each system functions and develops or fails as communities or societies around it thrive or fail. Trade, wars, economic innovations, droughts, invasions by outsiders, colonization, and so forces of change can dramatically impact the life and ways of a society. The arrival of the Europeans, the wars, the forced moves to desolate lands and reservations, the imposition of White schools and religion, the technology of the dominant society, and the imposition of the Bureau of Indian Affairs (BIA) have caused great change in the last five hundred years. Yet, the cultures of the American Indian have survived and still exist.

The very existence of American Indian communities is testament to their resilience! They have existed in the Americas for 30,000–60,000 years, despite facing: ever-increasing contacts with diverse civilizations, cultures, and religions; attempts to destroy their cultures, religion, language, and way of life; as well as disease, war, and poverty that threatened their very existence (Brown 1982, 1–2). The European expansion to the West came at the expense of Mexicans, Spaniards, and American Indians who already lived there, to the American Indians who resisted, as well as to those who were peaceful and were forced into reservations. The Cherokee who were farmers in the Carolinas and Georgia, who had an alphabet, a constitution, published a newspaper, and were peaceful, were forced into camps and forced to take on a long trip of 1,200 miles to Oklahoma, causing four thousand Cherokee deaths (Lockard 2015, 483). While many still view American Indians as a historical people who once existed, yet they are part of the present and have endured. The American Indian cultures are still evolving.

American Indian resilience stems from a way of life, rather than from an organized religion. The origins of this resilience predate organized religion. In spite of the many attacks upon their way of life having only oral traditions for carrying on their practices over time, the American Indian has been able to maintain their experiential faith. While American Indians are not one tribe, but many diverse groups, clans, tribes, languages, religions, and many different concepts of spirituality, the idea that all is sacred and all is related would be generally accepted by most if not all tribes. There is no place where the Great Spirit or Creator, or whatever name might be used, is not present. The resilience is a way of life, of living, of breathing, of existing! While the American Indians did not have a Bible or sacred writings where truths are taught, truths are still taught by elders, family, and mentors. One observes the harmony in nature, the interconnectedness of all things, and one's place in the universe.

POWER

The concept of power is another source of resilience. Power does not mean domination over others as it seems to be in the White world, but rather power emerges from relationships with rocks, animals, plants, other people, and all things. Hunters may see themselves having power over the animal that is being hunted and finally killed, but the animal also has power. The hunter is dependent upon the animal to survive, so the animal must give the power to dominate to the human. The hunter has power with, not over the animal.

Power is not taken but given to be shared by rocks, animals, plants, or other things in nature.

American Indians are taught to respect all peoples and all ways, and thus it is not unusual to integrate their own spiritual and religious practices with those of other religions. Becoming a Christian or following Christian teachings does not keep one from following traditional spirituality or the traditional religion. Every tribe, clan, and family would have their own customs, traditions, ceremonies, rituals, and prayers which may or may not be incorporated into Christian practices. Depending upon the tribe while they may take part in Christian ceremonies, they may also participate in rain ceremonies, cleansing rituals, sweat or purification ceremonies, giveaway or potlatch ceremonies, memorials, Moon Lodge ceremonies, Coming of Age ceremonies, Blessing ceremonies, healing ceremonies, and many others as well. Unlike Christianity, Muslims, and other religions, those who practice American Indian spirituality or American Indian religion does not proselytize, evangelize, or encourage anyone who shows interest to join. Organized religion focuses upon having a religious leader to teach, guide, and lead the members to spiritual growth. In American Indian spirituality, there is no intermediary or clergy to act as a go-between for the person and the spirits. One can ask for the aid of another on their spiritual journey. Each person is expected to follow the guidance and direction of his or her heart rather than what others may direct. The guidance and direction will come in the form of prayer, dreams, solitude, words and teachings and guidance of the elders, and from the power of the physical, natural, and human world.

Power is found in many sources ranging from other humans, nonhumans, spirits, monsters, inanimate objects, and many other forms in nature. Medicine bags, medicine bundles, and other forms of sacred bundles are other sources of power. The Blackfeet of Montana are known for their use of medicine bundles and the rituals associated with them. What a person puts into a medicine bundle may be learned from a dream about what to include in the bundle, what songs should be sung, what images to paint on one's body, and what clothes to wear. It is common to bury one's medicine bundle with a person who dies. The bundle might be used to heal, to help in hunting or war, in times of suffering, and on the journey to the next life. The Lakota would have a sacred pipe bundle. The Crow would often have shields in their bundles. Both the Crow and the Cheyenne also had arrow bundles. The Pawnee would have included corn. Each village, clan, tribe, and family would have distinct local bundles to give them power in situations where additional help might be needed. Grief is certainly one such situation where one might use their bundle. Morris Opler uses an oral history to describe how a Chiricahua Apache's father obtained his power from the bear, the wolf, and other animals while on a journey (Opler 1969, 41). For the Apache or Inde, power comes from one of two ways. Either power finds you in the form of dreams, spirits, animals, or vision, and other outside sources, or the person seeks power on his or her own by learning appropriate prayers, rituals, and so forth, rather than having contact with animals or receiving offers of any kind for power (Basso 1970, 40–42). Possessing power is key to understanding American Indian resilience. This book celebrates that resilience.

PROPER WORDS

One of the issues that must be presented when discussing "Indians of the Americas" is what to call them. Words like "Native Americans," "First Nations," "indigenous people," and "American Indians" are all terms that have been used to describe the people who first settled in the Americas. All have been commonly used and all have those who support their use and who object to their use. Some tribes prefer "American Indian" while others may prefer "First Nations." While clearly not the traditional name, the author will use the term "American Indian" as accepted by a number of North American tribes. The names for tribes are also problematic. The name Navajo was not even used in the language of the tribe. Their preferred name was Dine or Dineh. The name "Sioux" comes from the Chippewa word for a snake, while the word "Apache" comes from the Zuni word for enemy, and the word "Iroquois" comes from the Algonquian word for real adders or snakes (Alvarez 2016, 6). While the traditional tribal name is what I prefer, I will also use the more commonly recognized names to describe each tribe to avoid confusing the reader.

PEOPLING OF THE AMERICAS

While there is much debate on the peopling of America, there is little question that people arrived in the Americas long before the arrival of the Vikings and the much later arrival of Christopher Columbus and the European invasion. Archaeologist Louis Leakey suggested that people arrived as long ago as hundred thousand years. Others argue that they arrived 10,000–15,000 years ago across the Bering Straits. The development of genetic evidence has more recently suggested that people have been in the Americas for at least forty thousand years. None of the exact patterns for the arrival of people to the Americas have been determined and are still being debated, but generally, it is thought that the hunting of bison, elk, bear, and other animals is at least in part why people came to the Americas. Following animals on the hunt is thought to have brought them to the Americas.

When the first Europeans arrived in the Americas they only knew of the existing civilizations in the Americas. Because few of the America Indians had a written language or a spoken language that the Europeans could learn quickly, the Europeans had no knowledge or appreciation for the great ancient civilizations that had existed in the Americas. The Aztecs were the last of the great civilized societies that had existed in both North and South America. While this book's focus is only on half of the Americas, there were many other early civilizations that existed on both continents with the Anasazi, Olmecs, Mayans, Incans, and others. The people who developed these civilizations were able to build temples, pyramids, cliff dwellings, and to develop mathematics, hieroglyphs, calendars, markets, irrigation systems, communication systems, and so much more that would have amazed the conquering Europeans had they taken the time and effort to learn more about the cultures of the Americas rather than trying to destroy them. The Indians have their own views of how they were created, though tribes often differ in their creation stories.

CREATION STORIES

The oral histories of the Indians of North and South America tell very different stories of where they came from than the Europeans who have written the books on their origins. Among the ancient civilizations of the Andes and Western coastal areas of South America, two supreme creator gods, Viracocha and Pachacamac, were the most prominent among the numerous gods that were thought to have once walked the earth and taught the people that the God created the world and all that is in it, but all tribes had beliefs about where their people came from and how they came into being, but with less emphasis upon the how or why than the Europeans (Jones and Molyneaux 2004, 186). While lacking in detail, humans living in the Americas generally thought that they came from the sky or the underground, and that after creating the world, the gods did not take much interest in humans' day-to-day existence (Jones and Molyneaux 2004, 186. Another often found explanation is that jaguars were the masters of the earth before humans and that the jaguars' powers were acquired by humans after they were adopted by jaguars and had betrayed them (Jones and Molyneaux 2004, 186). Similar creation stories are found among the tribes of North America.

The Snohomish and other Northwestern coastal tribes believed that animals were the original inhabitants of the earth and that the large wild dog could take off its fur and reveal a man inside. Perhaps that was the inspiration for the "Twilight" series where wolves who transformed into people and vampires conflicted with each other. The Indians of the South, Central, and

North America all believe that their origins began at many sacred sites rather than coming across a land bridge, and from the underground or another world in the sky (McMaster and Trafzer 2004, 15). The Serrano people of Southern California believe that the first people followed a great White Eagle south until it landed on the top of the San Bernardino Mountains, the origin place of the people (McMaster and Trafzer 2004, 15). The Iroquoian people also believe that they are the children of Aataentsic, the Woman Who Fell from the Sky who used her own creative powers and those of the Big Turtle and Little Turtle to make an island known today as North America (McMaster and Trafzer 2004, 16). The Shoshones suggest that the Coyote carried humans in a basket and then released them into the world. The Shoshones also suggest that the world was created from nothing. The Cherokee tell stories of the Water Beetle who plunged into the water beneath the sky and brought up the dirt that became the earth. Despite being an inland tribe, the Cherokee describe the earth as an island in the ocean that one day the cords that hold it will break and the earth will fall into the ocean (Starkey 1995, 8). The Cherokee suggest that long ago when everything was covered with water, the Water Beetle dove into the water and brought up soil that was attached to the earth island to the rock sky with four rawhide cords stretching to the four sacred mountains of the four sacred directions (Leeming and Leeming 1994, 45–46).

By contrast, the Navajo creation stories are far more complex and have great detail to their stories. Paul Zolbrod (1984) draws from Navajo oral history to write a complete book to tell the Navajo creation story. The story is that beauty, balance, and harmony are the pivotal elements in managing good and evil by developing a relationship between the supernaturals and among themselves (Zolbrod 1984, 5). Like many other tribes, the name Navajo is not the traditional name for the tribe, nor is the word "Navajo" found in their language, but rather they call themselves "Earth People" or Dineh or Dene (Underhill 1956, 4). Rather than coming from the North, the Navajo saga, like the books of Genesis and Exodus, describe them as being created in the "western sea" and then coming east or as being created in the old Navajo country of what is now New Mexico (Underhill 1956, 19). Like other tribes, supernatural beings are part of the creation story. For the Navajo, First Man and First Woman and later Changing Woman provided the four sacred mountains that defined their homeland. The story is that the Holy People (Dine) lived beneath the surface of the earth, and as they moved from one subterranean world to the next driven by magic forces, they split into two factions causing discord that produced the two sexes with the female Holy People giving birth to monsters (Lindig 1991, 172). A great flood washed the Holy People to the surface of the earth, where they created "first things," and then death took one of the Holy People, but at the same time Changing

Woman was born who was impregnated by the sun and waterfall giving her hero twins who had many adventures and slewed all of the monsters except for hunger, poverty, old age, and dirt (Lindig 1991, 172). Changing woman, her husband, and the twins form the Holy Family that created the world and the earth surface people, the ancestors of the Navajo, and taught them how to feed and house themselves, marry, travel, trade, and protect themselves from disease, hunger, and war before vanishing from the earth (Lindig 1991, 172–173). These stories are the Old Testament of American Indian spirituality and religion. While the Jewish people used their book to pass the stories down from one generation to the next, like tribes in Africa and other places, the American Indians used their oral tradition to pass on their theology.

These stories were told to grandchildren who told them to their grandchildren who then told them to their grandchildren for centuries. More than just stories, the legends that were passed down were teaching tools that taught children the history of their people and their beliefs. The stories taught them what was expected of them in life as well as what to expect from others. It also taught what was expected of them and their obligations and responsibilities to others. Hundreds if not thousands of similar stories about creation exist that defy the European view that the tribes crossed the straits to arrive in the Americas. The European arrivals are also subject to question through their many stories.

CONTACT WITH EUROPEANS

Many suggest that the Vikings were the first Europeans to arrive in the Americas. It is thought that the Norsemen were blown off course as they tried to sail from Iceland to their colonies in Greenland, and it was the same Vikings that made the first contact with the Native inhabitants of the Americas (Alvarez 2016, 9). The Vikings are thought to have begun their conquests, explorations, and raids during the period of climate change known as the Medieval Warm Period that lasted for about five hundred years of unusually warm and stable weather that led to a population explosion in Scandinavia that in turn led to land shortages leading young men to take to the seas in search of plunder, land, and opportunity (Alvarez 2016, 9). Around 982, Erik Thorvaldsson the Red sailed from Iceland where he found an uninhabited land where fish were plentiful and grazing grass was plentiful and green which led him to name the place "Green Land" which it bears even today (Fagan 2000, 17). Unlike the Viking raids in Europe, the Vikings were not able to conquer or make subjects of the American Indians.

While there are no clear records of voyages and explorations of the Americas by the Vikings, there remains a strong debate as to how far from

Norway the Vikings were able to travel into the Americas. Archaeologist have generally agreed that the Vikings did establish a settlement in Labrador where eight structures and Norse artifacts have been found as well as Norwegian coin that was found in Maine's Penobscot Bay and some disputed longhouse foundations on Ungava Bay that some call Inuit structures rather than Viking construction (Fagan 2000, 18–19). The presence of Norse artifacts in Hudson Bay, in Inuit High Arctic settlements, and even the towers in New England or the Kensington Stone in Minnesota may be evidence of Viking exploration or of Viking trading practices with the Inuit and American Indians (Fagan 2000, 18–20). Archaeologists have also suggested that the Vikings were able to establish 220 farms in the southern colony and 80 more in a more northerly colony that supported between two thousand and four thousand people to raise sheep and cattle and farm (Alvarez 2016, 10). Alvarez (2016) argues that the Vikings explored the American mainland, perhaps as far south as New York and as far west as Quebec City, but that the Vikings never settled even though the climate and land were more congenial and resource rich than Greenland (Alvarez 2016, 11). The Vikings had contact with the Beothuk, a hunting and gathering people living in Newfoundland, who used red ochre for adornment, leading the Vikings to call them "Red Indians"—a name that was used by later explorers (Alvarez 2016, 11). While the extent of European contact before the arrival of Christopher Columbus is still being determined, there is little question that there was contact with American Indian groups. Like other attitudes toward American Indians, the European view of their origins is based upon European views of the world rather than the views of Indians.

The European view of the origins of humans in the Americas is based upon their knowledge of what occurred in both Europe and Asia generally leaving out not only events that occurred in the Americas, but also in Africa. For most Europeans, the history of the Americas begins when they arrived. The general view of today's archaeologists is that around forty thousand years ago, Stone Age groups moved into the arctic plains and somehow learned to live in the treeless, cold regions. Europeans typically dismiss the creation stories of the tribes because they originate from oral traditions. The general consensus is that oral histories are not as valid as those that are written down as in the Torah, the Bible, the Runes, or other documented sources. These stories are no less pure than those of the sacred texts accepted by the Europeans. Like the Bible and other accepted sources, origin stories teach moral challenges, traditional values, and ways of coping with life's challenges to those who listen to the stories. While the stories of the origins differ, the American Indians continue to exist and tell their stories today.

Perhaps a major reason for the European dismissal of the stories of the American Indians is that Europeans telling stories often embellish or change stories as they wish. American Indians have always told their stories with great concern for keeping the details consistent over time. Navajo rituals that last for days must be performed with exact words that may take years to learn before one can perform them. Sacred stories and sacred rituals are taught from one generation to the next with great care that no changes will occur. Origin stories must be reenacted as if they were the actual recreation of the beginning of the world and as such, must be recreated through song, dance, and prayer with great precision and accuracy to not offend the gods. These rituals and stories were highly developed over the centuries. While the Europeans took centuries to model the American Indian ways of storytelling with radio and movies, American Indians for centuries have told their stories in ways that brought them to life with song, dance, and prayer that may have included Kachinas, masked figures, chanting, costumed people, and many other representations of the gods and other figures in the stories. The rich traditions of storytelling have survived for centuries. While many think that American Indians are something from the past, yet hundreds of tribes maintain their traditions and are present in modern society.

WHAT THE EUROPEANS FOUND IN THE AMERICAS

Almost everything written about North and South American Indians, whether discussing their history, culture, civilizations, art, music, and religion, covers the era from the time of the first contact to around 1890 as if the tribes did not exist before their "discovery" by the Europeans and that they disappeared after the end of the Indian wars by 1890. When Christopher Columbus landed in the Bahamas in 1492, he did not actually reach the mainland, but he opened the door for two worlds that had no knowledge of each other to collide after thousands of years of developing separate cultures and ways of life. While many books focus upon what the Europeans brought to the Americas, little is written about what the Americas brought to the Europeans. Those native to the Americas gave the Europeans corn, beans, potatoes, and other foods as well as medicines such as aspirin, quinine, coca, and strychnine, not to mention their contributions to the artistic heritage of the world with their masks, pottery, blankets, robes, and so much more. The Europeans not only brought their culture, religion, and way of life, but they also brought disease, destruction, and violent death to thousands and thousands of American Indians.

Those who first came to the Americas from Europe must have asked many questions about the people that they found in the Americas, Who were these people? Where did they come from? Are they in the Bible? Do they have souls? Are they barbarians or noble savages? While incorrect, the development of archaeology was spurred by the study of American Indian tribes as living examples of the European tribes written about by the Greeks and Romans, suggesting that the American Indians were living examples of the Stone, Bronze, and Iron Ages. The myth that the American Indians represented primitive cultures was present in the writings of early archaeologists and others, and yet, they somehow neglected to give any credit to the accomplishments of the Aztecs and other civilizations that they destroyed upon their arrival as being empires that rivaled those in Europe, Asia, and elsewhere.

Like Africa, the Americas are vast continents with immense geographical, cultural, and ethnic diversity. From polar ice caps to vast deserts to rugged mountains to fertile plains, the Americas contain all known geographic areas. The hundreds of tribes who populated the Americas before the arrival of the first Europeans were *Homo sapiens* with no evidence of any other human forms being found to precede them so far. The Americas were replete with a wide variety of animals ranging from reindeer, wild horses, rhinoceros, musk ox, bison, antelope, bear, and others for the early Stone Age hunters for a thousand years (Fagan 2000, 69). Even earlier, the Americas had dinosaurs that roamed the vast areas that offered plenty of food and shelter for them. While there is strong evidence that the dental morphology of the American Indians is similar to that of those ancients living in Northern Asia and not like those living in Stone Age Siberia there is still debate about their origins (Fagan 2000, 72).

Similarly, the question of how long people have lived in the Americas has been the subject of much debate. Frank Joseph and others have promoted theories that people have been in the Americas for hundreds of thousands of years; that they sailed the seas long before Columbus made his voyage; and that many artifacts, cave art, and other items have been found that support their thesis that not only did people live in the Americas far longer than previously thought, but that those living in the Americas had contact with peoples in Europe, Asia, and elsewhere far before the time of Columbus (Joseph 2017, 11–12). Other scholars are more conservative in accepting Joseph's evidence, but there is little doubt that people have lived here longer than suggested by the land bridge theory of around 20,000–12,000 years ago. The arguments that ancients crossed the land bridge in their migration to the Americas do not explain the early settlements found in South America that have similar evidence of people in the area around the same time. While open to arguments, artifacts found in what is now Chile and Brazil date back forty thousand years ago, but the question remains whether they were human made or naturally evolved (Fagan 2000, 81). Either way, they have found evidence of ancient civilizations in the Americas long before the Europeans arrived.

When the Spanish arrived in the Americas, it is estimated that there were around 75 million people living in the Americas who spoke two thousand different languages, had endured countless cultural rises and falls, and had an incalculable numbers of rich and distinct American Indian cultures (Thomas 1994, xix). The view that the American Indians were uncivilized and inferior to the Europeans defies belief. It is generally thought that in North America there were around four hundred different languages spoken by hundreds of tribes with much greater variety and difference than in all of Europe and that just in California alone, there are more numerous linguistic extremes than in all of Europe (Jeanne 1996, 330). Like many European languages, there are families of languages among American Indians. The Tohono O'odham and Hopi share a language family with the Ute, Paiute, Comanche, Shoshone, Yaqui, and others, while the Navajo share the same family linguistically with the Apache, Dgorib, Sarsi, Chipewyan, and Koyukon among others with 104 language families having been identified in the Americas (Jeanne 1997, 333). Linguist John Wesley Powell is noted for classifying many of those language families in the late 1800s and early 1900s (Tooker 1997, 244). Having such great diversity of languages suggests that the various tribes had long periods of both physical and social isolation.

DIVERSITY OF THE AMERICAS

The Americas are much smaller than the land mass of Eurasia and Africa, but at the same time, the Americas have a much more varied environment than Eurasia and Africa. With the tribes ranging from the Polar Inuits of northern Greenland to the Fuegians of southern most South America, there is no single environment that would lead to similar cultural development. Perhaps, the most formidable geographical feature would be the mountain chains of the cordillera extending from Alaska through the Rocky Mountains of North America to the Andes of South America. The Andes isolated the Incas from those who lived on the Eastern side of the range. Rivers and their basins also spawned the development of still different cultures. The existence of large river basins of the Mississippi in North America to the Amazon and Orinoco basins in South America greatly influenced the development of different cultures. The mountains formed barriers that kept tribes apart. Those living in mountains had to develop different crops, different clothing, and different habitats for living in quite different environments. Corn, beans, peppers, and squashes grew more easily in the lower latitudes where food was more abundant allowing for larger towns and cities to develop. Rice required a moist environment and could grow only in an environment that had frost. Climate, geography, and environment led to cultural and lifeway differences.

It was not by chance that the Incas, Mayans, and Aztecs civilizations were found in tropical regions. The Inuit people had to develop clothing that would allow them to tolerate the frigid temperatures of the polar region. They also had to develop food sources other than traditional farming. The tribes living on the coasts or rivers were able to develop sophisticated techniques for fishing as well as boats that could survive in the oceans and the rivers that fed them. By contrast, those living in the dry, arid environment of Death Valley were forced by the shortage of water, the inability to grow crops abundantly, and by the extreme heat to live in small bands while those living along the coasts or major rivers could build large settlements with a thousand or so people and be able to supply them with food, clothing, and other necessities. Perhaps the most famous lifestyle of the American Indian would be the Plains Indians and their bison culture. The "buffalo" or more properly termed, the bison, was the center of the cultural activities of the Plains tribes. The Plains Indians used every part of the bison which gave them food, clothing, and tools, and forced technological development to follow and kill the bison.

IMPACT OF THE EUROPEANS' ARRIVAL

While most date the arrival of Europeans to the Americas with the arrival of Columbus, there are legends of the earlier arrival of the Irish and the Vikings. While teaching in Ireland, I heard stories of an Irish monk, Brendan, who sailed to the New World in the sixth century. While there is no archaeological evidence that the monks ever arrived in the Americas, they did reach Shetland, the Faroes, and possibly Iceland. As discussed earlier, there is more support for the journeys of Erick the Red who colonized Iceland and Greenland and possibly the arctic of North America around one thousand years ago. While there is debate about when the Europeans arrived in the New World, there is little doubt that the arrival of Columbus and those who followed him wreaked havoc upon the American Indians on both continents as well as upon the islands of the Caribbean.

The collision of the two worlds was disastrous for the Americas. The Europeans brought with them guns, cross bows, iron weapons, armor, and horses, which gave them a significant advantage over the stone tool military technology of the American Indians. They also brought with them smallpox, measles, cholera, influenza, diphtheria, malaria, the bubonic plague, and scarlet fever. The people of the Americas had no immunity to these diseases which killed millions from just 1545 to 1548 (Dobyns 1997, 163). Their views of those who lived in the Americas were based upon those that they first met in the Caribbean islands and not the more dominant empires on the mainland.

Because the Europeans first came to the Caribbean tropical environment where the tribes lived in huts, not because they could not build more solid homes as the Europeans built, but because they saw no need to build

European-style homes since they had to live with the hurricanes that often annually destroyed their homes, with a temperature climate, and with strong rainy seasons. Because they did not see the advanced civilizations of the Americas when they first arrived, the Europeans developed the belief that the New World people were barely human which allowed them to justify the taking of their lands, their conquest of people that they viewed as inferior which justified making them slaves, and ultimately, led to their genocide. Rather than viewing the Americas as a cultural find, they saw them as a resource to be exploited.

The Americas were viewed as the land of opportunity by the Europeans and others around the world. It was also viewed as a violent, uncivilized place with battles between "cowboys and Indians" and with shootouts between violent men as portrayed in novels about the Americas and particularly about the West. The "dime novels" were supported by the writings of many authors such as Frederick Jackson Turner who wrote about the free land, opportunity, and peril from the Indians and outlaws of the West. Newspaper editor Horace Greeley encouraged young men to go West to the frontier for opportunity, and still others encouraged young men to join the military to fight the "savage" Indian. The Europeans brought with them the belief that they were a more advanced culture arising out of the greater European civilizations. The belief in the superiority of the Judeo-Christian ethical and religious heritage and that they were superior biologically was used to justify their treatment of the Indians. Yet, the supposedly superior invading Europeans cut down the giant redwoods that were hundreds of years old, destroyed forests for planting crops, dug up graves for buried treasures, and generally desecrated the land and its peoples.

The concept of "Manifest destiny" gave license to the Europeans to take the land, to enslave the Indians, and to force their way of life or acculturation upon them. Sadly, the view of the American Indians has not improved dramatically from the sixteenth century to the twenty-first century. American Indians have become a people without a history. The view that they were uncivilized, lacking in faith, ethics, accomplishments, and lacked a proper understanding of government and private property. The truth presents a different picture. While there were over 1,470 fights that have been researched and verified in the 270 years of Indian wars or battles with the U.S. military, there were without doubt hundreds of other minor conflicts (Michno 2003, 1). While most modern movies and novels portray gun battles, Indian raids, and cowboys fighting Indians, the Old West was far tamer than the popular image that is still being put forth today. Many novels and movies focus upon the perils faced by wagon trains heading West and the violence that they faced. It is fairly well documented that Whites killed more Indians than Indians killed Whites and that the average casualty to troop ratio was higher during

Indian battles than the casualty to troop ratio during the Civil War (Michno 2003, 360). While there were not the many attacks on wagon trains as portrayed in the movies, books, and other media, most wagon trains were able to reach their destination; the attacks that did occur did lead to deaths, rapes, and torture at the hands of Indian attackers (Michno 2003, 361). While there are those who write that the West was not as violent or wild as the media presents, it was certainly wild and violent, yet, most of those who traveled to the West were able to survive and build their futures. Perhaps, the more important problem was how the views of the Europeans were so different than the Indians on the land and its resources.

CONFLICTING VALUES

The American Indians did not have property rights as was the common practice of the Europeans. They saw themselves as being one with the land and as keepers of the natural environment rather than exploiting it for profit. In trying to explain how the Indians arrived in the Americas, the Europeans saw them as possibly being the Lost Tribes of Israel, or perhaps Egyptians, or even the descendants of seagoing Welshmen, or other mythological explanations for their existence. Later, the common explanation is that they were Asian people who crossed the Bering Straits into what is now Alaska. The Indian people have far different explanations for how they arrived. Each tribe or clan has a biblical narrative or story that was formed by their oral traditions that have been handed down through many generations and forming the basis for their norms, values, and beliefs that does not concentrate on a Supreme Being but rather upon the interdependence of all beings, that people must honor all living creatures and forces of nature. Unlike the Europeans, they had no religious orthodoxy with rules for behavior. Each person is expected to be responsible for his or her relationship with the Creator and with other human beings and creatures who share the world with him or her. Sociologically, the American Indian spirituality is based upon the concept of "reciprocity." Each person has the responsibility to contribute his or her own unique gift or ability to keep the world in balance, to see the kinship and sacredness of all life, and to remember that they are related to all beings and forces in the universe. The concept of kinship is based upon a reciprocal relationship where responsible cooperation and mutual respect and affection were expected.

Spirituality has always formed the basis for tribal life. John Morgan (2000) suggests that spirituality is not a new concept, having been defined during the Renaissance and having its origins with Plato's teachings, and defines spirituality as both an awareness that things are not limited to this time and space and that the human mind can reflect and think upon itself

(Morgan 2000, 1). Morgan also saw activities such as humor, ethical reasoning, and religious concern as manifestations of spirituality with religion being just one of many aspects of spirituality (Morgan 2000, 2). This ability to think and reflect upon oneself forms the basis for American Indian spirituality.

All acts are spiritually guided, including meetings, governing, work, play, and simply every aspect of daily life. This means that each Indian would say a prayer for the plant or animal that they are about to eat, or for the plant that yields the cloth that will be used to make a blanket or rug. Each individual is to have a "good heart" or a personal relationship with the sacred. Life is a journey that must be taken with a good heart. American Indians live for today rather than focusing upon the future. The focus is upon the here and now rather than upon becoming. If one has enough to eat today, tomorrow will take care of itself. If individuals take care of the land and what is on it, the land and its resources will take care of them. While the cultures and peoples of the Americas were far more advanced than civilized than their European conquers seemed to believe, they were also a problem by their very presence for those who wanted their lands and resources. When two worlds collide, one loses.

COMPASSION AND LOSS

Sociology as an academic discipline tries to make sense of how people manage to the many disparities in their social lives. Sociology attempts to explain how people are able to manage the incredible power of social forces and social structures that they cannot see, how people are able to develop meaning in their lives in the face of massive social differences that they encounter in their daily lives, and how people are able to find their place in society as a positive contributor to others or as one who makes life more difficult for others. Humans may do such socially condemned acts like stealing, robbing, murdering, or plundering, and yet, the same societies have people who are also giving to charities, helping the homeless, showing kindness to strangers, and caring about the starving in other countries. Sociology begins as people remember, talk, put into words their thoughts, and by the use of logic to try to make sense out of their experiences. Sociological analysis is the attempt to make sense out of the many cultures and societies that make up our world; to better understand the differences of the people of the Americas, Africa, Asia, or Europe, and yet how similar they all really are; and to better understand why some are so violent, taking, and using others while some people are so giving, sharing, and concerned about the well-being of others. Compassion is valued in American Indian societies.

Compassion is defined as "sympathetic feeling" in the Merriam-Webster dictionary. Is the ability to have sympathetic feelings for others innate or a product of learning? From a sociological perspective, it would generally be thought that compassion is socially taught. Certainly not all people, nor do all groups of people, exhibit sympathetic feelings toward others. The very existence of prejudice, genocide, wars, discrimination, and ill will toward others belies the notion that it is inborn. The Nazis mass cremation of the millions of Jews, Pole, and others that they considered unworthy of human life has been considered to be an immoral form of destruction (Davies 1997, 34). Sadly similar genocidal acts occurred in the Americas. While there are many examples of genocide, a few would include: Tenochtitlan 100,000–240,000 (Waldman 2009, 119); Acoma 800 (Waldman 2009, 130); Wounded Knee 130–250 (Waldman 2009, 316); Washita 150–250 (Waldman 2009, 198); Sand Creek 160 (Waldman 2009, 185). The massacres by the Europeans of American Indians rival those of the Nazis. Yet, as there were certainly those who opposed the massacres of the American Indians, many others strongly supported the massacres. Kit Carson who was part of the Canyon de Chelly and the Sand Creek massacres was outspoken in his opposition to both events (Alvarez 2016, 94, 127). Generally, from a sociological point of view, the massacres were justified by the prevailing biased attitudes of the time toward the American Indians. As in Australia, Africa, and elsewhere, there was considerable outcry against the acts of the government and other groups in their treatment of the indigenous populations across the globe. Racism, fear, and dehumanizing attitudes toward the American Indians on the part of Whites living in the West were fairly commonplace with many believing that extermination was the only real answer to the problem while those of the wider public and those of government officials were more compassionate than those of the frontier culture (Alvarez 2016, 99–100). Some of the Europeans had compassion toward the American Indians even in the face of cruelty and outright attempts to exterminate them.

By contrast to the treatment of the Plains and other Western frontier experiences, the California Indians, rather than being exterminated, were colonized and exploited by the mission movement of the Spanish. The cultural model in California was to Christianize and civilize the Indians rather than to exterminate them. While cruelly treating the Indians with floggings, incarceration, and other punishments and ultimately virtual slavery, the California Indians for the most part were coerced into becoming a docile and obedient workforce (Alvarez 2016, 107). While the Spanish had a cultural view of "saving" the Indian, the Indian's cultural view was both to actively and passively resist the Spanish missionaries by work stoppages, slowdowns, becoming fugitives, guerrilla warfare, and even revolts (Alvarez 2016, 108). The Spanish rule was ended after sixty-five years of ruling when Mexico won its independence from Spain in 1821, finally ending the church's right to enslave the California Indians (Josephy 1994, 345).

Sadly, at the time when the Spanish rule was ended with Mexico losing sovereignty over California in 1848 and with the Indians helping the Americans throw out their hated oppressors, gold was discovered which led to the massacre of thousands of California Indians. The American culture who wanted gold, land, but no Indians, brought with them not only a change of cultures but unlike the Spanish who for all of their violence and injustice wanted to establish a society in which the Indians belonged even as second-class citizens while the culture of the Americans who wanted the riches that the gold offered rather than having the Indians belong in their new society, saw fit to exterminate the Indians (Alvarez 2016, 108). The number of Indians living in what is now California in the mid-1700s was more than three hundred thousand and yet by 1900, there were only sixteen thousand Indians living in California (McMaster and Trafzer 2004, 250). While it may be argued that the treatment of the Indians in the East, the Plains, and the Southwest was not genocide, there is little question that the California experience was genocide. Not only were the cultural attitudes toward the Indians based upon fear, racism, and dehumanizing beliefs, but the governments of many towns and other levels of government offered bounties for scalps, paid for bullets, and in many other ways supported the killing of Indians of all ages. It was in California that the campaign to exterminate the American Indian had its greatest success. It should be mentioned that many also died of disease as well as from overwork as slaves, due to starvation, and other ways and not just from deliberate attempts to kill them.

The American Indians have a history of compassion and caring for others, but there is also a history of human sacrifice and eating those who were sacrificed. The Mayans, Aztecs, and Incas have a history of sacrificing their enemies, but their numbers are far less than those of the Nazis in the Holocaust or the Europeans who came to the Americas with their attempts to destroy the Indian population. The attempts to destroy the Aboriginal population in Australia offer a similar example of unsympathetic feelings toward another group. As there are cultural examples of the lack of sympathetic feelings toward other groups, there are also examples of groups showing sympathetic feelings toward other groups.

CONCLUSIONS

Cultural differences between the American Indians and the Europeans led to conflict and to the extermination of many tribes and to the ultimate destruction of the American Indian way of life for many other tribes. Basic disagreements about values, property rights, and kinship led to even more conflicts. Different views about the origins of people, of spirituality, and compassion fueled the division between the two cultures.

Norms and values are principles for thoughts and actions that are shared with others. Norms are the rules or standards for right and wrong. Values are the basis for setting goals. The linking of personal worth based upon achieving wealth is a social value. Concern for orphans, those living in poverty, or those suffering from illness is based upon social values. As a member of various social groups, each individual will have many shared as well as many conflicting values that will influence his or her choices and behavior. The same individual can show compassion for members of groups that share values with the individual, and at the same time, show great distain for those who have quite different values. When two worlds collide, one often loses.

Part I

SOCIOLOGY OF DYING, DEATH, AND THE AMERICAN INDIAN

The topic of dying and death is receiving considerable attention these days. In recent years, the death awareness movement had its start with the work of Herman Feifel, Robert Fulton, Elizabeth Kubler-Ross, Cicely Saunders, and others in the 1950s and 1960s. The acceptance of hospice and palliative care has made it socially acceptable to discuss, research, and write about the sociology of dying and death. The recent COVID-19 crisis and the many deaths that it brought has made the discussion even more appropriate. Likewise, the American Indian has been the subject of many books over the centuries, but most are written with the attitude of discussing a past or extinct culture. The topic of dying and death has primarily been written and studied from a narrow, mostly psychological point of view. The literature of dying and death has generally paid little or no attention to the wider social factors or to the role of the community. It neglects the multidimensional phenomenon that merits a more holistic approach. Part I is an attempt to provide the foundations for this more holistic approach by incorporating sociological insights to complement and counterbalance the more traditional psychological views.

Ancient societies were generally collective cultures as opposed to modern individually focused cultures. In a collective culture, the focus is upon the well-being of the collectivity, group, clan, tribe, or whatever is the nature of the community in which one lives. The individual views his or her own welfare as less important than that of the group. The community response is evident in the funeral, disposal, and mourning practices of ancient societies. The entire community will be the base of support for those who have experienced a loss. The community will be there to help the survivors economically, socially, and spiritually. By examining the social and institutional structures of various societies and cultural groups, the hope is to help provide a framework for a better understanding of the study about dying, death, and bereavement from all cultural perspectives. The discipline of sociology offers a way to analyze the processes and institutional responses to dying and death in the same way that it analyzes cities, crime, or any other sociological subject. Using the perspective of sociology, dying and death can be studied in a way to teach how to face dying and death in a healthy manner. By learning about approaches of other groups around the world, we can learn how to better manage our own losses. The sociological analysis of the mortuary practices of groups around the world will offer a more clear understanding of our own practices. By studying other cultures, people can learn to better manage their own fears concerning dying and death. It is possible to learn that one need not fear or avoid dying and death as a topic. Each cultural group encourages and develops attitudes toward dying and death.

All can gain an understanding of dying and death as the natural end of the life cycle. By focusing upon the social processes and interactions involved in the dying and death process, one can develop an understanding of the social nature of dying and death and can develop his or her own personal views of dying and death. Our views impact the ways in which we are able to manage or not manage our losses.

The diversity within the various sociological approaches facilitates critical thinking, develops the sociological imagination, and assists the process of reality construction, both personal and societal. An understanding of dying and death in its personal, social, institution, and comparative dimensions facilitates the integration of complex emotional and intellectual phenomena in one's life. This will allow individuals to give life more meaning, to clarify its purposes, and to engage in social exchanges with more assurance and self-confidence. The sociology of death and dying is rewarding, intellectually stimulating, and definitely sociological.

Sociology as an academic discipline helps make sense of how people are able to manage the incredible power of social structures, processes, institutions, discourses, expectations, and relations that they cannot see; how we are able to develop meaning in our lives in the face of massive social differences that we encounter; and how we are able to find our place in society as positive contributors to the well-being of others (or as people who make life more difficult for others). As humans we give and take, whether stealing, robbing, selling drugs, murder, or scams; and yet, we also give to charities, helping homeless people, showing kindness to strangers, and caring about the starving in other countries. Humans can be cruel or kind.

Sociology gives us a basis for understanding the many cultures and societies that make up our world; to better understand the differences of the people while also recognizing how similar they all really are; and to better understand why some are so violent, taking, and using others while some people are so giving, sharing, and concerned about the well-being of others.

Traditionally, such matters have been addressed from a psychological point of view, with a focus on the inner workings of the mind. Sociology counterbalances this by considering the wider social context and its role in promoting (or preventing) compassion.

Sociologically, there may be many differences between ancient societies and modern societies, but the basic structural, cultural, social processes; institutions; and role of norms and values are found in societies of the past as well as the present. From a sociological perspective, there are structural, cultural, social processes, and social institutional impact on funeral and disposal practices. Every culture has norms and values that determine the acceptable behavior of its people. These norms and values are influenced by families, clans, religious institutions, governments, educational systems, social class, race, gender, and many other factors.

This section, like the entire book, tries to avoid the use of a highly technical style, drawing upon a great deal of the depersonalized academic and technical jargon that does not capture the very human nature or spiritual dimensions of the American Indian approach to dying and death. The first chapter, "Sociology of Dying and Death," offers a sociological approach to the study of dying and death. Chapter 2, "Why a Sociology of Dying and Death?," offers an examination of why the study of dying and death from a sociological perspective is both valuable and useful. Chapter 3, "Sociology of the American Indian," examines the societies, culture, and way of life from a sociological perspective. Chapter 4, "Burial and Mortuary Customs of American Indians," looks at the traditional disposal practices of the American Indians. Chapter 5, "Culture of the American Indians," provides a framework for examining the cultures of the American Indian. Chapter 6, "American Indian Cultural Denigration," examines the misuse of American Indian cultures by the wider culture. Chapter 7, "Problems in Understanding Other Cultures," looks at difficulties in accepting the ways of people other than ourselves.

Chapter 1

Sociology of Dying and Death

Everyone dies. The only real question is how and when. Dying and death are a part of everyone's life. The ability to manage our death and those of others is learned. Fears about dying and death are also learned. American Indians have much to offer and can teach non-Indians ways to improve their dying, bereavement, and grief. Ernest Becker (1968) argued that sociology is historically concerned with improving the lot of human beings and a form of consciousness rooted in moral experience (Becker 1968, 31). Sociology, then, functions for the betterment of human society. The attraction of sociology as a discipline of study has existential origins that are based upon the commitments and concerns about the human condition, suffering, crime, wars, violence, and other forms of human behavior that threaten or at least make the human condition less tolerable. From a sociological perspective, institutional structures characterize social expectations that form human behavior. Emile Durkheim, Claude Levi-Strauss, Karl Marx, Ida Wells-Barnett, Harriet Martineau, Jane Addams, Charlotte Perkins Stetson Gilman, Anna Julia Cooper, and other classical sociologists, while offering different approaches to structural sociology, would generally agree that social and institutional structures are major determinants of human behavior. Above all that as humans we are inherently social beings, living interdependently. They teach us that much of the pain and suffering in people's lives is socially produced.

Death, grief, and bereavement do not occur in a vacuum, but as the founding men and women demonstrate that oppression, discrimination, attitudes, and values all impact perceptions. While dying, death, and grief have been thought of as based upon individual responses, the founders of sociology argue that humans are inherently social beings and that grief and bereavement practices can be understood not only by looking at psychological and medical frameworks, but also by examining the understanding of humans as part of a complex structure of social arrangements, institutions, structures, and patterns. Oppression, discrimination, exclusion, and injustice impact perceptions of self, group, and community. One's grief is impacted by one's social position in society, by one's education or lack thereof, by one's spiritual or religious approach, and by what one has learned from those around him or her. By examining the social and institutional structures of various American Indian groups, my hope is to help provide a framework for a better understanding of the study about dying, death, and bereavement from all cultural perspectives. Richard Schafer (2015) suggests that all social interaction occurs within a social structure including those interactions that redefine social reality (Schaefer 2015, 106).

WHAT SOCIOLOGY HAS TO OFFER

The discipline of sociology offers a way to analyze the processes and institutional responses to dying and death in the same way that it analyzes cities, crime, or any other sociological subject. Using the perspective of sociology, dying and death can be studied in a way to teach how to face dying and death in a healthy manner. The approach of American Indians to facing dying and death has much to offer to those who are not American Indians. The sociological analysis of the American Indian approach to dying and death can enhance our understanding of how to face dying and death. By studying other cultures, people can learn to better manage their own fears concerning dying and death. It is possible to learn that one need not fear or avoid dying and death as a topic.

Attitudes toward dying and death are learned. Like prejudice and other attitudes, one's basic attitudes are learned from those closest to him or her. If one's parents and others close to the individual are very fearful toward dying and death and are unable to deal with dying and death in any sort of planned or enjoyable manner, then the individual will often adopt similar attitudes of fearfulness toward dying and death. Clearly, not all tribal groups had healthy views of dying and death, but more have healthy approaches than not. An examination of the healthy approaches and attitudes will at least make facing dying and death more manageable. There is no easy way to die. There is no easy way to mourn the death of another. Death is inevitable. All will face it eventually. How well one faces dying and death depends upon the attitudes one has toward dying and death. Some attitudes are healthy and make for less of a crisis. Other attitudes are less healthy and increase the amount of crisis and make the management of dying and death more painful and tragic laden. American Indians honor the elderly. It is not a bad thing to become old or even be dying. It is a very healthy attitude to accept and even enjoy aging and to be able to face dying by living until death occurs. For most those who are dying or care for those who are dying, the focus is upon the dying. If one focuses upon living until death occurs, the attitudes of the dying and those who care for them are improved.

Generally, social psychologists would argue that there is no inborn fear of death. Fears of death are learned at a very early age. The more that parents and others avoid the topic, the more their children will learn to fear it. How one explains dying and death to a child can add to his or her fears or allow them to have a healthy understanding of the events. While not all Indian groups teach constructive attitudes to their children about dying and death, most encourage a relationship with elders that can lead to less fear of growing old and ultimately facing dying and death.

Dying and death can be avoided as a topic for many reasons. It is often avoided because of fear of acknowledging one's own mortality. The topic may also be avoided because of fear of pain and suffering in the dying process. It may be avoided because of fear of the unknown. For most, it is easier to live in the present and avoid even thinking about loss of those that one loves or even one's own life. All can gain an understanding of dying and death as part of the natural end of the life cycle. By focusing upon the social processes and interactions involved in the dying and death process, one can develop an understanding of the social nature of dying and death and can develop his or her own personal views of dying and death.

The diversity within the various sociological approaches facilitates critical thinking, develops the sociological imagination, and assists the process of reality construction, both personal and societal. An understanding of dying and death in its personal, social, institution, and comparative dimensions facilitates the integration of complex emotional and intellectual phenomena in one's life. This will allow individuals to give life more meaning, to clarify its purposes, and to engage in social exchanges with more assurance and self-confidence. The sociology of death and dying is rewarding, intellectually stimulating, and definitely sociological.

ATTITUDES TOWARD DYING AND DEATH

Attitudes are social evaluations that influence one's reaction to the social world. Attitudes do not cause, but do influence social behavior. One's attitudes tend to change in the direction of reducing stress by trying to minimize the inconsistency or ambiguity with what one experiences.

There is no easy way to face death. There is no easy way to mourn the death of another. Since death is inevitable, attitudes toward dying and death determine how well one is able to manage death. Some attitudes toward dying and death are healthy and make for less of a crisis for either the individual or for the family. Yet, other attitudes toward dying and death are less healthy and increase the amount of crisis and make the ability to readjust more painful. Clearly, if one lives in a supportive, close-knit community that fosters positive attitudes toward dying and death, then one is far more likely to have positive attitudes toward dying and death. Jill Quadagno (2014) suggests that how individuals cope with death tends to be similar to how he or she responds to other stresses in life (Quadagno 2014, 302). How one is taught and how much support one is given in one's community will greatly influence his or her response to dying and death. Close-knit communities are being threatened as societies around the world become more secular.

Many talk about the fear of death, but the fear of death may actually be the fear of dying.

For most, fear is the basic attitude toward dying and death. To be fearful of dying is for many different than to be fearful of death. Fears of dying are fears that are related to living. Fears of being dead are the fears of what will happen after death. Typically these would include fears of:

1. Becoming dependent upon others,
2. Pain in the dying process,
3. The indignity of the dying process,
4. Isolation, rejection, and separation from loved ones,
5. Leaving loved ones,
6. What will happen to one's possessions, money, etc.,
7. Being a financial burden,
8. Not dying well,
9. The finality of death,
10. Being unable to face dying with dignity.

Fears of death typically include fears of:

1. What will happen to my body?
2. The spirit world,
3. Nothingness,
4. Is there life after death or not?
5. The judgment of others,
6. Not having proper rituals if family does not care,
7. Being buried or being buried alive,
8. End of all social relationships,
9. Never seeing loved ones again,
10. Loss of all physical and social identity.

These fears of dying and death are not innate or instinctive, but they are culturally created and sustained. All these fears can be managed.

Fears of whether there is life after death can best be resolved by accepting the fact that it doesn't really matter. One cannot change whichever is true. If there is life after death, then accept your fate. If there is no life after death, then you longer exist. Either way, worrying about it will not change it. Simply stated, deep anxieties about dying and death are not productive and are unnecessary. Robert Kastenbaum suggests that fear may be realistic or exaggerated, but it can be described or stated, while anxiety is a generalized state of being that cannot be articulated (Kastenbaum 1989, 81). Kastenbaum further suggests that studies on fear of death examining the dying find that the dying focus upon issues of pain, finances, well-being of loved ones, and not about being dead (Kastenbaum 1989, 83). The real question is that are people afraid of death or really just afraid of dying?

Dying and becoming dead are not the same for anyone. Those who are dying and those who think about how they wish to die share the goal of wanting to maintain autonomy, personal dignity, and quality in living until they die (Corr, McNabe, and Corr 2009, 144). There is little doubt that each of us will die some day. While we are not yet able to determine if plants, animals, and other forms found in nature are aware of their impending death, we do know that humans are aware of their fate. For many, the concept of dying with dignity would mean dying without tubes, being in a medically induced coma, being alone in a hospital or other institution, or being unable to respond to one's loved ones. Sadly, for many in the world, even those conditions would be an improvement over their dying experiences. Many are the victims of holocausts, wars, torture, murder, in-flight, famine, COVID and other epidemics, fires, building collapses, natural disasters, or any of hundreds of other undignified ways that humans die. Death in literature describes both dignified death and undignified death in the classics. Christians would describe the death of Jesus as undignified. Those who enjoy reading classics might describe the death of the fisherman in Steinbeck's *Old Man and the Sea* as dignified. The fear of dying an undignified death or having a love one die of an undignified death is one of the many possible fears.

Death fears are produced by the almost unimaginable. The thought of never being able to taste, smell, hear, see, or having any feeling of pain or pleasure is almost unbearable and at the same time beyond anything that we can imagine or have ever experienced (Fireston and Caltett 2009, 261). While most would prefer to have healthy attitudes toward dying and death, the ability to attain positive attitudes requires effort.

Healthy attitudes toward death are preferable to negative attitudes toward death. Negative attitudes toward death include having excessive fears of hospitals, nursing homes, funeral homes, funerals, cemeteries, dead bodies, and other symbols of death. People who cannot even talk about dying and death or have other problems such as an unwillingness to talk to those who are dying or even to the grieving exhibit negative attitudes toward death. Healthy attitudes toward death would include the ability to not only talk about death, but also a willingness to take part in the planning and other events before and after another person's death. The person with a healthy attitude toward dying and death will be able to not only deal with the deaths of others in an open fashion but also to imagine one's own death vividly and openly. A healthy imagination is also valuable. To imagine what it is like to be buried alive or even to imagine one's funeral is actually healthy. Negative attitudes, for example, might include being morbidly obsessed with one's death. If you knew for sure that there was no life after death, would you then change the way in which you were living? If you would, then you have an unhealthy attitude toward death. One should live the life one chooses to live because that is the one that you want rather than out of fear of what might happen when you die. If you attend Mass daily or become a minister or Rabbi to get a reward when you die, then you have a negative attitude toward dying and death. You should practice your religion because it makes your life better, not because of fear of what will happen when you die.

DEVELOPING HEALTHY ATTITUDES
TOWARD DYING AND DEATH

Death happens to all living things. Death is part of the pattern of universe. Birth is the leading cause of death. Had you never been born, you would not have to die. At the same time, for life to continue, we need loss and death. Losses are constant. Losses do hurt, but new generations follow as older generations pass away. The world is filled with beauty and goodness if we have the eyes to see the beauty and goodness around us. Change always brings loss, even when change is welcomed, like the child going to school for first time, both the parent and the child suffer loss. For the parent, the child has entered a new phase of life and will be less and less dependent upon the parent. For the child, the world will never be the same with added responsibilities, peer pressure, accountability, and answering to adults who do not have the same love that your parents showed to you. This change is both sought after and at the same time dreaded. Many of our attitudes have both positive and negative components.

There are many ways to foster healthy attitudes toward death. You can keep a journal, tell stories, or write letters to the deceased. Writing is a process of discovery. If you write for any length of time, you will probably state what is in your heart and on your mind. You will unearth much that you may not recognize about your own fears. Healthy attitudes toward death will follow. Humor leads to laughter, and laughter leads to inner peace. Humorous stories, particularly about yourself, are perhaps the easiest form of humor to use to aid the grieving or the dying. Music can also lead to positive attitudes, as can art, drama, puppeteering, clay, drawing, painting, and other art forms. People may be the best source of help. Friends share their joys and their sorrows. Rituals are also a major source of support and solace. Most tribal groups have a strong tradition of rituals that ease the burden of the grieving and help the dying find their way. Most clans or tribes teach that one must accept the life that one is given and to spend one's life living as he or she was called to live. Few have lives that they would want to trade with others.

Life is a series of blessings and burdens which provide balance and freedom. Each person has the opportunity to live fully until death overcomes them. Even those who are dying are not yet dead. Live life fully, each day, not someday. Healthy attitudes are learned. You live what you learn. Charles Corr (2018) suggests that dying people face challenges of not knowing the timetable or outcome, and as well face broad challenges that will end with his or her death, while survivors must cope with grief which applies to a much larger range of losses in coping with the actual death and its impact on their lives (Corr 2018, 11). That is not to say that dying is easier than grief, but the dying person's challenges end with their death, while the survivor's challenges may grow even larger after the death.

Families are the source of not only love, affection, and gratification, but they can also be the source of hostility, hate, and much frustration. The cultural emphasis upon loss at the time of death does not adequately represent the full range of emotions and feelings of the grieving person. While we tend to think of guilt as the result of the absence of feeling or being caused by having bad memories or relationships with the deceased person, the feeling of guilt may also be caused by the absence of any feelings when a person dies. The cultural directive to have grief and mourn for someone for whom you have no feelings can lead to emotional trauma, discomfort, and negative attitudes for failing to live up to cultural expectations. For those who are genuinely grieved, following the culturally prescribed role of being a bereaved person aids the management of their grief. Since the funeral is a major component of the culturally proscribed means of acknowledging the loss of the dead person from his or her social groups, a religious ritual, a way to commemorate the life of the deceased, and a means of asserting the families' solidarity, it is also a socially approved and a socially useful act of disposing of the dead body, over time, by culturally proscribed behavior changes.

As society becomes more secular and traditions are lost, so, too, are traditions about funerals, mourning, and grief altered over time. For many, funerals, expensive vaults and caskets, giveaway ceremonies, and other community activities are seen as wasteful. Many are choosing direct crema-tion, celebrations of life, donation of one's body to science, rather than tradi-tional funerals. The traditional black hearse, the black tie for the funeral, the black armband, the wreath on the door of the family who experienced a loss, and many other public signs of death, loss, and grief have disappeared in just a single generation (Fulton, Gottesman, and Owen 1982, 147).

All of us will die. So, will everyone that we know. Grandparents die. Children die. All of us have experienced the deaths of pets, friends, teachers, other students, neighbors, celebrities, and so many others. Death is part of our "biological package." Social scientists have only recently begun to conduct research in this area. In 1970, when I first taught a course in the sociology of death and dying, only a sparse amount of research and books were available. Now, there are thousands of books and resources available. Historically, we were forced to examine the work of theologians, poets, writers, philoso-phers, and artists to interpret this universal experience of dying and death. Research on human behavior is difficult when studying normal situations. It is much more difficult and troubling when studying extreme situations. The researcher's own thoughts and feelings compound the research process. While the study of dying and death is no longer a taboo topic, it is still dif-ficult to conduct meaningful research. As societies around the world move to become even more secularized, the need seems to have arisen to put forth rational explanations for behavior. Phenomena that previously were viewed as sacred are being examined with little regard for cultural traditions or ethi-cal concerns. In an era of concern for cultural survival and maintaining tradi-tions, many resist the efforts to study death management practices.

The entire death awareness movement has been popularized, and to some extent, has left the scientific community. Having said that the movement is less scientific, it is still important for scientists to continue to study the death management practices of humans and to learn as much as possible to enhance our own death management practices and those of future generations. The work in the field has been decidedly psychological. This work is an attempt to add a sociological perspective that has been lacking in the field. What we learn can be of value to those who face their own dying and death and those of others.

CONCLUSIONS

The final comment is a question: What do we wish to achieve by this kind of analysis that we are undertaking here? Why should researchers and scholars consider what happens to the dying, the dead, and their survivors be impor-tant? The answer is rather obvious, but I raise it as a way of pointing up the manner in which the subject of death reveals the social roots of existence. Dying and death are disruptive. They are disruptive precisely because the very meaning of our lives is based upon our interaction with other human beings. We are interdependent, and the removal of a member from the group reveals and emphasizes this interdependence. This is at the bottom of what we term grief which is, to put it negatively, an expression of our fear of aloneness. One of the things which we are expressing when we talk about the loss of a loved one is the loss of support, sustenance, and care. Thus, feelings of grief decline directly with our sense of dependence upon the deceased. There is a strong element of self-centeredness in our feelings of grief. Recognizing that phenomenon can aid our grieving process. Let me make this the first, although not necessarily the most important, substantive point, that part of the sting of grief is the revelation of our personal vulnerability and that this sting is accentuated by cultural prescriptions which make us reluctant to admit that this is the case. Our openness to cultural prescriptions other than our own may be the best approach to healing our own grief and continuing our lives in a healthy manner.

Chapter 2

Why a Sociology of Dying and Death?

The sociology of dying and death offers the opportunity to examine death management practices in different cultures; cultural practices for disposal of the deceased; to analysis of professions of funeral directors, clergy, medical staff, and other caregivers as they related to dying and death; the impact of dying and death on work environments, schools, and institutions; comparatively the ancient and modern death management practices; attitudes and values as related to dying and death; social death, legal death, biological death, and personal death; the violent nature of society and its impact on grief; theories of suicide and suicide prevention; the impact of religion on death management practices and grief processes; ethical issues relating to dying and death; and many, many more areas of interest to a sociologist.

Sociology is the science of choice making. The sociology of dying and death offers the opportunity to learn about the process of decision-making. To learn why some make choices that causes them to live life as they choose, to those who end up in the streets, those who get into drugs, those who raise their families in obscurity, and those who are able to retire and continue to live their dreams. The study of sociology allows us the opportunity to learn how society works. Sociology helps us understand the ways in which people make their living, pay taxes, invest, raise their children, face adversity, and eventually die. Sociology offers a way to understand how society is organized, and how we fit in this seeming maze.

People, like societies, must choose which of their wants to satisfy. Suppose you or your family wants to buy a car. The cost of the car would be the other things that you cannot buy. Going out to dinner? College expenses? A down payment on a better house? A trip to Europe? Which do you desire the most? If you buy the car, its real cost is the other most desired items that you cannot buy because you bought the car.

Life is basically the ability to make real cost choices. If one can make good money working on an oil rig, why go to college? College costs money. The real cost of college is the money that you are not able to earn while you are in school. One sacrifices income while in college. If one can get a house, new car, stereo, and more if one doesn't go to college, then why go to college. Unfortunately, when oil drops to $50.00 a barrel, one then lacks the training to go into another occupation when the oil field job ends. "Pay me now or pay me later." Many jobs and particularly those who are self-employed or own their own business do not have company paid retirement programs. Many truck drivers are owner operators who do not make money if they are too sick to drive or take a vacation. They also have to put aside their own money for their hoped-for retirement. If one's income is fixed, then every purchase is at the expense of another purchase that one might want to make.

As individuals make real cost decisions, so, too, do societies. High salaries paid to business graduates may attract more students to major in business. To society, the real cost of the additional business majors is not their high salary, but rather, it is in the artists, scientists, teachers, poets, and other occupations that these students might have become. Intelligent voting as a citizen requires that you recognize that the real cost of better roads or more national defense is that some other desired resource that must be given up. Paying a large amount to protect your borders means that schools, trash collection, safe water pipes, and so much more may be neglected.

Sociology then is the science of choice making. The sociology of death and dying will focus upon the science of choice making. What are the real costs to the people as a nation, society, or personally of suicide, murder, euthanasia, abortion, a large funeral, institutionalizing the elderly, or whatever? An attempt will be made to provide a framework to allow one to make real cost decisions which will allow one to live a more compassionate and caring existence. One will not need to second guess oneself or wonder if the correct decision was made. The grief that one feels for a loved one will be more manageable because the person is able to see that everything that happens is not in one's control. In short, one needs to learn how the system operates and how to live with it.

THE LESSON OF DEATH

The most important lesson that death has to teach is what is important in life. If one is not careful, one might begin to think that the newest model of car with 0.9 percent interest is really important. Who can afford to pass up such a deal? One cannot pass up such a deal even if buying the new vehicle means payments that will cause one to change his or her lifestyle. Can my family survive the current economic crisis affecting the entire nation and the world? If my family has food, clothing, and shelter to survive, is that enough? If one is not careful, one might start thinking that after several seasons of disappointments the Green Bay Packers may tear up the National Football League. One may start thinking that this is important. Obviously, many times people are not careful. While I want the Packers to be successful and do enjoy it when they have success, it does not make my life better. It is easy to be sidetracked about what is really important. "If only I had . . ." Often people lose sight of what is important. Often one feels that this is it. "If only I can have this . . ." Yet the new cars, bigger houses, winning sports teams, vacations, awards, recognition by others, and so on and on simply do not satisfy. Such things are not bad; they simply are not it! Such things can enhance one's life and can even make it better, or they can distract one from what is important and make it miserable.

When a loved one dies; when one's mother, father, wife, husband, sister, brother, son, or daughter lies in a casket; the car one drives; the Green Bay Packers record; the home one lives in; the clubs one belongs to; and the recognition one has in society simply do not matter so much. Death is not an easy lesson, but it is a lesson. The hurt will never truly end when someone who is loved dies. It will become more bearable, and life does go on. It will never be the same. But there is wisdom to be gained from the hurt. The death of someone who is loved causes one to stop the merry-go-round and to think about what one is doing with one's life. What is the value of life? What really is important? Is a genuine smile from a real friend worth more than having thousands of "fans" seeking autographs? Is taking two strokes off of your golf game worth more than an hour with your children on your day off? Is money in one's bank account worth more than what is given to help others when one dies?

Death is the gift that the dead give to the living. It can give them a new perspective on life. Each person has a unique contribution to make. For some, perhaps more is learned by one's failures and lost purpose in life. Others may teach by example. A good teacher must live by what he or she teaches. One may teach in the classroom or in the Hogan. Everyone can learn from others. Each person has something to teach to others. Is there a lesson to be learned when one dies from alcohol or suicide? Does one teach others to love their children as one loves his or her own? Does one teach others to complain and to prophesize doom? Everyone's deeds teach others even when one does not see oneself as a teacher. Elders help us to learn what is important in life. American Indians are not shy, but rather they listen more than they talk. Generally, American Indian values would encourage one to accept oneself as he or she is. Life has different paths for each person. Respect all people. No one is better or worse than you are. Those who serve us as leaders are not greater than us, but rather they have a different burden. Those who serve us as maids, clerks, who pick up our trash, or build our homes are not worse than us, but rather they have a path that gives them as much honor as our chiefs or other leaders. Wisdom of the elders requires that we do things in a good way, that we talk positively about others and about life, and that we honor the visions of the elders. Every life, the toad, the fox, the cow, the painter, the weaver, the trash collector, and so forth, has a purpose. One is not better than the other. All are needed and valued. The frog, the fox, the bear, the coyote, and the many others can help us face our own dying and death.

FACING ONE'S OWN DEATH

No matter how one prepares for death, it may cause one to be filled one with dread and fear. Most people will probably not be prepared to deal with their own death. Fear, in itself, is not bad. Fear is as natural as hunger and thirst. Cowardice starts when one gives in to fear, when one runs from danger, or when one neglects one's place in life. To be brave means to accept one's fear and then to act upon it. Courage is overcoming one's fear.

Death can be a frightening prospect. It is forced upon one. It takes one away from one's loved ones and one's way of life. As one faces the unknown, the fear of life after death or the fear of no life after death may overwhelm a person. Even Christ went through agony in the Garden of Gethsemane before facing His own death. How can one face the fear of death? People generally face death in one of two ways. People either evade death or defy it. Evading death seems to be the method that most people in modern society use. Somehow, by ignoring the unpleasant possibility of death, it is hoped that it might pass by. Before making any major decision in life, how many drink, play cards, watch television, or whatever to gain time to postpone or delay the decision. In facing death, gaining time is losing time.

One eagerly flings oneself into tasks such as work, raising one's children, civic causes, or whatever. Each person chooses how to pass one's life. The one thing that everyone has is time. One chooses to spend their time sleeping, using drugs, working, enjoying people, or whatever. The excuse that "I just don't have the time" is simply that. It is an excuse. You have the time. It is the only thing that you really do have. The most important question is "Is it worth my time?" rather than "do I have the time for this?" When you meet a new person, you must decide whether or not this person is worth investing your time into. This decision cannot be made based upon what this person can give to you. It is much more important to ask what you can give to them. If you have much to give, then you will also receive much from the relationship.

To find what relationships and what part of one's daily tasks are important, one should contemplate, "What would I do if I knew that I only had a few days, weeks or months to live?" If you have much that you would do, then one should do those things. One does not know the hour of one's death unless one faces the hangman. If your job is a burden, then find another job, but try to get hired before you resign your present job. If you want to tell your husband that he has made your life worthwhile, then tell him before one of you is no longer living. Life is based upon choices. What choices are keeping you from being fulfilled in your life? What choices give you happiness?

SOCIOLOGICAL CONCEPTS IN DYING AND DEATH

Sociologist William Isaac Thomas taught that all people define their situations in his concept of definition of the situation. A person defines himself or herself, one's family, one's marriage, one's job, those around one, and so forth. This is a never-ending process. Each person has the ability to make one's life miserable or happy. One can define one's world as a dirty, miserable place, or one can define the world as a challenge to make better, or any other definition that one chooses. The choice belongs to each person. One can be troubled with oneself and those around one. A person can allow others to get him or her angry, sad, or whatever. No one can make you angry. You choose to let them get you angry. By learning to be fully conscious of one's actions, one can take control of one's life. If one does not learn to make decisions and to take control, the person simply drifts along like a cork in the river allowing every mood or impulse of the river to control his or her life. The person becomes weak, helpless, and a slave to the whims of others who manipulate individuals like the cork bobber in the river. Some people may delude themselves into thinking that they can control their lives without making decisions, but does the cork control the fisherman? By letting others define one and one's situations, the person then tends to fulfill the prophecies of others rather than fulfilling one's own dreams.

The concept of self-fulfilling prophecy suggests that unless an individual takes control of one's life, then one will live up to the definitions or labels that others attach to an individual. Because one's teachers, parents, friends, and so forth define an individual, many then go through life believing that they can't do when they really can by taking the effort to examine oneself, one can then decide what he or she can do. By testing, one can discover that much is really possible. How many students invent excuses not to study for a test because of the fear that they will do poorly if they do study? The result is a lower self-concept.

Many people worry about what others think of them in a busy airport even though they will probably never see any of these people again. By making your own decisions of your self-worth, you rely less on the opinions of others. If nothing else, you will have less anxiety over what others think of you, which may allow you to live the life that you choose. If you can live the type of life and lifestyle that you choose, facing death becomes much easier. Too many people are filled with regrets and if onlys. If you live the life you choose to live, then there will be fewer regrets when you finally face your impending death. Perhaps everyone would like to see how one's children, friends, relatives, and so forth will turn out. Perhaps, one wonders who will win the Super Bowl. But if you have followed your own road instead of the road that others would have had you to follow, you will be content that you have lived your life. Each person must follow his or her own dreams. Don't say, "Someday." If you have a dream, follow it.

Our beliefs, attitudes, values about death, dying, grief, and loss come from the people and groups of which we are a part. Within our societies, our religion, philosophical position, and ethnic background help us develop and refine what are for us appropriate responses, feelings, behaviors, and rituals. While there are certainly wide differences among individuals even in the same family, there are also differences within any society or culture, particularly in their psychological processing of grief. These differences are often more subtle than profound. Differences among cultures as well as within cultures also exist. Societal and cultural influences may be difficult to recognize. Most of us are ethnocentric, or we view the world from the lens of their own culture. The world is as I live it is the way the world should be. Our world is based upon the context in which we live. Our contextual framework is fundamental to our way of viewing the world. As such, we often overlook the profound impact on how we feel and behave about loss.

The way that my parents grieve is the way that I learn to grieve. I may also learn styles of grieving from friends and other family members. Each of these people learned from their family members and friends. Each of them may have easily learned different or even conflicting styles of coping with grief. Our friend, family, schools, religions, and so forth make up our culture. We are what our culture makes to us, and yet, we are also what makes the culture what it is. Within each culture, there are many conflicting attitudes, values, feelings, responses, behaviors, and rituals. Yet, there is also continuity within culture. Because culture is so inclusiveness, it is also often difficult to know what comes from culture and what might be instinctive or natural as a part of our personality. How much of our response comes from our gender roles or from our religious upbringing or from our own spirituality? We are what we are because of our many cultural, familial, religious, and educational influences. Our attitudes impact our interpretation of our experiences.

Our experiences influence our attitudes. If our father's coping techniques for grief do not seem to work for him, we may adopt a different approach. Yet, each individual and each family is different. There are no guarantees that we learn from our mistakes. It is also not a given that we will choose the coping style that would work best for us. Colin Murray Parkes points out that adults whose parents expressed less grief often produce children who suffer protracted grief, anxiety, depression, and often turn to alcohol following bereavement (Parkes 2002, 23). Over time, each of us develops a coping style to manage loss. Many, if not most, people within a culture form similar styles of coping with loss. Yet, there are always many who have their own individual approaches that are influenced by personality, attitudes, spirituality, and gender. A given culture may offer many forms of institutionalized religion each with its own interpretation about the meaning of death in human life. Yet, while there is individual and family uniqueness within each culture, there are generally important culturally determined characteristics.

CULTURAL DIFFERENCE

Most people understand on the broadest level that there are differences among cultural, ethnic, and religious groups in all aspects of life from the food we eat and clothes we wear to the traditions we have about life's most important transitions such as birth, marriage, and death. These differences become most uncomfortable at sensitive and vulnerable times like death.

The broad social context and cultural environment is the key in determining an individual's reaction to death, dying, grief, and loss. Because death is universal, all societies have struggled with the reality of death and created a wide variety of responses to dealing with loss.

Precipitants of grief vary for families from different cultures after the death of a child. In the United States, parents often find that the holidays are very difficult, while Japanese parents may be painfully reminded of the death of their child when they pass by the school or see children walking to school in their yellow rain hats. The U.S. culture further emphasizes youth, beauty, and health. The United States has often been described as a death-denying society because it seems to want the dead to appear to be sleeping and to have others tend to the dead. Perhaps, they might also be described as a death-avoiding society for the same reasons. It might be more appropriate to describe the United States as a death-defying society because of the emphasis upon using any means possible to stay alive. In any case, the U.S. culture seems to deny the reality of dying, death, and grief. On the whole, American culture provides little support for grievers. Little time is given off work to deal with a family death since bereavement leave is generally one to three days. For the most part, we are expected to hide our feelings and emotions and to keep them private, to grieve alone, in silence and replace our loss as soon as possible. Those who work with us typically avoid us or change the subject if our grief becomes part of our conversations or behaviors. Little tolerance is shown to those who are grieving if they fail to perform successfully at work or school.

Even the language used to discuss dying and death is designed to make the pain less intense. We rarely speak of someone dying. Rather, we say that they passed away, passed on, expired, kicked the bucket, bought the farm, or whatever. Such euphemisms are designed to ease our sense of loss and emotional response of mourning. Our culture also discourages direct expressions of grief. When someone is actively grieving, crying, and expressing pain, we often say they are "not coping well." If we see someone who is sad, we attempt to cheer him or her. We say things like, "You have to be brave for the children" or "you are doing so well" which means that they are not expressing pain or causing us inconvenience. In the U.S. culture, grieving has come to represent a failure to adjust. It is not surprising therefore that we avoid grief and all things associated with it.

BECOMING CULTURALLY AWARE

Ideally, caregivers would be familiar with all the variations in cultural approaches to dying and death, so they could facilitate families as they carry out these important and comforting traditions of grief and bereavement, but there are significant variations between families and within cultures so to attempt to understand cultural similarities and differences is quite difficult. It is also important not to overgeneralize. Not only do funeral customs and rituals vary but also so do traditions in grieving and bereavement.

Nowhere in caregiving is it more evident that our personal experiences impact the care we give than in the area of death, dying, grief, and loss. Our conscious and unconscious reactions to our own grief experiences have had a profound influence on our past as well as current reactions to the grief of others. It is necessary for us to gain insights as to who we are and to our own responses to death. Our reactions and thoughts are related to our past experiences, personal attitudes, family traditions, religious or spiritual beliefs, and ethnic heritage. By knowing who we are, we can develop an attitude of curiosity and interest rather than being judgmental when talking with someone whose experiences and values are greatly different than ours. This generally means being aware, sensitive, caring, and open. One must develop cultural competence, cultural awareness, and cultural comfort zones. One needs to listen and ask questions rather than providing answers.

There is little doubt that socio-cultural characteristics of grief and death affect end-of-life care. The end of life is a vulnerable time for the dying and their families. The more deeply the caregiver understands each family's unique needs, values, rituals, and traditions related to dying, death, and grief, the less likely the caregiver will cause upset to families or those they are serving. Knowing the culture of those that they serve would also allow them to be more effective in aiding the dying and their friends and family in their journey through dying and grieving. We cannot know what people need unless we ask. In the U.S. culture, asking for help is not a cultural trait. Most people avoid using their button to call for the nurse for help when they are in the hospital or other institutions even when they desperately need help. Most of us do not want to be a bother. Caregivers need to let the family, dying person, and their friends know that they are there to serve them and that it is not a bother but rather a pleasure to serve. We need to be open to all family members and not just to those who are willing to talk. Children, in particular, need to be asked what they are feeling and if they have any questions about the process or illness or whatever. Questions can be woven into various discussions about the patient's terminal situation or impending death with family. You can also ask the family, dying person, or friends if they are willing to have a conversation with you about death-related things that could help you provide better care as this process unfolds. Allow children and adolescents to make their own choice about what they want to discuss. Children should decide how they wish to participate in funerals or other services. The question is not if children and adolescents should participate, but rather how. Adults must provide information, options, and support. Discussions can focus upon end-of-life care and decisions, styles of discussing dying and death, body disposal preferences, legal issues, grieving traditions, funeral practices, notification issues, or future issues such as remarriage or raising the children or whatever. As caregivers, we need to be culturally aware, culturally sensitive, caring, and open. Caregivers work with people who are vulnerable and often have difficulty coping with the situation. We can make the situation more tolerable by being a culturally aware person.

CONCLUSIONS

Sociology offers a unique window for studying dying and death. By studying other cultures, it is possible to better understand one's own culture. Sociology offers a way of enhancing choice making, facing one's own dying and death, and ways of helping others to manage their own situations of grief and bereavement. Those who work with the dying and grieving people can learn from other cultures how to better manage their situations as well as to better help others manage their situations.

Chapter 3

Sociology of the American Indian

The study of culture is basic to understanding any group. American Indians are subordinated in terms of power, privilege, education, housing, and economic status by the majority or dominant group. Like other minorities, American Indians are a minority not because of their smaller numbers, but by the unequal treatment, subordination, and classification as a separate and inferior group.

The subject matter of sociology is society. This, like other words in sociology, is borrowed from common everyday usage, but it takes on some special meaning or perhaps more precise meanings. Society can refer to a group, tribe, or band of people, or to people endowed with great prestige or privilege such as British Royalty, and sometimes it simply means the company of other people. However, the sociologist uses the more precise definition of a "system of interaction." This suggests that whenever you find a collectivity of humans, you find a set way of doing things, social organization, a large complex of human relationships, and rules for behavior. The six hundred or so societies that were in North America before the arrival of the Europeans developed set ways of behaving, social organization, definitions of behavior, and systems of interaction. You will also find that the word "social" has a common usage and a distinct sociological usage. The common use of the word social may refer to a meeting, to an event, or concern, but in sociology, the word social refers to activity which is oriented toward the behavior or actions of other people. The hunter who shares the spoils of his hunt with families other than his own does so for social prestige, to help other families, to encourage other hunters to share with his family when he is not successful in hunting, and as a way of following the rules of his culture.

Sociologists study patterns of behavior and then interpret those patterns. Social phenomena have two basic characteristics: recurrence in time and recurrence in space. Sociologists are interested, not in differing behavior, but in differing patterns. For example, rather than study the storytelling of a specific clan or tribe, sociologists look for the patterns of storytelling. It is a way of passing on sacred wisdom. While the stories differ immensely, the purpose of the stories remains a method to instruct and to entertain. Sociologists are also interested in complementary patterns: do the stories impact behavior, are they entertaining to listeners, do they impact the knowledge of the physical world, and how much impact do they have on rule making?

SOCIOLOGY AND SOCIAL LIFE

Social life is the product of human activity, the economic, social, political, and spiritual life of a people. Societies emerge from social life. Societies change, adapt, modify, fail, or survive over time. The society is the product of social interaction of people over time. The concept of social interaction is basic to the process of socio-economic formation. Every social aspect is part of a complex system of interacting elements. While the elements are often analyzed separately, the influence of other cultural elements is often overlooked or not accounted for by researchers. Interaction occurs between individuals, individuals and groups, groups and other groups, individuals and social institutions. Relationships that arise from specific systems of social interaction are called social relations. Social relations are relations among people under historically established social forms under specific conditions of time and place. In other words, social interaction, social relations, and relationships vary from one group to another. Social relations are studies as an aggregate from the social structure of a society. The social structure of a society provides people with their norms, values, patterns of behavior, and social forms in which their activities take place. These forms are called social institutions. The five basic institutions of all societies are religion, occupation, family, government, and education. A change in the social structure causes change in the social forms of human interaction which inevitably causes changes in norms, values, patterns, and social behavior which ultimately determine people's social attitudes.

Societies are greatly influenced by chance factors such as availability of building materials, environment, weather patterns, presence or absence of war, economic opportunities, educational systems, availability of natural resources, and choices of application of technology to the environment. Sociological analysis involves not simply the investigation of human motivation, but also the institutionalized social relations which determine the character and substance of human behavior. The task of sociology is to investigate the social forms which determine human activity. Sociological analysis involves more than simply the investigation of human motivation. It is the study of institutionalized social relations which allow understanding of the means of interaction of human activity and the social forms mediating these activities.

Social regulation is the product of social relations and relations between society's individual members. Some societies focus upon the individual while others focus upon the group. The conflict between the individual will and individual actions may lead to conflict and cross purposes. Society develops social regulations to ease the conflicts between individuals and groups. Marxist sociologists suggest that the lack of freedom allowed to the individual by the social regulations leads to alienation for the individual in his or her social life and working life. Other sociologists would suggest that it is not a question of self-awareness but rather a normal state of affairs that is the result of ultra-individualism. The ultra-individualism is the only way to retain individuality.

The organization of society requires that individuals follow rules that are developed by human societies to guide the behavior of individuals as they engage in activities with other individuals within the framework of cultural rules. Individual freedom is a consolidation of the individual's ties with society, cultural impositions, socialization, and requirements of the social organizations of which the individual is a part. Cultural groups also seek freedom. Individual freedom is typically subjugated to the freedom of the cultural group. Like individuals, cultural groups have to struggle to maintain their freedoms in the face of other cultural groups infringing upon their freedoms. American Indians struggle to maintain their cultural freedom from European groups who have attempted to destroy their cultures and to maintain their individual freedom in the face of rules and traditions developed by both their Indian heritage and the dominant "white" cultures. Learning new roles whether by force or choice while trying to maintain traditional roles produces conflict for American Indians.

SOCIAL LIFE AND SOCIAL RELATIONSHIPS

Human relationship infers that if there is behavior of two or more people rather than being the property of an individual, it becomes a double-headed arrow. More precisely, this inferred bond grows out of the interaction of persons-in-roles: mother-daughter, husband-wife, shaman-patient, follower-chief. So, social roles can be regarded as the essential element in the study of human relationships. Roles are the culturally prescribed performance of a person in a given social position within a group. Roles can be studies from direct observation of behavior such as watching a hunter prepare for the hunt, the hunt, and the behavior after the hunt; or indirectly by asking for descriptions of roles from people who have knowledge of how people behave in the roles. Roles may be defined quite differently in terms of the performance of these roles. Traditional American Indian discipline is unstructured. Discipline typically does not involve harsh words or physical punishment. Grandparents and less so parents instruct. Lakota believe that children acquire self-control and necessary knowledge from experience and would use shame or warnings rather than guilt or authoritarian methods. Cheyenne highly value children and would mold them with love and interest. While they would not punish children, they were taught patience, that life was harsh, and that they should put the interests of the tribe above self-interests. Apache children are taught the value of silence. Most groups value the ability to express ideas in few words, yet, most will relate that their grandfather answered their questions with long stories rather than simple sentences to teach about life and with prayers often are quite lengthy before meals or other rituals.

Typically, when people interact they may have different definitions of what is proper role behavior. A teacher working with Navajo students may expect them to engage in lengthy verbal discussions while they would typically offer short sentence answers. A relationship does not stand alone. It is implicated in an extended network of relationships. Relationships are a part of structures of interlocking relationships which exist within culture.

INFLUENCE OF SOCIAL GROUPS

At birth, individuals enter the group. The group changes every day with births, deaths, expulsion, punitive sanctions, wars, and thousands of other ways. How do people become members of the group? When a person moves to a new community as the spouse, child, worker, or relative of someone in the group, at what point are they accepted into the group? Most groups seem to never fully allow newcomers to fully become part of the group. The Apache welcomed those willing to fight with them, but they did not welcome men who would not join them (Terrell 1972, 102). Navajo are noted for integrating strangers into their group. Navajo took from refugees after making them part of their group. From the Pueblo they learned weaving, rug-making, pottery-making, rituals, mythology, sandpainting, jewelry-making, and ceremonies (Underhill 1956, 50–51). Some groups allow newcomers to become part of the group; others never seem to incorporate them into their groups. Like the Navajo, the Apache saw the wisdom of marrying the Pueblo and Mexican women who fled to them, who could give them children to make up for losses to disease and warfare (Terrell 1972, 102). People enter the group through migration, birth, capture, conquest, by living on land that is acquired, and by edict. The process of entering the group, the study of stability over time, and the processes of interaction are what was first developed by anthropologists and later by sociologists of culture.

INFLUENCE OF CULTURE

Culture provides the rules (norms), defines the roles that make the relationships that constitute the group, teaches the rules and roles to new generations, and attempts to preserve the group for future generations. Culture is a set of relationships that is not happenstance, a sometimes thing, but it is contrived, an artifact, the most significant of all human artifacts. A group is a creation; an enduring group is a continuous recreation. Sociologists see two processes: new members are recruited, and new members choose to join the group. Like the Navajo and Apache, the group that met John Smith and the other Pilgrims allowed Pocahontas to be a part of the Pilgrim's group and shared their group with them including the first Thanksgiving. Groups are participation units. It is not simply the two or more people who are first defined as a group, but groups such as the Western Apache or the Assiniboine that lasted long after their first members. Members are typically not involved in all aspects of the group. Shaman may conduct ceremonies, healings, and rituals, but they may not be involved in food gathering. Membership in the group would mean that the person learns to perform in a particular role that is intertwined with other's roles. Membership in the group presupposes that the individual has a shared understanding of what ought to be in member's interactions with other members of the group which leads to predictable interaction. It is hardly ever the case that all members agree on what is the proper way to play their role in the group. All of the six hundred tribal groups that were in the Americas when Columbus arrived had outlasted their individual members who began the tribes.

SOCIOLOGICAL CONCEPTS

All societies have developed specific patterns of behavior that are called cultural universals. These are elements common to all societies. Generally, these would include survival needs such as food, clothing, and shelter, and social needs such as recreation, sports, funerals, rituals, dancing, names, medicine, work, taboos, institutions, and health. While the cultural universals may be found in every culture, their application varies greatly. Not only do different groups have different definitions of what is adequate shelter, different generations, different groups may have even greater differences, but all would have adequate shelter. Available materials, knowledge of building, and financial means to obtain materials would influence the type of dwelling that a group would consider to be adequate. Lacking trees and other building materials, an Inuit would build a snow block home. A Navajo who rarely moved would live in a Hogan, a building with eight sides that was solidly constructed with stacked juniper logs and roofed. An Apache who moved often depending upon availability of hunting, weather, or safety lived in a wickiup made from branches and other materials that were very temporary dwellings. A Hopi who farmed and has not moved for many generations would live in a solidly built adobe dwelling. The Chippewa (Ojibwa) built wigwams from bent saplings that were covered with reed mats and bark. Because they were built in panels with separate frames and coverings, they were relatively easy to transport giving them freedom of movement. Iroquois and Huron groups were known for building longhouses, some of which were over 300 feet long, of many different styles using logs for posts, placing floors in the house, complete with bunks and storage racks, and roofed with cedar bark or elm bark. American Indians built many other forms of housing, but the point is that they all developed some form of dwelling—a cultural universal!

Ethnocentrism is another sociological concept that suggests that all peoples evaluate other people and groups according to their own standards using their cultural norms as a standard to judge others by. A Christian might view American Indian religion as inferior. A Muslim might view Christianity as inferior. One who works a 40-hour week and does not receive welfare or food stamps or other support would perhaps judge those who do so as lazy or inferior. Sociologist C. Wright Mills (1959) suggested that in order to better understand human behavior we need to use critical thinking. Mills developed a concept "The Sociological Imagination" or the ability to view one's own society or group as an outsider, to go beyond personal experiences and biases learned from one's own groups. Why would a Navajo choose to live in a dirt floor, eight-sided Hogan rather than in the modern house provided by the tribe or the government? Perhaps, the Navajo wanted to live in the way of his or her ancestors. Perhaps, the Navajo choose the Hogan because of religious or spiritual needs. Why is the Navajo unemployed? Because you work, you assume that the Navajo could also find a job. Perhaps, the Navajo lived more than 30 miles from the nearest place to find a job and has no car or public transportation available. Perhaps, the Navajo is serving as the caregiver, elder, or medicine person for the tribe, but does not get a pay check. The Sociological Imagination is looking at others or even our own group through a kaleidoscope or different lens than the lens that we use to look at ourselves. To look at one's own group without bias would entail becoming an outsider in one's own group. Honest criticism of one's own group is often met with harsh response. Describing other groups will often gain criticism from those same groups while one's own group may laud the criticisms.

Another sociological concept would be cultural relativism which calls for judging another culture from their perspective rather than that of your own culture. Rather than dismissing the ways of another group as strange or inferior, the sociologist uses a value neutral approach that was suggested by Max Weber. The United States choose to judge the American Indian cultures as inferior and attempted to force the American Indians to adopt European ways, religion, and values rather than trying to learn about the American Indian cultures and what might be gained from learning their ways.

An important attribute of culture is language. The importance of language cannot be understated. It is one of the major elements of culture. Without language, culture dies. As fewer and fewer American Indian languages are spoken, understood, and used by tribal groups, their knowledge of their own cultures is fading. As the dominant language of North America is British, groups who learn British and over generations forget their traditional language, their attachment to their traditional culture wanes. Navajo, Hopi, Apache, and other groups who have maintained their traditional language along with British have also been more successful at preserving traditional culture of their group.

Norms and values are two concepts that sociologists apply in their study of cultures. Norms are the standards of behavior or rules that are shared and understood by the group. Some norms or rules are considered to be more serious if violated than others. Norms that are considered to be rules that when violated will lead to serious sanctions are called "mores." Mores are considered to be so important that the very fabric of society would be threatened if violated, including such things as murder, treason, witchcraft, desecrating of sacred objects, rape, or other serious rules. Sanctions are penalties for violations of norms. For mores, the sanctions could include death, exile, imprisonment, or extensive physical punishment. For less serious rule violations, called folkways, the act may even be ignored. A Navajo child who speaks to an adult without being included in the adult conversation will not be exiled for the rule violation, but would get a look or be told, "You are not acting like a Navajo."

Values are collective ideas of what is considered by the group to be good, proper, desirable or to be bad, evil, improper, undesirable. In all societies, there are conflicting values. A Navajo youth may want an iPad, to not live in a Hogan, join a gang, and to wear baggy pants, while his parents want him to behave like a Navajo and not like a White person. Values differ across cultural lines. In the dominant white culture, teachers look students in the eye when teaching, often ask questions of students that they cannot answer, and give competitive grades, while Navajos are taught to not look people in the eyes who are not familiar or close, to not embarrass people by asking questions that the answers might not be known, and to cooperate rather than try to embarrass others by beating them in academic activities or sports.

The concept of cultural wars could be illustrated by the history of relations between American Indians and the dominant white culture. The current political cultural wars between the Trump followers and the Democrats are another obvious example. The Brexit struggles, the South African Apartheid, the "troubles" in Northern Ireland, the Israeli/Palestinian struggles, and so many more are examples of cultural wars.

CULTURAL CHANGE

Cultural change is another important sociological concept. Changes in culture occur in all groups. There is little question that all groups and all people change. The Hopi Kachinas have changed over time. As suggested, Hopi ceremonies were all directed at rain and fertility. Each clan had a specific area of religious responsibility. Each clan had specific roles and lessons to teach. Ceremonies followed specific times, calendar dates, and rituals. One-third to one-half of the year was devoted to ceremonies. Ritual work was the center of their existence! With the coming of European-style jobs, paying bills, driving cars, and living in a nontraditional world, many ceremonies have been lost. The two seasons of December through July with Kachina rituals and the August through November without Kachinas still are central. There are still three forms of Kachinas. The first would be spiritual beings who serve as intermediaries to the sacred world, numbering as many as 600 with around 250 being more commonly used. Such spirits are not considered to be gods or worshiped, but rather are viewed as friends and as having many human qualities. Some are viewed as kindly spirits who are benevolent, while others who inspire fear by their punishment of Hopi offenders. The second form of Kachina would be the dancers who impersonate both male and female Kachinas. By wearing the mask of a particular Kachina the dancer who is wearing the mask receives sacred powers, a loss of sense of self, and believes that they become the Kachina. The third form of Kachina would be the elaborate and finely carved dolls that Kachina dancers give to Hopi children during the ceremonies to teach them about Kachina beings. Traditionally, the Hopi taught that the two seasons were because the rituals of the first season were performed in the world below in the second season. The Kachinas had to be somewhere else during the second season which is why they could not dance in the mesas with the Hopi. Over time, the planting cycle has changed as has the timing of the dances. Fear of witchcraft and the fear that witches were becoming more numerous in the world above and the world below, traditional prophecies of the coming of whites and the resulting era of purification, the infusion of Christianity, and the development of different farming techniques that changed cycles all had their impact. The Hopi ceremonial cycle declined over time.

Like the Hopi who maintained their traditional ways and yet changed over time, the American Indians have experienced massive religious change. Over time, the Pueblo peoples have adopted many new festivals and ceremonies including various saint's days, All Souls' Day, Holy Week, Christmas, and other Catholic rituals that were modified to fit Hopi traditions. The ghost dance, which swept across the plains, is perhaps the most well-known new religious practice. When the traditional religious practices were forbidden by the white clergy and the Federal government and when lands and way of life were being lost, a Paiute Indian called Jack Wilson or Wovoka came with a vision that came to him in two near-death experiences that foretold of the destruction of the whites and the destruction of the earth with a new earth emerging after the flood which would be a reunification with ancestors, abundance, and plenty if only Indians would perform the ghost dance. The ghost dance spread quickly across the plains. For an excellent description of the ghost dance, see Mail (1978). The belief was that if enough people performed the ghost dance that the prediction would happen. Many came to a belief that the ghost shirts that they wore during the ghost dance made them bulletproof. Unfortunately, they were not bulletproof. The fear of the ghost dance by whites led to the massacre at Wounded Knee, South Dakota! After ordering tribes to not engage in the ghost dance rituals, the Seventh Cavalry was sent to stop the ghost dance. While it ended the public ghost dance, it did not end the ghost dance. For a more complete accounting of Wounded Knee, see Mails (1970), Brown (1970), Marin (2000), and Andrist (1964).

Another movement was the peyote religion. While it contained many Christian elements, it, too, was based upon a vision. Of course, peyote caused visions. The Peyote Cult is also known as the native American religion. Primarily, a twentieth-century movement, the movement has had great opposition from the government over its use of the mescal part of the peyote cactus. They have had some victories in court and have the general acceptance as a pan-Indian movement, but in 1990 the United States Supreme Court denied the use of peyote in their religious ceremonies, which drew the attention of other religious groups who feared that their practices would be threatened by the decision. The result was that Congress passed a law in 1993 that was challenged by the courts in 1997. Even though the practice of using peyote has been condemned in the courts, it has continued to flourish.

Not all religious movements among American Indians were feared or condemned by whites. The Seneca religion led by Handsome Lake, who like Wovoka, had three visions: offered an apocalyptic gospel that confirmed the existence of sin, the impending end of the world, and the need for salvation, none of which offended white Christians. He later called for temperance, moral reform, and the sacredness of the family. Cultural change is part of the fabric of all groups.

The term *First Nations* is used by Canadians to describe the peoples who are a part of the mainstream of American society—all of America, from the Arctic Circle to the tip of South America.

CONCLUSIONS

The study of the culture of American Indians from a sociological perspective requires the use of basic sociological concepts that frame the analysis and understanding of the many cultures. American Indians are subordinated in terms of power, privilege, education, housing, and economic status by the majority or dominant group. Like other minorities, American Indians are a minority not because of their smaller numbers, but by the unequal treatment, subordination, and classification as a separate and inferior group.

Chapter 4

Burial and Mortuary Customs
of American Indians

The study of burial and mortuary customs can provide the opportunity to learn much about the philosophy and the religion of a people. Sociologically, the study of the burial band mortuary customs will help uncover cultural universals in practices, or at the very least, the basis for diverse practices. Sociologist Emile Durkheim suggested that rituals were related to institutions and that while there was variety in form and structure, there were elements that were universal or common to all such practices (Durkheim 1915, 50). Today, mortuary practices are primarily conducted by funeral directors. Burial practices now include casket companies and vault companies and their personnel whom the survivors typically never even meet. Graves are opened and closed by backhoe operators also without the family being present.

The rich traditions of the six hundred or so North American Indian groups can be studied through an analysis of their mortuary and burial practices. American Indian cultures have been present for thirty thousand or more years and have left behind a record complete with rituals, artifacts, and customs. Burial practices are the one remnant that is found in all cultures. The practices of any specific culture are not universal to all cultures. The practices of the 574 federally recognized tribes are not the same from one group to another or within a single clan or tribe. At the same time, there are common elements that do exist in burial and mortuary practices. Depending upon the status of the person who died, the amount of public display will vary; the greater the display, the more highly valued the deceased. Public display suggests high social value. Tribal chiefs, great hunters, spiritual leaders, or even children maybe deemed to have high social status for one tribe or clan, and yet, another tribe or clan might assign greater social value to a grandfather, a storyteller, or to a holy person. The length and intensity of public grieving also tend to reflect one's social value to the tribe, clan, or family.

DISPOSAL METHODS OF AMERICAN INDIANS

Disposal methods may also reflect attitudes toward the dead. Cremation may be used as a method of sending the soul of the deceased skyward to an after-life. Cremation may be used to try to help the deceased on their journey to the next life out of our love and respect for the deceased. By contrast, cremation may also be used to destroy the corpse so that the deceased cannot come back to inflict injury or harm upon the living. By destroying the corpse, one is done with it, and the corpse can no longer harm the living (Malinowski 1925, 49).

Mummification as a means of disposal may be used to preserve the body from decay out of love for the deceased. Mummification may also provide aid to the grieving by helping them know that the body of the deceased has been preserved as the living reminder of him or her. On the other hand, mum-mification could be used to secure personal survival for the deceased to allow them to live in an afterworld (Malinowski 1925, 49).

The use of tree burial may reflect the cultural view that placing the dead among trees will allow the dead to return to their "roots." Tree burial may also simply be a product of trying to return the deceased to nature as quickly as possible by allowing animals, birds, and insects to consume the body. This practice reflects a naturalist philosophy. It is also possible that tree burial may be the chosen method of disposal because the person died in the winter when the ground was simply frozen so hard that it is nearly impossible to dig a grave until the spring thaw.

Mounds builders are also quite common, though quite diverse in practices across North America. Some mounds were simply pits, while others were foundations of houses, others were beneath houses, some were on top of the ground and covered, and still others were rocks that covered the grave that over time became mounds. The mounds may have included provisions and other items to aid the deceased in their journey to the afterworld. Even the conception of the afterworld varied from group to group. There are also dif-ferent concepts of where the afterworld is located, with some believing that it is in the sky, while others believe that it is in the center of the earth. Mounds building may also have been a method to keep the deceased from coming back to harm the living.

Those who used stones to cover the grave may have covered them to keep the ghost of the deceased from returning to haunt the living (Fraser 1886, 86). Covering them with rocks may also have been used to keep scavengers from ravaging the body of the deceased. Rocks may have been used to simply mark the grave. The Lakota used grave posts to mark graves. These markers were inserted into the ground or supported with stones. The stones themselves lasted longer than the markers. Other groups buried their dead by pulling down the wickiup, Hogan, or other type of dwelling over the dead body. Still others placed the body in a canoe, cave, urn, or other container designed to dispose of the body of the dead. Other groups would place the body into a crevasse or hole in the ground and then cover the body with rocks or by pulling a fallen tree over it. Many, many methods have been used.

The practice of leaving food and property for the dead person was also common. Such practices may have grown out of fear of the dead person. It may have also been believed that the dead person might return to disturb the living if they did not leave such items not left for the deceased. Such practices may have also resulted from the belief that it was a way to further honor the deceased by having treasured items buried with the person who was greatly loved by the living. Many cultures bury items with the deceased that are intended to show the love or fear of the living for the deceased. What is placed in the grave by the living will reflect who is in the grave. For a child, it might be toys, a favorite blanket, clothes, feeding items, and other trinkets that the child enjoyed in life. For a warrior's grave, one would expect to find favorite weapons, beads, medicine bags, or paint. In a woman's grave, one might find food or tools for tanning or making pottery. In a farmer's grave, one might find food, farm implements, or seeds (Atkinson 1935, 160).

ANALYSIS OF DISPOSAL PRACTICES, CEREMONIES, AND RITUALS

Since no two funerals will ever be exactly the same, it is impossible to offer a complete picture of the attitudes and values of a particular people toward dying and death. It would require the researcher to observe hundreds of funerals to be able to understand the subtle practices that might distinguish one funeral from another even in the same family. Each funeral will differ because of variances in the age, sex, social position, amount of disposable income, religious affiliation, spirituality, or other factors that characterize either the dead person or their survivors who plan and offer the funeral. Other factors might also include how the person died, the time of year in which the death occurred, or the personality or behavior of the person who died. The attitudes of the survivors toward the dead person or the dead person's behavior in life could also impact the type of funeral rituals and bereavement that ensue as well.

Generally, most tribes, clans, and families will have immediate or at least timely burial of the dead person. Most tribes would not include young children in the burial and bereavement rituals. The Dine would exclude not only children, but most people. Some tribes would bring gifts of food and other items for the spouse or family of the deceased while others would have the spouse and family of the deceased give away the possessions of the deceased

to those who attend the funeral and grieving ceremonies. A wake or some sort
of ritualistic telling of the tales and stories of the deceased would often follow
the burial. Warrior tribes would often regal in tales of the bravery or prowess
of the deceased. The more sedentary tribes would offer tales of the lore of the
tribe and the exploits of the deceased.

Generally in most tribes, men tell the stories about the dead person, but in
some tribes, it would be women who tell the stories. In either situation, those
listening to the stories are expected to try very hard to stay awake to listen
to the stories that may last for hours. Those who get too sleepy to properly
listen may quietly slip away for a time and silently slip into place at after a
brief rest. Food, drink, and smoking are common practices. Some tribes may
play games. If games are played, the surviving spouse would typically not
take part. Close relatives are expected to remain in a state of mourning until
the games are completed. For some tribes, this bereavement process may take
days. For others, it may only be for a short time.

Grieving by American Indians is like grief for any other group of people.
The responses to another's death are decidedly individual. Who died, the
relationship with them, how much experience one has with death, the spirituality of the griever, how traditional or "white" the griever has become,
and whether one is reservation or urban were among the many variables that
impact the grief of American Indian survivors.

Ceremonies and rituals are a part of everything that tribes do. While death
is accepted and is not the subject of great fear or dread, that does not mean
that American Indians do not mourn the loss of their people. Death is a natural part of life. Ceremonies and rituals are a celebration of every moment of
life and death. Perhaps only the American Indian has death songs that one
might compose spontaneously at the very moment of death or that are sung
when standing in the face of death.

While not as commonly used as other forms of body disposal, cremation
was the dominate form of disposal of the dead in three distinct areas: the
Yukon Sub-Arctic, adjacent parts of the Northwest coast, and the Mackensie
Sub-Arctic; California and adjacent parts of the Plateau, the Great Basin,
and the Southwest; Northeast Mexico and among a few people of Meso-
America (Driver 1969, 375). The Yuman-speaking tribes including the
Mohave, Cocopa, and Yuma of the Lower Colorado River and the Shoshone
of the Great Basin are among the tribes that used cremation. California
seems to be somewhat equally divided between those who burned their dead
and those who interred their dead. The Southern California Indians who
burned their dead along with the Northeastern Modoc as did the Central
California areas ranging from the Sierra Nevada to the San Joaquin Valley
to the lower Sacramento Valley while interment was used from Great Basin
to the Southern Sierras to the Chumash and Santa Barbara Islands as did

the Northwestern tribes also use interment (Kroeber 1971, 35). The choice to cremate or inter is decidedly cultural since both practices are found in both treeless and forested regions of California (Kroeber 1971, 35). Some Northwestern tribes and some Central and South American groups are also known to have used cremation.

Historically more than sixty tribes lived in what is now California. Some are still there. Many of these were small village groups whose tribal names were not used by them, but rather, were given to them by others. Linguistically, they are from many different language groups. The main northern California tribes, the Algonkian Yuroks, the Athabascan Hups, and the Karoks, are closest to the tribes on the Northwest coast cultures. The Yuma of the Colorado River Valley in Southeastern California were more similar in their culture to the corn-growing tribes of Arizona and New Mexico. The northern groups, while living mostly by hunting and fishing, were known to have developed greater technology, a more in-depth spiritual system, and had a property system. The majority of the California Indian cultures were similar to the Basin and Plateau cultures, and there were also food gatherers like them. Agriculture was not practiced anywhere. The primary food source was the acorn. Like other groups, they also did some fishing and hunting. Their major religious rituals were for puberty and death. The California Indians were noted for their fine baskets that were woven so tightly that you cannot see the stitches.

Like those on the East coast, everything changed for the California Indians when the Europeans arrived. While the first contacts were one hundred years after Columbus arrived with the Portuguese, English, and Spanish all making stops in what is now California, it was not until the 1700s that the Spanish began to establish their missions which began in 1769 and continued for the next fifty years to change the way of life for many of the California tribes. Unlike the Plains and the Southwestern tribes, the California Indians offered little resistance to the taking of their lands, their dislocation from their traditional areas, or to the decimation of the Mission Indians. After the gold rush of 1849, many of the names of cultures of historic tribes have been lost to history. There are still some remnants of the past that remain.

The Yuman family includes the Walapai, Yavapai, Havasupai, Mohave, Yuma, Cocopa, and Maricopa, the Diegueno, and other California groups. Today, around seven thousand California Indians reside on the more than hundred reservations and small rancherias in California. Fort Mohave Reservation has less than three hundred, while the Fort Yuma Reservation has around nine hundred Indians. This means that the numbers practicing cremation are dwindling. Many more tribal members live off of the reservation, including those who are self-identified Indians as well as those who are tribally identified. Those living off the reservation are less likely to use traditional cremation practices.

MISSION INDIANS AND NON-MISSION INDIANS

Mission Indians developed differently than non-Mission Indians. Mission life generally destroyed traditional life for most tribes. They were taught new arts and crafts, different ways of farming, new foods, new forms of housing, given a different religion, and crowded into towns. The results caused not only the death of individuals but also led to the death of their cultures. The Catholic missionaries who at the time opposed cremation tried to dissuade the tribes from using cremation and instead to practice earth burial. With great difficulty and much coercion, the missionaries were able to convince the Northwest Coast Indians to adopt the White people's use of a cemetery even though they viewed earth burial with horror. The non-Mission Indians, who had less contact with the Spanish and their missionaries, were able to keep more of their way of life and traditions intact. The Mohave have been able to keep their traditional cremation practices by missionaries (Gidley 1977, 113).

The Mohave are another California tribe that were able to resist the mission movement and continue to practice their traditional ways. When a death occurs among the Mohave, the dead person is quickly laid on a funeral pyre that will be prepared before death if the dying is anticipated and then cremated as quickly as possible. The funeral pyre is typically dug in sand, with logs placed above it with other burnable items piled on top of the logs and body by the mourners. After the fire is lit, mourners wail, throw own goods, and even their clothes on the fire. After the fire is complete, the mourners push the ashes and remaining debris into the trench or pit and covered it with sand. Generally, all of the dead person's property, clothes, goods, and even food is burned, and all evidence of them ever having lived is gone with no reminder that the person ever lived remaining. No mention of the name or even the existence of the dead person will ever be mentioned again (Gidley 1977, 113). Ceremonies will continue for four days, including the avoidance of eating meat, fish, salt, or drinking even water. Like most tribal groups, the Mohave include purification rituals as a part of the activities of the mourners. The Mohave believed that the soul remained for four days before departing. Those who prepared the body or touched the dead person or gave speeches about the deceased would typically be part of the purification activities. This would involve cutting hair, bathing, smoke ceremonies, and other more secret rituals. As a non-Mission tribe, the Mohave were able to keep their traditions longer than many other tribes. The European cultures did not invade their way of life until the nineteenth century. No missions were established in the

Mohave areas. The U.S. culture also did not impact them for many years as well. Horses and cows became part of their culture through raids and trading. Their trading of furs and other products gave them more cultural contact with other tribes and the White culture. While most of the old ways, foods, housing, dress, plants, and ways of making a living have disappeared, clan and cremation have remained among those who still try to live in the old way. While their religion is mostly gone, the Mohave have not become Christian like most tribes.

The Quechan or Yuma are also known for using cremation. Like the Mohave, the Yuma also were less impacted by the mission system. The Spanish attempted to build a mission, but the Yumans killed the priests and soldiers and were able to resist the influence of the Spanish (Bahti and Bahti 1999, 71). Near neighbors of the Mohave, the Yuma cremation practices are similar to those of the Mohave. The Yuma built funeral pyres that were house-high mass of logs upon which was placed the dead person dressed in his best clothes and piled with gifts while mourners danced and sang through the night (Underhill 1953, 272). Mourners would wail, cry, tear their clothes and throw them into the flames, scratch their faces, throw offerings or even money into the fire, request spirits to take this dead person and those who have died before, burn images of the dead person, and burn their personal items as well before fasting and giving speeches, singing, having mock battles, and mourning for four days (Underhill 1953, 272–273).

The Shoshone share their Wyoming reservation with the Northern Arapahos (Curtis 1987, 197). Explorers Lewis and Clark had Sacajawea, a Shoshone who served as their guide. The Shoshone lived in climates that varied from Death Valley to modern-day Yellowstone Park. The West Coast Shoshonean include Mono, Serrano, Gabrieleno, Luiseno, and Cahuilla (Underhill 1953, 291).

Of the Shoshonean grouping, the Cahuilla, another Southern California tribe, also practiced cremation. Some Cahuillas were Mission Indians, while others were not. Originally called Kawia, Cahuilla is a Hispanic name given to the tribe. The renaming follows a pattern that had many traditional tribal names which were replaced with a name in another language, including Dine by Navajo, Inde by Apache, Tohono O'odham by Papago, and Inuit by Eskimo.

Like the Mohave and the Yuma tribes, the mission system had less impact on the Cahuilla than it did on other tribes which allowed them to keep their political, legal, and religious systems (Hoxie 1996, 94). The Cahuilla also cremated their dead, burned their houses, mourned, and held mourning ceremonies for the dead each year (Oswalt 1973, 177).

Ancient tribes also practiced cremation. The Hopewell of the Middle Woodlands have been studied perhaps more than most Woodland cultures.

Their burial customs are well known because of the hundreds of burials that have been excavated, demonstrating that both burial and cremation were used (Fagan 2000, 426–428). The Hopewell people had perhaps the most elaborate burial practices of any of the tribes of the Eastern United States, burying their dead with great artifacts and treasures and yet as many as three-fourths of the Hopewell dead were cremated and laid to rest with no artifacts (Steele 1978, 51).

CONCLUSIONS

Basically, American Indian tribes used all known methods of disposal of their dead, ranging from burial (both ground and air), cremation, and mummification. It is also likely that the cause of death, where the death occurred, the age of the deceased, the sex of the deceased, and the social status of the deceased impacted the mortuary and burial practices of the tribe, but sufficient information about how such factors influence burial practices is not conclusive. It is also likely that climate, weather, availability of materials to dispose of the body, and religious beliefs were major determinants in how bodies of the dead were disposed. Almost universally, tribes provide provisions for a spirit journey whether for a single or for a group burial (Atkinson 1935, 159–160). If nothing else has been learned about their bereavement and disposal practices, it is clear that tribal groups did not abandon their dead. They provided them with ceremonies and dignified disposal. American Indians provide social support through the tribe or clan of the individual in the dying and burial process. That same social support system was used to sustain the bereaved after the disposal of the dead. The grief process includes the ceremony of the funeral, the cremation or other disposal method, and the bereavement ceremonies. Extreme emotions are usually managed by these ceremonies. The spiritual nature of the living and the dead is a part of the entire process.

Chapter 5

Culture of American Indians

The Inde, Dine, Hopi, Lakota, Ho Chunk, Oneida, or any other tribe that still exists today has much to teach to the dominant society. While their arts and crafts have drawn much attention ever worldwide, the cultures, values, and way of life may offer even more to the dominant society.

American Indians have managed to keep their cultural traditions by having a strong kinship system. In a kinship society, much of the social life, including how one makes a living, one's religion, the social learning that comes from others, and even social relationships, is the product of one's family and the community of which they are a part. For an American Indian, one's way of life and way of thinking is centered on people rather than things. One universal feature of American Indian culture would be that it is people centered.

While not all Indian peoples are spiritual, there is a tendency to overgeneralize and presume all Indian people to be spiritually centered. Over time, non-Indians have introduced cultural elements that have adapted to the challenge of a more materialistic culture such as was introduced by European settlers. Early settlers and traders brought disease, politics, religion, and an economic system that threatened the survival of the kinship, people-centered societies. The later introduction of "White" education even further eroded the traditional cultural system. While much of the culture has been lost, many American Indians are rediscovering their "roots" and trying to maintain or learn their traditional language and ways of life.

PEOPLE-ORIENTED CULTURE

Culturally, the focus on people rather than things has led to many cultural practices that distinguish American Indian culture from contemporary

mainstream culture. American Indians are generally quite aware of their kinship system and how they are related to others. Relatives are a part of their
social circle and friendship grouping. Children spend time and have experiences with grandparents and other older relatives. One's clan or lineage is
part of one's life. Each clan has duties and obligations that go with such
membership. One may be called upon to be a storyteller, dancer, singer, or
whatever based upon one's clan or lineage. Families care for the elderly at
home. People aspire to die among their clan or family groupings in keeping
with tribal customs. Perhaps the most striking characteristic of American
Indian cultures is the sense of community that pervades everything that one
does or feels. One is not alone in living, dying, death, or bereavement. The
community is always there to offer support, wisdom, counsel, and love. No
person is alone. While each has individuality and autonomy, each also is part
of a family that includes the extended family, the community, the tribe, and
even those all around the country who have been part of one's life. Death is
not only normal, but it is part of the natural life cycle and does not end one's
existence, but rather changes or transforms one's existence. While the community, family, and tribe are there to support the dying and bereaving, each
person remains autonomous and self-reliant. Resilience is a basic facet of the
culture of the American Indian. Some traditions have weakened with assimilation and the effects of oppression, poverty, and the attempts to destroy the
American Indian cultures and way of life.

There are nursing homes on some reservations and many now die in
hospitals, but traditionally, American Indians educate, respect, and work
together; they also care for the living, the dying, and the dead as family
groups. American Indians have patterns of sharing along kinship lines as
well; this may include money, childcare, housing, rides, help with work, or
whatever is needed. Generosity and sharing are strong cultural values. The
amassing of money and possessions is not a traditional practice. Goods are
to be shared and savings are to be used. The giveaway ceremonies are still
practiced among many groups. Public ceremonies are also still organized
along kinship lines. Ceremonies exist for all types of life events; even dying
has an important ceremony in most tribal cultures. Yet, traditional ways are
being challenged and even lost.

IMPACT OF DOMINANT CULTURE

It is probably not a realistic goal to try to live only a traditional lifestyle. The
traditional world of the American Indian has been invaded by the dominant
White culture. Hogans often have satellite dishes with pickup trucks parked
outside. A modern house may be next door to the Hogan with the family

living in the modern house and only using the Hogan for rituals and special occasions. Most make their living in mainstream occupations and participate in the White world at almost every level, reflecting the necessity of making a living in nontraditional ways.

It may be necessary to be a part of the wider culture, but it is also necessary to be a part of the traditional world. Only if one understands the culture and values of his or her own community is one able to broaden one's horizons and make possible a happier life. Only if one knows the dominant culture and one's own culture can one pick and choose the best from both cultures and thus build a way of life that is suitable for them as individuals. American Indian students need to learn as much as they can about both their own culture and that of the dominant society in order to best survive as American Indians.

Intermarriage has also become an issue of late as it has been of old. For hundreds, if not thousands, of years, people from one tribe have been marrying people from other tribes. Few contemporary Indian Americans are "full-bloods." Not only do people of one tribe often marry people from another tribe, but they also marry people who are not members of any tribe. Just as most of us are culturally mixed, so are members of most tribes. Cultural mixing has been occurring for a long time. In the United States, over half the people living on some reservations are not even American Indians. Often much of the land on the reservation is not even owned by tribal members or the tribe itself. Reservation schools are mixed tribally and often have as many White children as tribal children. Maintaining tradition in the face of cultural invasion is challenging.

SPORTS, ARTS, AND CREATIVITY
OF INDIAN CULTURES

From lacrosse, to darts, to a game with a hoop and a pole, to football, American Indians played hundreds of games, many of which we still play. Generally, American Indians amused themselves with many forms of games. For a more complete listing and discussion of Indian games, see Culin (1975), Vennum (1994), Oxendine (1988), and Balwin (1969). American Indians also have a history of running. While Billy Mills may be the most famous having been immortalized in a movie, thousands have run across the centuries. The "Winds" running series has spread running across the nation in recent years. For a history of running among American Indians, see Nabokow (1987). Jim Thorpe was perhaps the greatest athlete of all time, winning Olympic medals, playing professionally in both baseball and football, was an actor, and became the first president of the American Professional Football Association which became the National Football League.

Festivals and dances have been a part of American Indian culture. Dancing has existed in all American Indian groups. People dance alone, in rituals, and as performances for others. While many perform dances for paying audiences, most go to pow wows or other venues because they enjoy dancing, to honor their heritage, to honor the deities, to have fun, and to maintain their heritage. Sings, dances, ceremonies, and rituals are performed mostly on or near reservations. While most rituals and other activities are performed in traditional ways, in the modern society, some activities are now choreographed and professional dancers, professional musicians, and paid performers are used. Traditionally, most dance events were word-of-mouth events. Festivals would occur for each group based upon tradition. The Hopi have, for example, a fire ceremony in November, a winter solstice ceremony in December, and so forth for each month of the year. They would have multidances each month that occurred every year. All tribes had patterns to when their dances and festivals occurred. Some were to cause rain, to honor the dead, to appease the gods, to welcome the young to adulthood, and so forth. Rituals brought continuity to their lives.

THE ROLE OF RITUALS

People are social beings. We bond on athletic teams, with school mates, with fellow soldiers, with those with whom we play and grow, marry, have children, and so forth. Cultures have developed manhood ceremonies, bar Mitzvahs, baptism, confirmation, and many other ceremonies. Mortuary rituals are part of that process. Death rituals could be described as being pre-death, post-death, and long-term death. Every person, even those who are hermits or with similar lifestyles, is bound to others by family ties, clan, geographic location, ethnicity, social organization, spiritual beliefs, community associations for goods and services, for protection, and so much more!

Death rituals are not simply private, persona events, but rather they are a social event and a human experience that has tremendous social value for the dying or dead person, the bereavement family, for friends, and for the entire community. While we may die alone, our death has impact upon those who care about us, on those who receive the wares of our life's work, those who value our friendship, and so much more. The death rituals allow the mourner to accept that the death has occurred, to learn how much their deceased love one meant to so many people, to reconcile themselves to a life without their loved one, and to aid them in their grief process. Those who have disposed of their loved ones with no ritual are less likely to mourn effectively. Grief rituals allow and encourage the grieving to share their grief with others. Death rituals make social support from friends and family more likely to occur.

Simple acts like bringing food to the grieving family, writing a personal sympathy note, making donations to a favorite charity of the deceased, taking part in the death rituals, and so many more personal acts provide social support for the grieving. Funeral rituals not only support the grieving family, but they also support the grieving community. Death rituals are for the living. The living includes more than just close family members.

Death rituals of the American Indian are typically less predictable. For the Roman Catholic, the Mass of Christian burial is pretty much the same from church to church, country to country, year to year. While death rituals may vary by region, tribe, and place, they also may vary to meet the needs of those receiving them. The needs of the family may include having time alone with the deceased while a coworker may want to read a prayer, sing a song, give the eulogy, or other acts to show love to the deceased. Death rituals generally focus upon the needs of the family, but they also try to meet the needs of the community. While death rituals are at one level allowing the family to be socially supported, they are also giving care and attention to those who worked, hunted, played, or worshiped with the one who has died. Rituals that include the opportunity to share stories of fond memories, expression of love, or what the deceased meant to them give support to the community as well. When my friend and mentor, John "Jack" Morgan died, all of the mourners present at his burial were encouraged to place flowers on the casket that had been lowered into the grave and to use shovels to bury Jack. Those present indicated a strong sense of satisfaction that they were able to actively do something for Jack and that they felt a strong sense of completion. Some funeral directors encourage parents to wash and dress their infant child who died, offering them a chance to not only spend a little more time with the child but also to develop positive memories of doing what they could for the child that they lost. These pre- and post-death rituals do not end grief. Long-term death rituals may include rituals at the grave site on anniversaries of the birth, death, burial, or other special dates. It may also include simply visiting the grave site, tomb, or crypt where flowers may be placed; the area cleaned up of dirt, weeds, or whatever; and having conversations with the deceased. Other long-term rituals may include giving an age-appropriate gift to another person of what would have been the age of the deceased on their birthday, Christmas, or other occasions. It may lead to starting a charity, an endowment, the construction of a building or zoo or whatever, or having a scholarship in their honor, or working for gun control after the shooting death of a loved one. Community involvement is part of all death rituals. Rituals may also include the spiritual nature of arts and crafts.

The arts and crafts of American Indians included pottery, beadwork, woodwork, stonework, applied decoration, skinwork, textiles, basket-making, shellwork, featherwork, bonework, and cave art. All of these crafts at least partially embrace the spiritual dimension. Few recognize the degree of sophistication and development of the arts and crafts of American Indians. At the same time, most recognize that superior pottery was produced by the Hopi, Dine, Pueblo, and other Southwestern tribes, but few are aware of the glasswork, figurine-making, engraving, incising, and decorating of pots by the Great Lakes area tribes who also developed some of the first metallic tools ever produced (Whiteford 1970, 4). Most people are aware of the silverwork of the Southwest but not that of the Kiowa or the Iroquois (Whiteford 1970, 4). Many seek Dine rugs and blankets, but few know about the excellent weaving of the Northwest coast or the Great Lakes tribes (Whiteford 1970, 4). The most troubling aspect of the fine crafts that are produced is that the compensation is seldom adequate for the amount of time and work that it takes to make them.

Dine women have been weaving rugs for at least three hundred years. As early as 1850, Dine blankets would bring fifty dollars in gold which was an excellent price at the time (Rodee 1981, 2). Dine blankets have been found among the Shoshones of Idaho and Utah showing that Dine blankets were sought through trade by other tribes who did not make similar blankets (Hollister 1903, 49). Each blanket is unique. As the blanket is woven, it assumes its nature and purpose. Symbolically, the weaver tells the story of her life as she weaves. The colors, designs, symbols, and patterns are all part of the story, with each fabric having its own individuality (Hollister 1903, 113). Today, Dine blankets are quite expensive, but not very profitable for those who make them. It takes many hours to clean, dye, and to prepare the wool for weaving. It takes over 1,000 hours to make a blanket which may sell for $1200.00. They have to compete with cheaper imitations from Hong Kong, Mexico, and Taiwan which require far fewer hours to produce with machines rather than traditional looms. Many weavers work for wages rather than trying to sell their blankets. Fewer and fewer persons depend upon herds of sheep and summer harvests of crops for survival. Their blankets and rugs cost more than most American consumers are willing to pay. It may take two to three sheep to get the wool to make a rug that is 3 by 5 feet. It will take 15 hours to shear those sheep and clean the wool. To make the yarn from raw wool takes about 368 hours. To dye the yarn takes about 19 hours. To weave the rug takes 158 hours. The total blanket labor production time is 560 hours. If paid $1,120.00, the weaver would earn $2.00 per hour and yet, it would take three and one-half months to make a rug. For more information on marketing American Indian made products, see Bsumek (2008), Wilkins (2008), Harmsen (1977), James (1903), James (1927), and Kapoun (1997).

Basket-making was probably the first of the textile arts among American Indians. The weaving of baskets likely came before the weaving of cloth. Basket-making appears to have been practiced by many tribes who developed an almost endless variety of forms, styles, and patterns of baskets (Hollister 1903, 10).

The Hopi are noted for their pottery and Katcinas, but they also produce excellent drawings, paintings, mask-making, and garments. The Katcinas and masks are personations or symbols in the form of pictures, dolls, and masks of ancient gods with men representing them (Fewkes 1903, 15). Fewkes (1903) illustrates 260 individual Katcina figures, including many reproductions of Hopi artists. (See Mason (1946), Bromberg (1986), D'Amato and D'Amato (1968), and Salomon (1928) for more information on arts and crafts of tribes.)

Glubok's (1971) *The Art of the Southwest Indians*, Brody's (1971) *Indian Painters & White Patrons*, Keyser and Sundstrom's (1984) *Rock Art of Western South Dakota: The North Cave Hills and the Southern Black Hills*, Whiteford's (1970) *North American Indian Arts*, and Burton's (1974) *Indian Heritage, Indian Pride: Stories That Touched my Life* offer excellent discussions of American Indian arts.

IMPACT OF CULTURAL DIFFERENCES

The time dimension of tribal life is so strong in Native American cultures that it is often not noticed by White observers. John Collier writes about the Tewan pueblo, Tesuque, who were suffering from a famine that Whites wanted to help end. The Tesuques saw this as a diversion from the real issue which was the White man's plan to kill their past by shattering the bridge of tribal land and tribal religion which united past and present on the deathless two-way journey from living past to living future (Collier 1949, 7). Collier further argues that American Indians live in a time dimension that is different than others in society, one that is not linear, but rather places one's experience out in an eternity beyond years and beyond the stars (Collier 1949, 2–3).

For many tribes, life has been quite difficult. Unlike those in the dominant culture, the American Indian's way of life has not been a source of revolt, civil war, or riots. Contrary to widely held mistaken beliefs, the Federal government makes no payments to individual American Indians who, like other citizens, must make their own living (Reno 1972, 32). This is not to suggest that problems do not exist.

While people are no longer entering the United States in record numbers, it still remains the preferred destination for many people around the world. As people continue to enter into the United States, the concerns for the shrinking budget, the fiscal impact of the wars in Iraq and Afghanistan, the massive resignation movement, the loss of budget surpluses, the lack of funding for programs of health care and illness, the impact of the pandemic, and the masking and restrictions caused by the spread of COVID have caused more awareness of the gaps that divide the diverse peoples that make up the population of the United States. Traditionally, over half of all peoples who migrated to another country came to the United States. While the immigration policies of the Trump administration severely limited immigration, many people still see the United States as a place of opportunity. As the people enter with their own hopes and dreams, they put more and more pressure on the dreams and hopes of those already living in the United States. As more and more peoples bring their cultural ways and search for dreams to the United States, the First Nations or American Indians get pushed further and further from the mainstream of the dominant culture.

For those living on reservations, the emphasis has been upon HIV/AIDS, suicide, COVID, homicide, poverty, alcohol abuse, drug abuse, and other social weaknesses. Yet, those living on reservations also have illustrated great strength and resilience. Those of us working in health care, ministries, hospice, bereavement, education, and counseling need to learn about the culture and way of life of the American Indians to better be able to serve their needs and to learn from them how to better serve the needs of those of other cultures whom we also serve.

While any attempt to list the strengths of a culture may tend to foster stereotypes and to some degree ignorance, it is still helpful to better understand the Indian culture world to make some truthful generalizations. While not all tribes nor even all members of the same tribe follow these cultural values, enough do to make them important for non-Indians to enhance their grasp of Indian traditions. The values of American Indians are reflected in their spirituality.

CONCLUSIONS

The many cultures of the American Indians are a study of the encounters between ancient and modern societies. From the burials of the Neanderthals to the modern burials of royalty in Great Britain, humans have been fascinated with the practices of cultures other than their own. As people-centered and community-oriented cultures, the American Indians present a model of managing their needs with rituals and ceremonies that have existed for centuries. As their history has been neglected, so, too, have their many contributions to the larger societies in which they live. The lack of appreciation extends to their treatment, prejudices against them, and lack of proper support socially, financially, and spiritually.

Chapter 6

American Indian Cultural Denigration

Before the arrival of the White explorers, treasure seekers, and traders, the Americas had many thriving cultures many of whom had learned to live peacefully with each other. The ancient culture of the Incas covered one of the largest areas of land of any empire in world history. The earlier arrival of the Vikings had little or no impact on the Americas, but the arrival of the Spanish, English, French, and Portuguese forever changed the way of life for those living in the Americas.

In some areas, the Europeans were not as quick to use their weapons, enslave, destroy, loot, or violate the people that they found, but they still brought with them diseases that killed more than their weapons. Over time, the White explorers and traders shared their guns, horses, pigs, cows, religion, and language with those already living in the Americas. Seeing themselves as "discovering" the Americas as well as bringing a far superior culture and way of life, they saw little reason not to impose their way of life upon those living in the Americas. They also believed that the vast resources that they found in the Americas were there for the taking. While not in the early years, the new arrivals cut down over 90 percent of the redwoods that live for more than a thousand years. Over time, miners desecrated sacred places and murdered thousands to get to where the gold or other ores might be found. Millions of bison were slaughtered destroying the way of life for those living on the plains. Little regard was given to the damage that their acts of greed were doing to those already living in the Americas.

Tribes were forcefully moved from traditional homelands. The introduction of weapons changed tribal relations, tribal territories, intertribal relations, and just as importantly, tribal populations. Because the views of many of the new arrivals were that those that they found in the Americas represented an inferior way of life. The new arrivals had little appreciation for the cultures,

71

civilizations, and societies that they found. Few of the new arrivals were even slightly aware of the rich cultures and way of life for those who lived before. Even today with the concern for what is taught in schools with attacks on "Critical Race Theory," "Black Lives Matter," and "Holocaust Denial," much of what has been taught and learned about American Indians is based upon misinformation, stereotypes, and media creations that are simply false. These falsehoods have led to bias, disrespect, bad attitudes, and negative beliefs about American Indians that are in contrast with what are called "American values" of intellectual honesty, democracy, and fair scholarship. The very use of the word "Indian" stems from a misconception. The term "Redskin" is also a misnomer. Much of what is known about American Indians comes from the voices of European writers and their descendants.

Written and media presentations of American Indians often portray them as not as fully human as Whites. Movies and television shows depict them as not being able to speak full sentences or to use proper grammar. They are typically given ridiculous names and words used to describe them are equally negative such as savage, squaw, brutal, unskilled, lazy, wandering, heathen, massacre, primitive, buck, papoose, or stoic. The common usage of such words to describe American Indians has the consequence of perpetuating the cycle of stereotypes that have caused American Indians many problems.

REVISION OF AMERICAN INDIAN HISTORY

Like the Civil War, American Indians are the subject of many, many books since they were "discovered." The societies that lived in the Americas before the Europeans came passed knowledge from generation to generation through an oral rather than with a written tradition. The written history that has been chronicled since the arrival of the Europeans has primarily come from the European point of view. For most who have attempted to study the history of the Americas, it has been from the European perspective as opposed to the perspective of the Indians. The tribes that were here before the European cultures "discovered" them. The Indians also knew that they were here. The American Indians on both continents developed trading systems, governments, religion, families, and educational systems. The British, the French, the Spanish, and later, the United States saw their language, culture, education, government, childrearing practices, religion, criminal justice system, and economic system as superior to those of American Indians. Because the American Indian way of life was viewed as inferior, the invaders felt it necessary to change, modify, and even destroy the Indian way of life.

The destruction of the way of life of the American Indians was not entirely deliberate. The introduction of the horse changed the way of life for the Plains

Indians. Some of the ways of the Europeans had a positive impact upon the American Indians. The introduction of the horse along with the introduction of the gun allowed them to be more efficient in hunting, raiding, and traveling. The horse gave them the ability to have far greater mobility and greater ability to find and chase the bison and to have greater range to locate other foods and materials. It also allowed for faster and easier travel into enemy territory. Horses, themselves, became a source of wealth, prestige, and power. Horses also became an object worthy of stealing. On the negative side, the introduction of the horse led to an increase in raids, warfare, and hostilities between tribes. Yet, at the same time, the horse also led to expanded trade, or intermarriage between tribes, and to greater mobility for contact with new places and new peoples. Unfortunately, the Europeans also brought with them infectious diseases. The introduction of infectious diseases had only negative and no positive impact upon the tribes.

The never-ending desire for land and resources meant that nearly all American Indian tribes were forced from their homelands. A quick examination of a map of where tribes lived in 1492 and where they live today will more than make clear the relocation patterns. Not only was land taken from them, but schools were used to destroy the American Indian culture, language, religion, and way of life. The denigration of their culture led to cultural genocide. Yet, in spite of the attempts to destroy them, their cultures are not post-historical. In all of the Americas from the polar ice caps to the jungles of the Amazon, Indians have played a vital role in the evolution of the American experience. They were already here, helped settlers, gave them new crops and medicines, challenged them, were ultimately conquered, and seemingly, disappeared. While the American Indians seemingly disappeared from the contemporary awareness of the White society, their reality remains a vital one. American Indians are a vital part of our society today.

Columbus is viewed as both a hero and as a destroyer. There is little question that Columbus was unaware that there was a large mass of land between Europe and Asia. He called the Caribbean people Indians because he mistakenly believed he had discovered a short route to India. His greater misjudgment was to view the peoples and cultures he found from a European point of view (Josephy 1963, 4). Despite the presence of voluminous body of research and literature concerning American Indians, there is a colossal misrepresentation of the actual cultures of the indigenous peoples of America. Few have recognized the immense cultural diversity among American Indians that existed even before Columbus arrived. Cultural differences were denigrated by describing the American Indians as being different from Europeans as human beings. They were "savages," "pagans," or "uncivilized." They scalped people and wantonly killed without remorse. They needed to be "civilized." Boarding schools were started to destroy their languages and culture.

Their culture, way of life, religion, and even their languages were thought to be inferior to those of the invading cultures. Children play cowboys and Indians. They dress in loincloths and feathers. Do children play Irish, Jewish, Catholic, Hispanic, or White? Yet, while seeming the dominant point of view of Indians, there were many who did not share this view.

Among those who did not share this view was a notable and early chronicler of their lives and cultures of those living in the Americas, George Catlin (1796–1872). Catlin left behind a record of portraits and words describing the daily lives and artifacts of American tribes in both North and South America. Though he never published the book that he planned on North and South American groups, much of his material still exists along with two books that he wrote for children: *Life amongst the Indians: A Book for Youth* (1861), and *Last Rambles amongst the Indians of the Rocky Mountains and the Andes* (1866). Catlin (1913), Collier (1947), Parsons (1922), Cremony (1868), Embree (1939), Driver (1964), Alvord and Van Pelt (1999), Halsey (1971), Haig-Brown and Nock (2006), Hecht (1991), Ramirez (2007), Mails (1973, 1993, 1995), Coolidge (1930), La Farge (1956), Lindquist (1973), McKenney (1933), Terrell (1962, 1970), Underhill (1938, 1945, 1946, 1948, 1953), Kluckhohn and Leighton (1962), and Leighton and Kluckhohn (1969) are among other historical sources for learning about culture and daily life among the many diverse tribes. Many other texts are also available. While all these writers and researchers do not provide an accurate or even a positive view of the way of life and cultures they present, many do. If nothing else, they demonstrate an appreciation of what they did study. New analytic thinking and improved substantive data will continually change our understanding of how long people have existed in the Americas and how these ancient societies lived.

AMERICAN INDIAN HISTORY INTERPRETED

While many only think of a few tribes that still exist such as the Sioux or Lakota, Navajo or Dine, or Apache or Inde, over six hundred tribes are still trying to maintain their historical way of life. Countless others have been exterminated, assimilated, acculturated, or have forgotten their traditional ways. American Indians on both continents are a vital part of society today.

While no longer the feared and maligned people that they are portrayed as being, the Inde or Apache are dynamically evolving today. There are forty-one groups who call themselves Inde or Apache. For the most part, they still live on a few reservations including the Jicarilla, Mescalero, Fort Apache, and San Carlos in New Mexico and Arizona. The myth of the vanishing Indian has given rise to the belief of many that Indians are no longer among us or that they have fully assimilated into White society. The truth is that surviving Indian peoples of today all have very distinctively diverse tribal cultures. While for the most part, they are studied in the past tense, yet they continue to grow and evolve.

Because few tribes in the Americas had a written language, most history books of the Americas begin in 1492; the Aztec, Mayan, Mounds Builders, Pueblos, Oneota, Clovis, Incas, Mandan, Hidatsa, Arikara, Anasazi, Hohokam, Mogollon, Inuit, and others provide fascinating study for those who are willing to pre-date Columbus's arrival. Reed (2000); Richter (2001); Cattawich (1980); Browman (1980); Wicks and Roland (1999); McKenna and Truell (1986); Shetrone (2004); Erlandson, Rick, and Vellanoweth (2008); Jones and Klar (2007); and Ross 1989) are other excellent sources that provide an interesting analysis of America before Columbus.

Since the British and their descendants dominate most histories written about the study of European-American Indian relations, the impact of the Spanish, French, and Dutch has been decidedly neglected. Richter (2001) discusses contacts with Europeans prior to 1492 and presents a picture of the European invasion from the point of view of those who were already here. Comparative studies of the relationships between American Indians and the British and non-British are also insightful. Peckham and Gibson (1969), Delanglez (1935), Swanton (1984), Jaenen (1976), or Cronon (1983) is among many sources that examine the relations between American Indians and the Europeans, including Spanish, French, Dutch, as well as the British. It is more than a little bit important to note that Americans include not only those who live in what is now the United States but all of the Americas. The study of South American Indians has also been neglected.

To better understand the complexities of American Indian cultures, many excellent resources exist, including Silko (1981), Hyde (1937), Geertz and Lomatuway'ma (1987), Flood (1995), McGaa (1990), Voget (1995), Peters (1995), LaDuke (1999), Kehoe (2001), Grobsmith (1981), Hoebel (1960), Sarita (1995), Curtis (1972), Brasser (1974), or Dennis (1940).

For those who have taken history classes in the United States, the books that are used in their classes and what the teachers introduced about the Americas or the "New World" begin in 1492. Had history been written from the perspective of the American Indian, 1492 would be a point in history that forever changed their way of life, a turning point in their history as was the Holocaust for the Jewish people, but it would certainly not be the beginning of their history. The settlements at Cahokia, Moundville, and Natchez existed long before 1492. Plains tribes roamed the heart of the continent. The Siouan, Algonquian, Iroquoian, and others developed great societies. The Hidatsa, Mandan, Arikara, and many other tribes lived on the plains. Roper and Pauls (2005) are an excellent source for more information. The tribes in the Americas had no laws, courts, judges, prisons, police, or any need for a criminal justice system. Yet, those who arrived after 1492 felt that they needed not only to be civilized, but to have laws and courts to keep them from being savages. While they were thought to be lawless and described as savages, in fact, during the period of heaviest fighting from 1865 to 1898, the Plains Indians killed only a total of 919 U.S. soldiers and the large majority of these involved defensive battles in response to assaults by the U.S. Cavalry. More than a third of the 919 fatalities occurred at the Fetterman Massacre in 1866 and the Battle of Little Big Horn in 1876 (Deverell 2004). The term massacre applied to Indian victories is an Anglo-European usage of the term that is offensive to American Indians. The term massacre is seldom applied to the dominant slaughter of minorities whether Sand Creek and many others for Indians or Tulsa and many others for Blacks.

By the time of the U.S. Census of 1920 was taken, the American Indian population had fallen below hundred thousand people. While the media portrays the early American Indian as attacking Whites on their way Westward as well as upon isolated, lonely settlers, the record of history presents a different picture. There is little doubt that on some occasions Indians would kill White settlers; this sort of act was extremely rare. In fact, recent calculations of the total number of White settlers killed by Plains Indians from 1800 to 1870 measure deaths from such attacks causing fewer than four hundred to be killed during the entirety of the Westward wagon train movements across America (see Deverell 2004). This fact by itself goes a long way toward rebutting the savage stereotype of the Plains Indians.

CULTURAL GENOCIDE

While there is no doubt that some Europeans genuinely admired American Indians, the popular mainstream culture throughout the period of the Westward Movement portrayed them as savages. This prejudiced view of the American Indian ultimately led to genocide and a lack of concern for the suffering endured by Native peoples (see Altman 1995, Thornton 1987, and Churchill 1999). The Indian tale that every time a White man set foot on land, after crossing the Atlantic Ocean, an American Indian fell dead was not far from the reality of the time. While the precise number of American Indian populations in 1492 is not known, a good estimate is that it approached 10 million in North America alone (Schaefer 2012, 150). While the British are the most discussed in American history textbooks, the study of European and American Indian relations should not focus exclusively upon British colonists and their descendants, but also must include the Spanish, French, and Dutch as found in the insightful analyses offered by the comparative studies such as those of Peckham and Gibson (1969), Delanglez (1935), Jaenen (1976), or Brasser (1974).

As suggested, while the world of the plains tribes changed after 1492, it was mostly due to disease, introduction of the horse and guns, economic changes, and impact on the environment that came with the White settlers. There was not a great deal of battling between the groups, but prejudice ultimately led to genocide. The indifference to the suffering and loss of the Indians, the dehumanization, the response to resistance, and the ultimate attempts to destroy not only their cultures but the Indian people as well may be the basic reason for lack of respect for American Indian religion and culture today.

Racism was fueled by fear, fear led to hatred, and both led to genocide. Even today, while some view diversity as a source of strength, others view it as an obstruction to the purity of American identity. While the first major resistance probably occurred in 1622, it escalated after the United States was formed. In the early 1800s, there were over a quarter of a million American Indians in what is now California. By 1900, there were only around twenty thousand. Bounties were offered for scalps of Indians. The desire for land, for ores such as gold and silver, and for the opportunity to build settlements led to the demise of many vital and healthy American Indian civilizations. Those who did survive disease and genocide were not given U.S. citizenship and other rights such as owning property, voting, or citizenship rights until after 1924 when the Dual Citizenship Act was passed. Many states still blocked the ability to vote for American Indians. It was not until the Civil Rights Act of 1968 that civil rights were given to American Indians. While the "Indian Wars" ceased more than 125 years ago, the mistreatment of American Indians has not ended. The finding of gold in South Dakota and California and oil in Oklahoma resulted in more hardships for the tribal peoples. The United States does not bear full responsibility for taking away food sources, forcing groups to live in inhospitable lands, disease, land grabbing, and genocide since the British, French, and Spanish established the practice before the development of the United States (Schaefer 2012, 150). At the same time, the French and Spanish missionaries, fur traders, and mountain men were far more tolerant and did not deliberately cause loss of life.

IMPACT OF EUROPEAN INVASION

The first settlements in the United States were at St. Augustine in 1565 and the Plymouth Company which established Roanoke in 1587. While the survivors of nearly five hundred years of mistreatment, near genocide, and government dominance, sadly, problems continue to exist today. See Altman (1995), Thornton (1987), and Churchill (1999) for a more complete analysis of problems facing Indians today. Loss of tribal heritage and way of life has been linked to increased rates of suicide, diabetes, drug and alcohol abuse, poverty, and other problems on the reservations.

As many tribes today are now struggling to continue or have any hope of achieving the restoration of their cultural heritage and maintaining their traditional language, the image by the dominant society of those living on reservations continues to be as negative as the images that dominated in the past:

- Why don't the Indians on reservations get jobs?
- Why do so many get drunk, beg, use drugs, suicide, and die young?
- Why aren't they "more like us"?

Religious traditions and even dead bodies do not get respected if the people themselves are not given basic human respect. How many museums have displayed the bodies of Indians? As a child, I visited the Field Museum of Natural History in Chicago which housed not only Egyptian mummies but also American Indian bodies. American Indians are objects of prejudice for living the way they do, and yet, they must live that way to preserve their culture. To leave the reservation, to work in the White world, to live in the White world, to acquire property and goods as Whites do, to practice White people's religion, and to become successful, collectively means to no longer be a tribal person. Those who practice living in traditional ways are destined to fall below the poverty line and to be isolated, rural people. The urban, sophisticated culture does not respect the traditional ways, and yet, paradoxically, the urban, sophisticated culture seems to want to borrow from the sacred ways of a people who they do not respect.

From St. Augustine in 1865 all the way to the end of treaty-making, land was at the core of the destruction of American Indian cultures. Each newly encountered tribe was conquered and subordinated. By the 1890s, with the compete loss of full tribal sovereignty status, the lethal contact period had ended. Unlike other minorities, American Indians had nothing of value coveted by whites apart from their invaluable land rights that drove nearly all of the 374 treaties signed between 1778 and 1871. There was no conflict over labor, power, or jobs. The dominant group wanted only natural resources available on reservations or lands of American Indians. Even the later Civil Rights Movement of the mid-1900s was not the same for American Indians as for other minorities. American Indians wanted to be able to live their traditional lifestyles and not so much the desire to have the jobs, houses, cars, and other items of the White culture. While that may be changing for some, others still prefer to have their freedom to live in the traditional way.

In the process of taking all this land from the Indians, it was not just a few brave Europeans defeating the millions of Indians in bloody battles.

Only a few whites and Indians died in the "Indian" wars. Far more American Indians died from diseases brought from Europe by the White Europeans, ranging from smallpox to measles, tuberculosis, syphilis, and other illnesses for which the American Indians had developed no historical immunities. The wanton slaughter of over 6 million bison or buffalo may have contributed more to defeating the plains tribes than anything that the soldiers were able to accomplish. Rather than being European bravery, superior culture, or intellect, it was germs, disease, and wanton slaughter of bison and the traditional way of life that defeated the Indian peoples.

INDIAN COUNTRY TODAY

By the twentieth century, most tribal Indians were living on isolated, rural reservations that were remote, with little change. Many of the Pueblo societies live in housing that has been used for centuries. Unlike other minorities, American Indians were dominated by the U.S. government with rigid, paternalistic rules. While American Indians did not suffer Jim Crow laws, their isolation was just as complete. The control of their lives by the Federal government was not so much through Jim Crow-type laws but through the health care system, the reservation schools, the agency corruption, and the control of the BIA which rendered them marginalized, powerless, and isolated. The BIA, an agency of the Department of Interior, controlled everything from food, shelter, police, justice, schools, reservation budget, and even tribal membership, philosophy, and structure. Of the forty-five commissioners of Indian Affairs since 1824, six have been American Indians. While titles have changed, since 1977, all twelve leaders of the BIA have been American Indians giving some hope of change. While the American Indians lost most of their land, they did not lose all of their land. While American Indians lost most of their power, they did not lose all of their power either. American Indians have historic treaty rights that give them a different legal status than other citizens. Indian peoples view themselves as members of separate nations, hence the use of the term "First Nations" in Canada. Though the treaties and laws are often ignored and violated, that status has been endorsed by U.S. presidents and by Congress.

When the Civil Rights Movement emerged in the twentieth century, the Black protest movement remained primarily integrationist. The principal exception to this being the "Black Power" branch inspired as it was by Malcolm X and the numerical minority of American Blacks affiliated with the Black Muslim movement. By contrast, American Indians did not want integration, but rather wanted to preserve their heritage, culture, and reservations. American Indians have a different history and different goals than other minorities.

By 1900, American Indians were and remain today the most impoverished group in the United States. The poorest county in the United States is in South Dakota and is part of the Crow Creek Reservation. While states like Kentucky and other Appalachian areas are known for having poor counties, many American Indian reservations also have severe poverty rates. The traditional lifestyle has been difficult to maintain because the land where they have been forced to live is generally of poor quality, and whatever good land that was possessed has been systematically taken from them through treaty-making. Traditional hunting and farming practices were lost as traditional food sources were destroyed. For many, there were few ways to satisfy even subsistence needs. Over time, many became totally dependent upon the Federal government.

American Indians had few skills that were sought by the dominant White culture, lacked literacy, did not have Western work habits, and could only take Western jobs and lifestyles if they left the reservation. At the same time, the government attempted to dismantle kinship patterns by taking children from families and coercing the adoption of Western ways at reservation and boarding schools. Boarding schools forced acculturation with the historically tribal languages, style of dress, religion, and culture itself being forbidden. The abuse and exploitation at these schools is only recently coming to light. Children of different tribes, even warring tribes, were often boarded together. When school was not in session, children were often boarded with White families to keep them from renewing tribal ways by spending time with their own families. Children were often abused, neglected, and mistreated. The *Education of Little Tree* (1976) by Forrest Carter, while a controversial book, provides a picture of boarding school problems and conditions. As tribal control of education has increased in recent years, tribal colleges are now teaching tribal history, language, and culture. Still, coercive acculturation has led to loss of culture, tradition, and way of life for many tribes. (Deloria (1969), LaDuke (1999), Sheehan (1973), Steiner (1968), and Frazier (2000) offer an analysis of the consequences of coercive acculturation.)

Few in the dominant society respect or understand those who choose to live in traditional ways. Why would the Timbisha Shoshone want to live in what is now Death Valley National Park where it has negative rainfall, temperatures reaching about 120 Fahreneit degrees, and high priced goods and services with the remoteness of living in a two and one half million acre national park? Why would anyone want to live in poverty, suffer in the heat or cold, not have a job with opportunities for promotion, lack modern housing, and live in isolation away from cities? Other than perhaps scouting organizations or some school curricula, little is taught about American Indian culture.

Policies of the previous administration led to many suits against the Federal and State governments to stop or prevent pipelines, fracking, taking of sacred lands, and rights such as voting. The Trump administration did not seem to respect traditional ways or sacred lands. The BIA has not been focused on protecting traditional practices and way of life. The imposition of the White culture with technology, media outlets, and the emphasis upon possessions has made traditional ways more difficult. For the first time, the Biden administration has appointed Deb Haaland, a member of the Laguna Pueblo tribe, as the secretary of the Department of Interior, which will change the treatment of tribes and sacred lands.

Computers, video games, iPods, and technology in general have replaced historic fascination with the Old West and its ways. Even children living on reservations often lament not having what White children have. Many do not want to learn their traditional languages. Some wear gang colors, get tattoos, and engage in other nontraditional ways even on the reservations. It is only in recent years that tribal colleges, traditional curricula, American Indian teachers, and American Indian control of schools have increased. Many former boarding schools are now museums. Has the change come too late to save the cultures? For many generations, society constructed patterns of inequality, prejudice, discrimination, hatred, and genocide against the cultures of the American Indians. The recent interest in their spirituality and religion is not an attempt to save the cultures, but rather may be another way to destroy them.

All cultures have to work to preserve their heritage. Fortunately, American Indian cultures have recognized the need to develop tribal structures to preserve theirs. Elders and tribal councils are working hard to counteract the dominant culture's indifference, cultural attacks, and general lack of support. While this struggle is ongoing, hope remains, and strong spirits abound.

HOPE FOR THE FUTURE

After nearly five centuries of exploitation, discrimination, poverty, and despair, American Indian peoples can look forward to an improved future. Symbolic of the changing position of American Indians in U.S. society was the opening of the National Museum of the American Indian in the mall of Washington, D.C., in 2005. For the first time, there is something positive in Washington for American Indians.

There is also increased economic hope. Tribes have gone beyond gaming to entrepreneurship. Nonetheless, the casino industry has certainly emerged as a major source of economic revenue for large numbers of tribes. The tribal casino represents a relatively new policy shift of the Federal government intended to encourage tribal economic development, tribal self-sufficiency, and strong tribal government as cited by the Indian Gaming Regulatory Act (1998). Under this Federal policy, tribal casinos cannot be built without the approval of the Indian tribe upon whose land the casino is to be constructed nor can they be within a state that has prohibitions, as a matter of criminal law and public policy, against such gaming activity. It is important to note that a significant proportion of the jobs created by Indian casinos result in the hiring of non-Indian people. For example, in the state of Wisconsin, home to six different federally recognized Indian tribes, casinos produce 4,500 jobs of which 2,000 are filled by non-Indians. This also corresponds to the fact that about the same percentage of people residing on Indian lands nationwide are now non-Indian people. While the introduction of gaming has transformed the lives of some American Indians, about two-thirds of the tribes are not involved in gaming and of the one-third that are, only a small fraction earn substantial revenue from gambling ventures (Schaefer 2013, 268).

Of course, many Indian tribes do not enjoy the large revenue benefits to which the relatively small Wisconsin Potawatomi tribe, adjacent to a major city, has access. It is noteworthy also that in some states, such as Wisconsin, the growing Indian casino industry has significantly reduced the welfare rolls of tribal Indians. Monies from gaming are being put into developing tribal business, tourism, and other forms of economic development. The future will require more adjustments and accommodation to the dominant culture, but American Indian cultures will continue to survive.

The future will likely include a move away from gaming and toward more tourism, recreation, and service activities. Golf courses for tourists, camping, recreation, skiing, craft shows, pow wows, and other activities bring in more visitors and ultimately more money for tribes. Gaming has stigma that golf does not. Gaming is also becoming available at more and more locations that are not tribal owned which will ultimately hurt their ability to produce revenue.

American Indians have endured generations of illness, death, attacks, discrimination, as well as removal from their homelands. The Europeans brought with them disease, death, and hardship. Despite being a small minority (less than 1 percent of the population) in the United States, American Indians have been receiving increasing interest and attention in recent years. Part of the interest is that they have rekindled their ethnic awareness. Perhaps more attention is given to the social and economic plight of many of the tribes, as casinos, movies, and television have made them more visible. While there has been significant improvement to the quality of life on some reservations in recent years, many still face severe hardships and share less of the affluence of modern society than any other minority group.

CONTRIBUTIONS OF AMERICAN INDIANS

Perhaps the most damaging aspect toward American Indians is the lack of knowledge of their culture and way of life. Some of the misconceptions would include beliefs that:

- All Indians get a government check each month just for being "Indians,"
- Discrimination ended long ago,
- American Indians are forced to stay on reservations,
- American Indian religions are barbaric and lacking in spirituality,
- American Indians are lazy, drink a lot, and will not work.

Such views do not take into account the many accomplishments of American Indian civilizations and cultures. What they don't know is that American Indians had over hundred thousand people living in some pre-Columbian cities; that some practiced brain surgery; and that many practiced astronomy, mathematics, geology, art, and peace before the Anglo-British came. Hardoy suggest that three hundred thousand lived in Tenochtitlan, the ancient Aztec city in Mexico, in 1520 (Hardoy 1973, 141). Hardoy also suggests that as many as 150,000 lived in the city of Tenochtitlan by 150–250 CE (Hardoy 1973, 58). Five to six thousand years before the time of Christ, in the Southwest and Far West of what is now the United States, a maize horticulture emerged with beans, squash, and other varieties of maize and the development of pottery evolving over the next few centuries (Forbes 1982, 24). In what is now Southern Arizona, about two thousand years before the time of Christ, the Tohono O'odham engaged in horticulture, cremation, pottery-making, carved fine bowls, and made utensils from stone (Forbes 1982, 24). The later generations developed crafts, arts, crops, housing, and ways of life that have persisted to today.

American Indian societies gave much to the newly arriving Europeans. Foods given to the newcomers included pineapples, steamed lobster, barbecue, succotash, spoon bread, cranberry sauce, mincemeat pie, Irish potatoes, sweet potatoes, pumpkins, squash, maple sugar, corn, avocados, tomatoes, mesquite beans, cactus fruits, chili, guacamole, barbecue sauce, peppers, Boston baked beans, clambakes, broiled salmon, roasted buffalo, pecans, hickory nuts, peanut, kidney beans, string beans, navy beans, pole beans, Mexican frijoles, butter beans, lima beans, and sunflowers.

The clothing of American Indians was not just loin cloths and furs as often portrayed in the media. The clans and tribes of the Pacific Northwest are noted for their ability to weave and fashion clothing from plant and wood fibers. Blankets, rain hats, mats, and baskets were also woven. By contrast, the plains tribes mainly used buffalo and deer skins to make clothing including their moccasins. Some plains groups excelled in beadwork to adorn clothing while others used porcupine quills, feathers, elk teeth, bear claws, or shells for adornment. Those living in arctic or colder climates made parkas from hides with pants to clover their legs along with sunglasses to cover their eyes. Mittens and fur boots were worn. Tribes living in the desert wore very little in the heat of summer, but women generally wore more clothes than men. Woven grass and reeds were used to make clothing as was sagebrush and bark to make shirts and skirts. Cotton was used for clothing, and after the introduction of sheep, wool was also used by some groups. The Southeastern tribes used furs, bark, feathers, hair, and plants to make clothing. The clothing of all clans and tribes was functional, colorful, attractive, and durable. (See Solomon (1928) and Mason (1946) for illustrations and discussion of how to make clothing.)

The housing of American Indians was also unique and varied. Of the forty or so plains tribes, housing varied from dome-shaped lodges made of bark by the Sauk and Fox, to the dome-shaped houses thatched with grass made by the Wichita, to the log lodges covered with dirt built by the Mandan and Pawnee, to the tipi erected by the Lakota. The Pueblo tribes of the Southwest lived in adobe dwellings some of which have lasted for thousands of years and are still inhabited. Some have multiple stories that required wooden ladders to enter the higher levels. The Inde or Apache lived in oval-shaped wickiups covered with grass, brush, and matted materials. The Dine or Navajo, also of the Southwest, lived in Hogans made of logs and covered with dirt. The Anasazi lived in cliffs carved into the sides of mountains. Some have cedar beams that were 12–15 inches in diameter, but no trees are found near the cliffs, suggesting that they were transported from hundreds of miles away (Hollister 1903, 34).

The Aztecs have left behind ruins in New Mexico that were three stories high and had over five hundred rooms in what is now known as the Aztec Ruins National Monument. While little is known about the original inhabitants, later groups developed Kivas and other structures on the site. The Northeastern tribes lived in long houses with a frame of poles covered with strips of bark. Walls and doors typically were made from skins or blankets. The Seminole tribe in the Southeast made their homes on platforms with grass roofs and floors to keep them dry in the warm, wet climate. Northwestern tribes of Kwakiutl, Haida, and Tlingit used totem plank lodges for their dwellings with an ornate totem near the entrance. [See Nabokov and Easton (1989) for illustrations and examples of American Indian architecture.]

There are also many positives in the lives of America Indians who have learned their history and culture primarily from ceremonies, songs, and legends taught to them by tribal elders, and from scholarly sources (Reno 1972, 5). The music of American Indians has been preserved over the centuries and is still a part of the heritage of the culture of American Indians today. Peter La Farge who was of Pima heritage became a singer, songwriter, and guitarist who recorded many records that were part of the folk culture of the 1960s. While he died at the age of thirty-four in 1965, his recordings of "Ballad of Ira Hayes," "Coyote: My Little Brother," "As Long as the Grass Shall Grow," "Damn Redskins," and "Tecumseh" are examples of some of his hits and contributions to understanding the plight of the American Indians. In 1956, Gertrude Prokosch Kurath recorded "Songs and Dances of Great lake Indians," for Folkways Records. She was able to preserve the songs of the Ojibwa, the Meskwaki, Iroquois, and Algonquian tribes. Buddy Red Bow in 1983 produced another record, "Journey to the Life of American Indians Today" for Tatanka Records, and in 1977, he also produced for Tatanka Records, "Fools Crow," that recorded the songs of the Lakota to help understand the sun dance, the pipe, spiritual places like Bear Butte, and more with Frank Fools Crow providing the material. In 1953, Folkway Records produced "Songs & Dances of the Flathead Indians." In 1976, New World Records recorded "Songs of Earth, Water, Fire, and Sky," which recorded songs of the Navajo, Cherokee, Creek, Northern Arapaho, San Juan Pueblo, and the Northern and Southern Plains tribes. Canyon Records recorded "The Song of the Indian," which included songs from the Apache, Navajo, Cheyenne, Hopi, Zuni, Acoma, Sioux, and Taos tribes. New Worlds Records also produced in 1977, "Songs of Love, Luck, Animals, & Magic: Music of the Yurok and Tolowa Indians."

Perhaps more famously, Alan Lomax, working with the BIA, produced ten albums preserving the songs of the American Indians that are part of the Library of Congress Music Division from 1936 to 1951. Patrick Sky, of Creek heritage, was also a part of the Folk scene in the United States and introduced the Mouth Bow to Buffy Saint-Marie. Buffy Sainte-Marie is prob-ably the best known of the American Indian folk musicians. Her first hit was, "Universal Soldier," followed by many others including "Native American Child" and "Now That the Buffalo's Gone." Tony and Ida Isaacs formed Indian House Records in 1966 and were able to record the natural sounds of American Indian music without using sound effects or electronic devices. Floyd Westerman released "Custer Died for Your Sins" in 1969. R. Carlos Nakai is a Navajo flutist who has been nominated for a number of awards for his music. More recent American Indian performers would include peyote singer Blackfox, Jay Begaye with his contemporary Native folk music, rappers including Boyz from the Rez, and rock musicians like Tiger and Zit. Traditional Native music or folk music of American Indians has many different types and styles. Some have adopted the structure and harmony of Christian music. Others have combined traditional music with rock, rap, blues, folk, and activism. Most contemporary Native American music has abandoned the social activism of the 1960s and 1970s, and now focuses upon the music and performance. Connor Chee, a Navajo pianist, helped judge the Grammy's in 2019.

Traditional music is still being sung by several hundred tribal groups. Music is a basic component of culture. The word for music for many tribes is sing which is described as meaning to heal or to pray. Traditionally, music is thought to be a gift from the spirits, and as being a part of the oral tradition, serves as a way to keep in touch with the past. While the sun dance and other rituals were condemned by the government who also tried to keep the ritual from being performed, for over five hundred years, the sings have continued though modified over time as the influence of the White culture impacted the Native culture. For many American Indian groups, to sing a prayer is considered to be more powerful than to simply recite a prayer. While singing styles vary from tribe to tribe, generally, most used high-pitched, higher notes on the scale, and also with women singing higher octaves than men sing. Perhaps, the most unusual feature of American Indian music is the use of vowel sounds mixed in with words. The vowel sounds are used to give the melody or tune to the song. For some tribes, entire songs are simply vowel sounds with no words. It is rare to find a group, unless it is a contemporary version of the song, that sings with words only. Few instruments are used for a sing.

Drums are the most common musical instrument used, followed by rattles made of gourds or other natural materials, and flutes. Flutes also vary in style and material but are similar in sound. While music was a part of the culture, traditionally, unlike in the White world of music, musicians were not paid. Today, many artists and musicians make their living from their artistic endeavors. Many contemporary groups and individual performers are accepting bookings, gigs, and so forth. Many now consider themselves to be professional musicians like those who are their contemporary musicians from the dominant culture. Pow wows have become big business for performers, yet, the traditional music lives on.

PROBLEMS FACING NATIVE AMERICANS/ AMERICAN INDIANS TODAY

Other issues that plague contemporary American Indians who live on reservations include diabetes, cancer, heart disease, substance abuse, unemployment, not finishing their education, poverty, suicide, and alcoholism. Health care and health are among the most critical problems. American Indians are more likely to die before age forty-five than any other racial or ethnic group (Schaefer 2006, 174). COVID, murder of Native women, lack of safe water, lack of gainful employment, discrimination in voting practices, and so many more issues have made reservation life more difficult in the twenty-first century.

The government and corporations continue to exploit those living on reservations. Trust funds have been set up to pay for the resources taken from reservations, but little or nothing has been paid. From mining in Wisconsin to the disposal of nuclear waste in Yucca Mountain, few seem concerned with the misuse and abuse of reservations. Richardson (1991), Gedicks (1993, 2001), Steven (2004), LaDuke (1999), Churchill (1999), and Tinker (2008) provide an analysis of different forms of exploitation.

Other problems facing tribes today would include the loss of language which also leads to the loss of culture. Of the 154 surviving Native American languages only 20 have children actively learning the traditional language (Schaefer 2006, 150), and just under 50 percent of all the Indian language speakers in the United States today are Navajo. Seven hundred American Indian languages were spoken in 1500 (Schaefer 2006, 151), but by the year 2000, only 15.4 percent of all persons self-identified as American Indians reported speaking any Indian language at home. Fortunately, since tribal schools and colleges have been able to secure more control over what is taught in their schools, Native languages are now being taught in public as well as tribal schools.

IMPACT OF CULTURAL DENIGRATION ON DISPOSAL AND RITUALS

Like all people in all cultures, American Indians send their dead to the next life with rituals and practices that reflected their religious beliefs about death and the spiritual afterlife. Like other cultural groups, American Indians view desecration of the dead to be a serious and offensive act. Disease and even death are thought to happen to those who violate the dead and their resting places. Perhaps, the study of the Egyptians started the practice, but archaeologists have for generations been digging up human remains to study what was buried with them to learn about cultures. The tombs of Greeks and Egyptians have yielded great knowledge of their cultures. The pilgrims dug up the grave of an American Indian and took items from the grave only eight days after they anchored off the coast of Cape Cod (Watkins 2013, 695). Thomas Jefferson is reputed to have dug up a burial mound in Virginia. Physical anthropology has long studied skulls and human bones to provide a rationalization for our treatment of various indigenous peoples. Following the War Between the States, the Surgeon General of the United States ordered army personnel to obtain Indian skulls for study at the Army Medical Museum in Washington, D.C. (Watkins 2013, 697). The U.S. Army acquired heads from Arapahoe, Cheyenne, and Kiowa killed at the Sand Creek Massacre in Colorado. These and other such practices have made it far more difficult for contemporary researchers who seek information by ethical means. Many tribes are quite reluctant to discuss their practices because of the unethical acts in the past by anthropologists, archaeologists, and the U.S. government.

The practices of most tribes and cultural groups have been greatly influenced by Christian practices. Flathead and other plains groups have incorporated many Christian practices into their own practices. Flathead funerals include wakes and feast days. Like other religious groups, the Flathead believe that death will come to all, the young, old, rich, or poor, so we must always be ready for death. Every morning, one should thank God for the day, for life, and for help to get through the day. Before going to sleep, one should thank God for the day, to have rest, and to wake up for still another day. Death should not be feared. Death should be a joyous occasion. The Flathead see the wake as a spiritually uplifting experience for the bereaved family and for those who attend the wake. One should be there to greet the deceased and pray with the prayer leader. A person is expected to be with the deceased at all times. It can be a one-day, two-day, or three-day wake. Every morning prayers will be said that often bring tears to the mourners.

These tears are thought to prepare the mourners for the day. The prayers provide relief to help the mourner get through the day, to be able to smile when family and friends from far away and long ago arrive. Tears let others know that you need comfort. Tears are natural and a gift from God. Prayers will be offered while the grave is being opened and closed, during the procession to the church for the funeral, during the funeral, during the procession to the cemetery, and as well, during memorial and feast days. Years ago, feasts and memorial giveaways were planned for a year after the death, but today, most plan their memorial dinner and giveaways to happen immediately after the burial. The problem with this practice is that it is thought to hurry the mourning process. When the memorial dinner and giveaway are held immediately after the funeral, the family has little time to make decisions about the giveaway or the feast or even what to bury with the deceased because they are still in the state of mourning. The mourners who receive the keepsakes in honor of the deceased are thought to help take away the sorrow of the bereaved. The things that are given are not important, but the love that the items represent is important. Sorrow and sadness continue for a long time after the funeral. Traditionalists argue that by waiting for the feast day and for the memorial dinner, the family can then release their sorrow rather than feeling abandoned and alone after the funeral. The future of religious, burial, and bereavement practices will probably become more like those of the dominant religions.

The view of those living on reservations by those from the dominant culture has not improved the image of Indians from the views of the past. Why don't they get jobs? Why do so many American Indians drink excessively, beg, use drugs, suicide, and die younger than the rest of society? Religious traditions and even dead bodies do not get respected if the people themselves are not given basic human respect.

Many non-tribal members routinely hang dream catchers from the rearview mirrors of their vehicles, give Kachinas to their children for toys, use pipes as toys, have "sweats," and engage in traditional rituals in nontraditional ways. The emergent construction of anti-Indian prejudice and its resulting discrimination have led to disrespect and desecration of the dead and the spiritual ways of the plains tribes. By contrast, the "Blackrobes" and other clergy who worked with tribal groups have adored the Virgin Mary in traditional Hopi or other tribal garments; developed the "Black Madonna"; and have hung pipes, beaded items, shawls, and other traditional Native American items in their churches. Many non-tribal peoples attend, take part, respect, and become part of traditional American Indian ceremonies.

Few people in the dominant society seem to respect or understand those who choose to live in traditional ways. Why would anyone want to live in poverty, suffer in the heat or cold, not have a job with opportunities for promotion, lack modern housing, and live in isolation away from cities? Other than perhaps scouting organizations or some school curricula, little is taught about American Indian culture.

CONCLUSIONS

The denigration of the American Indian way of life paints a bleak picture for their future, yet hope still exists!

The future of Native American/American Indian cultures has both positives and negative. The economic future for some tribes is greatly improving. For other tribes, the economic picture is quite bleak. The lack of appreciation of the cultures, languages, and way of life by the dominant culture does not seem to be changing.

Chapter 7

Problems in Understanding Other Cultures

Judging another culture often presents a challenge for most people. For most of us, it is difficult to fairly judge the practices of another culture. Ethnocentrism, demographic variables, socio-psychological variables, and structural variables are factors that impact our ability to fairly or even competently judge and fully understand other cultures. Most judge others by their own standards or own ways of doing things.

Ethnocentrism is a sociological term that suggests that there is a tendency to judge others in not only other cultures, but also those in one's own culture, by one's own standards or ways of doing things to nudge how others are doing things. Coming from a culture where people are most often judged by what they do for a living, it is difficult to understand cultures that are able to accept individuals for who they are as people and allow them to maintain dignity of person even when they have no income-producing occupation. It is difficult for most Anglo-Europeans to understand people who communicate with spirits when science tells them that spirits do not exist, or to understand people who practice rituals that last for days when they have difficulty attending church services for more than an hour a week. Priests, Rabbis, and ministers will often get chastised if their services run too long. Can you imagine attending a ritual that lasts for ten days? Judging others is also influenced by other factors that would include variables that influence one's way of life.

Demographic variables would include such things as spatial arrangements, urban versus rural, race, and ethnicity. Clearly, it is difficult for an urban, sophisticated society to understand people who voluntarily choose to live in an isolated, rural, and often poverty-stricken wasteland when they could have all of the benefits of an urban life such as cars, constant entertainment, workaholic, and constantly busy lives. It is hard to understand a culture where words are precious and used sparingly and where silence is viewed as a cultural strength when one comes from a culture where talking is continuous and rarely meaningful. Is land to be owned or shared by all, or is the land to be exploited and used by those with the power to control it? Is one's personal space and territory intimate or distant? Should one be physically close to one another when talking to strangers? Should one look another person in the eye when talking or is that viewed as offensive? Should children be seen not to interrupt adults when they are talking or do children have something that is of value to offer in adult conversations? Different standards or norms of behavior can lead to judgmental reactions by those who do not share similar cultural attributes.

Socio-psychological variables would include income, education, social class, peer group, reference group, and personality. Some are more traditional or practice the "old ways" while others are more modern and follow the U.S., White cultural practices. Certainly, the educational system attempts to foster "White ways" of thinking and doing things.

Structural variables would include whether or not one maintains contact with aunts, uncles, cousins, parents, children, and long-term friends or whether one does not. Should one marry someone who lives locally and from a family that is known to one's family, or should a person marry someone from a different area and perhaps even a different cultural group? It may also involve practicing traditional religion versus adopting a different religion. Should one leave the religion of one's ancestors and join another people's religion? Should one continue to practice the traditional religion and actively attend and participate in traditional rituals or should one abandon the practices of their family? Does one still speak the traditional language or does one avoid speaking the traditional language especially when with nontraditional speakers when family is present? Is one educated in "White ways" or "traditional ways?" Is one future oriented or present oriented? Are children taught to respect tradition or to be "rugged individuals?"

TRADITIONAL VALUES

1. Most are taught that one should not amass too much property. Private property was not sought. Items were not produced for sale or trade. One should work hard, but only when work needed to be done.
2. American Indians have a network of sharing and assistance that is organized along kinship lines. American Indians are family centered and share with their families.
3. American Indian children spend time with the elderly and are taught to respect people, especially the elderly.

4. Indians are taught to respect the dignity and privacy of all people. One should mind one's own business and not interfere in the affairs of others.
5. Words are precious and are not to be wasted. Expressing one's personal opinion is not expected.
6. One is to speak in soft tones. It is not necessary to yell to make a point. Use of loud or angry tones ends a conversation.
7. Downcast eye rather than eye contact is preferred.
8. One not only talks less, but the Indian will also pause longer between words.
9. The preferred time is the present, not the past or the future.
10. Leisure is highly valued. One should take time to enjoy life.
11. One should live one's life in balance. One's good health depends upon balance.
12. One should live in harmony with the environment and nature.
13. One should have a sense of humor, but that does not require that one make fun at the expense of others. Stories, funny incidents, personal anecdotes, and poking fun of oneself are the sort of humor that is typical. Indians are also less boisterous when laughing.
14. One should have respect for ceremonies and tradition.
15. Honesty is highly valued.
16. There is a supreme creator.
17. Guardian spirits protect us.
18. Plants and animals are part of the spirit world and are neither lower nor higher nor better or worse than human beings. We all share the same world.
19. The spirit existed before it came into our physical body and will exist after the body dies.
20. Illness impacts the spirit and mind as well as the body.
21. The emphasis is on sharing and cooperation, not competition.

HEALTH TRADITIONS

Traditional methods of maintaining health would center upon physical, mental, and spiritual approaches. Think of health as a complex, interrelated phenomenon. How would a person try to maintain his or her health? In Western societies, people watch their diet, exercise, take vitamins and minerals, practice preventative or restorative medical programs, and have regular physical checkups. Some may also try to learn spiritual practices and teachings; interpretation of dreams; use of symbols; and cognitive actions such as examining genetic inheritance, one's body chemistry, and health history. People do things to avoid illness and will seek help when an illness does occur.

For most American Indians, illness is thought to be caused either by an intrusion into the body of a small semi-animate object that may be driven into one's body or by witchcraft, either by a contagious sort with an enemy who has cast spells over clothing, hair, or other objects; or by a wizard who sent or threw spells over bits of one's clothing, hair, or other objects (Drucker 1955, 159). The Tohono O'odham, also known as Papago of Arizona, view song as not just a way to express oneself, but as a form of magic that can constrain spirits. The Tohono O'odham believe that power can be turned to good or evil and that the same man can be a medicine man who cures or a witch who kills (Underhill 1938, 145). The Blackfeet Indians also believed that disease was caused by an evil spirit entering a person's body and that it could be cured by a healer who had the power to expel the spirit using many different methods, including curing the sick in dreams, singing, drumming, and calling upon supernatural helpers for assistance (Ewers 1958, 184). While the media has portrayed healers as typically being men, it was common for the healer to be a woman (Ewers 1958, 184). The belief that curses, voodoo, or other forms of spiritual attacks can kill a person was not limited to American Indian tribes, but was found throughout the world. Fear is a powerful and deep-rooted emotion that can affect a person physically as well as emotionally. If the medicine man or woman acting as a witch places a curse on someone, but the victim is then rescued by the prowess or power of another practitioner, the invading spirits might be directed back to the person who chanted the death prayer leading to fatal results for the chanter based upon the belief that the person who was to be cursed was not deserving of such a punishment (Steiger 1974, 108). Working with spirits is viewed as a dangerous business. Hospitals and other modern medical institutions do not address spiritual causes of illness. American Indians may very well use modern medicine for many, if not most, illnesses, but at the same time feel that they must be treated by those who understand spirits.

For the American Indian, health and health care would include using many different approaches that parallel the holistic medicine approach as well as using healers, shaman, and herbal treatments. They would also include healing relations with the family, culture, work, community, environment, and cultural heritage. Life is a constant state of flux. Our relations with others are continually in turmoil. To maintain health, a person needs to be in a state of balance with himself or herself, and with his or her family, community, culture, work, environment, and cultural heritage. One must live the life that was chosen for him or her. This may involve an extensive search to discover one's purpose. Learning one's place or purpose in life may come from a quest or spiritual journey.

Poor health, illness, and even death may happen because one is not in balance with one or all parts of the one's body, mind, and spirit. A person may be out of balance with one's family, community, work, culture, or heritage. This balance must be restored. For the American Indian, part of the task of healing is to determine the source of the imbalance. It is the healer's job to find the source of imbalance in the ill person's life.

Another part of the task of the healer is to restore the balance or harmony once the source of the imbalance is discovered. The restoration will include physical, mental, and spiritual acts. The physical will include medicines, shelter, food, clothing, massage, heating or cooling the body, and so forth. The mental will include relaxation, storytelling, family activities, ceremonies, rituals, entertainment, and cognitive activities such as concentration, meditation, focusing on the "rules," and so forth. The spiritual will include meditation, ritual, ceremonies, using sacred objects, prayers, and even exorcism.

Everyone is on a spiritual journey to find the meaning and purpose of their lives. Why was he or she born, why did my loved one die? Janice Winchester Nadeau (1998) writes about family meaning-making in grief. Her model certainly applies to the spiritual journey of American Indian peoples.

CULTURE AND HEALTH

Culture is more than the place where one lives, the objects that people own or use, or the physical surroundings that make up the area. Culture is the way of life of a people. It is made up of their values, morals, attitudes, assumptions, expectations, and behaviors. It is more than the material culture. It also includes the social organization, the environment, the way one communicates, and the time orientation that is used.

The social organization in which one grows, lives, and plays forms an essential role in cultural development and identification. It determines who we become as a person. Children learn to respond to the events in their lives from a cultural framework that is acquired from family, religion, education, government, and occupational institutions.

Those who live in an urban environment see the world quite differently than those who live in more isolated, rural environments. In the urban environment, one's occupation is far more important in your self-image or defining who you are as a person than in a tribal community. Being homeless, unemployed, underemployed, lacking health insurance, and so forth are far bigger handicaps in an urban environment. In a rural setting, one is more often judged for the person that one is than for the job that one has, or the house where one lives, or the car that one drives, and so forth. The advantage of the tribal community is its simplicity. A child learns a more consistent normative pattern; has security of knowing people around him or her; and has fewer roles to learn, identify, and develop. The extended family has far more influence on the person. People know what you do or don't do.

The communication styles that one learns are also important in cultural development and identification. Many differences exist among groups involving verbal and nonverbal behaviors and use of silence. How close does one stand when talking to another? How long does one take before responding to the words of another? How necessary is it to fill the air with words, or is it proper to continue to remain silent? Does one look the other in the eye when speaking to them or avert one's eyes? Generally, American Indians are far more comfortable with silence, standing close to another person, not looking another in the eyes when talking with them, and taking their time before responding to another person when talking with them.

American Indians generally value silence more than those in the dominant White culture. Personal space is not prized as in the White culture. Imagine giving a speech with the persons in the audience being within 1½ feet of you, or talking to a baby from a distance of 12 or more feet rather than holding them. Words are treasurers that must be sparingly used. Space is generally further away in the White culture. Yet, many elders report that children skip over their words suggesting that today's children no longer listen to what the elders really have to say. They hear words and not the lessons of life that the elders are teaching. Many other factors also influence cultural development and identification.

Environmental factors also contribute to cultural development and identification. Clearly, if one is used to folk medicine, traditional healers, ceremonials, rituals, and treatment at home or at least in the community, one may easily be intimidated by the environment of hospitals, nurses, physicians, bureaucrats, and pharmacies. Clipboards, strange machines, white clothes, stainless steel, and strange smells do not give confidence to those being served. Fear does not lead to healing or to the resolution of grief.

The time orientation of a culture is also important. The dominant White culture in both Canada and the United States tends to focus on the future with an eye on the past. It is not unusual to begin to make college plans for children who are not yet even in high school. American Indians tend to live in the present. One cannot change the past. The future has not yet happened. Why worry? Healing, illnesses, and even death are present issues, not future or past issues. If one drank or smoked or whatever in the past that led to his or her illness and ultimate death, one does not blame the ill person for their woes, but rather one should focus upon his or her failings. People are accepted for where they are now rather than for past accomplishments or even past mistakes. Grief is for today.

The White culture of Canada and the United States tends to focus on the future without the deceased. How will I pay bills, shop, maintain the house, or whatever is the focus of the dominant culture. The traditional American

Indian will focus on missing them today. Various actions will be taken to make tomorrow better than today. Folk beliefs are part of many cultures, not just American Indians. It may not be practiced anymore, but French-Canadian Catholics used to place a gold wedding ring on the eye of the person with an eye infection and make the sign of the cross three times. Folk practices are a part of most cultures. One should live every day as though it is the last day of one's life, but one should also enjoy today more than yesterday and tomorrow more than today. An appreciation of self is important in enjoying today. If one's skills are not highly valued, it can be more of a problem to enjoy today.

American Indian peoples often have skills that are not highly valued in today's world. Many have strengths and abilities in being able to remember visual patterns, to visualize spatial concepts, and to see images within rocks or metals. I was taught that when carving a piece of stone that I should study it to find what is in the marble or whatever type of stone that I was carving to let out the spirit or image that was in it. Perhaps, all people have such skills before they start school. The cognitive learning styles differ. Of course, not all students of any group learn well with any particular learning style. The emphasis upon skills involving reflecting and being observant is often used to explain the inordinate number of creative peoples in American Indian groups. The ability to become a successful artist may very well come from failure to adopt mainstream culture in any society. Hopefully, the young American Indian child will come to understand that even though their learning styles and skills are different, they are still valuable and provide meaning. American Indians are generally accepting of death. "We live, and then we live again."

CONCLUSIONS

Trying to understand another culture is difficult for all people. To try to judge another culture that is distinctly different from your own is exceedingly difficult. Sociologists use the concept of ethnocentrism to help explain why people have such difficulty in understanding why other people behave the way that they do. Those who have supported former president Trump have great difficulty in responding to those who support President Biden. Anger and even hatred of those on the other side have split families, caused people to lose friends, change jobs or churches, and have led to violence. The lack of empathy and understanding of other cultural groups has led to similar feeling about American Indians. Historically, many wanted to see them exterminated or at least completely out of sight. Bad feelings have emerged that led to the "Indian Wars," "Little Big Horn," "Wounded Knee," and so many more incidents. Judging another culture often presents a challenge for most people. Showing kindness and concern for those who are different seems to be a challenge for many.

Part II

SOCIOLOGY OF THE AMERICAN INDIAN SPIRITUALITY, DYING, AND DEATH

The chapters in part II are an attempt to use a sociological perspective to examine the way of life, approach to dying and death, and spiritual practices from a sociological perspective. The chapters will use knowledge and thinking from the thanatology or death awareness approach to managing dying and death. Chapter 8, "Sociology of American Indian Religion," uses a sociological framework developed by sociologist Emile Durkheim to analyze American Indian religious approach. Chapter 9, "American Indian Religion and Death," offers an examination of the spiritual and cultural approaches to death of the American Indians. Chapter 10, "The Sacred Way and Loss: American Indian Spirituality," provides a view of how death is managed by American Indians from a spiritual perspective. Chapter 11, "Death and Intimacy Impairment in Later Life," offers a way to understand the role of elders and the impact of aging to better understand the American Indian view of dying and death. Chapter 12, "American Indian Grief: The Healing Path," looks at the grief and bereavement practices of the American Indian.

Chapter 8

Sociology of American Indian Religion

While the writings of anthropologists, archaeologist, and even sociologists are not always correct culturally or even theoretically, they do offer a picture of the cultures of the American Indian both past and present. Emile Durkheim is considered to be not only one of the founding "fathers" of sociology, but also one of the most highly esteemed sociologists and is viewed as the founder of the sociology of religion. His work has been the basis of much of the work in sociology. The following is an attempt to apply his theoretical framework to American Indian religion.

Emile Durkheim defines religion as "the belief in Spiritual beings" (1915, 44). To have spirituality is to have renewal of the soul and spirit (Stolzman 1991, 74). American Indians traditionally believed in spirits and in an after-life. As in all religions, death management practices were developed to help manage loses. The practices in American Indian religions parallel those of other religions. American Indians, like Christians, view death with fear and yet as a spiritual release. For the American Indian, death is a separation of the body and the soul (Starkloff 1974, 45). Concepts of spirituality affect not only attitudes toward dying and death and the death management practices but also attitudes toward living. All spirituality is about one's roots. To be spiritual, one must live a rooted life, a life rooted in tradition and history (Fox 1979, 1). American Indian religion has many practices that have much in common with those of traditional Christian practices. While religion is a word that has no equivalent in the languages spoken by American Indians, they are at the same time intensely spiritual peoples whose spirituality is exhibited in their art and everyday living (Mander 1991, 200). Like Christians, American Indians do not view death as something to be ignored, but rather as a natural part of life. Death is a part of life as is birth. Death should not become an obsession nor be feared (DeSpelder and Strickland 1992, 58). Generally, American Indians are acceptant of dying and death.

Religion provides the believer with a belief system that defines the world and those in it, helps to clarify the mysteries of existence, forms a moral code to follow, gives meaning to life, adds to the sense of community by sharing a common faith with others, defines the sacred, offers a model for behavior in a secular world, enhances the sense of social order, and defines the nature of life and what is a good life.

ELEMENTS OF RELIGION

Fourteen elements of religion and death management practices will be presented. Each element will be based upon the model developed by Emile Durkheim.

The first element is the conception of the sacred. One visiting a religious place, a sacred person, or a sacred event would typically be struck by the fact that the situation is viewed by the people involved as holy rather than profane. It would also be an event that is characterized by a sense of awe or mystery. The American Indian is religious in totality or kind as opposed to practicing a religion. American Indians have a sense of the sacred that permeates even the most casual and personal attitudes of a person. The American Indian understands herself or himself and the world as part of a religious view (National Geographic Society 1974, 23). While the individual is basically spiritual, when faced with a spiritual crisis, the American Indian will turn to a priest or a shaman or other qualified person to deal with the sacred. These people have the knowledge of how to deal with the sacred. Among American Indians, those who deal with the holy were chosen in childhood for special religious training and eventually becoming spiritual leaders. As children and young adults, they would be taught the sacred ways of the people (Grimm 1981, 3). As the shaman might have a vision quest, Jesus had his vision quest in the wilderness (Myers 1994, 111). The traditions of Judaism and Christianity parallel those of the American Indians in many ways. The story of Samuel from the Hebrew Bible and the Seminaries for youths in Christianity historically are examples of similar traditions.

The second element of religion suggested by Durkheim would be that all religions contain magic as a basic element (1915, 58). Magic in religion could be typified by the basketball player who prays before shooting a free throw, by the child who prays for a bicycle or other special items, or by the parent who prays for a magical cure for a child who has no scientific or medical hope to survive a serious illness or injury. Certainly, the use of magic among American Indians could be seen in the practice of the Sun Dance ceremony of the Cheyenne and in the rites of the Lone Tipi (Hoebel 1960). Magic is similar to religion in that it serves some of the same functions. Both magic and religion deal with the supernatural, both use specialized personnel to work with the supernatural, both are based upon faith, and both explain why events occur. For the Dine, all sickness and disease, whether mental or physical, are caused by supernatural causes such as an attack by a witch or one of the Holy People, or by breaking one of the rules of life (Dutton 1975, 99). Certainly, many Christians believe that their misfortunes are due to the devil or their own breaking of the rules. Spiritual wholeness is given by religious identification and by sound moral teaching that results from such teaching (Starkloff 1974, 220). Following rules is a basic part of the American Indian way of life. Following rules is a basic part of the American Indian way of life.

David Brugge (1985) examined the records of the Roman Catholic Church of New Mexico from the years 1694 to 1875 and found that the basic cause of problems between the Navajo and the White was the basic reluctance of the Navajo to use coercive measures among themselves (1985, 132). The Navajo, like most tribes or clans, had no jails, no prisons, no police, no courts, or even a perceived need to have any of them. The Navajo, or more properly the Dine, were taught that one should take care of his or her own property, children, parents, the aged, those in need, and one's wife and her family (Ladd 1957, 255). There was no reason to have police, courts, prisons, or even punishment to know what was proper behavior. Dine values would include being generous to others, to avoid being mean to others, being dependable, being kind and respectful, and being willing to work hard. Lamphere (1970) saw the Dine as having values that would include not being stingy, mean, mad, lazy, sexually jealous, or envious of another's possessions (Lamphere 1977, 37). Many other rules of behavior also guide what one does.

For the most part, the Dine would not ask another person for help, but rather they would wait for people to notice that they need help. One should not act for another or speak for them or say what they think or feel, or judge them in a court or speak as a witness against them for their behavior. Basso (1970) argues that the Apache or Inde have similar rules for behavior and teach that one should behave as if everyone is your relative (Basso 1970, 228). Like other tribes or clans, the Inde would rarely order others as to how to act or behave, but would more likely simply offer observations as to possible outcomes for their actions.

Attitudes are the third element of religion. Magic is different than religion in that it is specific in its goals. In magic, those using magic command or order that another person falls in love, gets sick, dies, or whatever. In religion, the goals are more transcendental such as long life, unity with God, salvation, and freedom from sins. With magic, one not only has different goals but also has different attitudes as well.

In religion, the attitudes are generally typified by reverence, awe, respect, but the attitudes could also be ecstasy or terror as well. In magic, one commands that events happen while in religion one is more likely to plead or beg. Magic is more utilitarian and technical than is religion (Durkheim 1915, 405). For some Christian, Baptism seems to be able to magically guarantee one's entry into heaven. Communion magically gives the grace needed to live a Holy Life. For the American Indian, reverence for Earth Mother as an expression of the work of the Great Spirit in creating the environment in which the human beings live would more likely be a typical attitude.

A fourth element of religion would be ritual. Rituals serve the function of making objects sacred, teaching ways of doing things, and supporting beliefs. Rituals provide the routine that supports stability and provides predictability in life. Rituals might include the way one makes a piece of pottery, weaves a rug, carves a sculpture, makes a sandpainting, or casts a piece of metal. Before the Whites came, American Indians had beliefs and rituals that fit their way of life and their spiritual needs (Underhill 1965, 254). The Dine viewed themselves as being tied to the sacred earth, and to the materials that they used to weave or to make pottery or other items that had traditionally come from the earth: the wool from sheep, the dyes from wild plants and berries, the looms from the trees (Katz 1980).

Religious rituals provide order to one's life. This allows religion to help manage the strains of everyday living. The Blessing Way ritual of the Navajo is an example of a ritual in an American Indian religion. As an important ritual in the Navajo religion, the Blessing Way was a ceremonial that was concerned with peace, harmony, and good things (Wyman 1970, 2). Like the Catholic Sacraments, the Blessing Way is used for births, weddings, and other life events, but the Blessing Way is also used for good hope, to acquire property, protection against accidents, and to invoke a blessing on all aspects of domestic and social life, including childbirth, weddings, adolescent rites to install tribal officers, to bless a new house, and other blessings needed for daily life (Wyman 1970, 3). Lifeway rituals may be used to cure injuries caused by accidents or illnesses while the Mountainway Chant would be used to cure gastrointestinal and other illnesses (Wyman 1970, 3). Probably, most Christians would expect that being religious and spiritual would lead them to have good hope, to acquire property, to have protection against accidents, and to invoke a blessing on all aspects of their domestic and social life. The Dine also believed that the misfortunes such as sickness or premature death are caused by not following the rules and that performing the ceremonials could restore order in the individual and that by performing exact rituals that would require supernatural forces to withdraw their punishment or sickness from the individual (Dutton 1975, 98).

The Changing Woman is the favored people among the Holy People of the Dine. The Changing Woman had much to do with the creation of the Earth Surface people (Waters 1950, 214). Like Christ to the Christian, She is one with God. She also has an eternal presence (Waters 1950, 217). For the Pueblo Indians, contact with the supernatural is the aim of all ceremonies. Spiritual healing can occur with the aid of the supernatural (Laski 1958, 123). For the Inde, ceremonies were performed as cures, to set things right, or to ward off evil. The majority of ceremonies were carried out by the shaman (Dutton 1975, 135). Many rituals of the Catholic Church have their parallels in the Blessing Way and other Dine ceremonies. American Indian spirituality provides for those who are ill or who are dying, and their survivors a framework to cope with crises and trauma of life.

The fifth element focuses upon the concept that in all religions beliefs are an essential element. The major function of belief is to support religious rituals. Durkheim suggests that, in principle, religion is supported by beliefs, and yet beliefs are often modeled after rituals that account for them (1915, 121). As demonstrated by the book *The People: Sky Lore of the American Indian* (Littmann 1976), the American Indians had beliefs that are similar to those in Judaism and Christianity concerning the creation, the solar system, and the acts of nature. Oral traditions present stories similar to those of the ancient Jew as well as the early Christian. The beliefs of one religion are typically viewed as legends or myths to those who are not believers or those who practice different religions. Generally, most people believe that their religion is the only "true" religion which is an example of the sociological concept of ethnocentrism. Ethnocentrism conceptually suggests that one's culture is best. Our beliefs are religion while what others believe are mythology and superstition (Schaefer 2013, 62).

The origins of religious beliefs are the sixth element of all religions. Revealed truths typically come from deities or from the teachings of the prophets. God was described as speaking to Abraham and to Moses in the Old Testament and the Hebrew Bible. God spoke to Mohammed and told him what to write in the Koran. God also came to the Dine and also to give them the Blessing Way. After the original word is given to a people, the members of the religion and their leaders interpret what the word means. Christian groups who carried on the oral traditions of the Jewish word did not all follow the same text. The Yahwist, the Elohist, the Priestly, and the Deuteronomist sources all have slightly different versions of the word of God and the events of the people of God (Boadt 1984). The early Christian versions of the word of God vary depending upon whether one reads Matthew, Mark, Luke, John, or the words of Paul. Similarly, the word of God as exhibited in the Dine Blessing Way has more than one version (see Wyman 1970). The Monster Slayer who came to save the Navajo people is similar to the coming of Jesus for the Christians (Rapport 1954, 52). The traditions of the Dine combine belief, ritual, and ritual as a part of their view of social justice. The Dine Church focus is upon curing as was the focus of Jesus upon curing (Rapport 1954, 52). Spiritual healing is not only a part of American Indian religions, but it has been a basic part of the acceptance of the founders of religions, saints, and disciples as well (Sweet 1985, 124). In an oral tradition that covers many generations, stories have a way of changing as memories fade, word meanings change resulting in the possibility that revision may occur.

The seventh element of religion is animism. Durkheim would also view animism as an essential element of religion. He suggested that there were two kinds of phenomena occurring. One is nature in the form of the great cosmic forces such as the wind, rivers, stars, or the sky or as in the objects of nature such as plants, animals, and rocks that also have spiritual being. The second type of animism is that of souls who occupy the spirit world (Durkheim 1915, 65). In the first type, spirits are seen as becoming the wind, stars, sky, and other natural phenomena with the power to control their natural forces and to impact the lives of the people. These spirits are seen as responsible for what happens in the universe (Durkheim 1915, 333). Mother Nature, the Sun God, the Moon God, and the God of the River Nile are examples of this type of animism. The Blessing Way emphasis upon Gopher Man, Gopher Woman, Green Frog People, and the Maiden Who Became a Bear demonstrate the concept of the first type. The Changing Bear Maiden husband was killed by her brothers causing her to become a monster who killed all but the youngest brother who was able to kill her formed the belief that bear sickness could be caused by killing or offending a bear and could only be cured by a healing ceremony that included the Dine legend of the Maiden Who Became a Bear as a part of the healing ceremony (Pavlik 2014, 64). The concept that spirits of the people who occupy the bodies of animals is also accepted by many North American Indian groups. These spirit animals have their guardian spirits as well. The transition to guardians for people is a simple concept to accept. If animals have guardians, and if people can occupy the bodies of animals, then people have guardians as well (Hultkrantz 1980, 77). Spirits help people, befriend them, guide them, and for those who are blessed by the spirits, they become shaman (Wood 1982, 15).

Christians accept the concept of guardian spirits whom they describe as guardian angels. For the American Indian this can be one's guardian spirit (Hultkrantz 1982, 17). The second type of spirit of animism is seen in ghosts or spirits of another world who come to visit the people. In Christianity, the devil comes to tempt Jesus. The Blessing Way of the Navajo tells of the Horned Monster, the Eye Killers, the Big Centipedes, the Overwhelming Vagina, the Rock Monster Eagle, the Big Ye'i, and other world spirits that come to attack the people (Wyman 1970). The occult may have the similar threat of danger for Christians. Evil spirits come to take the souls of the living. The Black Mass and other occult activities are ways to attack Christianity and Christians as the monsters are to attack the Dine.

The eighth element of religion is veneration and worship of spirits (Durkheim 1915, 309). While it is probably true that humans have worshiped just about everything on earth that could be worshiped, it is generally not the object that is worshiped at all, but rather the spirit or being that inhabits the object, or the spirit that is represented by the object. For the Hopi, Kachinas were not deities, but rather Kachinas were the spirits of the people who lived in a way of obeying the laws and conforming to the perfect and pure pattern given to the Hopi by the Creator, who traveled to the next universe upon death (Waters 1963, 203). For the Roman Catholic, saints are venerated as Holy People, as those who lived spiritual lives in a sacred manner, as those who have died, and continue as living spirits may intercede for the living. Like the Catholics, the Dine worshiped a God. Most North American tribes worshiped a supreme deity (Hulkrantz 1980, 16).

The ninth element is that all religions also have myths. Myths can be viewed as a narrative projection of a cultural group's sense of its sacred past and its significant relationship with the deeper power of the surrounding world and the universe (Leeming and Leeming 1994, vii). Durkheim viewed myths as having an essential role in religion and suggested that if myth were withdrawn from religion that it would be necessary to withdraw ritual also because myth determines the character of the religion (1915, 100–101). Christian myths about Jonah, Abraham, Noah, the flood, and the parting of the Red Sea to allow the Passover are generally viewed as quasi-historical. The American Indian parallels the Orpheus tradition of the Ghost Dance (Hultkrantz 1957), the myth of the Navajo of the first humans ascending from the underworld, the origin myth of the Sun Dance of the Cheyenne (Hoebel 1960), and the Blessing Way myths of Changing Woman (Wyman 1979) are also quasi-historical. Such myths are typically so long ago that it is difficult to empirically test their validity. Myths are also part of the belief structure of the religion. Myths generally function to validate or justify beliefs and rituals. It is not important that myths actually be true to be supported or believed by followers of the religion. The function of myth is to support belief and ritual. It is not the basis for that belief.

The tenth element of religion is that all religions have a set of things which serves to designate the particular religious group that Durkheim called its totem (1915, 123). For the Roman Catholic, the totem would include the Rosary, the Sacraments, the church, religious artifacts, relics, clerical garb, and rituals. For the Dine, the totem would include the purification rituals of the sweat bath, the rituals of sandpainting, the weaving of the rug, and the making of pottery. These totems are social totems. Social totems give the members of the religion a sense of identity and a social solidarity that would not be possible without the totem. The members do the rituals and practices of the totem together and get a sense of belonging by doing so. The totem may also serve as a mystical presence that is found in birds, animals, rocks, mountains, or other natural objects. This type of totem would be called a mystical totem. Tribes that depended upon bison or other animals for survival would develop rituals and beliefs concerning the animal to give them power with the animal to allow its capture. The vision quest was a widespread belief that was undertaken to obtain a guardian spirit that would take the form of an animal, bird, or inanimate object (Hultkrantz 1980, 70–74). Durkheim describes such activities among the Australian clans and among some American Indian groups (1915, 122).

An eleventh element of religion would be the concept of ancestor worship. Like Christianity, American Indian groups generally had a belief in an afterlife though that did not include a concept of heaven and hell. The concept of a complete extension of the personality at death is not easily accepted. When a person has a close relationship for an extended time with another person or even an intense brief relationship with another person, the death of that person leaves a void. The dead can remain part of the life of the living. It is not unusual for a person to describe the visit of a deceased loved one in a dream ore semi-awake state. It is even more common for the living to describe experiencing a feeling of the presence of the deceased in their daily activities. The deceased are able to continue to influence and to be a part of the life of the living. Talking to a specific star or other object in the sky or to a bird or animal is used by many to communicate with the deceased. Catholics communicate with the deceased through prayer and meditation. The Dine may communicate with the deceased through animals. Death does not end life. It is part of life! Death permeates life! Death is not something which will only happen in the future. It is a part of the daily lives of people. Facing the future of death of one's own death makes life have more meaning and to be more livable. It makes life have a sense of urgency and causes an awareness of the importance of people in one's life. It makes death a goal rather than a threat to one's being. Everyone dies. Everyone that we know will die. When a loved one dies, those who survive have to continue their lives without the dead while at the same time, keeping them as a part of their lives. The living can continue to make the dead part of their life. Those in the afterlife may remain in an intimate relationship with the living (Klass 1999, 103).

A twelfth element of religion focuses upon attitudes toward death. Attitudes toward life and death are learned. Religion is one source of learning one's attitudes. American Indian and Christian attitudes are somewhat similar. Both share a concept human morality. Both have great emphasis upon prayer. The ritualistic prayers and chants of the Dine have their parallel in the

Catholic prayers and chants. A major difference is that the sacred words of the Catholic are written in a sacred book while the sacred words of the Dine have been passed down through an oral tradition. In the traditions of Judaism and Christianity, oral traditions are also a major part of their history as with the Dine. In recent years, the sacred words of the Dine are being written, but there are thirty-five major ceremonies and numerous variations of the thirty-five major ceremonies. A Catholic priest, Father Bernard Haile, who lived among the Dine for more than fifty years, not only developed a written form of the Dine language, but he also invented a typewriter to print it (Pavik 2014, 10). Generally, the ceremonies last from two to nine days, but regardless of how long the ritual takes, it is a community event. Like Catholics, the community of believers is critical to the success and durability of the rituals. Like the rituals of the Christian, the Dine rituals and ceremonies provide form, values, joy, virtue, structure, strength, and a sense of the sacred. As the personality of the Roman Catholic is represented by the Mass, the Rosary, and the sign of the cross, the personality of the Dine is represented by the Blessing Way, the sandpainting or dry painting, and the rituals of the Hogan. While most of the Dine ceremonies focus upon healing, the legends, songs, and prayers are also concerned with creation, the earth and sky, the sun and moon, sacred mountains and vegetation, clouds and mist, blessings and happiness, and burdens of life.

Like the Catholic religion, the Dine religion is essentially spiritual. The American Indian has been subjected to the religions of the white culture and will often turn to a priest or a shaman or other qualified person to deal with the sacred. Those who would learn the Blessing Way or other ceremonies will be chosen in childhood for special religious training. They would be taught the sacred ways of the people (Grimm 1981, 3). As the shaman performs rituals learned over many years, the Hogan is a major part of all ceremonies. The Hogan is a temple where ceremonial rituals are performed. As the priest performs rituals in the home of the sick, the shaman also performs rituals in the home of the sick. The Dine do not have churches as Christians do. There is also a difference in what they believe as to why people are sick. For the Dine, illness or even death can be caused by an attack on a person by a witch or one of the Holy People, or by breaking one of the rules of life (Dutton 1975, 99). Certainty is given by religious identification and by sound moral teaching that results from such teaching (Starkloff 1974, 220). Some chants of the Dine have their parallel in the Catholic prayers and chants. However, a central difference is that Christianity focuses upon belief and faith while the Dine focus upon ritual activity (Rapport 1954, 46). A major difference is that the sacred words of the Christian are written in a sacred book while the sacred words of the Dine are passed down in an oral tradition. In both the traditions of Judaism and Christianity, oral traditions were a major part of their history as with the Dine. In recent years, the sacred words of the Dine have been written, but mostly in English (see Wyman 1970, Zolbrod 1984, and Gill 1981). Death is a major subject in the oral tradition of the American Indian (Gill 1982) as is life to the Christian.

The thirteenth element of religion is the conception of a soul. Durkheim suggests that just as there is no known society without religion, there is no group that does not have a set of teachings regarding the soul, its origins, and its destiny (1915, 273). Not only do Christians have a concept of the soul, but so do American Indians. Durkheim further reports that American Indians believe that all people are descendants of a single soul and that makes everyone related (1915, 293). While all people are a product of what they receive from society and have more in common with those they live among, the soul though closely bound to the body is separate from the body and is distinct from what society has taught, the soul at the same time is what makes the human become human (Durkheim 1915, 307).

The last element of religion is the explanation for evil. Death is perhaps the greatest evil that religion explains. In Christianity God allows human freedom which explains evil; other religions have their anti-gods to explain evil (Durkheim 1915, 468). While there are many evils to be faced in life, death is one of the evils that all peoples must confront. Death is not simply an event which ends one's life, but death is a part of life. It is not simply a future event, but death is an ever-present event. The limits of time that one will live may force people to make the most of their lives while they have them. Death is a teacher for life and how to live one's life. Like all groups, American Indian tribes often lived a precarious existence. War, famine, natural disasters, accidents, or disease could easily end their lives. While all tribes did not talk of a separate place for the good and those who were evil in an afterlife as do Christians, at least most tribes believed in an afterlife (Rapport 1954, 45). Like the Christian, the American Indian is able to face death with less fear and apprehension because of a belief in an afterlife.

THE ROLE OF SPIRITUALITY

In the daily living of the American Indian, spirituality is a part of everything that they do. Spirituality and prayer are inseparable to the American Indian. To separate the spiritual and prayer would mean cultural death for the American Indian. Every day and every act is a holy event while for many Christians, only one day a week is a holy day. All that an American Indian undertakes begins and ends with the influence of a spiritual kinship with nature. Spirituality invades and benefits every part of the American Indian's daily life. Like the Christian, the American Indian looks to spirituality to explain the success and failures of daily life. The guiding spirit or force which rules nature can help or hurt one in his or her daily life and struggles. While the American Indian did not build churches, nor did they have a Bible, or hymnals, or whatever like Christians, American Indians are equally spiritual and religious in their daily lives. Every living thing including animals, plant life, stones, mountains, sun, moon, stars, and the elements are spiritual items. American Indians also show reverence to an all-powerful and ever-present spirit. The dead, too, are a part of the spirit world. In the American Indian theology, the abode of the dead is a blessed place and the death themselves are bringers of blessings. The funeral ceremony allayed not the fear of those who survived, but rather, allayed their grief (Underhill 1965).

While death beliefs varied from one clan or tribe to another, patterns do exist. Sedentary groups like the Pueblo and Dine seem to exhibit more fear of the dead body than groups that are hunters and gathering like the Sioux, Apache, and Flathead. The Hoogan (Anglicized to Hogan) was the center of every blessing in life: happy births, the home of one's children, where weddings are centered, the center of one's health, the origin of good crops and livestock, where old age is a goal of life, and where people perform ceremonies and visit. The Hogan means a long life of happiness. Those reaching old age in the Hogan have nothing to fear including death. The Dine pray the Blessing Way for the blessing of death in old age. The Hogan in which such a death occurs is not destroyed. The family may witness such a death. The four days of mourning which are otherwise customary are not observed. While some groups buried or burned items that belonged to the deceased including their dwellings, others simply could not afford to do so like the fishing tribes of the Northwest who had no fields to provide food and who lived in log houses that were not as easily replaced as a straw wickiup (Underhill 1965, 69). The Dine would prefer to no longer use a Hogan where someone died if the Blessing Way was not observed. The Dine had a purification ritual that would be performed on the items that the deceased left behind before giving them to survivors so that the dead cannot harm them. Other groups like the Tohono O'odham (called Papago by non-Indians) destroyed property that was not buried with the dead in order to keep survivors safe from the dead (Underhill 1965).

The Dine would bury their dead in their blanket and leave their jewelry on the body. Since American Indians did not embalm, normally, the dead were buried, cremated, or sent into the waters as soon as possible after the death. Funeral practices of American Indians are based upon their attitudes toward dying, death, and the dead. Some tribes mourn for a time such as the Dine who mourn for four days after the burial. Others like the Salish Sioux, who may mourn for up to a year after the death, will have a feast after the burial, a giveaway, with the clothing of the deceased being buried with the deceased along with any property that is not useful is burned, goods that will be inherited are ritualistically purified, and mourning will vary from as little as four days to an entire year (Habenstein and Lamers 1960, 698–702). Christians also mourn and feast after a death. While one may theologically celebrate the triumph of the soul over death, one still mourns the loss of a loved one. Funeral rituals are rites of passage. The rite of passage is designed to allow the dead to pass into the domain of the dead. For life to be meaningful, it must lead somewhere. Its destination is death. Therefore, death can be life's ultimate fulfillment or life's ultimate failure. Few moments can rival the moment of death as a significant moment in one's life.

CONCLUSIONS

All religions have many common elements. Fourteen elements of religion are presented based upon the work of sociologist Emile Durkheim. The spirituality of American Indians is similar to that of Christianity. Both American Indian religions and Christianity have much in common. Both exhibit similar patterns of spirituality. Both have similar death management practices. Spirituality of the people is shown through their management of death. Like Christianity, there is no single American Indian religion as there is no single Christian religion.

Chapter 9

American Indian Religion and Death

American Indian religion is often sought after for study and "borrowing." The respect that is generally accorded to the study of religions other than one's own is typically not given to American Indian religions. When visiting a Buddhist temple, we remove our shoes. When attending a Muslim prayer service, we might use a prayer rug. If we attend a Jewish service, a man would wear a yarmulke and remove his jacket and tie. The non-Jewish visitor would not wear the tallit or prayer shawl out of respect for Jewish traditions. American Indians generally prefer that strangers not attend spiritual services unless invited, yet many people come to watch and even take pictures, record, or videotape services without asking for permission. We would never take a Muslim prayer rug home after using it, yet many after watching American Indian rituals will take sandpaintings, dream catchers, pipes, or other sacred items. The lack of respect for American Indian religions by mainstream Americans has occurred for centuries and is not only unfortunate, disrespectful, and hurtful, but it needs to be stopped. What caused the United States and other cultures to disrespect Indian people's religions and spiritual ways and to subject them to unfair treatment?

SPIRITUAL PRACTICES

Many spiritual practices exist for all cultures. Disposing of the dead is a universal spiritual practice. Nowhere are losses of tradition in cultural practices more evident than in the realm of funeral practices. Immigrants in the dominant culture have not only lost their own traditions but they also have attempted to destroy the traditions and practices of those whom they conquered. American Indian religions do not focus upon sin, denial of personal pleasure, or fear of hell to guide them. The Protestant ethic of avoiding personal pleasure, working hard, and accumulating wealth are missing from Native faiths. Rather, the Indian religions focus upon spirituality and spiritual practices. In addition, Indians have often combined their religious practices with those of Christians.

The Flathead tribes, also known as the Salish, Bitterroot Salish, and as the Pend d'Oreille or Kalispel, have managed over time to integrate traditional practices with those of Christianity. The Flathead tribes are from the same language family. Other tribes in the language family would include the Spokane, Thompson, Coeur d'Alene, Shuswap, Lillooet, and others west of the Rocky Mountains.

Like many tribes on the plains and elsewhere, the Flathead were able to combine Christian and quite often Catholic traditions with their own sacred customs. A few "Blackrobes" or Catholic priests allowed them to keep some of their own traditions including peyote and sings and showed some respect for their ways and religion. Catholic hymns, prayers, and rituals have been translated into Kalispel dialect, the Salish or Flathead dialect, and the similar dialects of the other groups in the language family. Similar efforts have been made with some other tribes.

While there are those who do have great respect and admiration for the traditional religions and practices of American Indians, the pattern has not been adopted universally. Many clergy and Christian workers have abused, neglected, and generally mistreated those in their charge in boarding schools, mission, and reservation schools. Yet, the dominant, mainstream culture seems generally inclined to either ignore or suppress the indigenous cultures that it has tried to destroy since Europeans first arrived. Many "Blackrobes" and other clergy do go to great lengths to respect and preserve traditional ways. The Catholic Church in Crownpoint, New Mexico, was built in the shape of a Hogan with four stained glass windows representing the four sacred mountains of the Dine (Navajo) (McCloskey 2007, 9). The Stations of the Cross are Dine or Navajo sandpaintings which also acknowledge the traditions of the people, yet most Protestant fundamentalist and evangelical groups fiercely oppose incorporating American Indian traditions and ceremonies into their rituals (McClosky 2007, 10). The analysis of spiritual practices provides better understanding of the cultures and spiritual practices of others.

ACCEPTANCE OF SPIRITUAL PRACTICES OF OTHERS

The sociological approach called labeling theory suggests that while cultural groups have their own norms and values, they often do not respect those of other groups. Ethnocentrism or "my way is better than your way" seems to be the typical pattern. Those who do not practice the ways of the dominant group are often viewed as being inferior and having inferior ways. Those ways become "labeled" as inferior. They often become characterized by rhetoric that further labels them as inferior such as "savage, un-Christian, heathen, or Godless."

While it can be expected that individuals consistently believe their religion or spiritual practices are superior to those of others, it can also be expected that we could still have respect for different ways and traditions. It is not necessary to belittle or demean the practices of others. Cultural differences in how we present ourselves to others also often lead to conflicts. The Dine are generally reluctant to use coercive methods due to their strong respect for the individual. This has often been the root cause of disputes between Anglo-Europeans and the Dine (Brugge 1985, 132). The Dine approach of accepting people as they are rather than as we wish them to be does not mesh well with the typical Christian approach of trying to change the way people behave, who they are, and how they live. While many Catholic clergy also use this approach, more do not. Yet, even among clergy and those who call themselves religious, there are many who exploit, abuse, and ultimately denigrate cultures, beliefs, and peoples who are different. Not only do members of the clergy fail to respect or encourage traditional ways of bereavement and burial, but so, too, do funeral directors. Many funeral directors also go to great lengths to show respect for and to preserve traditional ways. Unfortunately, there are also funeral directors who are not cooperative with Native groups who want to follow traditional ways of disposing of their dead.

From the American Indian perspective, the blame for the lack of respect and unwillingness to not follow traditional ways of disposing of our dead is not just on the white culture or non-Indian influence, but rather that the elders failed to instill proper values in children or did not work hard enough to pass on traditional stories and ceremonies (Davies 2001, 109). Stronger efforts on the part of the people to insist that their religious traditions be respected and incorporated would have allowed fewer traditions and ceremonies to have been lost. [For further information on American Indian religions, see Wall and Arden (1990), Stolzman (1986), Archuleta and Strickland (1991), Curtis (1972), Powers (1972), Underhill (1953), Moskowitz and Collier (1949), Burland (1985), Taylor (1994), Marquis (1974), Fergusson (1931), and Anderson (1997).]

Like all people, American Indians want to send their dead to the next life with rituals and practices that reflect their spiritual and religious beliefs about dying, death, and the spiritual afterlife. Like other groups, American Indians view desecration of the dead or their burial sites as a serious and offensive act. Disease and even death can happen to those who violate the dead and their resting places.

Perhaps those who studied the Egyptians started the practice, but archaeologists have for generations been digging up human remains to study what was buried with them to learn about various cultures. The tombs of Greeks and Egyptians have yielded great knowledge of their worlds and ways of life. Thomas Jefferson is reputed to have dug up a burial mound in Virginia. Physical anthropology has long studied skulls and human bones to provide a rationalization for our treatment of various indigenous peoples. Following the Civil War, the Surgeon General of the United States ordered army personnel to obtain Indian skulls for study at the Army Medical Museum in Washington, D.C. The U.S. Army gathered heads from Arapahoe, Cheyenne, and Kiowa killed at the Sand Creek Massacre in Colorado. These and similar practices have made it far more difficult for contemporary researchers to learn about traditional ways by ethical means. Many tribes are quite reluctant to discuss their practices because of acts of the past by anthropologists, archaeologists, and even the U.S. government.

DENIGRATION OF AMERICAN INDIAN CULTURE

Many non-Indians take part in sweat ceremonies, hang dream catchers from the rearview mirrors of their vehicles or as wind chimes on their porches, give their children sacred objects as toys, share knowledge of sacred ceremonies, or otherwise denigrate traditional ways. The emergent construction of anti-Indian prejudice and its resulting discrimination have led to disrespect and desecration of the dead and the spiritual ways of the plains tribes. Mass unmarked graves of Indian children are vestiges of the mistreatment of the past, and yet some of those same well-meaning people have tried to make accommodations to the American Indian traditions. The Blackrobes and others have adorned the Virgin Mary in traditional Hopi or other tribal garments; developed the Black Madonna; and have hung pipes, beaded items, shawls, and other traditional American Indian items in their churches. Many non-tribal peoples respect traditional American Indian ceremonies and their sacred ways.

American Indian beliefs and traditions include reverence and respect for life. Death is not all that different than life. Everything is sacred. Every part of the dirt, rocks, trees, of all things, is sacred. The ashes of the dead are resting in sacred ground. Rather than disconnecting with the dead, American Indians continue to have a relationship with the dead. Rather than fearing death, it is rather part of life and to be accepted. One continues to love after someone has died. The dead do not cease to love us, to care for us, and to protect us. Of course, some of the dead did not do those things when they were alive. Chances are they will not do so from the afterlife. While the American Indian cultures continue to struggle to survive, the non-Indians view of them is often not based upon reality.

WHO ARE THE AMERICAN INDIANS?

For many, the stereotype American Indian is perhaps Iron Eyes Cody, St. Kateri Tekakwitha, or Sacagawea. While the stereotypes are not real nor is Iron Eyes Cody even an Indian, the image of the tears in the eyes of Iron Eyes Cody over the destruction of the environment may be more closely related to the sacred than leading Rogers and Clark on their journey. The image of tears in the eye is in keeping with American Indian spirituality and religion. Such images suggest that the American Indian has come to the end of their trail. Their way of life, their culture, and even their religion are being destroyed! American Indians have become a vanishing people who will soon be studied only by archaeologists and anthropologists. Yet, American Indians have experienced a new vigor, a sense of renewal of culture as well as religion. American Indians are not only militantly resisting their loss of culture and way of life, they are reclaiming the relics of their civilization that have been archived on shelves in museums and universities as well as reclaiming the bones of ancestors and reburying them (Echo-Hawk and Echo-Hawk 1994, 69–71). With the reclaiming of bodies and bones has come the resurgence of American Indian burial practices, religion, and spirituality.

While the image of Iron Eyes Cody as representative of the entire American Indians culture is false, so, too, is the image that all American Indians practice the same religion, follow the same spirituality, or even live the same way of life. Some were farmers who prayed for rain, others were warriors who prayed perhaps for months about hunting success or victory in battle, others who made objects or practiced the arts who prayed to make their objects sacred, or to those who prayed to animals or birds that held the souls of loved ones. For the European whether English, French, Spanish, Portuguese, or others who came to the Americas, religion and culture were separate worlds. To the American Indian, religion and culture were one and the same and not separate from each other. Sacred stories, the spirit world, rituals, and a way of life were traditional which is to them culture. American Indians would never try to convert others to their religion unless they intended to make them part of their clan or tribe. Europeans felt the need to convert "heathens" to their religion, to give them their European values, and to share their own view of the universal truth that their religion espoused. While there are as many American Indian religions as there are clans or tribes, there are common traits held by most groups.

SACRED STORIES

Sacred stories are common to most, if not all, American Indian groups. Rather than viewing the world as Europeans with a tri-level view of God, humans, and nature where each occupy different realms, for the American Indian, the world is tied together by kinship with those who made the earth and sky. For the Navajo, it was Changing Woman or Turquoise Woman who was sister of the moon and wife of the sun and who gave birth to the world. For the Pawnee, the maker of the world was Tirawa or Father Heaven, the husband of the female spirit who presides over the sky. For the Blackfeet of Montana, the Old Man was the creator of the earth and the one who directed where the prairies, mountains, animals, birds, and humans would live. For the Lakota, Wakan Tanka is the "power of the universe" and yet Wakan is a part of every object since every object has spirit (DeMallie 1987, 30).

Perhaps the use of sacred stories originates from the human anxiety about identity. Such questions, "who am I, and where did I come from," might lead to a search for metaphysical answers about life. At a metaphysical level the answer to "Who am I?" is tied to an existential concern about how my place on earth fits in with the vastness of the universe, with the world of spirits, my ancestors, and with sacred powers. My place in the universe is defined by my own social context. Who am I is defined by the sacred stories that taught me about my clans' sacred history, by what is passed on by my elders and my family, by learning the ways of my people, and by practicing rituals and conforming to social structures of my clan. Where I came from is answered by stories. For the Hopi, they were the first people to inhabit the Americas. It is believed that the Hopi village, Oraibi, is the oldest continuously occupied settlement in the Americas. The Hopi creation story describes ascending from the depths of the earth, wandering for a time, and eventually settling in the desert mesas of Southwestern North America. Children are taught that the "ancient ones" first came to earth from an underworld. They were three times given a world to care for, but every time, they became selfish and had not given respect to plants and animals, so they eventually lost all three worlds. Massau, who is the keeper of the Fourth World, told them that they must prove that they deserved a new place to live. After wandering for many years, they settled in the desert between four sacred mountains. The Star People taught them how to live in the harsh, dry land of the desert. The Hopi ask the Cloud People and other gods to bless them with rain. Besides pleasing the gods through prayer, the Hopi believe in working hard and living in balance with nature. They follow the "Hopi way." Their very name means "peaceful ones."

THE HOPI WAY

The Hopi are known as Pueblo people because they are among the many tribes that live in adobe or stone villages known as Pueblos. For thousands of years, the Hopi and their ancestors were scattered throughout the Southwestern United States. Hopi villages were for the most part built on mesas. Like most other tribes, the Hopi begin their day with the rising of the sun. A village crier calls people to greet the day! The Hopi believe that their harmonious and spiritual connection with nature is so important that it even impacts the design of their villages. For everyone, prayers, which are part of their spiritual way of life, begin early in the day. Men begin walking down the long trails that lead to the edge of the mesa to tend to their dry, cracked fields. Their prayers call for water to make the fields bloom. Women begin the day by preparing food. Older children help their parents. The Hopi have walled cities surrounding a central plaza where pithouses called kivas are the home to their ceremonies, instruction in Hopi ways, and where crafts are learned. There are no chiefs or central tribal leadership, but each village has someone who plays the role of leader that they inherited. Villages are divided into halves with each half having its own kiva. One half is for the Summer People and the other for the Winter People. Each half is further divided into clans that are often named after animals. Traditionally, men spent about half their time engaging in spiritual or religious activities.

The Hopi view of the world is of light and dark, good and evil sides of human existence. The Hopi believe that some of the spirits are good helpers while other spirits are bad witches and demons. In the summer, the Hopi pray for rain and a good harvest, and in winter, they pray for peace, health, and fertility. The various kiva clans had the duty of performing Hopi dances on special occasions. A holy man would lead the preparations for the sacred dances. Each kiva would focus upon specific aspects of their religious life. One might perform ceremonies to help farming while another would perform healing ceremonies. Still others might focus upon hunting or fertility. The Hopi are known to use prayer sticks, singing, dancing, and wearing costumes to ask the gods who live in the San Francisco Peaks, in the springs, lakes, and bodies of water to ask the spirits to come to their aid. Tradition says that the Kachinas came to earth, sang, danced, brought gifts, and taught the Hopi to farm, hunt, and do crafts. Though the Kachinas left the earth, they still bless deserving humans with peace, good health, rain, and crops. It is believed that at death, every Hopi becomes a Kachina. Kachinas are the link to one's ancestors in the spirit world with those who remain on earth.

THE LAKOTA WAY

The Oglala Sioux (Lakota), who were victims of the massacre at Wounded Knee, South Dakota, in 1890, are perhaps the best known of any American Indian group. Popularized in movies, novels, and Old West shows, the Oglala's traditional story of emergence tells of a Trickster, Inktomi the Spider, who lured the Oglala with food, clothing, and other gifts to try to get them to come to the upper world. A man, Tokahe, was convinced to go to the upper world to see what it was like. He took with him three strong companions and Inktomi gave them more gifts and promised them youth. They returned to the people in the world below and told stories regaling the upper world. Tokahe took six families to the upper world where they faced cold winds, a lack of food, and much hardship. The Old Man and Old Woman taught them to hunt, make clothes, and to make shelters. The six families were the first people in the world. The Lakota believed that everything had a life of its own, including rock spirits, tree spirits, and cloud spirits. Spirits could change their shapes and become animals or people or be invisible. The earth is the mother of all spirits. The sun has great power giving light and warmth. There were also spirits for the four directions and for the earth and the sky. The greatest power is Wakan Tanka who gave them the buffalo. Dreams and signs came from the spirits. Dreams and signs would bring them good luck and keep away from illness and death. The Lakota believed that after death, one would live with the spirits doing the same things that they had done on earth.

The White Buffalo Calf Woman gave ceremonies to the Lakota with the sacred pipe as its center for all religious rites. In ghost keeping, the soul or spirit of the deceased person could be kept for six months to two years or more. A ghost who is "kept" does not start on its road to its fate. Rather, it stays with close relatives. The elaborate rituals include a ghost bundle, a lock of hair from the dead person, and a special dwelling built for the bundle. When the "kept" ghost is released, equally elaborate ceremonies ensue. Other rituals include the sweat lodge ceremony, the vision quest, the sun dance, the "making of relatives," girl's puberty rituals, and a sacred ball game. Without giving away the specific rituals, the rituals are accompanied with specific rules, great attention to detail, adherence to direction, special numbers, purification, and specific gestures and actions.

The Lakota pray every day. They sing to the spirits! They dance and give gifts to the spirits. Sometimes they worship by themselves and sometimes with the entire tribe in a group ceremony. Everything that the Lakota did was to please the spirits. The way they ate, smoked their pipes, painted their faces, placing their tipis in a circle, placed stones for a sweat, fasting for four days, telling about dreams, painting tipis and shields, feasting, sewing, tanning, cooking, chopping wood, bathing, dancing, singing, praying, or healing others was to please the spirits. Medicine bundles were the most important method of keeping danger away. Each person made his own medicine bundle. A spiritual leader would tell each person what to put into their bundle. It might be an eagle feather, a tooth, a special pipe, rocks, and other special items. If a man is having bad luck, he might look for another medicine bundle. If another man is having good luck, he might try to borrow the lucky man's medicine bundle. Traditionally, the price would be high. War shields were also sources of good luck. These sacred items were highly prized, and others were not allowed to even touch them without permission. Shields were typically hung in the tipi with care to not let them touch the ground.

As a spiritual people, the Lakota had rules about good behavior. If a stranger came, you would greet them with a few words, and then both would sit quietly for a long time. It is good manners to be quiet. You would never show your feelings to a stranger. If you were happy, sad, angry, or whatever, you would not show it. You would be expected to share even with strangers your food, your pipe, and even your clothing.

CONCLUSIONS

Death may be viewed differently by American Indians. In funeral rites, the newly dead are often thought to be in an in-between state. The dead may be welcomed back as an ancestor. The dead may be feared as a potential source of death for the living. Rituals to manage dead spirits are developed to cope with grief and loss. Artistic expression may be used to aid with loss.

American Indian beliefs and traditions include reverence and respect for life. Death is not all that different than life. Everything is sacred. Every part of the dirt, rocks, trees, of all things, is sacred. The ashes of the dead are resting in sacred ground. Rather than disconnecting with the dead, American Indians continue to have a relationship with the dead. Rather than fearing death, it is rather part of life and to be accepted. One continues to love after someone has died. The dead do not cease to love us, to care for us, and to protect us. Of course, some of the dead did not do those things when they were alive. Chances are they will not do so from the afterlife.

Chapter 10

The Sacred Way and Loss

American Indian Spirituality

What truly makes us human has many dimensions. Much of what humans do and think are not related to the spiritual. Humans are concerned with power, physical needs, biological issues, historical memories, ways and results of communications, and psychological matters. Yet, no matter what areas of human behavior or human existence one may examine, there remain the need to examine the deeper issues of meaning and purpose of what one does with one's life. If a heinous act occurs, I may ask why? What is the meaning of the president's speech? Why is that happening at this time in history? Why did my loved one have to die? What responsibility do I have to my fellow human beings? Why is it that some people show such great concern for others? Why is living on the reservation seen by some as better than living in a city? Does the sacred way lead to spirituality? Would following the sacred way help me with my grief?

SPIRITUALITY

What is spirituality? As discussed earlier, John Morgan described spirituality as thinking and reflecting on ourselves and involving activities such as humor, ethical reasoning, and religious concern (Morgan 2000, 1). Thus, to be spiritual means to be involved with the realm of the sacred in thought, action, and social forms. Spirituality constitutes a total system of symbols with deep meaning that leads to a personal transformation through thinking and reflection. The concept of human involvement in the definition of spiritual suggests that humans who have a limited realm of experience and reality are connected with the sacred who seemingly has unlimited experience and reality. While humans may not know or even understand the realm of the sacred, the sacred can still transform their lives and their very existence. What is good and the ultimate good in human life has to do with relating to the sacred. While the idea of the sacred is distinctive in each religious tradition, it is possible to discern some general commonalities across religious boundaries. The shared humanness of all cultures should yield some general similarities in the way people describe their experiences of what they consider to be sacred. Humans tend to view the sacred with awe, reverence, and fascination. They tend to be drawn to the ultimate mystery of the sacred. The sacred becomes for humans the ultimate, the basis of life, and all that is in it. It holds the world together and accounts for everything, and yet, it is not dependent upon anything. The sacred is part of this world, but also wholly part of another somehow unreachable world for humans. Since the other world is unknowable, humans cannot find adequate words to describe it. Words refer to the human conditional reality, but the sacred is greater than that. The sacred is experienced with words that are inadequate and with symbols such as music, dance, silence, meditation, rituals, ceremonies, and so forth. Encounters with the sacred can evoke tremendous emotions and responses. Music, dance, drama, art, sculpture, and more can be deeply inspired by spiritual experiences.

All spiritual groups incorporate sacred stories, historical recollections, and a sense of meaning for humans, ritual, art, symbols, and so forth. They provide explanations of why things occur in our world, including birth, death, and even existence itself. Evil is also embellished with meaning. The ultimate evil is often portrayed as death. The world is a violent, dangerous place, and yet, spiritual worlds evoke images of peace and harmony. Lions lay with lambs, and humans take coup rather than kill. Humans become ugly and hateful. Life becomes filled with pain, death, and evil. Losses occur with great regularity. As spirituality is universal, so is loss. The spiritual offers a way to manage mundane loss as well as to transform those who have experienced tragic loss. The path of transformation involves deciding what is good and evil, and beginning the journey toward spiritual elevation. Change, repentance, seeking help from sacred powers, and following a new path to transform from our fractured existence are all part of the journey. Only then one can begin to live real life; only then can one begin to attain true healing. The sacred is taught in a way to give meaning and purpose to human existence. As human development matures, pollution is transformed by purification, ignorance by knowledge, evil by forgiveness, fracture by healing, and suffering by transformation to the spiritual path. All spiritual groups perceive that the power of the sacred transforms humans. As Christianity, Buddhism, and other religions recognize many paths to spirituality, so do American Indians.

LIFE VIEWS AND WAYS

American Indians generally believe that all life is predestined, but one can make his or her own destiny. Dreams assume greater importance to American Indians. One should strive to get rid of bad dreams because dreams can become one's destiny. Elders are teachers and can help one find his or her destiny. Elders are counselors, teachers, philosophers, mentors, and trusted. Many assume that because American Indians are quiet that they are shy. It is not shyness, but rather that the American Indian culture focuses more upon listening than talking. One does not just listen to words, but to animals, rocks, stars, and what is now called body language. Rather than trying to change others, American Indians generally accept people the way that they are. Elders and others with wisdom guide one through life by doing something in a good way, by talking positively about life, and by sharing their visions. By accepting life as it is, many would say that American Indians are content with living in poverty or suffering in the heat of Death Valley or wherever, but American Indians are not content, but rather ask how things happen rather than why things happen. Spiritual healing does not come from words. If one is sick, the sicker that one becomes, then fewer words are needed. Having goals are a major source of healing. The goal of the sick person is to become whole again rather than to be cured of the illness. Illnesses are to be appreciated as a gift. Illness is a gift because when one is made whole again, one has lost the sense of being indestructible, of reason, of connection to the world of the well, of central purpose, and of control. Illness makes one appreciate being well.

When one is ill, it affects the entire group. One is aided in illness by many who care for him or her. It allows one to better understand the love of others and his or her importance to others. One appreciates the beauty of life after illness. The drum allows one to feel the heartbeat of Mother Earth. Music is healing and helps one feel interconnected with nature and others. One is born in beauty as the new baby smells like sweetgrass, so do those who are made whole again feel like the reborn.

For all spiritual groups, the path to transformation is both a means and an end in itself. As a means, it is a method of moving toward the unattainable goal of a personal relationship with the sacred. The problems of human failure and evil remain until death. Most spiritual groups focus upon the future elevation of the human condition. The end may be in sight, but it is not achievable until death. By its very nature, the spiritual life is practical yet sacred; it needs to be lived and not just believed; it requires action, not just belief. Spiritual empowerment originates from ritual, sharing with family and community, and living according to the model of spirituality of the group. Yet, humans exhibit attraction toward the profane as well as the sacred. While some are motivated to become spiritual and develop a relationship with the sacred, others seem to not need or no longer need centers of meaning and purpose to their lives. For many, if not most, breaks in the path between the sacred and the profane are common. Special days, rites of passage, suffering, and pain are common precursors used to invoke a return to the sacred. Rituals, ceremonies, and sacred events may at least temporarily replace parties, sports, entertainment, vacations, holidays, and so forth.

SPIRITUAL LIFE AND LOSS

Of all of the events in life that challenge us to call upon our spiritual life or to need help from the spirits, loss, including death, seems to be the potentially most transforming. All cultures have rites of passage, such as birth, marriage, adulthood, aging, and death, to help people through transition periods of their lives. Rites of passage are developed by societies to help us through uncertain times. Death seems to have the greatest potential for transformation. Stories of children dying symbolic deaths, battling mythic monsters, battling with spirits, and so forth abound in the stories and lore of ancient cultures. For examples of traditional stories, see Thomas (2005), Thompson and Egesdal (2008), Matthews (1994), Burland (1985), Workers of South Dakota Writer's Project (1941), Leeming and Leeming (1994), Marriott and Rachlin (1975), Ramirez (2007), and Paige (1970).

In funeral rites, the newly dead are often thought to be in an in-between state from dwelling upon the earth while waiting to enter the afterlife. The dead may be welcomed back by those on earth as an ancestor, or the dead may be feared as a potential source of death for the living. Rituals that are designed to manage or control dead spirits are developed to cope with grief and loss. Artistic expression is also used to help with loss. Animals that are to become food for the group are often drawn to help the hunter to have a good hunt and to thank the animal for giving his or her life to the hunter. Death is a loss of immense proportions; it is the ultimate evil to be explained by the spiritual. Death is a loss not only for people, but also for the animals and plants that they eat to live.

Death is viewed as being as natural as birth for the American Indian. It is not one's choice to be born or one's choice to die. Many teach that those who take their own life may be condemned to wander as spirits in the next life. Spirituality offers us the opportunity to contemplate the basic questions of life. Why was I born? What is the purpose of my life?

There is no single American Indian religion. Nonetheless, all religions and spiritual orientations have similarities. American Indians perceive themselves as dwelling in a world filled with spirits. In the world, birds can carry messages, animals tell tales, rocks speak to us, and spirits roam the earth with us. Communication with mysterious beings is available to all. Dreams and visions provide messages or instructions that all may receive as a gift from the spirits. From this perspective, all life has a purpose. Each of us is here for a reason. We may spend our entire lives trying to determine that reason. Visions, dreams, rivers, rocks, animals, birds, and spirits can give messages if we would only listen. Cultures with oral traditions can travel back in time as far as the chain of memory will let them. In a world filled with spirits, the past provides a guide to those living in the present. Storyteller's tales of animals that talk, of spirits that roam the earth, of rocks that have messages both instruct and entertain those who listen. Storytellers do not just talk, they may drum, sing, and even dance as they weave their tales. Masks, costumes, regalia, and performance mark the stories. Knowledge of the spirit world is essential to practices relating to dying, death, and grief.

Generally, the storyteller's tell tales that demonstrate that all things have a soul. Rocks, plants, animals, and all living things are tied together. Each living thing has its place in the world. By living in harmony, the world is orderly and good. If disharmony occurs, bad things happen to living things such as sickness, accidents, disasters, and even death. Each living thing is responsible for other living things and each must protect the other. This would suggest that each must practice customary rituals and show forgiveness, patience, and sharing to others. It would also include living a spiritual life. In tribal cultures harmony does not mean viewing oneself as better, wealthier, having higher status, using one's power for personal gain, or other forms of self-aggrandizement. Success is not measured by occupation, money, or power, but rather a successful person is one who lives in harmony, works to acquire sacred knowledge, and tries to live his or her life and tries to perform his or her roles as well as possible. A storyteller, rug maker, grandparent, or whoever performs their roles in harmony and with spirituality will have good fortune and be admired by those around them. A person does not need to be a warrior, chief, or community leader to be admired. Having wealth is not a major determinant of tribal status. Children are also brought up without coercion or threats. They learn by watching older children, adults, and elder's role model what is correct behavior. Living in a world of spirituality makes it easier for children to develop a sense of the spiritual. The spiritual nature of everything in life becomes second nature. People also take part in rituals and ceremonies that reinforce their belief in the spiritual nature of the world. Fear is not the basis of life but being in harmony with the world is. Because they did not rush to work to accumulate property as did most Europeans, American Indians were thought to be lazy. Rather than being lazy, they are living a spiritual life.

LIVING THE SPIRITUAL LIFE

Life is to be lived; one engages in rituals, ceremonies, and community activities as one proceeds through childhood, adulthood, and becoming elderly just as the sun follows its cycle. Death is not to be feared. Death is natural and to be accepted. Even spirits meet death in stories. These sacred stories and myths teach us how and why to live. While many view myths as not real or not true, myths represent that which is "the Truth." Myths and stories provide the ultimate meaning by which one lives. As in Judaism and Christianity, the myths, sacred stories, songs, epics, and so forth are models or paradigms around which to live one's life. The oral traditions are taught to us by our ancestors and by sacred beings. The lessons from the stories permeate everything that we do. Stories cover all aspects of life. There are stories about marriage, hunting, work, play, art, war, and just about everything else that we do. The stories help define our culture, mold our orientation to the world, and help to develop our basic values. The stories and rituals of the ancient peoples are reborn in the present. This gives the living a place and role in the world that connects the past to the present in a meaningful way. The seemingly modern questions about why was one born? Why is there suffering in the world? What is the purpose of one's life? These are ancient questions that ancestors have also addressed and attempted to answer. We must accept life as it is. All of us have many human imperfections, but each of us should constantly strive toward an elevation of the human condition. The ancients have provided a model of how to live that continues to show us how to live in modern times as well as in ancient times. Our journey may not be easy nor painless, but with effort, we can have a fruitful, productive journey.

How one receives the sacred is also important. The response to the sacred can be intellectual, practical, or social. The intellectual can range from theology, scholarship, stories, myths, and so forth. The practical would include doing and saying spiritual things and acts. The social involves the acts of community and fellowship that evoke feelings and responses. The spiritual is not a solo action. It involves responses from others. Over time, the individual comes to identify with the spiritual community. While there are different social forms and structures of community depending upon cultural traditions, the individual even before birth and after death carries on those traditions through his or her clan, congregation, family, society, or nation. Spiritual leaders come in many forms. They may be kings, queens, priests, sages, prophets, monks, shaman, or whoever. Participation in the spiritual community provides continuity to the spiritual experience. The transformation of the human by spirituality suggests that spirituality is not only a system of beliefs and practices about the relationship with the sacred, but also a path or way of life for the spiritual. It is part of a search for ultimate meaning and purpose that leads to transformation. It is also thought that many people struggle in the search. It suggests that many are broken or fractured in their relationship with the spiritual.

All people live their lives facing basic troubles and the anxieties of daily living and human existence in general. All people seem to have an awareness of the human problem of explaining one's existence that is contrasted with the promise of the sacred. All may view the spiritual as a way to bridge this seemingly uncrossable gap. Spirituality provides a way to overcome this fracture, to restore the bridge to the sacred, and to transform the individual to attain the goal of life as expressed by one's spiritual group.

THE SPIRITUAL PATH

For all spiritual groups, the path to transformation is both a means to an end and an end in itself. As a means, it is a method of moving toward a goal that is never quite attained which is a relationship with the sacred. The problems of human failure and human evil are a part of life until death. Most spiritual groups focus upon the future human state as the place to achieve the ideal. The end may be in sight, but it is not achievable until death. By its very nature, the spiritual life is both practical and sacred. It needs to be lived and not just believed. It requires action, not just belief. The power for life comes from ritual, sharing with family and community, and living according to the model of spirituality of the group. Yet, humans seem to crave or at least choose to engage in the profane as well as the sacred. While some are motivated to become spiritual and develop a relationship with the sacred, others seem to either not need or no longer need centers of meaning and purpose to their lives. For many, if not most, breaks in the path or journey seem common. Special days, rites of passage, suffering, loss, grief, and pain lead to a return to the sacred. Rituals, ceremonies, and sacred events may at least temporarily replace parties, sports, entertainment, vacations, holidays, and other diversions. Of the events in life that call us to follow the spiritual life, loss seems to be the most transforming. Rites of passage, including the usual rites of passage of birth, marriage, adulthood, aging, and death that happen during our lives, may all lead to our transformation. Death seems to have the greatest potential for transformation. Stories of children dying symbolic deaths, battling mythic monsters, battling with spirits, and so forth are found among seemingly all tribes.

Storytellers typically have "snow on the mountain" which means that they have the wisdom that is shown by the white hair on their head. Stories can be about current times or ancient stories. All stories are expected to have a teaching component. The Mountaintop Way story of the Dine or Navajo presents

the bear as having a spirit that is both moody and sometimes even vengeful.
The story can be used to encourage rain and good crops, or it can be used
to heal. Other bear ceremonies focus upon the transformation of the bear.
Bears can be good or bad as can people. Bears can cause one to have good
luck or bad luck. Thinking about bears can cause bad events to happen. Like
people, bears and other animals can have a supernatural element or spirit.
The many stories of the coyote who seems to be able to become invincible
and then be able to come back to life after being killed are mostly the villain
in stories. The coyote often corrupts people or causes evil to exist in people.
The coyote is also responsible for the existence of snakes and other animals
in the world. Thousands of wonderful stories are told and retold in hundreds
of clans and groups. See Benton-Banai (1971), Bruchac (1995), Marriott and
Rachlin (1975), Hausman (1993), Leeming and Leeming (1994), Lavitt and
McDowell (1990), and Taylor (1994) for examples of stories. Many of these
stories that are told over and over are told about those who have already died.

SPIRITUALITY AND THE AFTERLIFE

Seemingly, all American Indian groups believe in the survival of the soul,
do not have much concern with the future, do not consider the afterlife as
having punishments or rewards, have no patterns of ancestor worship, and
view the afterlife as pretty much the same as what they experience while
alive (Drucker 1954, 180–181). The Winnebago or Ho Chunk tribe had at
least four secret societies in which membership was based upon blessings
from night spirits, buffaloes, grizzly bears, and ghosts (Radin 1970, 269).
The belief in spirits seems to also be generally accepted. The Tlingit, Haida,
and other Northwestern tribes were thought to believe in spirit helpers who
were part of their maternal heritage who would serve as "guardian spirits"
(Drucker 1955, 158). The Kwakiutl and Nootka developed masks and other
symbols of clan ancestors to have the right of succeeding generations to
receive gifts from spirits (Drucker 1955, 158). Margret Mead's study of the
Antlers, a name used to protect the idenity of the Omaha Indians, who were
a Mississippi Valley tribe that over time was also forced to accept reservation life, were able to accept the Christian idea of heaven and hell, but also
keep their traditional belief that ghosts of the dead were nearby (Mead 1966,
102). The ability to maintain the spiritual heritage and to continue to teach
the ancient stories are central to the survival of American Indian spirituality.

Chapter 11

Death and Intimacy
Impairment Later in Life

Being old is not a matter of chronology or how many years you have lived, but rather it is about how you feel about your age. While the United States has generally been a youth-based society and has devaluated the elderly and their way of life, the dominant culture, unlike the American Indian, has not developed positive attitudes toward aging and being aged. Few minorities have been subjected to so many stereotypes, generalizations and views rooted in prejudice, fear, and dread of one's own aging than those that plague older adults in the dominant society. The "old olds," those over age seventy, face even more challenges. Death becomes more of an impending reality as one ages. As we age, more and more people that we have known and love die. Close friends, older generations of relatives, spouses, and sadly, even children die. Yet, we can face death with a sense of purpose, dignity, and living fully each day, or one can face death with dread, fear, and loss, or in many other ways. Aging does not have to lead to intimacy impairment, loss of purpose, or fear. While there are many consequences of becoming old, being old does not have to mean that we cease to live before we die.

SOCIAL CHANGES WITH AGING

As we age, we know more and more people until we reach an age where more and more of the people that we know die, move away, retire to the Sun Belt, or move to a residential community or nursing home and withdraw from our life with them and from their previous social life. By age seventy, many, if not most have retired, cut back dramatically on their social activities and focus upon personal health and well-being as opposed to personal production and contributions to society, family, and occupations. For many, being old means that they are no longer productive. Yet, history has countless examples of people who achieved success after they were considered to be old. While not an exhaustive list, Colonel Sanders, Grandma Moses, Frank McCourt, Henry Ford, Harry Bernstein, Laura Ingalls Wilder, Charles Darwin, Ray Kroc, Sam Walton, J. K. Rowling, Morgan Freeman, Winston Churchill, to name a few. The point is that success may come early in life or it may come later or even much later. For the American Indian, success is expected to come when one becomes an elder. Many anticipate turning fifty so they can assume the role of being an elder.

The emotional attachments of friendship, spousal relations, and even close-ness to grandchildren and great-grandchildren are often compromised or even severed due to the traumas of aging and withdrawal. Upon reaching his early seventies, my own father lamented that all five of his lifelong friends had died. He had no one with whom to share his social life and his most intimate thoughts. Fortunately, he was able to find a new reason to get up in the morn-ing by buying a horse farm in the town of his birth, French Lick, Indiana. He was able to make new friends and to reconnect with the relatives of many people that he knew in his youth. He lived an active, productive life for the next twenty years. He found a new way to manage death and loss of intimacy. My father was an exception. Many old olds are coerced into living down to the expectations of society and often even their own families and friends.

Many in society label the aged as the population that is most demanding of the scarce resources that are available today and as the population that is most in need. Debates about Medicare, social security, retirement income, and lack of productivity focus upon the "drain" that the older adults cause to a society in economic peril. The concept of the elderly as being a "drain" on society has become a political issue that leaves many elderly feeling guilty for using resources, spending their retirement on themselves, or for enjoying their retirement by travel and recreational activities. The concept of being a burden adds to the stress of aging for many.

Being an older adult may mean that one is becoming a "burden" to fam-ily, friends, and community as well as being a "burden" to the economy. Detachment theory suggests that the old olds tend to withdraw from social relationships. The withdrawal negatively impacts intimacy. By not pursuing social relationships, one feels that he or she is less of a burden or negative presence. When one goes out to eat, couples as in the past, who pays for the widow? How can our group keep playing cards with only three players rather than four as in the past? How can I continue my medical treatment or go into assisted living when it would mean that my children will have no inheritance? How can I impose on friends and family when I reach the point that I am no longer able to safely drive myself? Communities are pressured to develop senior centers, programs for seniors, to provide medical care for seniors, to give discounts at businesses for seniors, develop specialized housing for seniors, and of course, build the dreaded nursing homes for them, as well. Historically, seniors have been among those most likely to vote which has led to developing programs for them as a political necessity. The current discussion of social security and Medicare as entitlements that need to be cut to help trim the deficit has caused a lot of backlash against politicians who have supported that view. Fear of losing seniors vote has forced many politicians to rethink their position.

Grown children often have problems that ultimately become problems for the older adults who raised them. Drugs, drinking, poverty, divorce, prison, and other issues often make them absent as parents. More and more often, grandparents are being called upon to raise their grandchildren. Over 6 million grandparents live with grandchildren in their home (U.S. Census Bureau 2009, 57) in the early 2000s. With COVID and other issues, the 2020 census will likely demonstrate that the trend is continuing to happen. At a time when many older adults are contemplating how to face their own aging, infirmities, and declining income and health, they are being called upon to be active as parents for their grandchildren. While there are many raising grandchildren, for some it is welcomed as an opportunity and a burden to the health and financial well-being of others. For many older adults, the major goal is to live a meaningful, productive, and fulfilling life in a society that offers the opposite. By contrast, American Indians value the elderly and generally anticipate becoming an elder and they are also expected to be a major figure in the raising of children whether or not the parents are present and participating. It is not an end of life burden, but an expected role to be played.

For American Indians the opportunity to live a meaningful, productive, and fulfilling life is enhanced by the honor given for their contributions to their groups, and for their wisdom, as well as to be respected for their age. In the American Indian cultures, status is not based upon money, fame, property, or societal accomplishments, but rather upon worth as a person. Elders represent a living legacy of the history of their people. Those who are older can bring valuable wisdom, experience, knowledge, compassion, history, values, and love that are not given to all around us. Not all of those who are older are poor. They are a major contributor to our economy, provide financial support to their families, and spend a major portion of the money generated in society. Rather than being a burden, the opportunity to raise one's grandchildren could be something to be cherished rather than dreaded. Living in a cross-cultural society as in the United States or Canada, there are other models of aging that might be useful. Being older can be a blessing. Having to raise one's grandchildren could be viewed as an opportunity rather than a burden. Not only is being older a contrast, but, so too, are the rules for behavior.

AMERICAN INDIAN SPIRITUALITY AND AGING

As noted, spirituality can be defined in many ways. The Apache or Inde are noted for the silence of words (Basso 1970). Spirituality is the opposite of the noise of modern life with its sirens, cars and trucks, construction, and forms of media and noise that bombard our psyche. Silence or solitude, that is intentionally quiet, is an essential part of spiritual life that allows one to move closer to people rather than away from them through compassion (Nouwen 1981, 39). Spiritual silence does not mean to merely not talk, but rather to open oneself to higher powers or God. Like the Inde or Apache, Christian spirituality teaches that one can have a poverty of spirit by focusing upon service to others rather than on one's egoistic, selfish, personal needs. Like the Inde, the Christian is obligated to care for the elderly, orphans, and widows. As deacons in the early Catholic Church were expected to care for the elderly, orphans, and widows, the Inde were also expected to devote a part of their food, shelter, and goods to aid the elderly, widows, and orphans. For both the Inde and Christians, it was seen as a spiritual act. For the Christian, sin is the refusal of spiritual life that is a rejection of the inner order and peace that comes from our union with the divine will (Merton 1963, 12). For the Inde, a lack of spirituality would be seen as a rejection of becoming what we were willed to become or the rejection of becoming what we truly are. For both, spirituality is the way one lives more than the acts that one does. For both, the way one lives impacts the way one faces death. For both groups, being spiritual would require that we should focus upon the needs of others. We can maintain intimacy in our relationships. American Indian elderly spend time with children and develop a special closeness to them.

Spiritual growth is a journey that does not have a timetable or finish line. Adults can teach children what they have learned on their own journey, but they must also recognize that their children's journey is not the same as their own journey. Each person's journey is different. Our spirituality can be an important component in that journey. The pattern of the universe is that to have life continue, there will have to be losses. Losses are constant as friends move, people die, graduations cause life changes, toys get broken, people change jobs, and so many more losses happen to everyone. Yet, the universe is filled with beauty and goodness. We can only see the beauty and goodness if our eyes are able to enjoy and appreciate the beauty and goodness around us. Those experiencing loss may ask questions that are painful and confronting when they are in pain. Elders are often able to listen to the pain of loved ones without judging or lecturing on the rightness or wrongness of their actions (McKissock 1998, 111–112). While we can never fully understand the process of our journey, it is still important to try to understand the pattern of loss and growth to be able to help others who are grieving.

SHARING

American Indians have patterns of sharing along kinship lines. This may include sharing money, childcare, housing, transportation, help with work, or whatever is needed. Generosity and sharing are dominant cultural values, but they are often missing in an urban environment. While many factors contribute to the loss of traditional lifestyles, intermarriage with other tribal groups, with non-Indians, with people of other cultures also take their toll. People in all cultural groups are quite diverse as are tribal groups. Yet, there are generalizations that can still be made about tribal groups that are still on reservations. It is not unusual for reservations to have Catholic and Protestant churches that have incorporated rituals, customs, and ceremonies that include hymns in Native languages, ceremonies honoring the earth and pipe, and incenses (Schaefer 2015, 161). For the elderly or the old that are American Indians, sharing may take on a different role than what is typically experienced in the White world. In some tribes, the elderly give their social security or other retirement check to their children or other family members and live as best as they can in the traditional way. The elderly may not only teach and become close to their grandchildren both by birth and by assuming the role to help those without grandparents, but they may also do the child care activities expected of parents. The elderly may also do repairs, babysit, shovel snow, and many, many other tasks to aid their children and grandchildren. The role is to be of help and service to others, especially one's own family. Sharing is more than writing a check!

The main differences between Jews, Muslims, Christians, and American Indians are that the former follow a single deity, often confine spiritual expression to designated sites, and have congregations who may barely or only superficially even know each other while American Indians embrace a broader spirituality that has more relevance in the whole of the world, including animals, earth, water, and wind (Schaefer 2015, 161). American Indians have the advantage of having greater community participation, more intimacy, more complete knowledge of who others in their group are, and are able to address spirits in many forms including rocks, animals, plants, and nature in many forms. To the Dine or Navajo, for example, a tree is not just a member of the plant kingdom; a spring is not merely water rising from the ground; a mountain is not just a mass of rock and earth; a bear, snake, owl, and coyote are not just animals because in the tree, spring, rock, mountain, or animal dwell spirits, not in the sense of ghosts, but happy, friendly, benevolent elves closely akin to the Navajo that are not to be questioned and yet can be communed with by the hour (Kneale 1950, 341). The bear that kills your sheep cannot be killed. It might contain the spirit of a deceased loved one. One only kills to save a life or for food. To kill the bear for killing your sheep would be wrong since it would only save sheep (Kneale 1950, 142).

Accumulation of wealth is not a traditional value on the reservation; rather, goods are to be shared and savings are to be used. The elderly are not valued for their wealth in money, but rather they are valued for their wealth in wisdom and knowledge. When the elderly died, those that still practice giveaway ceremonies will give their possessions to others. The honor of the dead person is not measured by how much that they had left to give away, but by what kind of person he or she was. The honor and value of receiving one of their possessions is not the economic value of the item or items, but rather, the honor of being given something by a true role model with a cherished memory that is found in the item or item that is being given that is far more valuable than any monetary value. Culturally, the focus upon people rather than things has led to many cultural practices that distinguish the American Indian culture. American Indians are generally quite aware of their kinship and how they are related to each other. Relatives are a major part of their social circle and friendship groupings. Golden (1996) suggests that the rituals of the Potlatch Ceremony of the Athabaskan tribes of Northwest North America allow the entire community and not just the grieving family to move from grief into a more joyous ceremony (Golden 1996, 65). Many elderly American Indians live in poverty economically, but they are rich in community.

LEARNING FROM THE COMMUNITY

Family, clan, tribe, and even the BIA can do much to help those who live on the reservation. Indigenous knowledge and practices are being used to design and deliver services that would otherwise be unavailable. The advantage of the tribal community lies in its simplicity. The child learns a consistent normative pattern, has the security of knowing the people around him or her, and has fewer roles to identify and develop. The extended family has more influence on the person. People know what to do and not to do. As mentioned earlier, the teaching of right and wrong meant that tribes did not make laws, build prisons, or even have police. While it may be that a majority of humans could get along with each other without laws, laws are not made for those who observe the "Golden Rule," and the American Indian is the closest to observing the "Golden Rule" of any culture (Kneale 1950, 132). A mainstay of the extended family is the elders who are both teachers and keepers of the history of their people.

As previously suggested, there is no single American Indian religion. The spiritual view of the world would suggest that communication with mysterious beings is there for all to experience that can lead to dreams and visions and provide messages or instructions that anyone can receive as a gift from the spirits. All life is thought to have a purpose, and everyone and every living being was born for a reason, but it may take a lifetime to discover that reason. Visions, dreams, rivers, rocks, animals, birds, and spirits will offer messages to us if we listen; as suggested earlier, cultures that have oral traditions can travel back as far as the chain of memory will allow. In a world filled with spirits, the past provides a guide to the present. The elderly tell the stories to children to help them develop morally and spiritually. To be an elder means that one is a living model for how to live life and to face one's ultimate death.

LIVING WITH THE DEATH

While accepting that death is natural, normal, and inevitable, American Indians like all people will still experience a deep sense of loss. Grieving ceremonies are very important to all tribes and clans because generally it is believed that what the living do can impact the dead and what the dead do can impact the living. All deaths take away from the clan. Life has a purpose, a reason for being. If the coyote becomes extinct, the message of the coyote is lost forever. The world will be less for not learning that message. Each death must be mourned whether human or animal. When death occurs, the person leaves the world and can choose to leave the world and go on a spirit trail or remain on earth. When death occurs, the dead one will see all of his or her relatives and then be able to wait for one's descendants to join them.

Most clans exhibit a people-centered approach to life with values that include less attachment to material things. In recent years, casinos and other sources of revenue and exposure to the lifestyle of the dominant culture can certainly change that approach to life. Death is to be faced with the belief that the dead are still alive as long as the living continue to remember them. Death is natural and normal. "We live and then we live again."

Life is to be lived even when dying. The sacred stories and myths teach people how and why to live and die. For example, a Dine or Navajo story teaches that the sun must be placated by human death. Each day someone must die, or the sun will not move. A part of the story is that those who die and go to the Fifth World must return to live in the Fourth World after death. The First World had three beings in darkness, First Man, First Woman, and Coyote, but the First World was too small for them so they traveled to the Second World where there were two men who became the Sun and the Moon (Burland 1985, 92). When the three beings arrived in the Second World, Sun tried to make love to the First Woman and discord began; and after Coyote was called upon to solve the discord, the people of the North, South, East, and West decided that the Second World was too small and that they should all climb to the Third World where there would be enough room for Sun to separate from First Woman (Burland 1985, 93). Then the journey was made to the Third World, they were welcomed and warned that all would be well as long as the water monster, Tieholtsodi, was left in peace, but Coyote went to the Eastern waters and took two of the children to his home which caused Tieholtsodi to fill the four oceans causing floods (Burland 1985, 93). After holding council, the people tried to escape the flood by removing the mountains of the Four Directions and pile them on top of each other, but the flood continued leading them to plant a giant reed on top of the piled up mountain which grew into the sky into the Fourth World of the ancestors and animals where men and women learned that they were indispensable to each other which brought hope of peace and social discipline (Burland 1985, 96). Coyote still held the children of Tieholtsodi, so the world became flooded leading to the piling up of the Four Mountains and ultimately the planting of the reed leading to the Fifth World (Burland 1985, 96). After death, people must leave the safer Fifth World and return to the Fourth World where the dead reside (Burland 1985, 96).

THE TRICKSTER

Many groups around the world including the Greeks, Druids, Mexicans, Polynesians, Ashanti, and the American Indians have developed a mischievous character described as the Trickster. Tales of tricks and pranks, especially when played by the lowly, poor, and least against the big, rich, and powerful, have delighted audiences since storytelling began (Erdoes and Ortiz 1984, 335). In Europe, the Trickster was usually portrayed as the fox while in North America, the Trickster was typically a coyote (Erdoes and Ortiz 1984, 335). The Trickster motif is found in Pink Panther movies, road runner cartoons, Brer Rabbit stories, Sponge Bob Square Pants cartoons, and any other story that has a character that is both wise and foolish, a doer of tricks, and yet the butt of his own jokes.

Children who watch Sponge Bob Square Pants cartoons are thoroughly entertained by the cartoons, but they are also learning moral lessons. Square Bob Sponge Pants is creative, outrageous in his ideas and behavior, and yet at the same time, he is caring, charming, and sensitive. The Trickster is the animal found in all people. A bit of a fool, and yet at the same time, symbolic of how one can solve problems while creating problems. The Trickster is always funny, but also instructive for humans. Among American Indians, the coyote is known for his ability to alternate his cleverness with buffoonery, his lechery and ability to cheat and destroy his enemies, and his enormous appetite (Erdoes and Ortiz 1984, 335). Trickster stories can help those in intimate relationships to better understand the frailties and weaknesses of humans that can impair intimacy or to help strengthen intimacy. As one ages, such stories often include facing death.

Death is viewed as not being the end of life but rather a change of life. The coyote, the interpreter of signs, told the Dine that someone had to die every night, though it did not necessarily have to be one of the People or Dine. The coyote also said that death would come quickly to those who gazed upon the face of the dead. The Dine, therefore, cover the faces of the dead and bury them quickly. Being old and possibly being close to one's dying is not viewed as a burden. Many clans celebrate when turning age fifty which allows them to be treated as elders in some groups. Others may not have a specific age but look forward to becoming an elder as well. As one ages, the status of elder increases rather than decreases. One is respected for his or her knowledge which is thought to increase with age. The cultures of the many American Indian societies can teach the dominant culture a lot about aging and intimacy and ultimate dying. Aging does not have to lead to intimacy impairment, loss of purpose, or great fear.

ROLE OF ELDERS IN THE FAMILY

Elders are very important in their communities and are treated in special ways. Children are taught to respect them and listen to them. Elders may or may not be tribal leaders, but they help make decisions in all things that are important to the group, including education, jobs, health and health care, housing, hunting, fishing, and general living. One of the main tasks of an elder is to teach the young. They sing songs, tell stories, and teach children to respect their culture and themselves. They teach the three R's: respect, reciprocity, and relationships. A fourth *R* might be responsibility as it is also taught by the elders. By teaching the four "R's," the elders offer a means of easing grief by focusing upon proper behavior and behaving in a prescribed manner which might also enhance intimacy.

Grandparents are expected to be teachers even if parents are present. If the parents are not present, the role of teacher is still there. Grandparents are active in the rearing of children. Field (2007) suggests that there is "grand-motherese," that grandmothers talk differently to grandchildren (Field 2007, 167). The extended family is expected to babysit, share housing, share food and money, and help prepare and carry out ceremonies (McClosky 2007, 126). Grandparents and other relatives who care for children are not paid or compensated for providing childcare; nor is it considered to be a burden.

When groups gather for events, the elders are always asked to begin the ceremonies with prayers. Elders are generally always served first at meals and are acknowledged before others speak. Elders are expected to live in a way that earns the respect of others and to be models so that others can learn to respect themselves. Elders are also supposed to look forward to their role as elders and to be active as a part of the community, to continue to learn, and to teach.

ROLE OF THE ELDERS

Protocols exist for interacting with elders, such as allowing them to talk first and hear first, be seated first, not interrupted when speaking, and so forth. Other important norms would include those related to personal sovereignty or autonomy. Elders do not make choices for others, interfere with the decisions of others, or judge others. An elder may offer suggestions but does not make the decision. A chief or leader may say that a course of action should be taken, but the group or individual makes the final decision. One does not tell others how to live. Elder epistemology suggests that elders are the window to roots of tribal identity, the vision of Mother Earth, and life.

As suggested, elders are teachers. The role of an elder as teacher does not occur because parents die or are absent. Elders are expected to be teachers even if parents are also present. For the Navajo or Dine, the mother's brothers would assume the role of father even if the biological father is present. Many would say that they have three fathers, their father and their two uncles who are also their fathers. The biological father's brothers would not ordinarily assume this role. The level of contact by children with elders, their uncles, and their biological father offers a level of intimacy that provides a safe, stable environment for children. In the case of divorce, children always remain with the mother, or in the case of death of the mother, children remain with the maternal grandmother or with a maternal aunt who is viewed as a "second mother" (Locke 1992, 19). If parents die or are absent, grandparents, uncles, aunts, and other members of the mother's clan assume responsibility for their upbringing.

Being a single mother does not have the stigma that is found in some cultures. A female-headed household is viewed as being strong and capable (McClosky 2007, 16). A child is not left alone while the mother works in an American Indian community. The child still has plenty of teachers and adults around for company and instruction. They may very likely miss their father if he is absent or even their mother, but the adjustment is not as devastating as it would be in the dominant society. While all children grieve the loss of parents or even the family care, children seem to adjust well even though the child's personal past resides in things that are still there (Simms 2008, 149). That is to say, children may still miss their parents, but that they are able to adjust far better than might be expected.

The model of having the community or village raise the child may be far more important to the Anglo-European culture than might be expected. In the current economic chaos that is spreading around the world, many parents simply do not have the ability to care for their own children. The state of Nebraska passed a law in 2008 that allowed parents to hand children up to age eighteen over to the state with no threat of prosecution. They were forced to change the law to only infants because so many parents were abandoning their children who were much older than infants and often nearly eighteen. For the Anglo-European world, the inability to care for children requires major adjustments. For the American Indian, to have grandparents and others help raise a child is viewed as normal childrearing practice.

For the Dine or Navajo, when poverty occurs, children are taught by their mothers and grandmothers to endure (McClosky 2007, 5). Parents do not have to leave because of poverty, but rather, they endure it with their children. The Dine are generally economically dependent upon older relatives. While every adult may have his or her separate account at the trading store, the older or more prosperous members of the family will see to it that credit is extended to the more dependent if food or clothing is really needed (Kluckhohn and Leighton 1946, 103). For the Navajo, clan membership is passed down through mother and is multigenerational with the clan membership being headed by the senior female (McClosky 2007, 16).

Children are highly valued. For the Navajo or Dine, wealth is measured by the number of children that one has. The children are not valued for their labor or even their future income, but by the help and blessing given to them by the Holy People. As the Holy Family (the Dine Holy Family like Jesus, Mary, and Joseph) is a model for raising children, parents are to raise their children in a gentle, caring way as the Holy Family did their twins. The Holy Family would include the First Woman and First Man and their twin children. They are part of the creation story that is told in terms of days. The model of parenting the twins by the First Woman and First Man demonstrates how to properly rear children in the Dine culture. The Dine creation story is framed by the Five Worlds. For a more complete discussion of their creation story, see Paul G. Zolbrod's *Dine Bahane: The Navajo Creation Story*.

WHAT THE AMERICAN INDIAN CAN TEACH ABOUT BEING OLD

In the Anglo-European model, children often act as servants waiting on their parents and doing their biding such as chores, making their beds, setting the table, and later caring for parents by putting them in nursing homes. Many families in the Anglo-American world are overworked, too busy, and facing economic challenges that keep them from developing intimate relationships. Yet, at the same time, there are many families that, like the Dine, view children as a blessing and needing the care and love of adults rather than being there to serve the adults. Intimacy is found in all cultures, and those who have intimate relationships with their parents are more likely to do whatever they can to make the lives of the old olds more productive and to maintain intimacy with them. In the Dine world, children are seen as a blessing by being the person that they were destined to become. If one's child becomes a drunk or abandons his or her family, one does not judge the child or assign blame. Drinking was not part of the life that was intended, but rather is a result of the evil intentions of beings such as the coyote that led them to this end (Schwartz 2001, 169). People are generally accepted as they are. Social workers, clergy, and others who try to change those living on reservations often face opposition because they are viewed as judging or blaming those they are trying to help.

When children fail, the blame should not be placed just on the imposition of the Anglo-European culture or upon young people or non-Indian influence, but even the elders are to blame for failing to instill proper values in children or not working hard enough to pass on traditional stories and ceremonies and not conducting proper ceremonies (Davies 2001, 109). Children may fail, but their failures are also the product of other's failures.

Even if your child divorces or abandons his or her children and leaves you to raise them, it is still a blessing, as is the child. Perhaps your destiny was to be a wonderful grandparent to your grandchildren. Without your child having his or her children and without him or her leaving you to raise them, you could not have fulfilled your destiny. It may require great personal and financial sacrifice as an older person, but rather than being a source of agony or lamentation, it is a source of blessing.

Children help us to stay young, give us a reason to get up in the morning, and help us to stay alive even if those children are our grandchildren or our sibling's children. The typical Anglo-European elderly person often fears of being lonely, of being a burden, needing assistance and support are less of an issue for the elderly in Dine society. While the Anglo-Europeans cannot adopt the Dine culture and way of life, they can certainly learn from them that aging need not be a burden, that grandchildren can be a blessing, that one should not be so judgmental of children and others, and that one's family is there for them.

TRADITION AND LOSS

In both the United States and Canada, First Nations peoples have been socialized, acculturated, assimilated, had their cultures taken away, and have experienced a general loss of their traditions. Traditional patterns of grief are much less often practiced and generally have become less effective. Those who have maintained their traditional languages are generally more successful in maintaining their cultural traditions. While it is common to use funeral directors and modern caskets and vaults to dispose of the dead today, there are still groups that try to include traditional disposal methods and rituals. There is considerable evidence that all groups developed ways to provide provisions for a spirit journey for those who died whether for one person or for a group burial (Atkinson 1935, 159). As all groups provide rituals and dignified disposal of the dead, they also offer the same social support for the grieving. Socialization is the process of learning to survival in a particular culture. First Nations peoples also had their own ways of surviving. As the French, British, and other immigrants moved into their land, First Nations peoples learned or were forced to learn the ways of survival of other cultures. Education was either forced or permitted to teach the ways of the white culture. Science has replaced tradition. Some maintain a foothold in both cultures. Some abandon traditional culture for the dominant culture. Some attempt to remain traditional ways. Socialization to a new culture or to many new cultures leads to loss of tradition and heritage.

Acculturation is the process of becoming a competent participant in the dominant culture. That means giving up one's traditional ways and adopting new ways. Sociologist Robert Park suggested that this process takes immigrants three generations to accomplish. The first generation is tied to the old country or old ways, the second generation is not tied to either country or to the old ways, and the third generation is tied to the new country and abandons or rejects the old ways. While the American Indian is not an immigrant to a new country, they have been forced to learn the language of their conquerors, their religion, and adopt their culture. Park suggested that by the second generation a Norwegian or Pole could not be distinguished from an American born of Native parents (Schaefer 2015, 114). Like other Classical sociologists, Park saw the social world changing from the traditional to the modern, or from the rural to the city (Goldberg 2017, 78). If Park and his students equated rural with traditional culture and urban with modern civilization, then they also saw mobility as the main way to transition from the traditional to the modern (Goldberg 2017, 79). Perhaps, Park unwittingly created a model of the rural people leaving the farm and going to the city as a way to assimilate into the dominant culture. His model of three generations to assimilate is not an adequate model to explain how First Nations people acculturate. Many more than three generations have passed with many still not acculturated, but those who have left the reservation for the allure of the city have been able to assimilate.

CONSEQUENCES OF ASSIMILATION

Assimilation, which is the process of assuming a new cultural identity, is a process that has weakened traditions. This means that the Native person abandons his or her traditional ways and culture. The process of assimilation leads to the traditional culture being lost and replaced with a new or different culture. For most, the inability to speak their Native tongue is the first step in losing traditional ways and becoming assimilated. Culture is very much tied to language. There are 350–400 languages spoken in North America. When cultures clash, indigenous cultures usually lose. Like the loss of the animal with its knowledge and gifts, if the languages of the many tribes are lost, the learning and lore of these tribes will also be lost. Knowledge of other cultures and their ways is beneficial not only for those in their culture, but also for those in other cultures. History is written by those who have written language and have attained power. Stories told by Native voice that are from an oral tradition are far more difficult to hear and remember. Those told in the era of Tekakwitha and Metacom came at a time when few Indians were literate in their own language or those of the Europeans (Richter 2001, 119). Europeans have transcribed some of the speeches made by Native speakers that reveal Indian people trying to adapt traditional ideals of human relationships based upon reciprocity and mutual respect in an era when Europeans were becoming dominant in North America (Richter 2001, 111).

The Eastern tribes were forced to become emigrants to western lands. As they were forced to move, when they went to the new lands assigned to them, they were forced to compete with the tribes that were already there and with the ever-increasing numbers of Whites who entered their lands. Coercive and compassionate Christian missionaries brought with them White education and culture for the Indian children. For many children, this meant boarding schools and even schools that were outside of their own reservations. Generally, the Catholic mission schools on reservations spread the Catholic faith and preserved the faith of those converted by earlier missionaries, and thus, became a problem for the public school system that was maintained by the Federal government which infused their education programs with the Protestant outlook and ideas (Prucha 1979, x). Catholics were forced to fund and maintain their own schools separate from the government-run reservation schools. After some time, the doctrine of separation of church and state which kept the Catholics out of reservation schools also forced out the Protestants (Prucha 1979, 133).

The boarding schools, which grew rapidly after the 1890s, were largely controlled by Protestants who insisted that nonsectarian schools would be godless and cause failure in attempts to civilize the Indians (Prucha 1979, 162). The United States had many policies through the years, including extermination, termination, relocation, isolation, and assimilation. There is little question that many who worked in or ran the boarding schools abused many Indian children.

Seemingly, the U.S. government is finally resigned to the idea of allowing the American Indians to maintain their culture and exist with a pluralistic society. While pluralism is viewed as positive by most, many others would rather have the American Indian cultures to simply go away or disappear. Thousands of Indian families live in Chicago, San Francisco, New York, Boston, Minneapolis, Cleveland, Dallas, and other large, urban centers. Education, casinos, bingo, and other intrusions have weakened traditional lifestyles. Alaskan tribes have experienced settlement by Europeans and other Whites in waves beginning in the 1700s by Vitus Bering from Russia. The Inuit probably had the least intrusion by the culture and coercion of the Anglo-Europeans. Since the twentieth century, they have been "discovered" by anthropologists and others who are dramatically changing their culture. Arts and crafts were introduced in the 1960s which has dramatically changed their lifestyle as has snowmobiles, weapons, and communications. This has negatively affected their intimacy.

Becoming modern has destroyed many traditional cultures. Much of the classic literature of the world concerns loss of tradition. While many, many great writings exist, to mention a few, Milton's *Paradise Lost* imitates the writings of some of the great writers of antiquity such as Virgil, Homer, Sophocles, and Euripides in style and choice of subjects. The epic is profound and deep. It analyzes, among many other issues, the choices made by the first human beings to disobey God, and the resulting loss of way of life that results. Many write about the loss of the traditional life in poems including Alexander Pushkin who laments leaving the rural lifestyle for the city. John Dunne describes his pain at the challenge of religion by science in "An Anatomy of the World." French poet, Alfred de Musset, describes the breakdown of French society after the revolutions in *Confessions of a Child of the Century*, Denis Diderot in *Romeau's Nephew* discusses the loss of grounding with the loss of norms as does Fyodor Dostoevsky in *The Underground*. Charles Dickens, in *Smart Dealings in America*, and Ambrose Bierce in *Crime and Its Correctives*, lament the conflict between cultural values and social relations. Yet, the tribes persist.

RELATIONSHIPS WITH THE DEAD

Tribes exhibit reverence and respect for life. For many of the dominant religions, death is to be feared. While generalizations are dangerous, the variety of cultural expressions of dying and death among American Indians do have some commonalities. Most would support a willingness to surrender to death at any time without great fear. The Lakota, Chief Crazy Horse, was noted for his chant before going into battle, "Today is a good day to die." Every day is a good day to die if one has fully lived life. The philosophy is to enjoy life and live fully each day. Death is not all that different than life. As one cannot buy the land, nor can one buy life, death is waiting for us all. While none of us can escape death, we should not seek death before its time. One should not avoid death or try to delay death. For the American Indian, there is no death, but rather a change of worlds (Steiger 1974, 25). Most tribes teach that death is not all that different than life. Just as modern science teaches that nothing is lost in the universe, that matter simply changes form and is not destroyed, the First Nation's peoples generally believe that everything is eternal. Nothing is lost!

Rather than disconnecting with the dead, American Indians continue to have a relationship with them. People are able to continue to have a relationship with their deceased loved ones. American Indians have been doing so for a long time. Rather than fearing death, it is rather part of life and to be accepted. American Indians generally believe that the dead do not cease to love the living, to care for them, or to protect them. Of course, some of the dead did not do those things when they were alive, so chances are they will not care or protect them from the afterlife. The Hopi, like many other groups, believe that the dead are able to influence the lives of the living. The breath-body or spirit of humans is believed to continue to exist after the death of the body, keeping the powers of both good and bad actions (Fewkes 1991, 16). For the Hopi, who live in an arid climate, rain is basic to survival. Corn is specifically looked upon as the basis of survival for the "peaceful people" as the Hopi describe themselves. Because weather is so unpredictable, the Hopi have long felt a pressing need to have supernatural assistance to have adequate amounts of rain to ensure that their corn will grow, and they have formalized that belief into rituals that are similar to other Pueblo peoples that involve supernatural beings known as Kachinas who are visualized in human form but coming from the underworld as cloud-like spirits who can help the living (Smithsonian 1979, 17). Hopi children are expected to learn ceremonies along with the understanding that the knowledge that the ceremonies offer will impact their life, work, good conduct, and respect for the cloud-like spirits (Dennis 1940, 38). Like other Southwestern groups, the Hopi grandparents are expected to be teachers, but they are not expected to discipline or enforce obedience of grandchildren (Dennis 1940, 38). Generally, the old olds have an important role in the life of children. Like other groups, the Hopi are a matrilineal culture with the home belonging to the mother and the mother's kin and particularly the eldest maternal uncle having more of a role in raising the child and imposing discipline than the father (Dennis 1949, 163).

As most groups teach that all life, not just human life, is important. Not only human life is important, but also other forms of life. As you must thank the plants and animals that gave up their life for you to eat this meal, you must also thank the soil that nourished the plants and animals, thank Mother Earth for providing that one might live, and thank the least in our societies who also contribute to the survival of the people.

CONCLUSIONS

Death is a natural occurrence in life. American Indians generally teach that death is not to be feared but rather should be accepted. Fear of death can be greatly reduced by understanding and accepting one's place in the world. The concept of quest or discovering one's place in the world is common to many American Indian groups. While American Indians, like all peoples, may still have fears of death, the intimacy that results from community that is found on reservations helps to alleviate those fear. For the old olds, the quest is usually mostly completed. As they face the end of their lives and the ultimate impending death, they can have the support and power of knowing that they have lived a life that was in balance and that they still have purpose and meaning. The life of each person has a meaning and place in the larger scheme of things. What one does impacts the entire world.

Intimacy impairment can be lessened if one accepts the importance of each life in the larger scheme of the world. If each person has a place in the scheme of life, then each person remains important whether rich or poor, homeless or thriving. Each can maintain their dignity, self-respect, and sense of being even as an old old, and can feel that he or she is still contributing to the group, culture, and larger society even if one no longer works or is productive by Anglo-European standards. The challenge is to empower all peoples so that they value their roles and support the roles of their children and grandchildren in a spirit of community that values and welcomes all members of the society of the world as significant and valuable to each other as human beings and part of the spirit world. Accepting this challenge will allow the elderly to maintain intimacy in the face of aging and death.

Chapter 12

American Indian Grief

The Healing Path

People in all cultures must manage the deaths of those that they love. People die everywhere. The analysis of the dying process, the burial practices, and grief management of a people give us a better understanding of their values and culture. Maintaining health is of primary concern for people in all cultures. Caring for the terminally ill can raise questions of the meaning of life, lead to tragedy and tears, relief from pent-up emotions, and at the same time can offer those giving care immense gratification.

NORTH AMERICAN INDIAN CARE OF
THE DYING AND GRIEVING

The care of the dying by American Indians differs from the care offered by the White society in the United States. Generally in the dominant culture, doctors and nurses see themselves as being in positions of power over their patients and their families. Doctors and nurses also use a scientific model to treat disease that often leads to impersonal care.

The medical care of American Indians over time has been fragmented and confused. As many have been forced to live on reservations or restricted areas that are maintained by the Federal government, many traditional practices for caring for the dying and grieving have been lost. White medicine has also been introduced and even forced upon American Indians over the years. In the early years, missionaries, clergy, trading post owners, soldiers, and many others assumed the role of parent for many Indians who they saw as lacking in knowledge. Because of their fear that they might get the disease that the Indian was suffering from, they often forced their "charges" to use White treatments rather than traditional healing practices. Today, many American

Indians live in cities and are using White medicine and treatments as their primary way to deal with illness. While each of the approximately six hundred plus tribes had their own beliefs and practices regarding health and illness, generally, most would believe that health was the result of living in harmony or balance with nature and having the ability to survive under extremely difficult circumstances. Humans should have an intimate, personal relationship with nature. The earth is alive and also wants to be healthy. Like humans, the earth is occasionally ill and at other times it is healthy. The earth, too, can be out of balance. The earth is the friend of the human. It provides food, shelter, clothing, and medicine to humans. The earth belongs to life. Life belongs to the land. The land belongs to itself. A person who is in harmony with the earth will live in balance and will be healthy. Health is in the control of each person.

Tribes exhibit reverence and respect for life. For many of the dominant religions, death is to be feared. For the American Indian, death is not all that different than life. Just as modern science teaches that nothing is lost in the universe, that matter simply changes form and is not destroyed, the American Indians generally believe that everything is sacred. Every part of the dirt, rocks, trees, of all things, is sacred. The ashes of the dead are resting in sacred ground. Rather than disconnecting with the dead, American Indians continue to have a relationship with them. As Tom Attig (2001) suggests that we should continue to have a relationship with our deceased loved ones (Attig 2001, 46), American Indians have been doing so for a long time. Rather than fearing death, it is rather part of life and to be accepted.

Everything in life has a purpose. The land feeds and clothes humans. Every illness or pain has a purpose. Illnesses teach us to appreciate being healthy. Each of us must pay the price for what we do. Every human has the power to control themselves. Spirit power is the source of illness and pain. We must pay the price for our acts whether they occurred in the past or in the future. Science views the causes of disease as coming from bacteria, viruses, germs, or other empirically controlled causes. The American Indian views illness as being the price that one pays for their acts rather than as the result of bacteria or germs or whatever.

American Indians often feel a sense of distance or coldness from those who care for them in hospitals. They are close to the shaman and other healers, and know that they care about them and not just for them. For those who are White medical caregivers, American Indians tend to be thought of as difficult patients. The White culture, until the pandemic, has been greatly attached to science and its ways. COVID may have made the position of the American Indians more acceptable to the White culture. American Indians respond differently to hospital rules and ways than White patients. A Lakota may have as many relatives as possible in the hospital room. They may want to use smoke for purification, which would set off smoke detectors. An Inde or Apache who is dying may not have any visitors so that he or she is allowed to die with dignity by being alone. The Dine or Navajo may want to leave the hospital to have a "sing" which might baffle a physician or other hospital worker. Science has not been a major part of the way of life of the American Indian.

The basis of the care for the dying by American Indians lies in natural treatments and healing rituals. The use of medicine by American Indians was a major part of their healing or caring practices for the ill and dying. Weiner (1980) lists over 150 plants and trees that were used for healing by North American Indians (Weiner 1980). American Indian healing arts have also included sweat baths, rituals, and herb medicines.

Nature is the foundation of the healing process. Even the medicines administered are from nature. The spiritual nature of healing does not begin with the treatment of the sick or dying, but rather the spiritual nature of healing begins with rituals that are used when picking the plants, processing the plants for use, and later when administering the medicines to patients. The health care of the White culture also includes medicine, but generally, it does not include rituals. When White medicine does allow the use of the shaman and healers with their rituals, the serenity, healing, or calmness of the dying is enhanced.

Quite often, the American Indian perceives his or her illness to be caused by something other than what the white physician has diagnosed. The hospitals are strange and unfamiliar. The patient is often forced to wait, often alone, for prolonged periods of time without any explanation or reason being given to them. The patient will be asked many personal questions that seem to have no relevance to their illness—questions that are often taboo subjects in tribal life. Physicians and caregivers at White institutions are often demanding and impatient with American Indan patients because they are not aware of the tradition of many tribes of thinking before you answer questions. This often results in the American Indian patient reacting by silence, fear, or simply leaving the hospital or institution.

White medicine is typically not explained to the patient. The healer or shaman would tell the story of the medicine that she or he is offering to the patient. When the White doctor or nurse offers medicine to an Indian, they usually talk about drug interactions, reaction to the drug, symptoms to be wary of, and so forth. Without the story, many will refuse to take the drug, will take it home, but not use it, or simply throw it away when the caregivers are no longer present. White medicine appears to be unnatural when it is administered in bottle, capsules, or syringes with no rituals or stories.

The staff of the hospital may feel just as estranged as the American Indian patient who comes to use their services. Hospital staff often resent the substantial number of American Indians who enter the patient's room. They also often come when it is not visiting time and seemingly stay forever. They may also want to burn items to make the room sacred. The cleansing smoke may set off alarms and sprinklers. Their methods of bathing, their refusal to wear hospital gowns, and their loud singing make it quite difficult for the staff to accept them. By contrast, the lack of visitors for the dying Inde or Apache also puzzles them.

While many in the White world are quick to blame the doctor or hospital when a loved one dies and may even sue or bring legal actions against the doctor or hospital, traditional American Indians rarely blame the doctor of the hospital. For American Indians in general accepting death is a normal response. It is inevitable. It is not the fault of the shaman or caregiver or doctor or even the hospital. It was the person's time to die or else the spirits were stronger than the shaman.

The traditional healer for the American Indian is the shaman. The traditional American Indian culture has generally maintained the belief that the shaman is a healer. The shaman is expected to be knowledgeable in the ways of the earth, humans, spirits, and nature. To be the recipient of medicine power, one must live one's life in balance. There are four directions, four seasons, four ages of humans, and four kingdoms of life. One must renew the commitment to this balance every day (Steiger 1974, 62). The shaman's task is first to determine the cause of the illness or pain and second, she or he then must develop the proper treatment of the illness or pain. The special ceremonies may take from a few minutes to several days.

A shaman is taught by another shaman. It takes years to a lifetime to learn the craft. As with any education, one is never finished with the learning. The shaman tries to determine not only the physical causes of illness but the spiritual causes of the illness as well. Holistic medicine may be the result of the recognition that illness has both physical and spiritual causes and components. Just as each life has a purpose, each illness has a purpose. The shaman attempts to determine the cause of the illness and to cure it.

To be able to heal an individual, the shaman does not stop with the idea that a drug or other medicine can cure. To cure, the shaman may very well administer physical medicines, but she or he will also administer spiritual medicine. The treatment is a process that heals not only the physical illness, but also administers to the spiritual needs that must be addressed to bring the person back to harmony or balance. Medicine power enables the possessor of the spirit to personally contact with the invisible world of the spirits (Steiger 1974, 63). If it is one's time to die, then there is little that the shaman can do. We cannot defy nature. What can be done will be done. Doing more than that is unnecessary may be an affront to nature. Administering treatments in the White hospital that are administered to a person who is brain dead or living in a vegetative state would be unacceptable for the traditional American Indian. Natural dying and death are the proper ways to die. Death is not something to be feared, but life is to be appreciated for oneself and for one's loved ones.

SOCIOLOGY OF AMERICAN INDIAN
BONDING WITH THE DYING AND DEAD

Are all of the people you love with you at this moment? Can you love people from whom you are separated? Can we continue to love after someone has died? Of course, you can. The dead do not cease to love us, to care for us, and to protect us. As suggested earlier, those who did not love, care, and protect us while they were alive are not expected to do so when they are dead, but the possibility still exists that they might. Death is a natural occurrence within life. It is not to be feared but rather should be accepted. Each of us has lives that have a meaning, purpose, and place in the larger scheme of things. What we do as individuals may impact the entire world. How many of the natural resources have each of us consumed during our lifetime? How much air have we breathed, and how much carbon dioxide have we produced?

PATH TO MUTUAL UNDERSTANDING

Like people, cultures have good and bad points. In days when warriors went first to protect the women and children, the women and children carried all items and walked behind the men who were ready to face potential attackers. As time passed, the practice of walking behind and having women and children carry heavy objects to free the men to protect and be better able to protect them was lost. Now most women walk next to their men and children are no longer beasts of burden. It was not a lack of respect for women that led to this practice, but when we look at other cultures, we often fail to see the origins and nature of cultural practices.

Most tribes exhibit a people-centered, group-centered approach to life. As we discussed with values, this means that they are less attached to material things. Of course, casinos and other sources of revenue and exposure to white lifestyle can certainly be changing this tradition.

Death does change the lives of our survivors. Each of us will, hopefully, have others who care and mourn that we are no longer among the living, but each of us is still alive as long as the living remember us. Death is part of the design of the universe. Life cannot exist without death. We live and then we live again. Time and space do not change our existence. Death is a painful separation for the living, but when we die, we have the opportunity to join our ancestors, and we are given the hope that for our descendants to join us.

GRIEF AND THE AMERICAN INDIAN

Grief is experienced differently for each person. At the same time, grief is decidedly cultural. People in the same cultures, while having individual response to loss, still have common consistent patterns in their response to loss. Because all cultures are ethnocentric, each society seems to think that its ways are the best ways. If my ancestors grieved in a certain fashion, then we must as well. At the same time, all cultures "borrow" from other cultures. Knowledge of cultural practices pertaining to grief and bereavement used in another culture may have many benefits for those seeking to manage their own grief and bereavement. One can learn management practices that are successfully used elsewhere and apply them to your social group. Learning about other cultures might also provide a better understanding of how people of other cultures respond differently and provide better services and care to their own people who are grieving. American Indian burial and bereavement practices are similar to those of other cultures, but they are also different enough to puzzle, stifle, and even anger caregivers who work with them.

The many cultures of the Americas before the arrival of the Europeans included the islands in the Caribbean, South and Central America, and North America. In just the area north of what is now Mexico, over seven hundred distinct languages were spoken (Schaefer 2015, 167). While it is not possible to discuss over seven hundred cultures, the death management practices of a few of the larger or more well-known cultures will be presented.

For those who work with grieving American Indians, it is important to gain an understanding of the culture and attitudes of the particular clan with whom you are working. To enhance successful grieving, it is imperative to understand what success means to the American Indian. Too often, non-Indians define success by their own terms without considering that others might have a different definition of success. The emphasis should be on the positive, the good things that can be done to help the grieving person, and not disparaging looks, glances, or sneers indicating a lack of respect for the views of your patients. Many speak of American Indians as being disadvantaged, lacking skills that prepare them to survive in modern culture. Generally, American Indians have a double advantage of living and knowing in two cultures. They may be more aware of the caregiver's attitudes and values than the caregiver is of their attitudes. Most also define the American Indian cultures as "dying."

While many American Indian cultures have been greatly impacted by change and loss of tradition, many are still thriving and experiencing a resurgence. Caregivers are often not aware of the difficulties of being Indian in a non-Indian world. When asked about their traditional grieving practices, the typical response by many American Indians is to say what the Indian thinks that the caregiver wants to hear. Cultural diversity is like an orchestra. Each section of the orchestra has its own identity. Each makes its own sound. All become part of the whole which makes the sound from the entire orchestra more pleasing and rich in its sound. No part of the orchestra is superior to another part. The differences make the orchestra better! We need to grow in our appreciation of differences.

Culture has many components. It is not just buildings, places, objects, or environment, but it is the way of life of a group of people. Culture also is made up of their attitudes, values, customs, beliefs, assumptions, expectations, behaviors, spirituality, artifacts, and the buildings and other physical artifacts as well. As suggested earlier, for American Indians, spirituality is not a separate part of their lives. Spirituality is present in everything we do, say, think, or make. While the names vary for different groups, names for the supernatural would be for the Dakota *Wakan Tanka*, for the Algonquin *Manito*, for the Iroquois *orenda*, and for the Ojibwa *Kitche Manitou*. A supernatural force exists in everything in the world. Spirits are in everything: the mountains, trees, animals, streams, rocks, plants, Father Sun, Mother Earth, the moon, the stars, and all other things found in the world. Rituals provide a systematic framework which is both recognizable and comforting to those taking part in the rituals. Rituals allow us to combine the psychological aspects of grief with the sociological familiarities of the rituals which not only comforts the grieving, but it also helps resolve the guilt of survivors (Hicks 310). Rituals are often designed to invite the spirits to look favorably upon the living, to aid them in battles, growing crops, healing the sick, to have love, to bring rain, and most other human desires and wants. The spirits have to be thanked and honored through prayers and offerings of food and tobacco and often through a shaman (Bial 2000, 72). American Indians maintain their bonds with the dead.

BONDING WITH THE SPIRITS

Dreams and visions are important to most tribes and clans. Many believe that if they can understand their dreams that they can better understand themselves. Those who work with grieving Indians need to be aware of the power of dreams and the importance to those who are grieving. Dreams are often very important as part of the grieving process. It is quite common for the grieving to communicate with their lost loved ones in dreams.

Many groups commune with the spirits of the dead by using masks, false faces, and kacinas. The False Face Society of the Iroquois carved faces into trees and made masks that they believed held the power of the disease spirit as well as the life power of the tree which could be used for good, but if the spirit was offended, there was always danger of harm. The Iroquois generally believed that the more grotesque and ugly that they were able to make the mask, the more power that mask held! It was thought that when a person wore the mask that the spirit of the ugly flying head entered his body and his own personality was gone. The False Face Societies of the Iroquois were known for their ability to cure people in crowds by driving out evil spirits.

Their approach is more acceptable today because modern medicine recognizes the relationship between illness and the mind. While the caregiver may not see the value of the ritual, it may be a powerful tool in the grief process. Those who grieve have many rituals available to them: to cleanse, to release the deceased, to purify, to aid in the journey, or to appease the spirit world. Long after a person has died, the griever may feel the need to do a particular ceremony to honor the dead because of a dream or vision. For the Hopi, kacinas are supernatural beings and spirits of the dead. Children are given carved wooden dolls as images of them to help them learn about the Hopi religion. Like the False Face Society, the Hopi believe that when they dress as a kacina, that their spirit leaves their body and is replaced temporarily by that particular kacina. Clearly, the Hopi believe that the dead are still with us. The obvious message is that caregivers need to understand that the Hopi view of the afterlife is that the dead are still with the living.

Like the Hopi, the Zuni also wore masks. At the winter solstice, the masks worn by the Zuni make them appear to be 10 or more feet tall. Caregivers need to understand the importance of encouraging whatever rituals or ceremonies are sought by the grieving American Indian.

Medicine lodges and sweat lodges are common among many groups. Many would be found among Plains groups. Most would have the door facing the east into the rising sun. They would contain a sacred fire, an altar, and often four pillars. Four is an important number for most groups. Four winds, four seasons, and so forth. For the Arikara, the four pillars represented the sunrise, thunder, wind, and night. While sweat lodges have become popular among non-Indians, their purpose is primarily religious. For most clans, the purpose of the sweat is to purify spirituality and physically. While most benefits are mental, it is also beneficial for health and hygiene. Lodges may have medicine bundles around the walls along with special symbols and other artifacts. Medicine bundles are collections of objects that vary greatly from one group of individual to another, but medicine bundles are generally made from animal skins and contain stones, grasses, tobacco, the sacred pipe, skulls or bones, and other sacred objects. Many groups have tribal medicine bundles as well as individual bundles. It can be expected that most groups will have some sacred objects and places that may or may not be open to the caregiver.

JOURNEYS IN THE AFTERLIFE

For the most part, American Indians are concerned with the joys and problems of life and do not focus upon what happens to them when they are dead. The Ojibwa buried their dead in the ground with food and tobacco for the four-day journey to the land of the souls. The Iroquois would fast for ten days after a death, and the family would grieve for an entire year wearing mourning clothes and carrying the spirit bundle. The widow would sleep next to the spirit bundle and would place food before it (Bial 2000, 43). The widow would not remarry for a year. At the end of the year, a special ceremony was held in which mourners are given gifts and comforted which signaled the end of their time of grief and allowed them to rejoin the daily activities of the village (Bial 2000, 43). For the Dine or the Navajo, after the burial, there are four days of restricted behavior (Leighton and Kluckhohn 1969, 92). The Navajo are noted for their repulsion of contact with dead bodies. They have ceremonies for people who have touched dead bodies to remove the evil effects of such contact, but they also will use the same Blessing Way ceremony to neutralize the evil effects of contact with white people (Allen 1963, 59).

For the Navajo, grief is part of life. Each Navajo is reminded that as the medicine men and women spent a lifetime learning and performing ceremonies, the nature of the Navajo belief in a Supreme Being, the symbols and expression of this unknown power, is everywhere in all of creation and that it surrounds one's life and gives meaning and purpose to life (Greenberg and Greenberg 1996, 128). To survive grief, one must remember where one came from and who one is. Grief keeps a person from performing his or her purpose in life. For the Navajo, one must return to what being a Navaho means to be able to manage grief. The Lakota at the Sun Dance feed mourners who have lost someone in the last year—a ritual meal to reincorporate them back into the ordinary activities of the Lakota society (Medicine 1987, 168). The Lakota are expected to restrict behavior for four days and at the end of the year, to feed the ghost for one last time, distribute the belongings at a feast or giveaway, which releases them from their period of mourning and allows them to begin life anew (Grobsmith 1981, 66).

For the caregiver who is instructed in the stages of grief or even the process theory of grief, the usual methods of guiding people through grief do not work so well unless the Indian has fully acculturated in the dominant society. While there may very well be anger, depression, lack of wanting to go on with life, denial, and other common reactions, the means to helping the person through their grief is not group therapy, counseling, or medicine. Rather than therapy, the focus should be upon ritual, tradition, and return to what is important. The Lakota may want to "keep the ghost" of a dead relative, but they would still be expected to end their mourning, conduct a giveaway, and so forth, and they are also expected by their culture to end their mourning after a year and begin life anew (Grobsmith 1981, 66). Cultural expectations are more powerful than feelings. How does one learn cultural expectations? Those who work with American Indians need to better understand the cultural differences.

CAREGIVERS AND CULTURE

Caregivers should study information about whatever cultural group they might be working with as caregivers. If there is a community available, the caregiver can become involved in the community and learn valuable ideas about the culture, things that work with grieving people, the role of elders, the role of spirituality, and the importance of ritual and ceremonies. Visits with the people in the community at every opportunity are vital to successful caregiving. Listen to them more than talking to them. Particularly visit with the elders and with parents. Visit with the attitude of learning, respect, and value of the cultural group and the community. In most American Indian communities, life and thought are centered around people and not about things. People are more likely to be respected for their contributions to the group than for their status, possessions, or other individual accomplishments. Standing in the community is generally based upon helping others and contributing to the group rather than getting a job or achieving fame. The successful person is the wise elder, a good model for others, or who has benefited his or her people. Deep trust and reliance upon others are important. Sharing and cooperation are important. Defeating others or getting better grades or a bigger house or whatever is not a positive goal. Sharing includes sharing grief. The caregiver is expected to grieve with the griever and not just offer advice or comfort. When another is unhappy, so are you! If one is hunger and another has food, all will eat! For caregivers, this is often a problem. Some groups have the giveaway in six months rather than waiting a year. They may have given away all of their food. The caregiver has food but does not share! How can a selfish person aid those who share everything?

Most clans are relatively quiet. A traditional Navajo while being quite hospitable, friendly, and fun loving will typically enter a room where there are many friends, but will show them no sign of recognition for several minutes. After a socially acceptable length of time he will touch hands with all of them. Navajos are seldom loud or demonstrative in public. They may cry on each other's shoulder if there are no strangers present, but public displays of affection are rare. Navajos rarely speak louder than is necessary to make themselves heard by the person to whom they are speaking. Caregivers who are loud or speak when they walk into the room or hug when they meet the Navajo are generally looked upon as not showing respect. Their ability to work with Navajos is greatly compromised. Caregivers must show tremendous patience when working with American Indians. For a culture that focuses upon billable hours, having too large of a caseload, and little time for anything, it is extremely difficult to meet the needs and values of American Indians. A caregiver might want to have several visits with the family where they are before offering any kind of professional support. Certainly, the caregiver would want to visit neighbors, elders, and others in the community before offering professional advice. If the caregiver is well established in the community, it may not be necessary to spend so much time with others in the community. Elders need to be respected and should be consulted even if their advice or counsel is ignored.

To be able to work with American Indian communities, the caregivers must show respect for people, especially the elderly. Respect for people and their feelings are very important in American Indian societies. Relationships between family members are based upon mutual respect and care. People get great satisfaction in helping others. For the caregiver, these are the positive relationships that your care can be based upon! The American Indian will go to great lengths to avoid doing anything that will disrespect others. Children are taught restraint and self-control. They are taught particularly to respect the elderly. Caregivers must learn to show respect as well. As children are not to interrupt or speak before spoken to, so should caregivers oblige. It is important to not interrupt or correct elders when they speak.

CULTURAL VALUES AND CAREGIVING

Caregivers typically are from a society that honors children. In American Indian societies, people not only honor children, but they also honor the elderly. While perhaps not true of all tribes, most anticipate and celebrate reaching the age of fifty when they can become an elder. Having "snow on the mountain" or white or gray hair is looked upon as a good thing. It is also important to know that respect is earned, and not just the result of age. Being a respected elder is based upon gaining wisdom, humility, calm judgment, and being a model for others, particularly those who are younger. Non-Indians can be respected if they show the same traits.

American Indians are generally taught to respect the privacy of others. They should not interfere in other people's affairs. Personal dignity is highly valued. One does not give advice unless the other person asks for it. Most resent freely given advise that most caregivers offer. One should not make decisions for others. One is expected to fulfill one's duties to the family, clan, and community. One should be generous, control oneself, and mind his or her own business! The nature of caregiving is often counter to this approach. The extended family is also very important. Children spend far more time with extended family including grandparents than in the larger society. Generally, American Indians do not rush to make decisions or to make changes.

By contrast, caregivers are typically under a time constraint. The hospice program will only allow them to work with a family for a limited period of time. The government will only pay for so many visits. The management will not allow for non-billable hours. Time is viewed differently in American Indian cultures. One should not rush through life. If there is work that needs to be done, then do it. If not, spend time with your clan and friends. There is no rush to manage grief or anything else! Patience is normal, not expected in certain situations.

Caregivers who work with American Indians need to better understand the cultures of the people they are serving and to learn to respect that the ways of other people are just as valuable as their own ways. It is important to show respect for the values and way of life of the people they serve. Learning as much as you can about other cultures is an important step in gaining respect for those cultures and receiving respect from those you are serving.

TRIBAL PRACTICES IN DYING

The culture of American Indians also impacts the values, norms, patterns, and processes used to aid the dying. Their relationships with the white culture have also impacted these patterns and practices. Prejudices toward them have probably existed since before the colonists came into contact with them. Their treatment by the early explorers was not exemplary. Today many still describe them as incompetent and needing of government care and direction. The problems with suicide, high rates of infant mortality, alcohol abuse among both adults and children, and other social problems have led to negative opinions of most tribal cultures. The traditional views of Indians as treacherous and murderous have been passed down through the years. More recently, with American Indians playing key roles in the government, being elected to Congress, and having success in the arts in both music and artistic endeavors have greatly improved the views of American Indians.

While American Indians have diverse cultures and the lifestyle of the tribes differs greatly, but some cultural patterns do emerge. While the White culture is future oriented, Native Americans are more focused upon the present. Time is to be enjoyed and lived, not dreaded. Calendars and time are not important in the Native cultures. One is to live life with family and friends. There is no need to hurry. Life is full when one has food to share, family and friends to enjoy, and ceremonies to attend. Enjoy the present and the future will take care of itself. Facing death means living until it occurs. One does not stop enjoying life, people, ceremonies, or spiritual activity because one is dying, rather one engages in life, people, ceremonies, and spiritual activity because one is dying. In the Anglo-European culture, the dying are often encouraged to withdraw from active participation in life and its activities. While nursing home can be found on some reservations, the usual pattern is to care for the sick and elderly at home.

American Indians view leisure as a basic value. In the White culture, people often return to work to rest up after a vacation or holiday. American Indians work as needed not because it is there to do. The Navajo do not distinguish between work and play. One is to have fun at whatever one does. For the Navajo, good behavior means completing one's duties to one's family, being generous to others, minding one's business, and not bragging on oneself. For the Lakota, good behavior would include respecting others, being socially sensitive, and respecting others. How long or how hard one works is not highly valued. This does not mean that American Indians do not work hard or long hours. They might work 20 hours a day and then not show up at work the next day. It is not a question of being lazy. If my brother was moving to a different home, I would have an obligation to help him move which would be a higher obligation than working at my job. If one of my student's mother was sick and could not care for her family and children, my student would place that familial obligation before attending my class. Family and friends come first. If a relative or friend needs your services, that is more important than a job. American Indians do not work for the sake of work.

While generalizations are dangerous, the variety of cultural expressions of dying and death do have some commonalities for the various tribes. Most tribes express a willingness to surrender to death at any time with little fear. The Lakota Chief Crazy Horse was noted for his chant before going into battle that, "Today is a good day to die." Every day is a good day to die if one has lived one's life. Every day is to be lived as if it were one's last day. One must enjoy life and live fully.

Just as one cannot buy land, one cannot buy life. Death is waiting. We cannot escape death, and yet, at the same time, we should not seek death before its time. Nor do we avoid death or try to delay its occurrence. No one is ever truly alone. The dead are not altogether powerless. There is no death, but rather a change of worlds (Steiger 1974, 25).

Despite the high rates of suicide that occur among some tribes, generally tribes reject suicide. The Lakota teach that those who suicide will wander the earth lost and lonely.

American Indians also have a keen sense of humor. Carl Gorman, who taught me much of what I know of the ways of the Navajo, lived and taught that one is to maintain a sense of humor during good times and sad times. Humor is different in each society, but all societies have humor. Yet, even Carl went into a deep depression where he did not paint or work for many months after the death of his son. When he did start painting again, it brought him back to life. All of us need to find that reason to get up in the morning, that reason to continue to live, and that reason to be the person that we were born to become. There are many ways to face grief. Humor is one of them.

For American Indian peoples, all aspects of life, including death, are subjects of humor and laughter. The naturalistic philosophy of tribes generally means that when it is one's time to die, then one should die. They would not use medically futile interventions for the dying. One should die naturally without tubes and machines. One does not show love by trying to keep a person alive as long as possible. We should not allow our loved ones to continue to suffer needlessly to satisfy our desire to keep them with us. Being present is the best gift that we can give to the dying. Being present is also a gift to us as well. One does not allow a loved one to die alone with strangers. COVID has made that impossible for many of us. One of my sisters died with COVID, and none of our family was allowed to be with her.

American Indians are also more likely to be silent and to have periods of few words. One may go on a trip with an Apache and have few words exchanged. In the Anglo-European culture, those who travel together feel a social obligation to talk to fill the time. A smile or a touch is more highly valued than words in most American Indian groups. One should take time for thought before expressing oneself. In the dominant culture, words will fill the time rather than silence.

Spirituality is also a basic part of the American Indian culture. One achieves courage and optimism from one's spiritual life and religion. Balance with nature and spirituality is essential to good health. Healing ceremonies are designed to restore such balance. Everything in life has a purpose. Even pain has a purpose. Pain causes courage to grow. One cannot be brave if one has only experienced wonderful things in one's life.

One must also have respect for ceremonies. Among the Navajo, ceremonies exist for almost every event in one's life. A ceremony exists for the baby's first laugh, healing, welcome home events, birth, marriage, death, and other life events. The ceremonies teach about clan life, personal relationships, values, wholeness, and relationships. Dying is a part of life. One accepts whatever fate has to offer. The purpose of rituals and ceremonies is not to worship, but rather it serves as a renewal of the relationship between the group or clan and the supernatural or sacred. A person enters the world of the sacred to purify themselves so that they can then be able to return to the secular world. Ceremonies great and small are the very fabric of life for the American Indian. It is not a Sunday thing or what one does at church. For the American Indian, spirituality is not something that one does as part of an organized community, but rather, it is a part of everything that one does, thinks, and observes. Rituals and ceremonies are a way of life! We live, and then we live again.

CONCLUSIONS

Death is a constant in the university. Dying is a part of every culture. An analysis of the dying process, burial practices, and grief management of a people gives us a better understanding of their values and culture. Maintaining health is of primary concern for people in all cultures. Caring for the terminally ill requires a basic understanding of the people that you are serving. Working with those facing death can raise questions of the meaning of life, lead to tragedy and tears, relief from pent-up emotions, and at the same time can offer those giving care immense gratification.

Part III

TRIBAL PRACTICES IN DYING, DEATH, DISPOSAL, AND BEREAVEMENT

Ancient societies were generally collective cultures as opposed to modern individually focused cultures. In a collective culture, the focus is upon the well-being of the collectivity, group, clan, tribe, or whatever is the nature of the community in which one lives. The individual views his or her own welfare as less important than that of the group. The community response is evident in the funeral, disposal, and mourning practices of ancient societies. The entire community will be the base of support for those who have experienced a loss. The community will be there to help the survivors economically, socially, and spiritually.

Markers such as tombstones, items that the deceased wore or used, pictures and other mementos, and memories help keep them alive for the grieving. The success or failure of using these markers is dependent to a great extent upon community support or nonsupport.

Perhaps the most recognizable and documented response to death by societies and cultures would be the funeral process. Seemingly, from the earliest discovered cultural groups, humans have developed funeral rituals to accompany the deaths of their members and even those of their enemies. The patterns of notifying others about the death, the preparation of the body, the rituals to honor the deceased, the social development after the funeral activities, and the choice of how to dispose of the body are all products of social and institutional pressures. Even the way a person grieves for the loss of a loved one is subject to social norms and pressures. An understanding of the power of cultural and institutional forces of the ancients may open windows to understanding current practices and pressures.

By examining the social and institutional structures of various societies and cultural groups, the hope is to help provide a framework for a better understanding of the study about dying, death, and bereavement from all cultural perspectives. Disposal practices evolve over time with responses from those who are part of the community. Burials have been found from the earliest human social groups. Over time human cultures developed formalized rituals, burial containers, mourning practices, and patterns for remembering the dead. As with the kings in Egypt, some groups try to outdo previous kings or members of their community in building their tombs, grave markers, of funeral activities. Others simply follow the traditions set by their ancestors. The chapters will look at what is known about the more ancient societies and what is known about those that still exist.

Chapter 13, "Anasazi Disposal and Bereavement Practices," looks at what is known about the Anasazi people and their practices. Chapter 14, "Aztec Disposal and Bereavement Practices," looks at the practices of the Aztecs. Chapter 15, "Maya Disposal and Bereavement Practices," describes the ways of the Maya. Chapter 16, "Mounds Builders Disposal and Bereavement Practices," examines what is known about the Mounds peoples and their practices. Chapter 17, "The Dine (Navajo) Disposal and Bereavement Practices," looks at the practices of the Dine. Chapter 18, "The Inde (Apache) and Tohono O'Odham Disposal and Bereavement Practices," presents the practices of the Inde and Tohono O'Odham. Chapter 19, "Hopi Disposal and Bereavement Practices," offers a look at the practices of the Hopi. Chapter 20, "Lakota and Blackfeet Disposal and Bereavement Practices," uses two of the Plains tribes to examine the practices of those living on the plains. Chapter 21, "Cheyenne, Shawnee, and the Potawatomi Disposal and Bereavement Practices," examines the approaches of several tribes. Chapter 22, "Ojibwe/Anishinabe/Chippewa, Shoshone, and Stockbridge-Munsee Disposal and Bereavement Practices," examines the disposal and bereavement management of the three tribes.

Chapter 13

Anasazi Disposal and Bereavement Practices

The story of the Anasazi is the story of a people that adapted to and even thrived in what may have been one of the most difficult environments in the world. They were a people whose lives revolved around agriculture and religion in a culture that saw the performance of ritual, dance, and chanting as important and uplifting as tilling the soil. The Anasazi who built their homes in caves and cliffs, lived in an area with very little rain, that had mostly dry streams that would often have flash floods that could wash away what little fragile topsoil that made it possible for them to farm. They left behind close to 100,000 distinct sites that extended over 25,000 square miles of the Four Corners region with over 400 miles of ancient roadways without the use of draft animals or the wheel (Flaharty 1992, 125). They left behind 1,400-year-old baskets and sandals, human remains, furs and fabrics that clothed the dead that are far better preserved than those of the contemporary Mound Building cultures of the Eastern United States where moisture took a heavy toll on what was left for future study (Flaharty 1992, 125). The Dine work, Anasazi, was used to describe those of the ancient culture. It was thought to mean "ancient ones," but the Dine define the word as "ancient enemies." Because the Dine had a history of raiding and conflict with the pueblo people, that is probably the more correct meaning of the word "Anasazi."

WHO WERE THE ANASAZI?

The Anasazi culture has become perhaps the most famous of the ancient tribes in part because of Mesa Verde, Canyon de Chelly, and other national parks. It is also one of the newest prehistoric tribes with a rich cultural heritage. While little has been confirmed about their origins, the Anasazi are thought to have arrived in the Americas around thirty thousand years ago, and over time, settled in the Four Corners region around ten thousand years ago (Arnold 1992, 20). For over a thousand years, the Anasazi culture flourished. There are hundreds of long-ago abandoned Anasazi villages dotting the Colorado Plateau. The Four Corners area, where Colorado, New Mexico, Arizona, and Utah come together today, the remains of the great communities that stood on the wind-swept mesas and the depths of the desert can still be found. The Anasazi stretched from the lush foothills of Colorado's San Juan Mountains to the sun-baked deserts of New Mexico to the secluded, deep canyons of Utah and Arizona. Archaeologists generally recognize three major distinct variations of the Anasazi culture that became known by the region where they were found: Chaco Canyon, Mesa Verde, and Kayenta cultural group-ings. Other, less well-known groups would include the Virgin River Anasazi, the Little Colorado Anasazi, and the Rio Grande Anasazi also named by the regions where they dwelled.

CHACO CANYON

Chaco Canyon, New Mexico, is thought to be the one of the earliest pueb-los to develop, and it was one of the richest areas in its time. It has been researched for over a century and covers an area of 32 square miles contain-ing more than two thousand sites with eleven large pueblos and more than four hundred smaller ruins making it one of the richest archaeological places in North American (Noble 1981, 78). It is generally thought that the Anasazi people first came to this area around ten thousand years ago as nomadic hunters based upon the stone spear points that were left behind (Noble 1981, 78). The Chaco Canyon area was thought to have been thriving about two centuries before other Anasazi areas were developed. The Chaco pueblos were built along a 20 mile or so stretch of the Chaco Canyon. There were thirteen enormous pueblos called "great houses" that may have housed more than one thousand people in each pueblo. Some of their building had more than one hundred rooms, circular underground religious rooms called kivas with built-in benches, central firepits, ventilator shafts for air, and a Sipapu or symbolic hole of entry to the underworld (Naranjo 1993, 17). The ways of life and practices of the Chaco Anasazi were part of the larger Anasazi culture.

ANASAZI WAY OF LIFE

The later Pueblos saw the Sipapu as the sacred opening or the gateway to the world. They have taught for generations that their ancestors emerged from an underworld through a lake or underground passage to their present homeland. Like other tribes, the Pueblo people believed that they must keep life simple and live in harmony with nature. Religion was not something practiced on special occasions or on Sundays, but was part of what one did in every facet of one's daily life. The Anasazi saw themselves as caretakers of the earth and as holders of the responsibility to care for the earth. Kivas were believed to be used, as did the later Pueblo people, for sacred rituals. Each Kiva had an altar, sacred relics, and murals. Perhaps the most famous prehistoric figure was the pied piper known as Kokopelli. Petroglyphs are thought to have been first used in the Anasazi Four Corners region but have also been found on the Great Plains, the Hohokam areas, the Canadian Rockies, in Mexico, in the Mogollon areas, and in Utah's Fremont culture (Cheek 2004, 10). The Kokopelli is often described as the Casanova of the ancient ones. He is one of the few petroglyphs that is found among thousands of drawings, etchings, and paintings on rocks, in caves, and walls of the prehistory period that is not only found quite often, but also is definitely male and has a name (Young 1990, 1). The Kokopelli remains popular even to today being found on baskets, pottery, t-shirts, and other items for tourists. The Kokopelli might best be described as a hunchback flute player. Drawings of the Kokopelli are found in pueblos in all areas.

Perhaps the most famous pueblo would be "Pueblo Bonito" or beautiful village, which covers more than 3 acres, has eight hundred to nine hundred rooms, was four stories high, and housed around one thousand people. Chetro Ketl, a nearby pueblo named by the Navajo, is of similar size. These two pueblos are thought to be the most advanced of the pre-Columbian architecture in the United States (Nabokov and Easton 1989, 356). While there is much speculation, the existence of wide prehistoric roads built with stones or rocks cleared from soil and rocks and other materials stretch for hundreds of miles. They are thought to be the only American Indian group to have built roads in what is now the United States. Part of the puzzle is that the Anasazi did not develop the wheel, have horses, carts, or other obvious reasons to have built roads over 30 feet wide covering hundreds of miles in a desert area. There is little question that they somehow did bring in logs from other areas to use in building their great houses and kivas. The thirteen large pueblo towns were connected by these roads and water control systems that were also developed to enable them to farm more land than would have been possible with dry-farming techniques (Anderson and Anderson 1981, 5). Their survival skills were greatly advanced for any culture.

Around 200 miles North and West of Chaco Canyon are the ruins of three more amazing Anasazi communities in an aspen-filled canyon, Tsegi Canyon, in the heart of what is today is called the Painted Desert and is the center of what is called the Kayenta Anasazi culture. This culture thrived at a later time than the Chaco Canyon culture, but it lasted longer (Noble 1981, 55). The Kayenta people were also scattered along Black Mesa, in the depths of the Grand Canyon, and along the Escalante River. The three towns in the Tsegi Canyon represent the height of the Kayenta culture with Betatakin having 150 rooms, making it the largest cliff dwelling in Arizona, while Keet Seel and Inscription House are now part of the Navajo National Monument (Noble 1981, 59).

The third major Anasazi area was the Montelores Empire or the Mesa Verde culture. The Montelores Plateau is also called the Great Sage Plain and covers around 4,000 square miles. Next to the Montelores Plateau is the much higher Mesa Verde which became the center of that culture. Mesa Verde is about 75 miles northwest of Chaco Canyon. While more people are thought to have lived on the Montelores Plateau than in Mesa Verde, Mesa Verde is far more famous. Some pueblos that are still unexcavated have as many as one thousand or more rooms and as many as one hundred kivas in each pueblo. The Yellow Jacket site, for example, had around 1,820 rooms, 166 kivas, four plazas, twenty towers, and more people than even Chaco Canyon's Pueblo Bonito and the entire Mesa Verde region (Fagan 2000, 336). Like other early civilizations, the Anasazi were able to develop thriving cultures.

CONTRIBUTIONS OF THE ANASAZI

The people of the Pueblo cultures were able to maintain large villages of 1,000–2,500 people and were able to build clusters of a single architectural structure with each family maintaining its own cluster of structures with a living space, storage space, eating areas, and a kiva (Fagan 2000, 336). The Anasazi cultures were known for their stonework, basket-making, farming, water systems, roads, communication systems, pottery, and farming.

The Anasazi culture is known for developing weaving of baskets, foot coverings, utensils, clothing, and storage containers of many sizes and purposes (Terrell 1971, 13). The pit-house, which ultimately evolved into the Kiva, was developed along with basketry to include the making of burial shrouds (Ambler 1989, 53). The Anasazi culture was spread over a great deal of territory with numerous communities that supported hundreds of people. Many of the artifacts that were left behind still have the bright colors and exhibit the craft of their construction that belies their age of hundreds of years (Fagan 2000, 339). While no explanation exists as to what happened to these people, there is no evidence of any warfare or destruction by another culture (Terrell 1971, 21–22). Visits to the national parks and national monuments in the region would offer the opportunity to view artifacts from the Anasazi culture

The Anasazi were called the "ancient ones" by the Navajo, but since it is a Navajo name, the Hopi object to using that name because the Tavasuh, the ancestors of the Navajo, used rocks or stone clubs to bash the heads of captured enemies to kill them (Muench 1974, 12). Even less is known of the early Anasazi because they were nomadic basket-makers who rarely built permanent dwellings where artifacts could be found, but over time, they became more sedentary and moved from occasional caves and other temporary dwellings to building communities (Muench 1974, 45). While the Anasazi are thought of as one people, like most other tribes or clans, they were a diverse people. Those living in the Mesa Verde and Chaco Canyon regions developed differently than those living in the South with the Mogollon and Hohokam peoples. In a little more than thirteen centuries, the Anasazi went from small bands of hunters and gathers to great communities of farms and cities, living with what nature gave them in deserts and dry lands, and were able to develop basketry, pottery, building techniques, to a higher civilization that remains a mystery and contradiction of a people who left their ghosts among the rocks (Muench 1974, 20). The Mogollon and Hohokam cultures developed from the Cochise Culture or Desert Cultures that characterize the Mesa Verde and Chaco Canyon areas, not as a different group genetically, but they were culturally different with wickerwork, for mats and sandals, bracelets with seashells probably gained from trading, and having more water, were a more secure and ultimately sedentary culture (Muench 1974, 66). The Mogollon culture is thought to be the first to build houses and rather quickly, they were building pit-houses that were at first used for storage of jars and baskets of food, seed corn, and other crops that over time became kivas (Muench 1974, 69). The relics of their culture have provided a rich history.

The Hohokam culture is thought to have emerged about one hundred years after the Mogollon culture and is noted for building rectangular houses rather than round ones, and for sometimes within pit-houses without using the pit-house walls as house walls (Muench 1974, 70). Because they lived in an arid area, irrigation was vital to their survival. They not only developed sophisticated irrigation systems, but they also developed arts and recreation including mirrors, carving of stone bowls, stone human figurines, exceptional bows and arrows that were traded for goods, etching seashells with animals and other geometric motifs, and sports arenas and games that persist to today (Muench 1974, 71). The Anasazi also developed a passive solar system to allow them to control the temperatures in their apartment complexes to manage the heat in their arid environment (Churchill 1995, 348). The Anasazi were able to develop great irrigation systems, games, ballgame courts, mirrors, intensive pottery manufacturing systems, intensive horticultural activities, trading beyond their region, and exceptional construction techniques (Forbes 1982, 26). It has also been verified that the Anasazi in the Chaco Canyon area mined turquoise in the Cerrillos in northern New Mexico and traded it with other cultures (Warren and Mathien 1985, 93). How they lived and how and why they disappeared still remain a mystery.

It is generally believed that the Anasazi had a sophisticated communications system as early as the Chaco era. The National Park Service demonstrates how the communication system might have worked at several different sites in the region. The ability to have a line of sight that stretches from one ridge to another for many, many miles seems to have made this possible. There appears to be a clear pattern to the towers and other structures that would enable the ancient ones to have used some method to signal each other at long distances. The Kin Ya's is visible from the Penasco Blanco and is visible for distances of 27 miles to a tower kiva to the south and so forth to other towers and structures (Anderson and Anderson 1981, 33). While it is not known how they signaled, some possibilities might include horns, fire, pyrite, drums, or even flags, but the distances make drums, flags, horns much less likely (Anderson and Anderson 1981, 33). While the exact methods are not known, they were able to communicate over long distances in a fairly efficient, orderly, and speedy system. How and what they communicated is not known. Perhaps, the communications systems were warning towers for approaching enemies, or to notify people about rituals and ceremonies, or that traders were approaching, or many, many other possibilities. While much is left to speculation, at least, it is known that over the centuries, they were able to communicate by means that were much faster than humans could travel on foot. So, many questions remain about the Anasazi and their way of life, but some answers do exist.

MYSTERIES OF THE ANASAZI

There are many, many unanswered questions about the Anasazi. Not only are there questions about how they communicated, but there are also questions about their huge warehouses that were much bigger than anything that they could have produced. What sort of political systems did they use? What were the religious practices that they follow? How much trade were they able to do with other tribes? What did they do with their dead? Only a handful of burial sites have been found anywhere in the region. Clearly, with a history that covered over a thousand years, there would have been a large number of people who would have been buried or otherwise disposed after they died. In just Chaco Canyon alone, based upon the number of rooms, there could have been as many as fifteen thousand people living in the canyon, but there are not enough burial sites or even enough area to grow enough corn to feed that many people (Anderson and Anderson 1981, 85). Did they supplement their crop production by trade? Were they great traders? Were there other people in the region that would have traded with them? There is still much to be learned about the Anasazi.

BURIAL PRACTICES OF THE ANASAZI

While not much is known of their burial practices, they did leave behind artifacts that provide clues to some of their basic practices. When a death occurred, the Anasazi placed the deceased in a tight flexed position with the knees to the chest and buried them with many possessions such as beads, sandals, digging sticks, blankets, smoking pipes, and mats. The body was placed in a basket and mats were laid over the body before the grave was covered (Spencer and Jennings 1965, 96). Seemingly, they must have believed in an afterlife, because they would not only wrap the dead in furs or woven blankets or deerskins, but they would also place new or unused sandals in the grave as well as ornaments, stone knives, clothing, food, and even cradles (Terrell 1973, 77). Fortunately, they often choose to inter their dead in caves where moisture did not reach them, and the dry air preserved over time mummified many of them (Terrell 1973, 77). At times, the Anasazi apparently buried their dead beneath garbage piles and rockslides, though it could be that the dead fell to their deaths into the garbage piles or were crushed to death by rockslides. In other eras, there is no evidence of burials of any sort. Perhaps the dead are sealed into places that have not yet been discovered. At other times, the Anasazi sealed their dead in rooms of their houses where they still remain (Ambler 1989, 51).

Like the later Hopi and Zuni tribes, the Anasazi made Kivas of two distinct types. Some were circular, while others were rectangular. Some Kivas had roofs, and other Kivas had none (Muench 1974, 115–116). Since the Anasazi buried their dead where they lived and provided them with possessions for an afterlife, it would seem that they had little fear of the dead or of ghosts. The many mysteries of the Anasazi add to their mystique. Visits to the national and state parks that have pueblos, cliff dwellings, and other sites are excellent sources of visual as well as physical knowledge of the Anasazi.

CONCLUSIONS

While there has been little or no consensus as to why the Anasazi left or what caused them to disappear, some archaeologists suggest that the drought of 1276–1299 may have caused them to move to where there was water (Terrell 1973, 84). Whether they were forced to leave, lost battles causing them to leave, or left simply because of a drought or famine, the impact of the Anasazi on the Pueblo peoples has been profound. The Anasazi were the people who developed bows and arrows that changed life for those living on the plains and elsewhere. The sports and games developed by the Anasazi exist today as do their dwellings and artifacts that have fascinated thousands for generations. It is believed that the ancient places with their artifacts, pottery, buildings, and rock art are still here because the Navajo taught that they were supposed to stay away from the places of the ancient ones which is like the National Park Service edict to "preserve and protect" (Simonelli 2008, 11). To learn more about the "ancient ones," see Watson (1961). Today in New Mexico alone, there are nineteen Pueblo groups included in the census. The Indian Pueblo Cultural Center in Albuquerque offers an excellent introduction to the Pueblo people with hand-crafted jewelry, pottery, painting, baskets, and other ancient and modern items for viewing and for sale. It also provides a history of the Pueblo people and gives information on all of the Pueblos in New Mexico. Many Pueblos require that visitors obtain permits, some charge for taking pictures while others do not allow picture taking, require permits for painting or drawing, and some allow visitors to observe and possibly take part in tours of kivas, graveyards, and some ceremonies. Others do not allow visitors to kivas, graveyards, or ceremonies. The National Park Service maintains many of the historical sites of the Anasazi. Their parks are the source of a wealth of information and offer many beautiful sites to learn about the Anasazi and their ways. The Anasazi were able to thrive for over one thousand years. Their cliff dwellings were only a century of their history when their people moved into caves as a response to strong enemy pressure and built the cliff dwellings for which Mesa Verde and other sites are famous (Watson 1961a, 50). Yet, it is this century that has continued to fascinate the study of the Anasazi.

Chapter 14

Aztec Disposal and Bereavement Practices

The Aztecs were a civilization that conjures up images of Egypt, Romans, or even the Greeks, not only because they were a warlike people who established a great empire, but also because they built not only great cities, but also built pyramids, golden objects, had feathered priests, and offered human sacrifices (Waldman 1988, 26). Growing from a group of nomadic hunters, the Aztecs were able to establish a great civilization that had the misfortune to be at the height of their culture achievements when the Spanish arrived.

The Aztecs lived in what is called Mesoamerican in the area where North and South America are joined. The Aztec lands included much of what are now Mexico, Guatemala, Honduras, El Salvador, and Belize. This region has historically been the home for many great civilizations, including the Aztecs, Mayans, Toltecs, and the Olmecs. As each civilization built upon the ashes of the previous civilization, so, too, did the Aztec culture was built on the ruins and successes of those who came before them. Each of the previous civilizations made possible even greater innovations, progress, and dominance of the succeeding civilizations. The progress of each culture added knowledge and practices that could be used by the next civilization.

AZTEC CULTURE AND WAY OF LIFE

The Aztecs were able to dominate a very large area without the technology and weapons that the Spanish brought with them to the Americas. The Aztecs ruled 400–500 small states. The states were taken over by both conquest and trade. As dominant and powerful as the Aztecs were, they fell to the Spaniards who came with their guns and cannons in search of gold and other treasures.

175

Like the Incas and the Maya, the Aztecs borrowed from other cultures. From the Olmec and Maya, they learned to carve jade, make pottery, develop irrigation systems, write, paint walls, use masonry building techniques, apply stucco, farming, language, enact laws, and many other skills. The Mayans are thought to be the only American Indian group to develop their own writing. They also inherited the practice of making slaves of those who were criminals, captives, enemies who were captured, or simply poor people who lost their freedom in return for food and shelter. Like the Incas, the Aztecs left behind buildings, books, pottery, jewelry, tombs, and temples. Much of the knowledge that we have of the Aztecs comes from their writings and artifacts that they left behind, and from the journals and logs of the Spanish conquers, missionaries, and traders who were able to provide a more clear record of their successful culture that were able to dominate their regions for many generations.

As in most early civilizations, nobles, soldiers, priests, and government workers formed the highest social classes, while most people worked as farmers, fished, or were servants. The middle class was made up of craftspeople and merchants. Like many early cultures, the empire was built upon the products of farming. Beans, maize, peppers, squashes, turkeys, ducks, bees, rabbits, and even dogs were food staples for the empire. Like many civilizations around the world, the peasant farmers were forced to fight in the armies, made to build public projects, and required to pay taxes from the products that they produced whether by farming, hunting, crafting, or artistic endeavors. The strong class divisions meant that generations generally remained in the same level of social class as their ancestors. It was only by becoming a great warrior, becoming a member of the clergy, or marrying someone from a different social class that social mobility was possible for most people.

The Aztecs were known for making arts and crafts. They made cloth; worked with gold, mosaics; made creations with feathers; sculpted stone and wood; made jewelry; and made brilliant, colored clothes. As in the Egyptian, Roman, and many other ancient cultures, those with artistic abilities were greatly respected by the Aztecs. As in all cultures, children were trained for adult roles. Peasant boys were taught how to become farmers, to be soldiers, to be laborers, or other skills suitable for their social class position. By contrast, the child of a wealthy or noble person would probably be taught the skills to become a leader in government or to be a priest. The child of a merchant would be taught the family trade. Unlike most American Indian groups, the Aztecs had schools for the different career paths that included art, reading, and writing. Writing was considered to be an important skill for more than two thousand years in what is now Mexico (Mann 2006, 447). Not only did the Olmec develop writing about two thousand years ago, but they also excelled at mathematics and developed the concept of zero around the same time and centuries before its development in India (Mann 2006, 241). Schools taught reading, writing, mathematics, religion, and astronomy. The image of the American Indian as lacking culture or being inferior is debunked by what the Aztecs were able to accomplish.

Like other traditional indigenous groups, for the Aztecs, family, clan, religion, and what was considered to be proper behavior were the pillars of the Aztecs' way of life. Clans were responsible for the needy, for those who broke laws or codes, for meting out punishments, for ceremonials, and for educating the young. Unlike the tribes in northern parts of the Americas who had no laws, police, courts, or prisons, the Aztecs saw the need to police their people. Like other indigenous societies, families spent most of their day finding food, preparing food, washing clothes, spinning thread, weaving cloth, tending for the sick and elderly, and teaching children. As in early United States and Canada, most people lived in villages while others lived in cities like Teotihuacan which had 150,000 people 1,400 years ago.

Like the Incas and Mayas, the Aztec peasants lived a fairly simple life typically living in a one-room home with little furniture. The Aztecs used reeds to make their beds. They developed chests to hold their clothes. Most would also have shrines to honor the gods. The Aztec and Mayan homes were typically made from adobe while the Incans used stones. The use of adobe was also a part of the Anasazi culture. Perhaps, the use of adobe was another cultural trait borrowed from those who came before. Like many other indigenous groups, the Aztecs, Incas, and Mayans all had separate building for their bathrooms. The Mesoamerican groups' major foods were maize cakes, tortillas, and tamales which have been passed down through the ages to those who still live in the area. Foods that are now known as Mexican foods were their staples. The Incas brought the potato to Mesoamerica from South America through trade. Those living in Mesoamerica and those in the Andean region developed strong trade routes stretching thousands of miles that spread the cultural practices as well as goods. Trade and conquest were the major ways that the empires of the Aztecs, Incas, and Mayas were spread.

AZTEC EMPIRE

The Spanish conquers must have been somewhat surprised to discover that there was such an advanced civilization when they stumbled upon the Aztec empire. Likewise, the Incas must have also surprised the Spanish when they found their advanced culture in South America that covered more than 4,000 miles of territory. By contrast, Spain is the third largest country in Europe and covers an area that is far larger than the area that was covered by the Aztecs. Yet, the Inca empire stretched for more than 3,000 miles. Spain is less than

700 miles across at its widest point. Spain had the advantage of borrowing and building upon the technological developments from the many cultures of Europe and Asia to aid their ability to have greater technological success that included the weapons of war and the ability to have armor and other protections against the simpler weapons of both the Aztecs and Incas.

The Aztecs, or more properly the Tenochca or Mexica, were late comers to Mesoamerica who came to the unstable frontier and were able to gain control and bring some stability to the region (Spencer and Jennings 1977, 477). Like the Incas, the Aztecs were able to develop a large empire though both began as simply a small group of hunters and farmers. While an exact date is not known for when the region was first settled, it is argued that the first people settled in the Americas around thirty thousand years ago. Both the Aztecs and Incas ruled for a century, and both cultures were destroyed by the Spanish. Generally, it is thought that the Aztecs moved into the region from Northern Mexico, and after being dominated by local groups who were descendants of the Toltecs, the Aztecs were able to begin to build their great civilization. The Aztecs were forced to live in a marshy area where they were able to fish and farm. Over time, they were able to build a settlement and began to conquer some of their neighbors as their emerging empire began to form. Their legend is that they claimed the marshy area because it was prophesized that they would find a spot where an eagle on a cactus holding a snake was where they were to settle (Mann 2006, 130). The spot where it is believed to be where they say an eagle on a cactus holding a snake is where they built what would become the city of Tenochtitlan which ultimately housed over five hundred thousand people. Tenochtitlan would ultimately become a city with towering buildings, temples, public buildings, palaces, zoos, gardens, plazas for trade, and sprawling suburbs for the many people who lived there. Like New Orleans and Chicago, the city built on a swamp was able to grow and thrive.

AZTEC DEATH AND AFTERLIFE BELIEFS

The groups of people living in Mesoamerica had a highly developed understanding of death. They lived in an ear of low life expectancy, high infant mortality, human sacrifice, and almost constant war (Phillips 2006, 78). Like all cultures, the Aztecs developed rituals and ceremonies surrounding dying, death, and bereavement. Unlike most cultures they also developed practices relating to human sacrifice.

Aztec warriors were described as fierce fighters who were noted for capturing enemy soldiers and other people for human sacrifice. Like the Incas, for the Aztecs, religion touched every part of their daily life. As with the Lakota and Navajo, religion was not something that one practiced, but rather was everything that one does in life. The Aztecs believed that they were living in the world of the fifth sun and that the world would end violently and that the only way to delay that fate was human sacrifice (Mann 2006, 132). The thought was that feeding the gods with human blood would keep the sun alive. The Aztecs captured people through warfare for human sacrifice to appease the war god Huitzilopochtli who demanded the most blood leading priests to sacrifice thousands of prisoners on a scale that was far above any other Mesoamerican civilization (Waldman 1988, 27). It is also argued that human sacrifice and ritualized warfare were not only a religious cult-like activity, but it was also a way to maintain and build social power (D'Altroy 2003, 39). Like other peoples of Mesoamerica as well as the Hopi and others, the Aztecs believed that they would go on living in another world. Like the Egyptians and many other societies, the Aztecs would bury their dead with the goods that they thought would be of use to them in the next world. Archaeologists, historians, and even colonial writings suggest that it was the way in which people died rather than the way that a person lived that determined what would happen to them in the next life (D'Altroy 2003, 193–194).

While the Aztecs believed that they lived in the world of the fifth sun, they, like the Maya, believed that there were thirteen tiers of heaven that rose above the earth, and that there were nine layers of Mictlan, the sinister underworld beneath the earth (Phillips 2006, 78). The Aztecs believed that only a select few were bound for the happy areas above while most would go below depending not upon how they lived, but how they died (Phillips 2006, 78). Simply dying a natural death would lead you to the underworld, but dying as a warrior in battle, in childbirth, or even suicide would spare you from the lower areas (Phillips 2006, 78). Those who might achieve the upper tiers would include those who drowned or were struck by lightning who would go to Tlalocan, the paradise presided over by the rain god, Tlaloc, where his life-giving waters fall in a constant light drizzle and flowers, fruit, and delectable foods grow abundantly without the need for human labor of irrigation, digging, or planting (Phillips 2006, 78).

Like Christians, the Mesoamerican societies venerated their ancestors. While they did not call them saints, they viewed the dead as having a spiritual essence, as having their spirits going to a place with no pain or suffering, believing that people who lead evil lives would descend into the underworld where they would be tormented by devils, and that ancestors could be part of the everyday world of the living (Sharer and Trazler 2006, 733–734). Such beliefs were helpful when the Spanish attempted to convert them to Catholicism. As suggested earlier, Emile Durkheim would suggest that there are cultural universals that are found in all religions.

As in all cultures, the royal, the wealthy, and the military leaders were given more elaborate funerals, burials, and more extravagant items were left in their tombs. The clergy and children would also be likely to have more elaborate funerals than those of the common worker. Archaeological evidence demonstrates that the less wealthy families would often entomb their dead beside, under, or at least near their homes to maintain their connection with them (Sharer and Traxler 2006, 734). Most Aztecs were cremated with only the prominent members of nobility and rulers being placed in stone vaults that might have included not only items of great wealth, but also wives, servants, dogs, and food items (Phillips 2006, 79). As with all cultures, social class impacted not only how one lived, but also what happens when one dies.

CONCLUSIONS

The Aztec culture was built upon the ruins of the cultures that existed before it as the Romans built upon the ashes of the Greek civilization using its knowledge, technology, and social organization to build their own empire. Like Egypt connecting with Nubia and other civilizations, the Aztec culture was part of a series of connected cultures across Mesoamerica, but like the Greeks, Egyptians, Romans, Vikings, and others, it was able to develop its civilization with its own distinctive features. Its use of human sacrifice is not unique in the experience of the world, but its religious beliefs supported the use of human sacrifice. Its view of the world as a hostile place that would soon be destroyed was not typical of most American civilizations. Its death management procedures offer some understanding of the social life, social structure, and class system of that time.

As with most early civilizations, contact with their conquerors ultimately led to the destruction of their traditional way of life. While their conquerors were Spanish, the pattern has been repeated in countless areas of the world. The indigenous population ultimately becomes marginalized with their way of life, being viewed by the dominant group as inferior. The dominant group tends to force the indigenous group to adopt the values, norms, and perspectives and practices of the dominant group. The "power elite" are able, by the use of their power and position, to force their views and perspectives to become shared with those that they rule. The "power elite" after using military force to conquer the indigenous people then turn to material conquest or conquering by goods and services to keep the indigenous people in line or obeying whatever rules and behaviors that they wish to impose. While many indigenous groups have been able to resist the total loss of their cultures, others have been completely destroyed. While their civilization has been destroyed, the Aztecs have left behind many descendants, much of their learning and lore, their foods, and their language.

Chapter 15

Maya Disposal and Bereavement Practices

Like the Aztecs, the Mayan culture emerged in what today is known as "Mesoamerica," and more specifically, in an area that covers a major part of Mexico, the entire present-day countries of Belize and Guatemala, and parts of what is now known as El Salvador and Honduras. Like the cultures of Egypt, China, Mesopotamia, and others, the Maya advanced from simple beginnings to an advanced and complex society. The Maya were able to build massive monuments, wonderful works of art, to grow crops on mountain sides, make advances in both astronomy and mathematics, and to live in elaborate cities. The Maya lived in a region that had farming four thousand years ago. The Maya, like the later Aztecs, both lived in the Mesoamerican region, Much earlier, the Olmecs built very large ceremonial centers, developed a religion, a calendar, writing, and established a cultural pattern that lasted more than two thousand years. There is strong archaeological evidence that people have lived in the region for at least twenty-two thousand years (Phillips 2006, 6).

ORIGINS OF THE MAYA CULTURE

Like the Aztecs, the Maya culture is often compared to the great cultures of Africa and Europe. While the Aztecs built pyramids like the Egyptians, the Maya are noted for their wonderful artistry and intellect that influenced the societies around them with their city-states, social class system, architectural knowledge, writing, mathematics skills, road paving, irrigation systems, calendar, artistic skills, and so much more (Waldman 1988, 126). While few of the Europeans who came to the Americas recognized the possibility of an intellectual society being found in the Americas, the Maya were without a doubt on a par intellectually with the elites of Europe.

The first people who came to the region were hunters and gathers like those in other early civilizations. It is generally thought that the switch from hunting and gathering was at least partially motivated by climate change. Around nine thousand years ago, the temperature rose worldwide causing many of the grasslands of Central America to become deserts or tropical forests leading to fewer animals to hunt, forcing the people to turn to more intensive food cultivation (Phillips 2006, 28). Over time, they learned to farm which allowed them to stay in one place. This further allowed them to be more free from hunting for food, to be able to learn new skills, to develop a division of labor, small communities, and to create and make things. The radical change in the way that they lived also led to making rules for working together which led to laws and punishment for violating those rules for behavior. As in other civilizations, this process took thousands of years. There were major differences between the Old World and the New World that greatly impacted their different paths to establishing great civilizations. Those living in the Americas did not have cows, pigs, or sheep and had to use small dogs and turkeys to supplement the fish and the meat that they hunted, nor did they have carts or even beasts of burden like oxen or horses nor did they use the llamas that were used by those living in the Andes to transport their goods (Phillips 2006, 28). Yet in spite of the lack of the wheel, handcarts, beasts of burden, and meat supplies, the people of Mesoamerica were able to develop great civilizations.

The first great civilization in the region was the Olmec society. While their dominance faded after about eight hundred years, their influence not only spread around the region, but also continued to influence the great civilizations that followed them. The Olmecs are often called the "mother civilization" of Mesoamerica, but the Maya culture took the Olmec cultural traits to even higher levels of refinement (Waldman 1988, 126). The Olmecs were able to build towering earthen platforms, pyramid mounds, stone drainage systems, remarkable stone heads towering 10 feet in height, to control an area from El Salvador to Mexico City, and develop a hierarchical society (Phillips 2006, 29). While there is no evidence that the Olmec developed an empire, there is little doubt that their civilization influenced the large area through its cultural influence that left behind ceremonial centers, stone carving across the region, religious rituals that persisted through descendants, human sacrifice also continued in later cultures, possibly a system of writing that may have led to its development in later cultures, and Olmec-style grave objects are found across the region (Phillips 2006, 29). The Zapotec lived in the mountains of Southern Mexico. Like the Olmecs, they built elaborate tombs, temples, pyramids, underground passageways, ball courts, and the city of Monte

Alban which flourished for around six hundred years. As the Zapotec civilizations declined, the Mixtec civilization emerged. As Monte Alban flourished in Oaxaca, Teotihuacan emerged in central Mexico near what is now Mexico City. It was arguably the greatest city in the Americas before the arrival of the Europeans. At its peak around 2,700 years ago, it is thought to have had 150,000 people, great plazas, palaces, administrative buildings, courtyards, burial grounds, temples, 600 pyramids, and some 2,000 single story apartment buildings that fell into ruin possibly by war or rebellion (Phillips 2006, 55). At its peak, Teotihuacan was one of the largest cities in the world.

As the other cultures rose and fell in the highlands, the Maya built their civilization in the lowlands, building upon the model of the other civilizations with many of the same patterns of temples, palaces, pyramids, tombs, and so forth. The Maya civilization is generally thought to be representative of the Classical period. Teotihuacan was a planned city 2,500 years ago in a civilization that had writing, division of labor, a specialized priesthood, secular planning and management, complex construction techniques, and systems of government that lasted hundreds of years (Spencer and Jennings 1977, 451). Located in Teotihuacan, the Pyramid of the Sun is thought to be the third largest pyramid in the world. The Mayas had more than forty cities including Teotihuacan that had populations ranging from 5,000 to 50,000 people (Phillips 2006, 33). The population estimates ranging from one and one half million to thirteen million (Spencer and Jennings 1977, 458). The many Maya city-states were in almost constant conflict, and yet, the Maya were able to build imposing temples, palaces, and pyramids; advanced irrigation systems; a sophisticated calendar; a sophisticated astronomical science; and a highly developed writing system (Phillips 2006, 33). The Maya were also known as the most peaceful of the Mesoamerican civilizations though at the same time, their games were especially violent with captives playing for their lives and using human heads instead of rubber balls, their city-states made war with each other, and they sacrificed their captives to the gods (Waldman 1988, 127). Whatever the truth may be, the Maya were able to develop a flourishing civilization.

BELIEFS ABOUT DEATH AND THE AFTERLIFE

As was true of the Aztecs, the Maya believed that a steady stream of human victims was necessary to appease the gods and that their approach to investigate the human spirit's destiny ranks alongside the *Egyptian Book of the Dead* and the *Tibetan Book of the Dead* (Phillips 2006, 78). Like the Aztecs, the Maya believed that some would progress to a life of heavenly ease, but unlike the Aztecs the Maya vision was of shaded trees, drinking chocolate, and leisure, but the great majority of the dead were doomed to the dark and dangerous realms of the underworld where they would face trials and tribulations at the hands of foul and sadistic divinities (Phillips 2006, 78–79). Like the Hopi who saw the Kiva as the doorway to the next life, the Maya built great plazas to mimic lakes. The Maya believed that the voyage to the underworld began on water and often depicted nobles traveling in canoes on water to start their journey to the next life (Phillips 2006, 79).

METHODS OF DISPOSAL

In the Maya culture, both the rich and the poor were buried with the intention of helping them on their journey to the next life as was the practice in most ancient civilizations. Death retuned the Maya to where they came from, not just to their neighborhoods, but to the cluster of houses where they grew up and even to the home in which they were born beneath whose floor they would be buried (Restall and Solari 2020, 59). People were buried with the tools of their trade, such as hunters with spears, fishermen with harpoons and nets, nobles with generous supplies and even helpers, crafts people with the tools of their trade, and so forth (Phillips 2006, 79). A priest or a scribe might be buried with hieroglyphic books, royalty might be buried in a splendid royal tomb beneath a towering pyramid filled with the sacred wealth of treasure, while the poor might have a jade bead in their mouth, small carved statues, a few pieces of pottery, or some beads (Restall and Solari 2020, 60).

CONCLUSIONS

The emergence of the Maya took place at around the same time as the Old World militarized states of China, Rome, India, Greece, and Persia, and the other Mesoamerican and Andean militarized states. The Maya civilization rather than being a military dominated state was a series of ritualized states. Though many of the city-states warred with each other, the Maya were not characterized as a military state. In both the Old World and in the New World, the change from hunting and gathering took thousands of years, While many scholars would dismiss the comparisons of the Maya and the Greeks and other Old World civilizations, the Maya were able to construct enormous pyramids, spectacular monuments, develop writing and other scientific advancements, and to have thriving cities of more than 150,000 which had lasting influence on those societies around them as did the Greeks, Romans, Egyptians, and others. Perhaps the biggest difference between the Maya and the Old World civilizations would be found in the system of social class. In the Old World, the development of technology, writing, advances in agriculture, and so forth improved the lives to some degree of the larger population, whereas in the Maya civilization, the advances in technology, writing, and so forth greatly improved life for the elites, but for the larger population, they were left behind still living a Stone Age lifestyle.

As with most civilizations, scholars focus upon the elites and how they lived when they study a civilization. There is little doubt that the hallmarks of the Maya culture were its spectacular buildings, sprawling cities, intriguing texts, stunning carvings and paintings, dazzling architecture and art, which have presented a distorted view of the ancient Maya (Restall and Solari 2020, 57). The way of life and how the nonelite Maya lived were far more simple and filled with challenges, ever present death, hard work, disease, suffering, and forced labor. Yet the power of their religious beliefs sustained their way of life and made it tolerable. While education was limited to the elite, the nonelite did have some opportunities through the priesthood and the military. The Maya were perhaps the most advanced civilization in the Americas at the time of the arrival of the Spanish to their area, yet they were seldom even considered to be an advanced ancient civilization.

Chapter 16

Mounds Builders Disposal and Bereavement Practices

Mounds are found stretching across North America. In just the eastern region of North America, there are thousands of mounds. While there were perhaps as many mounds in the Midwestern region of North America, most of the mounds in the Midwest have been destroyed by the later arriving Europeans who wanted to use the areas where the mounds were found for farmland and other purposes. Many of the mounds were constructed in the shape of animals and at least a few were in the shape of humans. While little is known of the way of life of the early Mounds Builders, they are thought to have established farming, house building, villager life, pottery-making, weaving, some technological advances, and perhaps the most complex and organized way of life of all of the Indians north of Mexico some three thousand years ago (Waldman 1988, 147). The many cultures of the Mounds Builders have left behind a historical record that yields a picture of their way of life.

The Mounds Builders were not a single cultural group, nor were they of the same clan or tribe. There is considerable variety in the practices, style, and form of the mounds that are spread across North America. While there is little consensus on when American Indians first arrived in North America, little has been substantiated about the early history of North American tribes. Perhaps forty thousand years ago, the first tribes began to occupy what is now the United States (Aguirre and Turner 2004, 105). The early Folsom discovery suggested that the early tribes were skilled hunters who destroyed mammoths, muskox, and bison, but they did not keep any records or leave any remains to allow knowledge of what kind of culture and people that they were. Because they were nomadic, they did not build permanent settlements that would have left behind relics or other historical records that would have provided accurate information about their culture and way of life. What has been left behind for study is the enormous number of burial mounds that are scattered from Southern Mexico to the Great Lakes to Florida. There still remains a great deal of controversy surrounding who the Mounds Builders were.

MOUNDS BUILDERS SOCIETY

Many different interpretations of who the Mounds Builders were have been developed. One argument is that the Mounds Builders were a superior group when compared to ordinary American Indian groups and are a vanished people who were of the Israelite tribe of Joseph, and they are the ones who built the mounds (Silverberg 1968, 52–53). Powell (1881) suggests that it was not a single group or tribe who built the mounds and that any search for the original tribe was simply fruitless. Henry C. Schoolcraft (1860), in a masterful six-volume text, argues that there is nothing to suggest that the Mounds Builders had Asiatic or European origins from the artifacts that they left behind nor that any of the tribes who built mounds were in any way connected to each other.

While the Angel site, the Clovis site, the Cahokia site, the Hopewell site, Moundsville (Alabama), and numerous others are similar to each other, there is not adequate evidence of what rituals or attitudes the people who buried their deceased practiced. Nor is there any evidence of social differentiation of those who were buried. The burial mounds do not have the social class differences of burial between the elites and commoners that were found in the Incas, Aztecs, and Maya, for example. By contrast, the mounds range from rooms constructed for burial as in the Angel site to burial in a trash heap in Arizona. While there are thousands of mounds all across North America, much of what was buried has rotted and disappeared leaving behind only things made of stone, copper, shell, and bones that were left behind (Fagan 2000, 409). Most of the mounds that have been excavated are in damp climates that are less likely to leave behind relics, intact bodies, or other funerary items than those in the Southwest. Those in the Anasazi or other regions that have yielded far more items for study. The little information that is available suggests that the peoples who built mounds must have had a farming culture and that they were able to support a large population. It is possible that North American tribes began farming as early as 9,000–11,000 years ago (Terrell 1971, 5). Mounds range in size from small hills to hundreds of acres. Mounds vary in shapes from small mounds of dirt to a pyramid shape (Terrell 1971, 123). They also constructed temple mounds. Monk's Mound at the Cahokia site in what is now Illinois covered over 14 acres and stood 100 feet high in Cahokia, a great village that is believed to have had as many as forty thousand people living in it with the village covering about 4,000 acres (Waldman 1988, 149). In one burial mound, archaeologists have found the remains of 110 young women who were probably sacrifices to the gods (Waldman 1988, 149). The Mounds Builders were able to thrive along the Mississippi and other rivers for hundreds of years.

Mounds vary immensely. Mounds have been found that were constructed with many different materials. Mounds have been constructed with flat stones, dirt, poles, twigs, grass, mud coatings, mud plaster, slab lids, shells, or whatever else that could be used including garbage, and they also contained gifts and supplies for the deceased to use on their journey (Fagan 2000, 410). Rather than being a culture of Mounds Builders, it may be that the existence of mounds was that the various tribes disposed of their dead in similar ways. Lacking shovels or other tools to dig graves, it might have been easier to simply put together graves on top of the ground and to cover them in some fashion. Those who lived in forests were more likely to use logs, while those who lived in rain areas were more likely to use mud. Some tribes built pyramids while others built humps. Typically, not only Mounds Builders, but most tribes have placed goods and gifts in the grave to aid the deceased on their journey to the next life. The Mounds Builders may have placed the gifts and the body on the ground. After the body was covered, it may have created a mound over time. Again, lack of digging tools or whatever could explain their practices.

Little is known about the people who built the mounds in ancient times. The arrival of the Spanish and the French, has yielded some knowledge. The French painter Jacques Le Moyne's depiction of a group of Indians mourning at a chief's burial ground with a mound of a few feet high and a few yards across, containing his body and his great cup with arrows set around it at least, demonstrates some idea of how the mounds were used (Silverberg 1968, 24–25). The explorer Hernando de Soto had earlier found mounds in Florida, Tennessee, Georgia, the Carolinas, Arkansas, Alabama, Mississippi, and Louisiana (Silverberg 1968, 24). In the Ohio/Kentucky area, the Adena/ Hopewell cultures lavished much care upon the dead with log tombs that were built into shallow rectangular pits that were roofed with logs after the burial and dirt piled up on the walls and roof with some being cremated or just buried on their backs with one to as many as three people to a grave (Spencer and Jennings 1965, 60–61). The Adena Indians were primarily hunters and gatherers who found enough game and plants to be able to live in permanent settlements, and they are also thought to have grown sunflowers and pumpkins for food and as well to cultivate tobacco for rituals (Waldman 1988, 147). As with other cultures, burials included grave furniture, objects of value, ornate stone tablets, pipes of stone, animal jaws, and other ritual objects (Spencer and Jennings 1965, 61). The existence of these items in their graves demonstrates the care and respect that the Mounds Builders had for their dead.

While the mounds that were built in the Americas lacked the beauty and elegance of the stone pyramids built in Egypt, the mounds of the Americas are still impressive. The mounds of the Americas are quite diverse. They range from the colossal Cahokia Mound in Illinois which is more than 100 feet high and covers 14 acres to others that were simply piles of earth, but all of the mounds constructed demonstrate that when they were cleared there was regularity and symmetry of shape and contained many artifacts (Silverberg 1968, 10). Studies of the Mississippian era demonstrate that the influence of the Hopewell culture is present with burial mounds and temple mounds being placed side by side with plaza arrangements and rectangular truncated pyramids as a typical plan (Spencer and Jennings 1965, 76). It is speculated that the plaza space between the mounds was used for ceremonies (Spencer and Jennings 1965, 78). The Effigy Mounds which have been found in what is now Illinois, Iowa, Wisconsin, and Minnesota have mostly been destroyed by plowing, looting, and construction, but they ranged from a few feet to rather large effigies of bears, felines, deer, wolves, foxes, buffalos, turtles, eagles, swallows, geese, and with just two have been found that were constructed in human form (Barrett and Markowitz 2004, 258–259).

Perhaps because of being close to the sea, the California Mounds Builders used a far different plan for their mounds. The California Mounds Builders built their mounds quite close to the ocean shores using shell heaps that were either oval or oblong ranging from a few feet deep to over 36 feet deep and from 30 to 600 feet in length with at least thirty being quite large (Nelson 1971, 144–147). What makes these mounds unique from those made by other Mounds Builders is that the construction is made with loose material that has not weathered appreciably over time even though many are below sea level and are often pounded by waves (Nelson 1971, 147). Studies of the shell mounds and their artifacts found that objects found at the top of mounds in later cultures were also found at the bottom from earlier cultures which demonstrates that the people who lived there were hunters, used fire, prepared vegetable foods, fished, made musical devices, used body paint, buried their dead, and over time, were able to learn basketry and skin dressing (Nelson 1971, 156). Unfortunately, most of the mounds have been destroyed by builders and farmers who used the land without concern for the destruction of knowledge of the shell mounds people. As often occurs even today, construction crews often fail to report that they have found relics or other evidence of ancient cultures in their building sites because they know that they will have their construction shut down to allow archaeologists and others to examine the site.

CONCLUSIONS

The various Mounds Builders around the Americas seemed to each have their own ideas on what to include into the burial mounds and what form they would take. Since most have been destroyed, we lack the ability to determine how well they were built and what shape most of them had for designs. While their specific practices and rituals may never be known, it is clear that they went to great lengths to care for their dead.

Chapter 17

The Dine (Navajo) Disposal and Bereavement Practices

One of the more famous tribes, the Navajo, has lived in the Southwest of the United States for hundreds of years. The Navajo, or more properly, the Dine or Dinah, which translates as "the People," are the largest tribe in the United States who also live on the largest reservation. Like the Apache or Inde and the Sioux with many names like Lakota, Dakota, and so forth, the name for the tribe known as the Navajo is not what they have traditionally called themselves. The word Navajo was not even used in their language (Terrell 1974, 47). The Dine reservation spreads across four states: New Mexico, Arizona, Colorado, and Utah. Because most of the reservation is a mile or so above sea level, it is rarely brutally hot in the summer and offers quite cool nights for sleeping, but in the winter, "Navajoland" can be quite cold and can have severe weather.

The Dine are of the Athapascan linguistic group. Although their language was spoken by many other tribes, the Dine did not speak many other languages or even use sign language; but rather, they did use gestures to make points. As English is the universal language for communicating in many countries around the world, the Dine language is the universal language of their region. The Dine language is one of the more difficult languages to learn. Perhaps, that is one of the reasons that it was chosen to be used as a code during World War II. While other tribes and their languages were also used as code talkers, the Navajo or Dine have become the most famous tribe for their work as codetalkers. The movie *Windtalkers* helped spread the awareness of their importance. Their language is entirely differently from the other Southwestern languages with words from their northern heritage where they fished and used boats (Underhill 1956, 4). The word that they use for the flight of an owl is one from the north which meant to paddle a canoe (Underhill 1956, 5). Traditionally, the Dine had only one day of the week with a name which was Sunday. The other days were counted before or after Sunday. They also did not have swear words. To insult someone would be to call them a coyote or say that they are not acting like a Navajo. Such a language certainly confused the Japanese during World War II. The Dine can express very complex ideas using a single word which makes it very difficult language to translate into English or any other language.

While the exact time of their arrival in the Southwest is not known, nor is it known if they came across the Bering Straits to journey to the Southwest or rather as they teach, from the center of the earth. Perhaps, they did come from below from the underworld where there was no light from the sun or stars (Coolidge 1930, 3). The Dine are generally a loosely knit group of individualists. The extended family is the basic unit of social organization that is part of the larger community. It is also matrilineal and matrilocal where the man belongs to the clan of his mother, and in his wife's home, he is a permanent guest unless his wife decides to divorce him. Since the Dine have had a pattern of borrowing from other cultures, they learned many of the ways of the Pueblo people living in their region. While being more nomadic than the Pueblo people, they did learn to grow corn, to use the Pueblo loom, to grow cotton, and to weave cloth. The Dine religion is basically concerned with maintaining harmony with nature. Ritually, the Dine religion has adapted many of the surrounding Pueblo cultures' ceremonies and rituals. When the Spanish arrived, the Dine were able to have horses, sheep, wool, and ultimately silversmithing.

VALUES AND CULTURE OF THE NAVAJO

The Dine, like all cultures, have rituals and ceremonies as part of their culture. For the Dine, art and religion were intertwined so that a sandpainting or rug or any other art item has a spiritual element (Waldman 1988, 154). The rituals and ceremonies in the dying and funeral process would often involve artistic creations. The intermingling of art and religion is basic to understanding the values and culture of the Dine.

The Dine are known for being friendly, hospitable, and having fun. Humor is a strong part of the culture. As a group, they tend to talk softly. Rarely do they raise their voice. Anger is rare. For teachers, it is important to know that they do not like to be asked direct questions. Dine do not brag on themselves, but they enjoy others saying great things about their deeds and accomplishments. Most people whether Dine or not find it quite satisfying when others extol their knowledge or skills. It is considered improper behavior to show affection in public. Traditionally, there was no police to enforce their many norms of behavior. One is expected to be a Dine and act like one without the use of discipline.

Like seemingly all tribes, the Dine are a very religious people. God(s) are democratic, industrious, kind, hospitable, yet unmerciful, subject to human weaknesses and human passions. Evil comes from the wrath of the Dine or the people from animals, winds, and lightening. Disease and death are caused by those who are evil or as a consequence of witchcraft, spells, and dreams. One encounters evil by two forms of worship: one against evil and one for blessings. Ceremonies that are against evil also include blessing ceremonies, but blessing ceremonies do not always include those against evil. God as the creator of all things is an idea not known to them. Nor is the idea of heaven or hell. The Dine believe in a life after death where there will be happiness with peoples of the lower worlds who are deceased. The dead may hurt the living. Death does not represent the end of life, but a journey to the next life.

The Dine do not have the type of stratification that is found in the Anglo-European world. Leaders are equal to other members of the clan and not their superiors. As a democratic culture, leaders remain leaders as long as they continue to have the support of their people. The Dine were not a war-like people. Dine society is based primarily on kinship established by clan affiliation. Children are protected from death and other social ills. When a person is dying, he or she is taken from the Hogan where he or she lives to an unused Hogan or to a neighboring shelter. While some suggest that this is because they are afraid of the spirit of the dead person, but Dine people would argue that it is to allow the spirit of the dead person to begin the journey more quickly and easily. The goal is to keep the spirit from lingering around the Hogan. They would dress the dead person in his or her finest clothes and jewelry. If one is poor and does not have fine clothes and jewelry, others in the clan will provide it. The person will be dressed in the finest apparel regardless of the cost or pain that may be caused by burying valuable items. Only adult members of the family and those tending to them will remain with the dying person. As death nears and hope wanes, all but one or two will leave. Only those closest to the dying will remain to possibly expose themselves to the evil effects of death.

Usually, an older male relative, father, maternal uncle, or male cousin; and the mother, the mother's sister, or female cousin, is expected to be the chief mourner. If there are no men, then women will take care of the body. If there are no clan relatives, then the deceased person's spouse's relatives would take care of the body. If there is no spouse or relatives, then someone can be hired to take care of the body. Since one's clan is on the mother's side, one of the mourners would be from the clan and one from the father's clan. It is sometimes difficult to find people willing to take care of the dead body. Generally, it is considered to be a duty to take care of the dead. The care of the dead is performed for the sake of the dead relative, but it is hardly an honor. Children are not allowed to be part of the process, and most other adults avoid the process as well. The death ceremonies are complex but fascinating. The rituals must be performed properly to protect the mourners from harm. After the ceremonies, mourners are expected to take part in cleansing ceremonies to protect themselves from harm. Grief is the cause of great weeping in the Dine culture. A mother will weep for the loss of a child for a long time. One will cry at the death of a friend or relative, but it should not last.

Dine men tend to grieve more silently than Dine women. Deep depression is common. It is not unusual for a man to not be able to return to work or "normal" life for an extended period of time. Women seem to focus more on the grief of others than on their own grief. They often encourage men to find the strength within themselves to return to life. Women are also more vocal in their grief than men. They are more likely to cry publicly than men. Like the British, Germans, and many other tribes, men are expected to be strong and not as public with their grief. Dine children are less sheltered from death during their early years than are Anglo-European children (Leighton and Kluckhohn 1969, 39). Dine children also have far more community support in their grief than Anglo-European children in part due to their extended clan and closeness to their grandparents and other relatives.

To be an elder is honored in American Indian cultures. For the Dine, maturity and old age will bring prestige and authority, but if senility or Alzheimer's sets in, the elderly lose their esteemed status. The elderly have a special relationship with children. Like White grandparents, they are indulgent and giving to grandchildren. The traditional Dine child would spend more time with the mother's parents than the father's parents as long as the mother, her sisters, and her parents are still alive. Grandparents generally have much more say about the training and raising of children than in the Anglo-European world. Children may even live in the Hogan with the grandparents rather than the parents for a time. In the Anglo-European world, the actions of grandparents toward grand children would often be viewed as interference and the cause of tension. By spending more time with grandparents, Dine children spend less time with other Dine children. Grandparents are also known forgiving tasks to their grandchildren. They may be asked to tend sheep, do chores, and basically to serve the needs of the grandparents. Unlike the Anglo-European culture, the mother is the dominant parent. Fathers are neither the source of discipline or of authority. Fathers seem to have no problem with this arrangement. The mother's clan is the dominant family in a child's life. If parents' divorce or otherwise separate, the child stays with the mother or her family. The absent or missing father is common. Unlike the Anglo-European culture, children are not taught to resent the missing father. Children may feel that the father is less dependable than their mother, but it is not viewed as a great failing or cause for dislike of the father. Children are taught that to be disobedient to one's parents will lead to unhappiness. Many Dine stories and tales have that theme. Like many cultures, children are taught to always be kind to one's mother. Unlike the Anglo-European culture, sisters remain close even after they become adults. Historically, they might have even shared a husband. Today, many still feel responsible for their sisters economically and socially. This closeness is not as common for brothers. Brothers move to the clan of their wife when they marry. This means that they are less close after becoming an adult. They are also economically independent. One sister might feel responsible to help her sister out of debt, but not her brother. Brothers will help each other as brothers would in the Anglo-European world. When an estate is divided among children, a sister will often be expected to maintain the sheep or land or whatever of a brother. Even the brother's inheritance will go to the sister's children at the expense of his own children. Brothers are also expected to help sisters instruct and rear her children. It is likely that when a death occurs, the brother will tell the children and explain grief and rituals to the children.

Dine children typically grow up in very isolated conditions. Yet, perhaps because of the traditional Dine culture is remarkably inquisitive, they ask lots of questions about things that Anglo-European people would not ask. Though they are isolated, they seem to be aware of world news. Of course, today, many Hogans or the nontraditional house next to the Hogan will have a satellite dish. While not yet common, internet is likely to increase that knowledge as internet becomes available to the isolated homes on the large reservation. Children are taught that one does not ask questions that would embarrass people which is important for teachers to become aware of this norm. Grief is a source of possible embarrassment. Like the Hopi, the Dine rarely talk about grief with those who are not Dine. Even though the child may have significant questions, they will often not ask the person who is grieving because they have been taught to respect adults and particularly the elderly. Because respect is carefully taught, children learn to respect elders for the respect that they receive from others. Grandparents are given a lot of respect. The child will listen to what they have to say about life, death, and grief. Throughout the life span the Dine passively accept death and other traumas of life. It is often difficult to know what a Dine is feeling. Withdrawing into oneself is a common response to grief and loss. Women are more likely than men to cry openly, especially mothers and sisters. Men also cry, but more often not publicly. Men and women both are likely to have prolonged periods of nonproductivity and loss of interest in life and its pleasures. It may be months before the grandfather returns to his craft or sheep or whatever. Mothers and sisters, in part because they normally do much of the work, typically continue to work during loss and grief. A child will typically withdraw for shorter periods of time than an adult. Life is interesting and much remains to be learned. Children return to their curious ways more quickly than adults.

Dine time is also different than Anglo-European time. Most Dine have excellent memories. They can tell stories and tales of events at great length. They are not so good at remembering dates, anniversaries, one's age, and what happened on what day. They are frustrating to lawyers when they testify because they can remember with great detail an event, but they cannot say when it occurred with any degree of accuracy. Events are related to other events. A Dine can often say that the event occurred when so and so was born, or when we visited the mountain, or it was during lambing time, or whatever. Even remembering one's own age is often a problem. One may remember that an event occurred with grandfather died or some other personally important life transition. This seems to make grief more manageable.

Dine are known for their ability to enjoy life, for laughing, and for having a good time. Yet, at the same time, the Dine are also known for worrying and sadness. Like White people, they are often preoccupied with questions of health and illness and worry that loved ones will become ill and die. Life is precarious, and bad things do happen to good people. At the same time, there is a joy in living each day. Perhaps, because children are protected from the trials and tribulations of life, life seems harsher as they grow older. Adults seem to crave social support. One is taught not to brag on oneself, but it seems that most want others to do the bragging. Dine are often described as moody, but my own experience is that they are quite stable. The Dine religion may be part of the explanation. Things happen for a reason. Bad things may happen because you have offended a ghost or someone put a curse on you.

The Dine believe that life begins when the wind enters your body through your ears and ends when it leaves your body through your fingers (Leighton and Kluckhohn 1948, 91). Perhaps, the Dine obsession with wind led to that belief. Because being sensitive to the wind is important for hunters who must approach their prey who can better smell them if the wind is strong and in their direction, the Dine describe the wind as holy and that the holy wind is within and without of all bodies (Nabokov 2006, 129). Death is the end of all good things. The Dine do not look forward to life in the next world as a reward for good deeds in this life. At best, life in the afterworld is uninviting. As surely as life enters your body through your ears and leaves through your ears, you can expect life to be full of both good and bad things. The universe is silent. Why complain about the weather, you cannot change the weather. You do not need to talk about all of the events of the universe. It is what it is. Evidence is all around. The stories and tales of your childhood provide answers that science cannot give. Our inner and exterior life must be in balance. What I am is on the inside. The Dine are generally better than Anglo-European people at sensing the feelings, including grief and loss of other people. Words do not need to be spoken to the person who is grieving. Silence is not bad as in the Anglo-European world.

The difficulty with discussing the Dine reactions to death across the life span is that the Anglo-European culture has changed that story for most, if not all Dine families. For most, both cultures impact their way of life. Anglo-European patterns of grief and loss have become more common among those who live and work in the Anglo-European world. Yet, the traditions still have meaning. Those who remain on the 17 million acres of the Dine reservations generally are more likely to live the old ways of the people.

CULTURAL BELIEFS OF THE NAVAJO

American Indians did not have a name for the continent that is now called America nor did they call themselves Indians. Their land was taken and divided among the Europeans who "discovered" their land. Of course, the American Indian's peoples knew that it was here before the Europeans came. The Dine believe that they emerged from the center of the earth already fully human. Before the beginning of time, "the people" were with the holy people who are supernatural beings with supernatural powers. It is from this underworld that all things were created. Ceremonies and rituals were created at that time to help the human beings to be in a state of balance or harmony. Ceremonies and rituals were also created to help the human beings to restore their balance or harmony when they lost it. Illness, disharmony, and even death are mainly caused by offending spirits, curses, or being out of balance in one's life. One could also get ghost sickness by touching dead bodies, disinterring a body, misuse of sacred objects or ceremonies, neglecting ritual or ceremony, or tampering with witches or witchcraft.

The Dine have been able to maintain a relatively more consistent culture than the Apache or Inde. The Dine would steal and capture not only goods and technology but also people. They would marry them and borrow the cultural ways as well (Terrell 1974, 46). While it is not known whether the Dine moved to the Anasazi lands or were descendants of the Anasazi, but they choose not to inhabit their deserted big towns. Instead, they built their traditional Hogans of mud, logs, bushes, and sticks (Terrell 1974, 45).

Like the Inde, the Dine believe that illness has a spiritual basis. The Dine also believe that the Great Spirit would never put an illness on the earth without also making a remedy for it (Leighton and Kluckhohn 1948, 39). The shaman's task is to name the disease and to find a cure for it. A person becomes ill by breaking a taboo, an attack of a witch, offending a ghost, or by failing to live one's life in balance. For the Dine, the hatqali, chanter, or shaman is the person who knows the chants, songs, and requirements of the chants. An elderly shaman will choose someone to learn the ways of the chanter. They will often choose a son, brother, or other male relative. After many years of study, the chosen one may also become a chanter. It could take as long as eight years to learn the songs and methods of painting in the sand (Shorris 1971, 177).

Like the shaman of the Inde and the Sioux, the Dine healer may refuse requests for services. The healer may refuse after discerning the cause of the illness and the condition of the patient. Most of the time, the chanter will accept the patient. Usually, women do not serve as chanters, but some are able to be chanters. Often women learn a great deal about medicine and are sought by the shaman to use their medicines to heal. If the chanter can't find the cause of the illness, a diviner may be called upon. After the treatment, the shaman will perform a sing for the person. Each person who performs a task in the healing ritual will expect to be given fee for his or her services.

The ceremonies and rituals of the Dine are very complex and must be performed accurately to ensure success. It may take as long as three or four years to learn just two ceremonies (Steiger 1984, 49). Some rituals may last for as long as nine days, and each part of the ritual must be recited accurately from memory. If the healer fails to chant even a small part of the ritual or omits a detail from a sandpainting, or neglects a detail from a prayer stick, it is believed that the patient will die.

The practice of the motion of the hand is one of the gifts of the diviner. Like those searching for water, the diviner knows when the hand needs to move in a certain way, when that the cause of the disease has been found, and what might be done to cure it. Sandpaintings, star gazing, and other ways are often used to discover the cause of an illness. Like the Lakota, the Dine listen to learn. What they hear may also tell them the cause of the illness. As with the Inde and the Lakota, the goal is to achieve harmony or balance.

The Dine may have the most complex healing rituals of any tribe. Many items ranging from charms, sandpaintings, cornmeal paintings, prayer sticks, masks, and many more are used. Dine ceremonies are far more unchanging and traditional than most other tribes. Modern Dine generally recognize that their traditional healing rituals are not as effective against "Anglo-European" diseases. If you have a heart attack, you would likely have your family take you to a hospital and not to a healer. Like many other tribes, the Dine use both Anglo-European medicine as well as their own traditional medicine to try to manage disease today.

DEATH AND BURIAL PRACTICES

Many who have studied the Dine suggest that they are afraid of the dead. Perry writes that the dead are viewed as objects of horror that must be buried with elaborate precautions to protect the living from having problems with the ghosts of the dead (Perry 1991, 99). Habenstein and Lamers saw that fear as coming out in the belief that people must even avoid whistling after dark to avoid attracting ghosts (Habenstein and Lamers 1963, 704). Weiss-Krejci applied it to the Dine taboo against touching anyone whose body has been struck by lightning, killed by a tornado, or drowned (Weiss-Krejci 2013, 286). Many Dine deny these claims and instead suggest that it is out of honor for the dead that these practices have emerged. Most dead are not to be feared.

Those who prepare and bury the dead must themselves prepare by going through cleansing rituals. The rituals may include removing one's clothes and bathing, covering oneself with a yucca leaf, using sign language to communicate, and eating only certain foods (Habenstein and Lamers 1963, 704). After the arrival of the Europeans, the Dine would ask a White person who may serve as a teacher or missionary to the tribe to do the burial. If that was not possible, then the Dine might hire another Dine who is not a relative or clan member to conduct the burial and other duties (Leighton and Klockhohn 1948, 92). Today, most would simply hire a funeral director to perform the preparation and burial. Traditional ceremonies are often combined with Christian ceremonies, but most who still live on the reservation use more traditional rituals.

Burial practices can vary immensely. Traditionally, depending upon the age of the deceased, the Dine chose two or four people to be mourners for the deceased. One of these would typically be a close relative or member of the clan of the deceased. Another would often be from the clan of the father, wife, or husband of the deceased. One of the mourners would be chosen to direct the rites. They would bathe the body, dress it in fine clothes, and put the right moccasin on the left foot and the left moccasin on the right foot. If the person was not removed from the Hogan before death, the body will be taken out of the Hogan through a hole that was made in the North side of the Hogan. The door of a Hogan is on the East to allow the sun to greet those who live there. Depending upon the view of the spirit of the deceased, the Hogan may or may not ever be used again. If the person was not a good person in life, he or she would not be expected to help the survivors in death. Traditionally, the mourners would carry the body to the burial site in a prescribed fashion using only sign language to communicate. The mourners will bury the body in a deep hole far from the Hogan and place in the grave the saddle, blankets, jewelry, and other treasures with the body, and they would also kill the horse at the gravesite and leave it and the tools used to dig the grave broken on the gravesite as well (Habenstein and Lamers 1963, 705). As with the custom of taking the dying person from the Hogan, it is believed that the horse should be killed and buried along with the body and possessions so that the spirit of the dead person can move on with its journey.

Each of the four mourners would have specific tasks. One would lead the horse carrying the possession of the one who died to the gravesite. Two would carry the body. The fourth would warn those that that might meet along the way who might cross the death line to not cross the death line or the circle route taken with the body until the four days of mourning are completed (Habenstein and Lamers 1963, 706). Mourners are also expected to remain quiet, to not spit, to avoid turning even a stone on its side, to skip and hop on their return, to avoid stepping on a cactus or brush and to return by a different route so that the ghost, chindi, cannot follow (Habenstein and Lamers 1963, 706).

The Dine traditionally buried valuable items with the body which makes grave robbing a problem. To rob a grave was a serious offense. Those who rob graves take significant risk of getting ghost sickness, which could even kill them. Since the ghost of the deceased is at the very bottom of the grave, those who rob graves must purify themselves after robbing a grave before they can touch another person (Habenstein and Lamers 1963, 706). Grave robbery led to the practice of not marking graves, but the presence of broken shovels generally gave the secret away.

During the mourning period, mourners may kill horses or sheep, break dishes, destroy the Hogan, avoid eating, and other ways to manage their grief. Family members might weep silently in another Hogan, people may remain apart for four days of the mourning period, while other mourners will purify themselves with the smoke of a sage fire (Leighton and Kluckhohn 1948, 91–92). Should the ground be too hard to dig during the winter weather, the body would be placed in the Hogan, and the Hogan would be crushed in on top of the body (Leighton and Kluckhohn 1948, 93). Like the Inde, the Dine speak very little when mourning, while men might embrace one another and cry together, women would hold one another's hands and cry together (Basso 1970, 228). All cultures find ways to give support to the grieving.

Dine death beliefs are filled with dreams, omens, and portents relating to death and to the dead. The Dine do not have a belief in a glorious afterlife for the soul, but rather have a vague conception of an afterlife as an ephemeral and shadowy existence with an end to all that is good (Habenstein and Lamers 1963, 703). Not only is death to be avoided as long as possible, but those who are dead could be a threat to the living. Homes of the dead may be haunted as are the ruins of the Anasazi and other ancient peoples. The Ghostway and Ghost Dance rituals are used to stave off offended ghosts (Wyman 1970, 2). All ghosts are feared. The dead are thought to be the source of all sickness and disease whether physical or mental. Holy Way Chants, Life Way Chants, Ghost Dance rituals, astrological rituals, and other rituals are used to manage malevolent ghosts. Even the Hogan is constructed and blessed with an awareness of astronomical directs and concern for the traditions of the past (Monroe and Williamson 1987, 29).

In recent years, the Dine no longer use many of their traditional ways to disposing of their dead. As suggested earlier, today, the preparation and burial of the dead is given to Anglo-European people whenever possible. Reservation and boarding schools have been provided with coffins or at least lumber for them, and staff members have taken responsibility for burial (Leighton and Kluckhohn 1948, 93). Sadly, many of those same schools abused and mistreated their students and may have caused the deaths of many of them. Since World War II, even more changes have occurred. Since Anglo-European soldiers were publicly buried with honor, the Dine gave their own dead soldiers public burial (Underhill 1956, 242).

After the death, the Hogan in which one died is often burned unless the person was moved outside before he or she died. After the person dies, the family will sit for four days facing east and chant prayers to help his or her soul on its journey. Friends wait on them and take care of the dead body. The last ceremony is that the purification of the family will take place. The prayers end with, "In beauty, it is finished."

CONCLUSIONS

The Dine have been able to maintain their traditional language and much of their traditional way of life. The Dine reservation spreads across parts of four states. While lacking adequate roads, water, housing, schools, and so much more, the Dine remain a proud people who have shown resilience in the face of colossal attempts to end their way of life and to take their land from them. Their kinship system remains strong! They have organized and have adapted to the ways of the dominant culture, yet they still manage to maintain their traditional culture. At the same time, the Dine struggle with the vast distances between towns, lack of roads, services, internet, and so much more. While there is knowledge of their bereavement and burial practices, there are rituals and practices that they prefer to remain sacred and not shared. I have chosen to honor that tradition.

Chapter 18

The Inde (Apache) and Tohono O'odham Disposal and Bereavement Practices

The Apache or Inde are thought to have entered the southwest over three thousand years ago. They are thought to have been a nomadic band of the Athapascan language-speaking group who were known for being fierce fighters. The Inde were the last of the hostile tribes to submit to the Whites. While there is debate as to when and where the Apache arrived, as with the Dine, they quickly left their mark as a fierce tribe. Like the Dine, the Inde engaged in banditry, but unlike the Dine, they also engaged in warfare as a way of life. It is necessary and important to remember that the Europeans were the invaders of the Inde homeland. The hostility of the Inde (Apache) was their way to protect their families, their homelands, and their way of life.

The American Indians on the Eastern coastal areas at first welcomed the European settlers. The atrocities that we associate with the "Indian" wars occurred on both sides as happens in all wars. Our uniformed stereotypes of American Indians as wild savages or as Indians fighting losing battles with cowboys and the Calvary keep us from appreciating the oratory, beautiful languages, and humanity that American Indians have shown to one another. Like the Maya, Mounds Builders, and many other groups, the Inde are not one tribe but are spread among many clans.

WHO ARE THE APACHE?

Historically, the early Inde were nomadic raiding bands that were part of particular clans that used the mountains and canyons for protection and concealment. Like the Dine, the Inde had a strong clan system. Rather than raising their own crops, they stole them from other tribes and after the arrival of the Europeans they stole from the Spanish ranchers and White settlers. By the time that the Spanish arrived around 1540, the Inde were already known as raiders and murderers by the Pueblo Indians and other tribes living in the region. The Inde were described as masters of concealment and combat. The discovery of gold in California led many to cross Inde land which caused the Inde to feel greatly endangered. For the next forty or so years, Inde led by Cochise, Geronimo, Diablo, and Mangas Colorado also known as Mangas Coloradas led their people against the soldiers who battled to kill, subdue, and force them on reservations. By 1875, most of the Inde had been rounded up and forced onto reservations, but many refused to either go there or to stay on reservations. With the surrender of Geronimo in 1886, the Inde subdued. Most Inde today live on reservations in New Mexico and Arizona. Their cultural history of individualism and aggressive ways has continued to be a part of their culture and has led to them being able to have more say in tribal governance and in business ventures.

INDE CULTURE AND WAY OF LIFE

The Inde or Apache have been a dynamically evolving tribe in the United States. There are sixty-two clans with twenty-seven being active today call themselves Inde or Apache. For the most part, they still live on a few reservations including the Jicarilla, Mescalero, Fort Apache, and San Carlos in New Mexico and Arizona. Among the Inde there are seven basic clans. The word Apache comes from the Spanish word Apachu which means enemy (Terrell 1971, 47). The Apache call themselves, "the People." This is translated the same as Lacotah or Dakotah or Dine or Inuit—all meaning "the people." The Jicarilla and Mescalero Apaches seem to have borrowed from the Plains Indians and lived in tipis, wore braids, and used buckskin for clothing as did the Plains Indians. The Chiricahua and other Inde groups lived in wickiups which are basically grass and bush covering over young trees. Unlike the Dine, the Inde historically did not develop arts and crafts to any extent. They did develop utilitarian crafts. Each Inde group developed its own baskets, pots, and so forth. Rather than being decorative, the items were functional. Unlike most other tribes, the Inde believed that natural colors were beautiful and did not change the color of baskets, pots, or skins from their natural colors. The revival of interest in American Indian arts and crafts in the 1960s led to a resurgence of basket weaving, the introduction of "Navajo rug dyes," and as prices increased the adoption of other crafts as well. For more information on Inde or Apache basket weaving, see Roberts (1931) and Mason (1904).

   The Inde culture is not a simple culture. To be an Apache is not a traditional part of the culture. As noted, the word Apache was not used by the tribe itself. It means enemy and was used by their foes to describe them. Like the Dine, the Inde are a matrilineal and matrilocal society that trace their descent through the female side and like the Dine will have the groom move in with his wife's people (Sherman 1996, 104). Their childrearing practices were thought to be permissive and lacking in discipline by the Anglo-Europeans. Boarding schools sought to impose discipline, order, and "the Protestant Ethic" upon their children. Rather than having formal schools, the Inde grandmothers instruct their grandchildren on the proper ways of the people. Girls were considered to be more valuable to the tribe than boys. Both receive the same physical training on foot and on horseback as they grow toward becoming adults (Sherman 1996, 124). Unlike the Dine who developed into a single tribe, the Inde developed into several divisions or tribal groups. The Inde are not one tribe; their ways are not the same for all groups. The Western Apache are noted for their lack of words. As with other tribes and clans, the Inde believe that words themselves have the power to make things happen. Prayers, poems, songs, and spells are not differentiated. All words have spiritual powers to cause things to happen. One rarely sings or says poems for entertainment. Sings and other word forms are used in ceremonies and in times of crises and for any undertaking in one's life. Other clans and tribes have their own cultural orientation and way of life.

FACING ILLNESS AND DEATH AS AN APACHE

If a person is suffering from an illness or injury, he or she might be "sung over." In describing the healing ceremonies of the Inde, Basso suggests that when one is the object of a ceremony, it is considered wrong to talk to the person (Basso 1970, 228). Silence is an important virtue for the Inde. The only people who are able to talk to the patient are the shaman and the relative who is in charge of the ceremony. The patient only speaks openly when he or she is asked to pray. Imagine their surprise when a nurse or physician asks the Inde patient questions about their pillow, medicine, food, health, well-being, or to fill out forms while they are receiving treatment in a hospital.

As with most other tribes, the patient or the family will ask the shaman to do a ritual or ceremonial when some is suffering from illness or injury. Like the Dine, the Inde shaman may or may not accept an invitation to do a ceremonial. If the shaman accepts, then a ritual will be performed. Like the Dine, the Inde seem to have a fear of the dangers of witchcraft, animals that could cause misfortune, and the evil that may result from failing to properly respect the supernatural forces and supreme deities that watch over humans (Sherman 1996, 135). Disease has a cause. Those who can cause disease can assume the form of a snake or owl, enter our dreams, or materialize as a ghost and cause one to suffer from disease and illness or other forms of misfortune (Opler 1941, 229–232). The job of the shaman is to counteract their evil, to exorcise the harm that might be associated with the rituals, and to manage the elaborate ceremonies such as sandpaintings, which like the Dine are destroyed after the healing ritual (Parezo 1983, 19–21). For a more complete description of the healing ritual, read Opler (1941).

For the non-Inde who might be invited to attend a curing ceremony, the ceremony will usually begin in the early evening and continue until nearly dawn of the next day. Some ceremonies might last as long as four days. Normally close friends and relatives attend the ceremonies. The rituals typically do not include children.

Like the Dine, the Inde are described as having a great fear of death and communicate this fear to children at an early age. While many Inde deny this fear, it continues to be a part of most works on the subject. The Inde also practiced methods with children that are generally not recommended today by thanatologists, such as not allowing children to be around the dying or even viewing the dead and preventing children from associating with other children who are grieving until they have been cleansed (Tiller 1983, 18). The Inde generally believe that children should be protected from the ravages of illness and death. When an Inde dies, he or she prefers to die alone if possible. Children would rarely be present.

If ceremonies last more than one day, they are typically last from dark until after midnight. There will be abundant food provided by the patient's relatives. There will be numerous ritual articles that are fully described in Opler (1941) that will be used in the ceremony. The shaman will sing, pray, and perform various rituals to try to determine what are the causes of the illness or injury and what can be done to overcome the injury or cure the illness.

The ceremonies are often quite loud. Music is associated with the supernatural and religious life in all civilizations, and it is a therapeutic tool that promotes a religious attitude that encourages spiritual development (Lewis and Hughs 1997, 46). The drum is the heartbeat of the earth that creates a sound as old as the earth and beats within each of us as our heart (Gustafson 1997, 94). Music is a basic part of American Indian way of life. It is used to treat the sick, to win wars, to hunt animals, and in everything that requires extra strength, cunning, or ability. While the dominate cultures influence has lessened the ceremonial significance of the merits of music, it still has great appeal and is viewed as having ceremonial power. Like the Dine, for the Inde, every ceremony and ritual is conducted to accomplish a specific purpose (Terrell 1972, 57). Rituals and ceremonies not only aid those who need healing, but they also enhance the sense of community among those who are involved in them.

Everyone from the shaman to the patient to the participants gains from the healing rituals and ceremonies. If the patient dies, it was because it was the person's time to die or that the spirits were simply too strong. If one lives or dies, it was meant to be. Suffering is a natural part of life. Each person must confront whatever destiny each faces and all must eventually face death with a spirit of acceptance (Starkloff 1974, 119–121). Most Inde view the illness of the Spanish and other European people as being too strong for the shaman and that if the shaman does not cure these diseases, the shaman is not at fault (Stoekel 1993, 29).

Like the Dine, the Inde are thought of as being a gay people who love to laugh and always seem to appreciate something funny and are forever joking and laughing (Goodwin 1942, 556). The Inde are also known to use clowns and dancers to keep illness away (Opler 1941, 276–279). The Inde use strong communications, humor, music, art, and social support to help cure those with illnesses and injuries.

The Inde believe that when a person dies his or her spirit does not go immediately to the underworld, but rather, the spirit stays around for a while. Therefore, relatives who touch the body are likely to get ghost sickness and may themselves need healing ceremonies conducted for them (Haley 1981, 165). Like most other ancient cultures, the Inde bury their dead with grave goods. One of the reasons given for burying the dead person's goods with their body is to prevent ghost sickness (Cremony 1983, 251). Probably a more important reason to bury a person's goods with them is to honor them and their memory. The Inde also view the human soul as having two components: one was air, vapor, or breath identified with life and which disappears when one dies; and the other is shadow which tends to linger near or at the scene of death and which may appear at night as a ghost (Perry 1991, 33). Like seemingly all groups, the Inde recognize a Supreme Being, but unlike most groups, the Inde do not see the Supreme Being as either benevolent or punitive and therefore, does not worship the Supreme Being, nor do they have any conception of a hereafter similar to the Christian idea of heaven and hell (Terrell 1972, 57). Like any human, the Inde try to prolong their lives but they do not live in morbid fear of dying, but rather the Inde see death as the normal end of the life cycle where they will become one with the cosmos (Terrell 1972, 57). Death is not to be feared, but rather it should be accepted as the natural end to one's life.

When an Inde dies, the dead person's body is dressed in their best clothes, wrapped in a blanket, carried to the hills, placed into a crevice in the rocks, or buried in a shallow grave (Cremony 1983, 251). In early historic eras, cremation was widely used (Perry 1991, 33). For the Western Apache, ashes and pollen would be sprinkled in a circle around the grave beginning at the southwest corner to offer the soul a safe journey to heaven. After which the crevice or shallow grave would be covered to prevent coyotes or other animals from getting to the corpse (Cremony 1983, 250). The Apache would use as small of a place as possible to put the corpse such as a place where a rock had shifted, or a stump had fallen, and then they would put back the rock or stump to cover the body (Cremony 1983, 250). The Inde who pride themselves on caring for those in need, such as the elderly, ill, orphans, and so forth, often leave a jug of water for the deceased to drink. This practice can be traced back to an earlier legend that the Gahan or Mountain Spirit will come to rescue the thirsty and take them to the mountains to dwell with the mountain spirits (Opler 1941, 280).

The Inde held a wake and cried and wailed for the deceased. The Inde would also set aside a part of their fields for the dead and would not cultivate the field for a period of time to honor the deceased (Mails 1974, 221). Like the Dine with the dead person's Hogan, the Inde would sometimes leave the body in the wickiup and push it down on top of the body (Mails 1974, 221). The Chiricahua Apache wives and children would often cut their hair short, cover their faces with mud and ashes, and dance to keep the ghosts from capturing them after the death of a warrior (Mails 1974, 176). The Mescalero Apache saw death as the final foe and did not perform rites upon the death of a loved one (Mails 1974, 393). For all Inde groups, the death of a warrior aroused much grief while the death of the woman seemed almost unnoticed except of intimate friends and relatives (Mails 1974, 174). The Yuma Apache are the only Inde group that used cremation. Not only do they cremate the body, but they also cremated all of the person's possessions including their wickiup. In recent years, funerals and wakes have become customary practice (Perry 1991, 193).

"Being with people who are sad," describes the state of people who are emerging from intense mourning and begin to return to their normal activities as members of the Inde community which suggests that they are still experiencing intense grief, and that if one encounters such people, one generally makes the effort to meet the mourning person with a minimum of speech (Basso 1970, 222). For most deaths, the Inde mourn for a few days and make strong cries. As suggested, they often cut their hair quite short and then continue to mourn until their hair grows out again. The Inde generally believe that intense grief, like intense rage, often produces changes in the personality of the person who experiences it, causing them to likely be disturbed and unstable because of the emotional strain of dealing with death and a sense of irrevocable loss making them abusive, hostile, and physically violent (Basso 1970, 223). Today, the term used to describe such behavior would be traumatic grief.

Like the Dine, the Inde saw death as the enemy and expressed no great desire to be among the dead or their ghosts. Both tribes also view ghosts as being responsible for sickness and death and fear the threat of deceased relatives, and yet, because of their fear of the dead, both tribes felt a tremendous need to properly dispose of the dead to protect themselves (Stoekel 1993,

13). At the same time, the Inde did not have great fears of death or of being dead.

The following is a transcription of an oral history from an Inde (Apache).

My name is_____, and I'm with the Cibecue Apache band, but living here in San Carlos. And, my grandparents are from Camp Verde area and my dad's side of the family is from Cibecue area, the southern part of Cibecue, the Cibecue band, um, known as the Black Hills clan, and uh, my grandmother's clan is the Black Walnut clan. And my dad's clan is Black Hills clan, so, we follow on our mother's side more than on our dad's side. Um, as far as history, don't know too much about it, only from what I learned when I was growing up, when I was five years old, on up, I saw some very highly spiritual dances, um, that I had a lot of questions about, but never got them answered. There was a lot of traditions and customs that, um, were introduced as well and I didn't know anything about it, and again I asked questions, but never got any answers. And sometime when I went away to school, back in 64 to 68 I was in Santa Fe at the Institute of American Indian Arts and graduated from there, but I started reading a lot of books in the library and what I didn't understand I would bring it home in the summer and ask my grandparents if it's true. And they said that part of it is, not all of it. So, to this day when I do my lectures, I tell people, "Don't ask me what year, what month, what day, what hour, what time because we lived day to day." And I think most Native American Indians are like that. We get up early in the morning, just before the sun comes up, have breakfast, put everything away, then go do our daily chores, for lunch probably a light snack and then for the evening um . . . again a light breakfast or a heavy breakfast depending on what type of activity you've done, and then put everything away before the sun goes down because we didn't have any electricity.

But very, very little of history I've heard from my grandmother's talking about Geronimo and that's neither here nor there either, so, it sounded like they didn't care too much for him. But there were some old songs that they sang, and stories they told, very interesting, but I keep that to myself, and I don't tell it unless a subject comes up between different people, or the community members. So, um, so I know very little about the history. In fact, I know the word Apache didn't come from us, or from another tribe, it was an British name that was given to Apaches. Of course, we just call ourselves Inde just like the Navajo call themselves Dine, but again, there is similarity there, it is the same thing.

And the beliefs about dying. I know for a fact that we're not supposed to burn the dead, we're supposed to bury it. We don't believe in reincarnation I don't think, um, there's a lot of beliefs about what's going to happen, now what's not going to happen. But then some people say they're back and they're here, and yet people pray when they die and around when they bury it, and they pray and use different stuff so [woman walks in who he helps] Uh, where was I? Ok, some of the beliefs about dying only the older people have beliefs about dying, but not the younger people. And beliefs as to like when they bury you and they say their prayers and the reason why they say their prayers is that they want you to go to where ever it is you're supposed to be going to. And they believed in that. But now, nobody really cares for that, and a lot of people say, "Well, so and so died a year ago, so we're going to have an anniversary dinner." Well, I don't believe in that anniversary dinner, because that's a white man's way, and it's with us, to my understanding that we're calling that spirit back when it should be on its way to someplace else.

Um, burial practices, most of these are way, way before me so I can't tell you about burial practices. There's a lot of people that tell me what was practiced during the time of the burial, um, the only thing I saw was . . . again, as a young person you're not supposed to go where they're burying somebody, not even your own relative, not even your own sister. You're not supposed to look at it . . . as a young person, so I can't tell you anything on that. Um, grief, I guess the only people who would be grieving would be the elderly or either the mother of the child or the mother, um, if they really liked the person I guess it would be more like a grief I guess, but there again, I . . . . for me I was closer to my mom when she died, and when they brought the body back you're supposed to visit it four times when they bring the body home in the afternoon, then at midnight, and then early in the morning and then just before they head off to church. And that's what my grandmother used to always say.

But, at that time, for me, I was in, I was like a zombie, I didn't know, because I was real close to my mother, um that I didn't even know she died, and again, I don't remember how her funeral went, but the only thing that was upsetting me was my, one of my sisters was very upset with the rest of us, because of greed I guess you might say. And she kept saying, "Well, you guys are going to get this, you guys are going to get that." Oh no, that was my Dad, that was my Dad, because my mom didn't have nothing. It was my dad she was worried about. So, she was yelling at us, in fact I didn't even stay for the mass at the church during my Dad's funeral and I didn't see them bury until after it was all over, and I walked up to the cemetery and said my prayers and then came back down. So, um, afterlife, there's no comment on that one. So . . .

The following is a transcription of a member of the White Mountain Apache tribe at Fort Apache.

Um, my name is _____, *I'm a member of the White Mountain Apache tribe and live here on the Fort Apache Indian Reservation all my life. And uh . . . what I know about tribal history . . . what my mom told me and what other information I got from elders that we've always lived here . . . since time immemorial and we have mountains that are named in Apache and all the way down into Mexico all the way down into to uh . . . to uh . . . to I guess the Northern part of Mexico. And, my mom used to say that the migration of Athabascans are Apache is the other way around. You know, we didn't come from Bering Straits, that's the scientific theory she used to say, because we have our own creation story and that creation story puts us right on this reservation. I guess, uh, we're the only ones that still retained our land during the war. A lot of indigenous people were moved to different areas, but for us we still live on the same reservation our creator gave us. And, uh, our creation story talks about the land base here in this area, and uh, so that's why I knew that we have always been here. I've been working elders for the last I guess ten years and uh, through their knowledge the things that they told me they, you know, it all makes sense that we do come from this area, original people that lived here. Other archaeologists, or other people might argue, but that's another scientific theory to me. It dates back to when the first Spaniards first came. You know, we were here. My ancestors tell me that we were here then, we were up in the mountains and we didn't want to be taken prisoners or didn't want to fight with them. And that's why, you know, we never showed our presence and we were a mountain people and mountain is our sanctuary, and that's why some of the early, um, people who came through here, the Spaniards, um, you know, never wrote about us until later on. So . . . [talks briefly with his wife in background] . . . the archaeologists, several people like that, you know, they might argue about it, but my people tell me. I believe it because these incidents that happened started from here.*

Burial Practices, you know we are a people that are, are uh, that don't associate with the dying, and even talk about them, even mention their name. You know, it was taboo to do that. And even going to the burial grounds, you know, you never take any kids over there, you never take . . . uh . . . you brush yourself off and smudge yourself when you come back to get rid of the "death disease" as they say. And dying, uh, to Apache's we believe in the spiritual world, that we all go there after we die. Our ancestors that fought for this land, you know, they believed that there is a world for us, and, they don't call it hell, you know, there's just, once you die you go to this, uh, "happy hunting grounds" as they say. So, that's what we believed in, and uh, we did what we could to retain our land and, you know, we were called savages, but we are a people of our prayers every day, and uh, that uh, when we die we go to another spiritual world, happy hunting grounds where you live forever. That's what the Apache people believe, and uh,

Burial practices, uh, we only had certain people that did it. I guess they would be considered as, uh, as uh, undertakers nowadays, but there were people that the only thing they did was that because most of the Apache people they have to prepare the body to put it away in crevices back then and there were certain people that did this, and that once you bury a person you don't speak of it anymore. Before you leave you put ashes around the burial and it is a practice that has been done by my people for years and years And uh, you know, you didn't have kids go over there. It's only done by the elders and uh people that were in charge of doing this uh you know we don't have that anymore, that's why you know we take anyone that dies today we take them to the mortuary and uh, and it seems like that . . . that uh . . . that's the way it's done today, you know we don't have anyone that's uh, that does this, that takes care of burial. That was just modern day living, we just take it to them . . . uh . . . people that do these things. And uh, there was a grieving period that for women if they lost . . . if she loses her husband you know she cuts her hair and she doesn't go anywhere, just dresses in dark clothing and, uh, for a year, and uh and they cry, they wail, and uh, some of them don't even go to the grave, because it was taboo to go to the grave.

But now, in the modern-day era you know, you uh, do what's done today, because of armistice day, or memorial day, they go over there and put the flowers on which is done by the non-Indians practice. And now we do, we go to clean up the burial grounds and put flowers on it, which isn't our way at all. But, uh, the grieving period is, uh, you know, it took years, and for a family it took, uh, they don't participate in ceremonies, they don't go out in the public for about a year. And, uh, so, ahh, the same way with the men, I guess if they, if their wife dies, or if their family relatives, you know, they don't go anywhere, they're not seen in public. It's not good to be like that. They say, "They're having fun over there, even though one of their relatives died." Because people say that, you know, so that's why. And then, uh, you know, we, like I said, we are a people of prayer. Everything we did we prayed. And even, I don't know if you heard that [garbled] . . . and even making a (garbled) which is a corn fermented drink, when you make that, you know, you prayed, and that anything you did you prayed. Any baskets you make, any material you make you pray. We're a people of prayers, the morning we get up before the sun comes up, about four o'clock in the morning you stand there and pray, you stand into the east. They say when you do that you know God is more present then, And so, all the witches are asleep at the time, people that are bad people are asleep at that time, they don't get up early. So, you know, that's why the creator is out there. You can, you know, it's more present early in the morning.

And, our people knew who our creator was before the white people came. We have stories similar to the bible for some reason. But, uh, nobody wrote this, my people, they didn't have written stories, it's all oral history, and, uh, they believed that there was an afterlife, and you I just mentioned a while ago that when you die you go through your turquoise bead and you meet your creator on the other side. That's the afterlife, they knew about the dying, where we came from, who our creator was, and uh, you know, we knew about the afterlife, even though we didn't read it anywhere, not, surely, the bible, but we knew about it. And so, we believe in afterlife, even though we were called savages . . . people that call us savages is, uh, people that didn't understand us. We were fighting for our land, you know, our land had been stolen here and there, and . . . uh, bloodthirsty, and that's what . . . uh, to get rid of the foreign people to stop taking our land we had to do that, and still they prayed when they came back, they go into a sweat lodge, before they go to war they go to sweat lodge and pray. When they come back, to cleanse themselves, they pray again.

So, these are the things that we have done, our people of prayer, and to me all indigenous people are like that. They believe in a mother earth that, uh, that we are here to take care of the mother earth and it will take care of us. Even taking the medicine, we have to pray when we do that, so it would be more for the kids coming behind. So, we knew about afterlife, and that we are good people until Columbus came . . . heh heh . . . that's it.

TOHONO O'ODHAM

The Tohono O'odham tribes are of the Pima linguistic group and have been friendly neighbors with the Pima for centuries. Both of their reservations are found in Arizona. Unlike most tribes, the Tohono O'odham live in their ancient homeland. Some scholars suggest that the Tohono O'odham are descendants of the ancient Hohokam agricultural people who irrigated the desert with a series of canals (Rasmussen 2000, 515). The Tohono O'odham believe that they have lived on these lands for ten thousand years. Archaeologists have found relics and other evidence of a modified Hohokam culture living there from the first century to around 1400. While the Tohono O'odham describe themselves as being the descendants of the "ancient ones," who they descended from has not yet been verified. The word "pima" means nothing and the word "Papago" means bean in Spanish. Neither tribe used that name for themselves before the arrival of the Spanish.

THE TOHONO O'ODHAM LIFEWAYS

There is no historical record of where the Tohono O'odham originated. They may be the descendants of the Hohokam canal builders, or just as likely, the enemies of the Hohokam and the cause of their disappearance. The members of the Tohono O'odham tribe are a desert people who live on the Sonora desert south of the Gila River in Arizona. Their largest reservation is in both the United States and Mexico. The Gadsden Purchase of 1853 caused the Tohono O'odham to lose their territory in Mexico, and even though they ignored the international border for many years and were able to keep contact with their relatives and friends living in Sonora, more recent concerns about the border have made that interaction much more difficult (Pritzker 1998, 130).

Living in a desert environment has made life difficult for the Tohono O'odham over the centuries. Being at the mercy of nature to provide them water and food has meant that they have experienced both thriving periods and as well periods of famine and starvation. Their relationship with the Spanish and the U.S. government has generally been positive. With the Pima, they fought with the U.S. troops against the Apaches in the 1860s, they allowed the Anglos to use their waterholes, they lost their best lands when the reservations were formed, and they lost more when the railroad came through their lands, but they gained cattle that were lost by the cattlemen of the area, and they were able to sell their goods to the growing town of Tucson (Pritzker 1998, 130).

Even though they live in a desert environment, they are surrounded by mountains and valleys with freshwater springs and abundant plant life. They were known for their success as farmers, growing beans, corn, and squash. As the people of the Hohokam culture irrigated water from rivers to grow their crops, so, too, did the Tohono O'odham and the Pima which allowed them to grow their squash, tobacco, corn, cotton, and beans, and to be able to live in their permanent villages year round (Waldman 1988, 177). Like the Hopi and many other groups, the Tohono O'odham were dependent upon rain. Because the rain did not always come, they learned to use the many desert plants for food as well.

Perhaps, while corn was their most abundant crop, they were called Papago or "Bean People" by other tribes. They are part of the Pima tribe who lived in the Gila River region. Historically, they were able to trade their excess corn to other tribes in the region for meat and other food items. They were able to recover salt from their lagoons, which was their main trade item. The beans that others named them for were from the mesquite, the saguaro cactus from whose fruits they used to make syrup and preserves. The men hunted deer and other small animals. The Tohono O'odham baskets are expertly made in the style and patterns of the Pima. The neighbors of the Tohono O'odham included other Pueblo tribes such as Jemez, Acoma, Laguna, Tabira, and others; the Apache or Inde, Navajo or Dine, and Yuma who spread from Arizona into Southern California.

Other than their ways of obtaining food, the lifeways of the Pima and the Tohono O'odham are very similar since they both lived in house covered with brush and mud, both had armadas or open areas for socializing, both wore cotton and leather clothing, both wore sandals rather than moccasins, and both made beautiful coiled baskets out of a variety of materials (Waldman 1988, 177). Like those of the Pimas, Tohono O'odham dwellings are circular and built with saguaro and ocotillo ribs and mesquite covered with mud and brush while their ceremonial house are similar, but much larger (Pritzker 1998, 131).

Their first contact with the Spanish was in 1540, but it was not until the late 1600s that they had any extensive contact with the Spanish (Pritzker 1998, 130). When the Spanish arrived, they found a peaceful farming tribe that lived in small villages. They wore cotton clothing that they made themselves after using the wool to make cloth. They also made and wore leather sandals that they made.

Before the Europeans came with their diseases the Tohono O'odham, like other Pima groups, thought that disease came from being out of harmony with the natural world. If one does an act that is an insult to parts of nature ranging from butterflies to bears to the wind and so forth, negative power enters the body causing an illness. Harming an eagle might cause nosebleeds while killing a gopher might cause gastric distress. If it is found that the sickness is caused by being out of harmony with nature, then a shaman performs a ceremony and identifies the source of the illness. Then, a healer, not the shaman, will perform rituals including such acts as using fetishes on the sick person's body, singing, dancing, and possibly sandpainting to help the person recover. Like other Pueblo tribes, the Tohono O'odham had many rainmaking rituals, used masked dancers and sacred clowns, and held annual ceremonies culminating in the summer climax where they drank fermented juice from the saguaro cactus until they were drunk to encourage the rain spirits (Maxwell 1978, 232). Those who have visited their reservations may be away of the saguaro wine feast which is the first public ritual of the Tohono O'odham each year. Typically, families with gather saguaro fruits and make syrup from them. After the syrup is fermented, it becomes wine. The making of wine goes back centuries for the tribe.

The Tohono O'odham had two clans, the Coyote and the Buzzard clans where children took their clan membership from their fathers, and like the neighboring Pima tribe, believed in two main deities, Earthmaker and Elder Brother (Maxwell 1978, 232). While the Pueblo tribes were successful farmers and welcomed the Spanish and later people seeking gold, they were not treated well by their invaders. The Gila River, which was the source of their irrigation for centuries, was drained by the invaders. The Spanish forced them to build their homes and churches and converted them to Catholicism. Today, they mostly work off the reservation. They also face the problem of being one of the areas where illegal immigrants and those trafficking in drugs and humans often cross the border since their reservation is on both sides of the border. Building a wall would separate families and make the tribe suffer great hardships of not being able to shop, work, and visit freely on both sides of the border. The Tohono O'odham face a strong battle to maintain their way of life in a period of harsh border policies, declining revenue, and less and less water.

The following is a transcription for a member of the Tohono O'odham tribe:

Respondent (R1); Woman in the room (W); Gerry (G):

R1: [leads in with something about Bull Durham tobacco in little sacks] They call it Bull Durham, I don't think they make it anymore, it comes in a little sack

W: Yeah, I know what that is, that's a very famous, that's the most famous of all tobaccos.

R1: And even like tobacco or tequila in a bottle, or even like clothing

W: They put that on the grave?

R1: No, at the, where we set our table. See it's supposed to be quiet too, you know, and the cloths you hang on the wall. Like my aunt would buy a hat or shirt, mom would buy little baby things for, because I lost two sisters when they were young, you know, babies, so she place like baby bottle or at that time cloth diapers, and after, it's supposed to be going until after midnight and then we go to sleep, have to go inside and not be going around outside. In today's time, maybe no TV or radio, you know how kids play the radio real loud, you know, but it's supposed to be quite until after midnight. And then you can go and partake of the food, and it's . . . but some places, some villages, they put the table at the cemetery.

W: R. do you take . . . [long pause] . . . whichever you like, do you take milk in your coffee? This is cream, and this is 1%, but you can have this

R1: Cream's ok

W: Cream looks OK, sure it is

R1: But also, like my aunt and my mom bake, after, and then after midnight people come around now and they eat. It's like a trick or treat, because in my village we don't have trick or treat on the Halloween. So, people come around and I tell them back the second. But like ??? they do have trick or treat, kids go out and collect candy, but in my village we don't. But we do have something similar to trick or treat on the second. People come . . .

W: So, it doesn't get confused with the more . . .

R1: People come, and we do hand candy and things. In the past we've had these old-time musicians, because they go from house to house and we . . . they us ["*woman interrupts to give artificial sugar and to give Gerry something to drink—"my favorite elixir"*]. *It would definitely help you if you went down to see what goes on, instead of just over . . .*

G: *Well, I saw your movie too, and that was very informative.*

R1: *Yeah, but that doesn't really tell everything. *I tell people, you have to live with the people to understand it. People call and ask questions, and I tell them to come out and see what we do . . . so you can see and experience it, you know. You're so close to the reservation, that you could do that. So, what happens to this recorded material.*

G: *Well, just say a little bit first and tell a little bit about your tribe.*

R1: *Well, I'm . . . of the Tohono O'odham tribe in Arizona.*

G: *and then tell about your tribe, a little bit of their history, like you told us they went clear down to Mexico and whatever*

W: *Yeah, where they came from*

R1: *Well, with what's been here, here in this place because, we're desert people and uh we never got moved like other tribes did, those that were pushed out by the government, military, so forth. Because of their land, the railroads, the timber, and so forth, the gold. But in here it's just a desert, it's hot, hard to be out here except the real strong. We have people in the Sonora, people on that side cause many of them are mixed, you know, And uh, but the main part of the tribe is here in southern Arizona, and that's alright.*

G: *And you want to talk a little bit about how you treat dying people*

R1: *What do you mean?*

G: *you have children come and visit them, and some tribes don't do that, and some do, or . . .*

R1: *I don't think we have any problem with that, not that I know of.*

W: *When someone falls ill, everyone can come and visit.*

R1: *I would think we'd hope they would. That's what we'd hope with our people, you know. That relatives would come and see the person. And I'm sure, if I was standing conscious, I'd want my people to come, my grandkids, and . . .*

G: *And you're burial practices?*

R1: *What do you mean now?*

G: *What kinds of things you do for funerals and . . .*

R1: *you're talking about a funeral?*

G: *Yeah, I know, but traditionally what would you have done?*

R1: *To bury the person?*

G: *uh hmm.*

R1: *Bury the person*

G: *Do you just have the men do it? Or everybody?*

[short pause]

W: Remember the video? Of Florence's brother?

R1: Well, today, the men, I think probably always the men have . . . because they have do the hard work that they . . . there on the side of mountains . . . uh . . . I'm sure the men would make the clearing where they place the body, while women do other things, you know.

G: How do you manage grief? What do people do when they're grieving? Do they have any particular rituals or customs?

R1: [pause] hmm . . . well like what?

G: Well like the Apache women cut their hair, or anything of that sort, or wear black or take a year off from going to parties and things

R1: I would hope they would! I don't think we have. I know we pray for four nights after . . . but that's from the Spanish, they uh after the burial they used to have four nights of prayer. Say the prayer, I guess we can do it ourselves, but they come and say the rosary.

G: Do you believe in an afterlife? Where do they go when they die?

R1: Well, if they're good persons, they go to heaven, to live with God and fight fire with the angels in heaven. And, uh, bad people go straight down and burn in hell for ever and ever, that's what the sister's told us anyway. And that's their belief [chuckles].

G: Some groups talk about people going to the core of the earth, or staying on earth as ghosts. Do you have any traditions of that sort

[long pause]

R1: Traditionally, we used to say we go east, a spirit, you know, before the heaven and hell thing, that's the way we went east. We didn't know there was such a thing as heaven and hell, and our spirit went east and lived there. There was a saying, I wish I could say it in British, but there's a place where there's plenty of prickly pear fruit.

W: Like a paradise.

R1: You know, according what we had then, it was a land of plenty for there was always something to eat like the prickly pear, you know, it's a place where I guess, when you think about it, you never went hungry, like in the human life. And that's where the . . . uh . . . your spirits go . . . someplace below the east, where the deceased people go and they say there is continual dancing, we called it dancing, for power, It's kind of like when I think about it's the kind of place where, you know, they've got a celebration . . . you know . . . uh . . . I don't want to call it a party, because back then we didn't know what a party was . . . you know, what people do today . . . but it was just a place where there was like a . . . I guess I would say that dance, you know content, and people just dancing and not having to worry about anything.

W: That's what we all hope for.

G: *Being a desert people, do you have any different ideas about life and death than other people might have?*

R1: *Like, well, what I just told you.*

G: *Yeah, the death part, what about the living, are we . . . because you're born you have to die, is death something you seek or something you just accept?*

R1: *[laughs] well I don't know that anybody seeks death, but uh, it's just something that's to be expected.*

G: *It's just natural?*

R1: *It's something to be expected when you're an elder. Someday you'll be gone. That's OK, you've lived your life, but in today's culture, it doesn't seem to happen that way. An elder was talking to me over at the hospital now, and we got to talking about all these people dying, you know, anyway, at one point he said You know, Danny, us elders, we're burying the young people, when they should be burying us. Because, uh, people younger than us are dying off, and this man had a wake last night in (garbled), and he was around 45. In my home village in a matter of two weeks we lost two brothers 43 and I think 47, brothers, and then the following week another man died, uh, I think he was 54. To me that's young. I'm 67, and they're not even, they haven't even reached the elderly age. And that's from different things today, just to mention what that's like, it's diabetes, violence, alcohol, cancer, you know, people are dying off. You know, people don't take care of themselves. But anyway, that's what's happening compared to years ago when they say people lived a long time. My mother is 91 but she's still going. Course her legs are weak, but her mind is very good, and that's the way I hope to be someday, in fact not that long, because, you know, there are some people who get a certain age and they can't remember things anymore.*

G: *What can we do to help the young people keep the traditions, and not drink and so forth? And not die early deaths?*

R1: *What can you do? Uh, I don't know, what can you do?*

G: *Well, I hope if we teach them traditional ways, they'd be less likely to do some of that, but uh . . .*

R1: *You or who?*

G: *We as a society . . . as a country, culture.*

R1: *Well, I don't know, I think each region has to work with their own people, you know, like we've been told by people in the past . . . people have come on the land "do it this way, do it this way," and people are always telling us what to do. I think that the Indian population has to take control of their own lives. Again, we've been told since people came out here . . . and you're talking about something that's very hard, teaching the traditions, I think we have to teach them early. Because when they get older, they're too into games, drugs . . . because we have a lot of drugs coming to our land, because we're right by Mexico. An officer just told me last week, the police chief, that more of them* *are being arrested today for hauling marijuana and illegals, because we have illegals come through our land day and night. And some people are not working and they're looking for that fast money. I think . . . one thing I heard was how much marijuana you bring to Tucson, one amount I heard was like $5000 a trip. That's very . . . you know if you don't have anything to do.*

W: *That's very appealing isn't it?*

R1: *Yeah . . . and yet, I feel that people can go and do something if they want to . . . IF they want to. IF they want to. Go to school, have a job, but a lot of people can't get a job because of the alcohol. My own son Mark, you know, sad to say. He had a job at the hospital, you know, and many, many people are like that.*

W: *It's not just your society, it's our society too.*

R1: *It's not just there it's here, it's on the reservations.*

W: *We're having the same problems that you are, with our children.*

R1: *Today, it's . . . every time I turn on the TV to watch the news, it's somebody else got killed in Tucson. It's almost a daily thing now. And out there, kids carry weapons, you know, maybe buy with the drug money. I was looking a pistol, man they're expensive 800 or more. I thought maybe something like a hundred dollars, or . . . it's kind of nice to keep a weapon handy because . . .*

W: *That's why you need $5000 runs of marijuana, so you can buy the . . .*

R1: *Yes, it's really not safe out there anymore. Before, there was a time, years ago, when you could sleep outside. I remember we slept on the ground with our blankets and just laid on the ground and looked at the stars, but it not safe to do that anymore. Especially the elders, a lot of things go on today. It's uh . . . I used to walk across the border to go home, because I'd get up at my cousin's house and my aunt would say, "You better go, it's getting dark," and so I'd just walk and be safe. But today, I don't let my grandkids do that. Maybe we're getting off the subject . . .*

G: *No, it's fine. I enjoy listening to you*

R1: *Yeah, a lot of things go on today that are bad. I keep stressing to my language classes that, and the parents that we need to teach our children the values at a young age. Don't wait until they're teenagers, because by then they're so hooked up to something else. And the language, the dances, the traditional dances. We have to teach them when they're little, and language is almost a daily thing that the kids have to do, because, it's all British. And my concern is the next generation. You know we talk about endangered languages, even though there are tapes and paper, but the language that's good, but the spoken language is what I'm concerned about. It's so much British to be . . . there's nothing wrong with it, because we have to talk British to come to you, but on the other hand, there's no reason to lose our own language.*

W: *No, you just found it . . . you just got it in print in the last 40 years or so.*

R1: *Yeah, it's one of the newer languages to be written. Compared to Navajo, they've been at it a long time, probably the other tribes too, you know. So, I*

encourage the parents to teach the values. You know, even if they're Christian
. . . teach your teachings, live your teachings. Don't just say you're Catholic or
protestant and not practice the teaching of the church. A lot of us do that. We
go to church if someone gets married, or a child gets baptized. Other times, the
church is almost empty. I mean, I try to relate that to the goat culture, where
people just . . . when they didn't have Christianity, but the healer talks about
values like sharing and respect, kinship, being industrious. You know, it's just
a part of their lives. That's how they lived, they just lived it. They didn't have
to think because it was pounded into their heads. They talk it in the evening,
and in the morning, the kids were still in bed, because grandpa talking about
this. And then making the kids work, for exercise, but also something with their
mind. I guess that's what runners talk about today on the land . . . floating on
the air. They say some spirit will meet you out there to give you some kind of
knowledge, you could be a singer, or to ??? songs, or to be a medicine man,
you know. [long pause]

G: *In teaching the children the traditions, today they mostly use funeral directors,*
you know, and have funerals at churches or whatever. How did you do them
before?

R1: *We've always had them at churches, I mean since my time, because . . .*

G: *I mean before your time, then, or do you know those?*

W: *The old traditional way*

G: *How did you do them before you had the missionaries and all?*

R1: *Well, back then it was, well, I do know that people buried really fast, you know*
like the same day. Because back we didn't have a freezer, like today we have a
morgue.

G: *Did you still use the same songs that you used to use?*

R1: *Shouldn't forget our own customs, but we have?*

G: *well, the Blackfeet use Christian songs, but they also use theirs too.*

R1: *Well, today what we do is we sing . . . especially about a person who was*
involved in ceremony, we do sing traditional songs. And then the Christian
books also But also, the burial, when they start burying the person, when
they make their last viewing, lower the casket down in the ground, at a cer-
tain point the ladies sing the rosary. So, they get through and we start sing-
ing. Not many people are involved in some kind of ceremony. Maybe if the
person was a singer. Especially the elders we do that to a lot of people my
age or older. But as I mentioned, also the burial sites were on the sides of
mounds, on hills. We just kind of like dig a hole and place the body there,
then put wood, well not wood, but like branches and rocks over it. Uh . . .
but also at times they were just kind of, no like just left, but this in the foot
hills, they were laid this way, across. And they put branches across this hole,
branches because they're strong, and they cover them with rocks . . . that's
a long time ago

W: Well these are these are holy sites now, aren't they? Places where you buried people. Aren't they . . . holy sacred grounds?

R1: To me they are, I don't know what other people think. Any burial site is. That's what I think. But, again, because what Christianity into our thought has changed, uh, . . . there's still a traditional burial site covered with rocks, but down below in the flat it's not very much difference in height, maybe the top of the house was sloped down, and down here it's flat, but there's a mound . . . the old burial site. But down here it's all modern. You see the wooden crosses . . .

W: Yeah, that's a Christian symbol

R1: . . . head stones with their names on there. Uh, . . . I do respect that, but they have this picture in my . . . and they must costs a lot.

W: Oh, the stone headstones, the granite ones that they buy and have things written on them?

R1: Yes, because my mother's is kinda square, but it slopes and it's about so high. I think it was like uh . . . it was quite a bit, I don't know maybe five hundred. But if you can imagine the picture you know, you have to like see it to believe it, and it cost maybe three thousand. You know, it's not free. And also, see the other thing, I mean it's just me that thinks this way, you want like a rosary on there, you know, a rosary? And uh, you know, some of these people, of course people own, I don't say ??? [garbled], some of them are drinkers, but we try to uh, we try to Christianize them after they're gone, they didn't lead a Christian life.

W: Try to grease the wheels or whatever you call it.

R1: Yeah, it's kind of like the other way, when they should have lived that way when they were alive, a human being and maybe it's OK to have that when you're dead. But it's just my thinking.

G: Do you do anything to honor the dead, like at the cemetery site or later. Do you bring things and leave them there?

W: That's what he was starting out with . . .

R1: But also, during . . . do you have a napkin? But also, uh anytime of the year sometimes we go and do that . . . like my family will go and just clean my parents grave and my sister's graves, and maybe put up a new wreath or flowers throughout the year. That's what we do. Other people tend to do that. Except folks that are not taking care of, you know, but also on the notes when the person dies . . . it's kind of like a memorial, they might have a mass and framed. Again, once in a while, at one of these anniversaries, you might have a singing group, you know traditional singing. But according to my mother in law, those things were not traditional. Again, with today somebody dies today, maybe they might not bury the person until four days or seven days because maybe families are over in LA or someplace and they have to wait for that son or daughter or family to come in and be there for the, what we call the wake, and then the funeral the next day. But what I beginning to notice, though, is that they'll let . . . this last man in the village, they had the mass and the services throughout the day and then, usually they'll have the all-night vigil and then the burial the next day. But I think it will become more, with more people, just they just have the one day. I think in future, and also like cremations.

W: *Is that new too?*

R1: *Well, yeah, to be cremated. But that's not too often. But once in a while you might say, you know, they got cremated. There was silence and finally somebody said, "Oh she was cremated in Tucson." You know . . .*

W: *That's why we didn't bury her . . .*

R1: *Well, they uh . . . I know one family they asked to come . . . the lady came to me and said, "Can you come and do a blessing?" I said, "For what?" She said, "We're going to release my mom," you know, the ashes. I said, "Well, I never did that, I wouldn't know what to do with the ashes. What prayer do you say, what song do you sing? I don't know, but I do blessings for like gatherings like I do a blessing. Certain things like, yesterday they had an opening at this one place for a new building for the WIC program, well it's been open. I think, and they just got a new place and they want me to do a blessing, so I did. So, I said 'I think you probably have to get somebody else because I don't know, to be honest really don't . . . I wish I could help you because she's a friend of mine." And so I guess that's what . . . they kept the ashes I hear and I guess let it go. But see that's the other thing too is to keep ashes in your house of the deceased. Some people are really spooky about those kinds of things".*

W: *Yes, people ask me make vessels to put their ashes in. Somebody just asked me last week if I would make a vessel, you know a pottery vessel, for them to have ashes put in.*

R1: *I think that's kept in a room or something . . . I think I'd be scared at night, but you know, but that's me.*

W: *Well, I think my mind could go a little wild.*

R1: *Yeah, getting up a night, and uh, but I think we've become more modern*

W: *These are new innovations, or new ideas, non-traditional*

R1: *I know a tribe, I think it's Quechan, they do burial. I think they laid them . . . I don't know, I've never been there, the Yuma, I guess they lay the body. I think it's the Quechan tribe. But that's what's always buried. But also like you don't . . . like you see . . . especially the old grave stake, the cross pieces rot and they fall in and sometimes you can see things in there, like maybe bones you know. People are spooky about . . . some people.*

G: *Do you bury things with people*

R1: *Oh, the belongings, in the old culture, maybe their clay pots or maybe a bow and arrow. Because, now I don't know, but it comes from my mother, when this light came about we call it the lantern, and I guess what my mother heard years ago that's when this man walked in the mine shafts out there where there were a lot of prospectors, and she said that what she heard how this light came about was when they buried this elder with lantern because that's a custom, you bury things with them. Some of the things that they valued, and she said that this one people, they started noticing this thing walking around at night, so they call it the lantern, the lantern, they call it, lantern. Because of that lantern, I guess [for some it was scary?] I never saw it, but I . . . some years ago I interviewed some, these are younger women, to see if even the younger people ever saw it. And a number of those younger ladies said they did including my sister. And she said she saw that in our village, this light. But one of the stories that my mother told me, because our people used to travel at night, you know in the summer it's hot, so they travel at night to go to another community, because it's cold you know, it's so hot in the day time. Well, this girl going and her younger sister forgot a doll, a little doll she stuffed in the walls at the house and they were quite aways from the village and she remembered that, and she got upset, she's one those little kids, you know, "I want go get my doll." And my grandma said it's too far off, we can't go back, she was just hanging on the back part of the wagon and threatening to jump off and walk all the way back for her doll, and they tried to scare her . . . I never want those kind of kids . . . anyway they got into this village, and there's big river you have to cross, and they went down into this bank, into the sand, and there's a big bush and my grandmother told her to get in or the lantern will come around. I guess she was upset for a long ways, cause from home a good ten miles, and going by wagon is slow, they went in dark. And my grandmother said "get in, get in" and my mother said that all the leaves on this bush just lit up, and she said the horses, the animals or the horses, she said they spooked and they kind of ran, and so grandpap held the reins to settle them down, and I said "how about your little sister? I never knew the lady, she died a long time ago, she'd have been my aunt, but she was younger than my mother, and she said "You should have seen her boy, she just kind of flew up and sat in front with us.*

W: *Hopped right up into that wagon.*

R1: *Yeah, because the ladies sat in back of the wagon and the seats up here where the driver sits. She really learned her lesson. But it's superstitions. You know, don't look at it. Even like when we used to go over to the cemetery, because it'd be kind of like in the dusk, what do you call it, in the evening, and I would just look straight ahead, because our old road used to go right by the cemetery, and I'd just look straight ahead and I'd try to whistle, but I couldn't whistle. Kids used to say that if you look in there you. . . . Something might come out, and I didn't want to see it.*

W: *You know it's superstitions and things like that, that all people, when you've heard stories before, something a little eerie about them, and you wonder, you wonder, and you go into a cemetery and you wonder about all the lives that are represented there and you know it's hard to say . . .*

R1: *But a lady told me she had to look, and she said "I saw the lights" you know. In my class at the community college and I got to talking about this and this* man said, he lives in . . . *my village, but he's married, and he takes classes out there, and he said that he saw the lights of the lantern, because . . .*

W: [interrupts—can't hear]

R1: . . . said it's a person, you know, a spirit.

W: So that still lives on, that legend. Is it a folktale now?

R1: Well, I don't know, because that man said, recently, I mean, recently

W: recently that he saw it.

R1: Well, this was some time ago that he saw it, but recently I guess his brother who lives up in the village took this lady home because she works at this store, gets up at night. So, he gave her a ride and they got to talking about that lantern. She lives on the west side of the village, and she said, uh she live on the east side, and they were talking about how sometimes that light comes around, that lantern. So, she told him come over sometime and just park there . . . sit in your car. So, I guess one night she did, and this was maybe in the past three or four months. So, I guess one night he drove over there and parked by the house in the dark and he said, "Sure enough this light came in the dark." It kinda came and made a circle and then it seemed to go that way and it just kinda faded out. You know, I've never seen it . . . I told somebody, you know, I'd like to see that, but man I'd probably faint. I've never seen it, that's why I wanted to ask these younger people if they did . . . but they did . . . some of them did, not all of them did, but some of them did. And when cowboys used to camp out a lot in the desert, you know, from roundup, they sometimes 'd see. So, they spook . . .

W: ready for Halloween.

R1: Hmm . . . today cowboys don't camp out any more, because they have trucks and they go in the day and do so many round-up and then come back next day and go again. But when I was a kid, cowboys had like a wagon, the chuck-wagon, and they'd camp out there someplace, several days and for the next cowpoke, but now they don't camp anymore. And, uh, like I said, I haven't seen it, uh, but it's superstition.

W: So, there are some superstitions, and that . . .

R1: And even when people die, I remember on this side of the, the Spanish crosses, and they used to say that if you go at night, some people say they see somebody standing by the road. And I told this in my class, and when you get close it just disappears, and this lady raised her hand and I looked at her and she said "My mother, she saw that, it was somebody on the road and it just disappears." I guess it's something that, you hear other people saying and it . . . one day at night you're thinking about it and may be, I don't know, a hallucination, I don't know, you know. But, uh, oh like when you get spooked, the people they see a shadow, you know, or even like when they, uh, a shadow, I think mainly a shadow, but I guess maybe they're still mourning, because I think it's the thought, you know you miss the person, and you long for them. Uh, cause like my mother in law used say, she lost her husband that she thought it was like a pact. She used to sit in her room and that maybe someday he'd come back, or he'd walk through the door, she'd hear walking, because they live here in town, on the sidewalk, you know "maybe that's him" you know, that longing. It took her a long time before she realized, he's never coming back. I think it's in our culture.

W: *I think it's in all cultures, too.*

R1: *Things that remind us of that person, you know, clothing, uh, but uh, also traditionally, somebody didn't tell him right, is that our belief is that when people die, their spirit comes back in the form of the owl. That's why even today, a lot of people don't mess with the owl. We got home and golly, there's this place kind of a ways from . . . we have this owl with this deep hooting, it's a sign. But I guess it was annoyed, because, I haven't heard it again. But that's our belief that, uh, it comes back in the form of* an owl, our spirits.*

W: *Every winter we get an owl that comes and perches in our pine tree out here, appears almost the same time every year, and there's two of them. I think they're mates. Do owls have mates, lifelong mates?*

R1: *I imagine, I don't know. But anyway, see the owl, the, and some years ago this man died. And there was an article in the paper that the family didn't want to have the autopsy done on their dad, because, the article said, because they were afraid if they had an autopsy that his spirit would come back in the form of an owl. Maybe somebody told them wrong, because in our community, and in other communities, some of us still have that belief that our spirits come back in the form of an owl. But all souls days, November the 2nd, is the day when we remember . . . again it picks up on the Spanish culture . . . maybe couple hundred years ago we didn't know anything about this kind, you know, but now we prepare food, ladies right now, some make their own hole, you know they cut cloth in a circle . . . and they cut hay, and make flowers. Some are good at that, you know. And they place those wreaths and like a coyote story, you what a coyote story is, see all these wreaths out . . . because the things you want to buy ahead of time, because when it gets close people are going to come in and start buying and sometimes you can't find it.*

W: *Stock up now . . .*

R1: *Or else you won't*

W: *. . . get it early or it will be gone . . .*

R1: *Won't have your wreaths when it's time. And there are certain people who make wreaths that I know men down in Churchill village he makes a wreath he takes them out to sell, I'm sure that Joe does well financially. But a lot of his money he gives away, it's not really for himself, or he gives it to the church. But he makes wreaths and people know him. Some people do that, some people buy them, and they sell them because they're Indian made. Also, crosses, the wooden crosses, after so many years, they rot and they fall over, so we replace them, and people are looking for crosses to replace the old one, the grave candles, uh the crosses. It's quite exciting to see the lit candles it just kind of looks like a city with all the lights, you know. It's because it's so close to town, you know the lights . . . but if you're out there someplace you can see all [women inter-rupting—garbled]. And also, like uh, like each family has uh a trail to their, from the cemetery to their home. There's a place that drag to kind of clear it, all the way back it's like a path, and uh, then that night after the candles are lit somebody will address the spirits and say, our family will say that, my parents and my sisters will say "We've prepared food for you to come over and eat," you know, the spirits, and the idea is that they will go on the trail. Kind of each family has their own trail. It's kinda cute in a way, yeah. But food has been placed that has taken a long time to prepare like tamales, or squash, again for the older people they eat, they must see traditional foods like maybe the roasted corn or tapery beans, but for the younger people they have maybe like fruit. Like watermelon, oranges, uh but I was just joking with some people and I said, "I wonder if anybody places a hamburger?" and this lady said "Yeah, uh, they did for her daughter, or somebody in that family, because, every time we went to town, they wanted to stop at a Burger King or something". They always wanted to stop, so they placed a burger. Again, tobacco, and also, I hear I think I heard someplace that people make, um, something alcoholic like a beer, because maybe they're an alcoholic. Uh, I heard or marijuana, now I know that has been placed in coffins, because I know when they uh had, a man who died in San Pedro on my wife's side and this guy stuck something in here and his brother was talking to him, but I guess it was a bit of money, it was for a beer he said. So, I guess, like a silver dollar. I guess we're all like that with our family, uh, our siblings, you know. But I've heard of marijuana being place in those plastic containers.*

And there was one that they did at a burial and I guess the man did that, this young man get in a car accident, and so when they buried him, they placed it. And I heard, somebody told me from that community that this will come out and spook people at night, and somebody said maybe it was all high because of that marijuana, that kind of thought. But I know that people do do that. Based on, I think they call it a lid. But I know also, that like with the . . . we went to ??? when my son was working at the hospital, this man died but I guess he grew up n LA and I guess he was like in a gang over there, because, again, he worked with my son. And my wife knew his mother, of that man who died. So, you know we went to pay our respects over in some, I know they had a banner on there like an East LA something something gang and I guess like gang colors. Uh, and that's happening toward the young people. At one place when the young people died, this one young man died, I didn't go, but his mother was telling me that this people came and bring all this ???? and she had to tell to.. "we don't do that" I guess because he was their buddy or a gang member or something, but he received a lot ????. I heard of one place in another community where a gang member died, and somebody said "oh it's the gang kids that really helped" because there is a lot of work that takes place like the cleaning around the house especially if you have the wake right there at your home. You clean around the house and the ladies cook, but I guess this young kids were there everyday helping them work. I guess when they carried out the casket to the cemetery it was the kids with their shirts on and that carried that coffin and that put in the work for their member. It's one thing I heard, I guess . . .

W: They do have that loyalty . . .

R1: Yeah, I guess in one way they . . . put in the work, that loyalty. And uh, but also the other thing too is like drunks, I remember this one place when this elder died, in my village as a matter of fact this one male he was up at the coffin talking for a long time and some of the men asked him to move because people were waiting because people had come from other villages to pay their respect. And, uh, he was kind of bothersome. I heard in one place on the west side, this man came in with his six pack and he . . . no, he just put it down back where he sat, you know, what kind of respect and the young kids who are not dressed, who come in shorts you know you think that when you go to a wake that you kind of dress, at least a shirt, which you know. Or I go to one place in San Pedro where this young man and girl were just hanging on to each other, you know they weren't thinking about the grieving, it was more the grown-ups. And uh, a lot of disrespect today, and even with the kids, uh, there was a time when you didn't let kids look inside the coffin, and today kids are kind of, like the parents don't really watch them, and also like at the burial, they're running around where the hole is and they want to look down there and years ago it was something that wasn't done. Kids were kept over there and . . .

W: That's right and we stood by silent and kept our mouths shut.

R1: . . . yeah, and because there's a fear that if you stared at the deceased you might, like at night come to you, you know, bad dreams, and it probably happens to so many kids.

W: I'm worried about you guys getting some supper.

R1: I'm trying to think about what I might have forgot. Speak to ???? that today we cleaned the cemetery, because, really, we cleaned every grave.

W: He did that this morning, he was there today with his son Mark

R1: Because in certain villages they just clean their own plot, and they don't clean these, but over there we clean everything, all the men come, and they work in the cemetery and at the feast house the ladies are there cooking. So, when they get through at noon, or the afternoon, the men go back to eat.

W: They did that today?

R1: Yes, we didn't eat because we had to leave early, we left about eleven. Uh

W: and then on the road a long time.

R1: . . . they clean the cemetery because of holy cross day and again that's sometimes when most families will place a new wreath and light candles so it's again a Christian traditions Holy Cross day, May the third.

W: You know that day?

R1: It's called Santa Cruz, Santa Cruz from Spain, it's Santa Cruz, which means Holy Cross. So that's another thing we do.

G: Hmm, my son's in the Holy Cross order, so . . .

W: Oh, that's how you know.

R1: And also, like I said, the anniversary, besides the service, uh most of the time they'll have a mass if the father can get there, because, those poor guys they have to go to a lot of places and they get called on a lot this past year. Priests like before you know there's a shortage. They have what call, but he can't do everything, he's limited but a priest they can say the mass and have prayer and feeding but what's happening to a lot of anniversaries is a celebration. This is because somebody said, "today was my dad's anniversary whether it was tenth anniversary or whatever". And some people leave it for ten years, but again, this is a new thing. Like I got from my mother in law, this things was done years ago, you know, and she says we're kind of outdoing . . . who is going to have the biggest anniversary, or you know, or the most, with a lot of food and you know kinda out do the Jones you know.

W: Wait until you get into a Bar Mitzvah, and all of that. You know, the Jewish people have Bar Mitzvahs for young men and that's where the competition for the biggest, most you know, I had a friend who used to cook for them and she said, "Why they're positive pageants," they're just theater.

R1: You know just mention like the Apache ceremony with the young woman, I saw it, this man showed us a video and this lady was talking and it takes several years to prepare when you're, because it's a big financial thing today, I mean that's the day they . . . this lady from the college attended one someplace, Santa Cruz or someplace, she had a friend that invited her so she went and she said "Oh those stacks, you know like TV" You know it's a little bit, are we doing . . . is this not for the money or for the girl, you know who are we doing it for. Because it's popular.

W: And you're out living your culture just like I am, that's what my husband tells me when I talk like this. It's a shame to watch this, it's hard to watch this

R1: trying to be in the biggest parties. And who's going to give the best, and like a wedding, who's going to . . . Well, is there anything that uh

G: Just fine, you've done a great job, if there's anything you want to say about your tribe that you haven't said that you want us to have on there

R1: Well, oh just talking about we're changing, our language, our traditional beliefs, there's a modern Christian way, but again just say everybody's sinning.

People like me who still pray in the traditional way with the sunrise. I really like that, you know, nothing about Christianity, I guess people do live it, but that's my way. I pray both ways, even though I don't always go to church, I try to say my rosary every day. I kind of made a promise to Saint Francis, because something about that at the mission and the majority of them are Catholic, October the fourth many of them go Mexico to worship the Saint, but also at the mission there's a Saint Francis, there's a festival on the reservation, in each year it changes from district to district, oh what do they call it, a big priest. They just had it in Santa Rosa and they'll have it in the next district, it kind of moves from each year except, but there's one in . . . there's a church on a hill and they call it the [auto?] chapel, but there's another in kind of like a village, they call it, on the map it says Saint Francis, but often call it ???? you know where the rabbit fell, I don't know the story about that, but they also have a big celebration and today they have three night. Years ago, we went, a long time ago when I was a little kid, we had a one-night celebration, just a small, I mean, a lot of Mexicans come and drank a lot of alcohol, you know, serves and tequila and you know. It wasn't really like that, there was some drunk people, but I guess they mostly just drink but not get drunk.

R1: I think it's 24,000, but I'm not sure on the main reservation and there's people out there, I think it's, but I not good at figures, I think it's about 28,000 people that's out there in LA or . . . When we went to Washington for the march after the celebration, this young lady came to us. A young girl, and she came all the way from Japan. She's in the military, but she wanted to be there. And she was way up in the military or someplace in Chicago, because that was a time called . . . we called it the relocation . . . the government relocated people to work. A lot of these people went off to Denver, Texas and even there in LA. Some came back later but some uh . . . there's a family from our village that's over there, some place in LA [unintelligible—background noise—counter#20] . . .

I know this young man from this family in charge of the library there someplace, but some don't, and some are working on . . . I think this one man, he's gone now, but I think he worked in the Dodger Stadium for years. Some are very commendable, and uh, our government it's just like uh . . . executive, legislative and judicial, and with what we have for our fourth lady chairman, chairlady, . . . who used to work at the college, her husband's police chief there, . . ., a nice man, but it's a huge job. He's trying to educate on his own, he's trying to educate the tribe what's happening with the drugs and the young people and the drugs and the weapons. Oh we have a lot of truancy . . . our education system is not too good, as matter of fact we keep scoring in the low . . . except the primer school. But the intermediate and high school and I think they're, I think maybe I heard that the state might take over. Because if they are Indians, I think the state can move in and try to do something. We have some kids that go to school here called Hoshing school, it's right off Westby, you know it's a charter school, but next year they're going to be offering an intermediate school. And I'm seriously thinking talking my other son to send my grandson up here . . . because again I'm concerned about the education up there . . . uh . . . a lot of things have to build up to and I think the, we hire somebody and they come don't want to make changes their way and I don't know, jeez, I think Indians need to be educated and take control of certain positions, because they're the ones that grew up here and lived the life and made it good, hopefully. But we have to teach the kids now . . . we can't wait until they're old and don't want to listen, because older people or hard to try to talk to, but Hoshing school is very good, they came to listen that night to learn about the school, now, I like Hoshing school. It's small classes. Another place I really like to go is Ontario.

Again, there's a lot of British today, there's some that speak our language, but the younger generation I think some really ought to learn, but again language can't be a go twice a week, it's kinda got to be a daily thing to really learn the language, but we're trying. Also, I think education will help us. I like learning, the education the Anglo system, I liked education, I tell the kids that I try to learn something new every day, but that's old school, but also the education in your community about your culture, you family history, about the rituals, songs, ceremonies, that's a world of learning out there, you know from your grandpa, uncles or somebody, how to chop a . . . how to use an axe. The other night all lights went out again, and we had to put candles and this men was telling me that he's got a kerosene lamp, well he brought that. We can't always rely on this out there, and if it goes out for days, cause it happened one time. It didn't come on till next day until about noon, you know, and people were upset and, but again technology screwed up, but you have to be prepared otherwise, how to hunt a rabbit or how to get the wild spinach and eat that to survive. So, anyway, I think that's it's an end. You're welcome to call me up sometime if I think of something else).

G: *And I send you what you said so that you can add to it if you want.*

Chapter 19

Hopi Disposal and
Bereavement Practices

The Hopi are a Southwestern tribe who live in the middle of the Dine reservation. The Hopi are called "the peaceful ones" or "peaceful people." Though some of the Dine may call them old women, the Hopi have also been called the Moqui (Moki) or the dead. The Hopi are the western most Pueblo group. Being pueblo people who lived in adobe housing, the Hopi left behind many ruins for the archaeologist to study. As a pueblo people living in an arid environment, they built and abandoned many sites due to the lack of water or having not enough water to continue to grow crops, and also because they were forced to move. Because they did not have carts, horses, or other animals to carry items, they left behind their exquisite basketry and pottery that marked their stay in the abandoned regions. After the arrival of the Spanish, the Hopi were subjected to the Spanish way of life and religion and their attempts to exploit, enslave, and control the Hopi. Over time the mission movement that attempted to end the Hopi religion and make Catholics of them was ended through a revolt by a number of pueblo tribes. The Spanish returned a few years later and reestablished their mission in 1700, but an uprising again ended the Spanish influence on the Hopi.

THE HOPI

The Hopi language is part of the Shoshone language group. They may be the descendants of the Anasazi, or it is possible that they simply moved into their areas. They have lived in the same region for ten thousand years and have been one of the Pueblo cultural centers along with the Zuni/Acoma and the Rio Grande pueblos (Pritzker 1998, 42). As the westernmost pueblo people, the Hopi also represent the most unique pueblo people. They are the only pueblo people that speak a dialect of the Uto-Aztecan language (Waldman 1988, 95). As a people who tried to avoid warfare and conflict, they moved to the protection of the Mesa to escape the raids of the Dine and later the invasion of the Spanish. Eventually, they were controlled by the Europeans who established the Hopi reservation in the midst of the Dine reservation in 1882 and with their power over the Hopi brought in the railroad that came with tourists, trading posts, missionaries, and scholars that not only changed the Hopi way of life, but it also killed many of the Hopi with the diseases that the Europeans carried with them (Pritzker 1998, 42). Of all of the tribes in North America, the Hopi probably live closest to their traditional way (Waldman 1988, 98). In spite of the changes that came with boarding schools, tourism, outside control, and so much more, the Hopi have been able to maintain their traditions.

HOPI BELIEFS AND PRACTICES

The Hopi view life as a journey or a process that begins in childhood, youth, adulthood, and old age that follows a path that leads to the sun (Thompson and Joseph 1994, 50). The Hopi also believe that long ago the Hopi people lived in the underworld where there was much rain and where crops grew very well. Sadly, the Hopi people began to quarrel as they do today, so they were forced to journey to the upper world and wander until the Bear Clan group finally arrived at Shungopavi and took possession of the land (Parsons 1964, 32). Like other tribes, the Hopi are a deeply spiritual people. Like the Catholic religion, the Hope is a religious system of yearlong ceremonies that are designed to help maintain the harmony of the universe (Waters 1963, xvi). To the Hopi, the perfect individual is the person who obeys the laws and conforms to the pure and perfect pattern laid down by the Creator who then becomes a Kachina when he dies, allowing him to go directly to the next universe without having to pass through all of the intermediate worlds or stages of existence (Thompson 1959, 125). Like the Jewish people, the Hopi see themselves as the "Chosen People" (Waters 1963, xviii). Their beliefs have allowed them to endure multiple hardships over the centuries.

Unlike the Dine, the Inde, and many other tribes, the Hopi do have a great fear of ghosts or malevolent spirits. The Hopi look to the dead to bring help to them. The Hopi believe that the dead return as Kachinas (or Katsinas or Katzinas), who are intermediaries or messengers rather than as gods, to help humankind on its evolutionary journey (Trimble 1993, 45). The famous, valuable, and often sought after Kachina dolls represent Kachinas, but they are not given power; rather, the dolls function to help children learn the masks and names of real Kachinas and that the dolls are not sacred objects with spiritual powers (James 1956, 169).

The Hopi view the journey of the individual through life as the model of the journey of the Hopi people. The Hopi must journey on the path of life and then at death, the person is allowed to return to the lower world through the place of emergence to the ultimate home where the souls of the dead live like those living on earth (Underhill 1953, 212–213). The Hopi believe that the souls of the dead often revisit the upper world in the form of clouds represented by the masked dancers called Kachinas to bring rain and other necessities to the living (Thompson and Joseph 1994, 50). The tie to their ancestors presents a model of how to live and to act as a Hopi.

Like the Inde and the Dine, the Hopi view excessive handling of the dead body as a possible cause of illnesses (Beaglehole and Beaglehole 1935, 14). While all three tribes seem to exhibit great fear of death and the dead, the Hopi remain in the house where the death took place and do not destroy the dwelling as the Inde and Dine often do (Beaglehole, and Beaglehole 1935, 14). For all three, the fear of the dead body and the disease that it might bring might be the more logical explanation rather than the fear of death and the dead.

DYING AND DEATH IN THE HOPI COMMUNITY

When a member of the Hopi is dying, the Hopi have their young children leave the house of death so they do not become frightened or even die from their fear, leaving only those brave remain with the dying (Beaglehole and Beaglehole 1936, 11). Perhaps the reason that the Hopi have children and others leave is to allow the dying the dignity of not having others watch them suffer. The elder or adult who chooses to stay will tend to the dying person and then will prepare the body after the person dies. A man would typically be wrapped in buckskin while a woman would be wrapped in her wedding blanket, and both would be buried in whatever clothes that he or she was wearing at the time of death (Beaglehole and Beaglehole 1935, 11). Unlike most other groups, the Hopi do not wash or prepare the body in any way other than to wash the hair with yucca suds and to also tie the person's hair with yucca fiber before they place the body in a sitting position with the knees and arms flexed and tied with yucca to hold them in place if necessary (Beaglehole and Beaglehole 1935, 11). Immediately after the death, the father of the dead person or another man from the clan of the deceased person will make prayer feathers with one tied one to the body's hair, another one to each foot for the journey to the next world, one over the navel where the breath of a man lives, and one under each hand (Beaglehole and Beaglehole 1935, 11).

The person's face would be covered with raw cotton to indicate the future existence of the deceased as a cloud. Piki bread and a small gourd of water would be placed in the pockets of the dead person to provide food for their journey to the next world (Beaglehole and Beaglehole 1935, 12). One of the men from the clan would carry the body of the deceased to the cemetery, dig the hole for the body, place the body into the hole, replace the dirt into the gravesite, and place a stick on the grave to provide a ladder for the deceased to climb to the next world (Beaglehole and Beaglehole 1935, 12). The Hopi believed that the dead spirits went to the underworld.

The Hopi belief was that Masau'u or the God of Death was in charge of the underworld where dead spirits go and that a touch of his club would bring death to the living. Masau'u is in the dark, which causes the Hopi to fear the dark (Kaiser 1991, 27). Traditionally, the Hopi made a great show of not mourning for their dead, but now they, like the Dine, let the missionaries bury their dead. The Hopi also have mourning rituals (Thompson and Joseph 1944, 64). Like the Anasazi, the Hopi use Kivas for rituals and bury their deceased beneath the Kivas (Thompson and Joseph 1944, 129). Like other Southwestern tribes, the Hopi teach that they came from the underworld. The hole in the floor of the Kiva represents the place of emergence in the path of life (Thompson 1950, 122).

HOPI SPIRITUAL LIFE

Living in an arid environment has led the Hopi to have many ceremonies that call for rain. Without rain, corn and other crops will not grow. Like most other tribes, the Hopi are a spiritual people. Not only do the Hopi pray, but they also believe that they must work hard and live in balance with nature. As a Pueblo society, the Hopi live in mesas in the Colorado Plateau in the Middle Rio Grande area. The Grand Canyon and the Painted Desert are in their region. Despite the arid climate and the lack of water, the Hopi have been able to survive in their dry land for centuries.

The Hopi are known for their religious, intellectual, and peaceful natures (Waldman 1988, 95). The Hopi culture does not have a church or teach its people specific religious prayers. Rather, prayers are part of their spiritual way of life. Prayers are a part of everything that a person does, says, or thinks. The Hopi constructed what they call "breath feathers" that are made with willow wands, hand-spun cotton cords, and with down from eagle's breast believing that these fluffy and light as air structures are the homes of rain-bringing spirits or Kachinas (Nabokov 2006, 129). As the breezes make the plumes of these sacred homes of the rain-bringing spirits, they seem to be alive. The Hopi believe that the wind is a blessing that flows through the lungs and heart and turns it into a living thing and that breathe is a blessing so the elders will breathe on the breath feathers to give them life (Nabokov 2006, 129–130). The Hopi use of breath feathers, prayer sticks, shrines, and so forth are examples of the sociological principle of reciprocity that each helps the other or the idea of a gift for a gift. The Hopi help the rain-bringing spirits, and then the rain-bringing spirits will help the Hopi.

Unlike the European newcomers and most other societies, the Hopi do not have a central government or leadership group. Each village has a leader with advisers. Most inherit the role rather than have elections or other means to be the leader. Villages often are divided into halves with one group being the Winter People and the other the Summer People. These two groups are divided into clans. While one can change his or her name, the clan member-ship is forever. Traditionally, women could ask her husband to leave, but this was a rare event since most marriages lasted anyway. Perhaps, the men were aware of the power of the wife and worked to make the marriage last. Property was sparse. Land was not owned by individuals, but rather clans would decide where a person could farm. Everyone was given enough to care for their family. If a man failed to use his land, it could go back to the clan or to his nephews. Women generally owned the homes though men built them. They were often four- to five-story apartment buildings. Men usually lived with their wives and children. Women not only owned the houses and household goods, but women also owned food, seeds, and water. Men could inherit property including a home from his mother or grandmother. Unlike the Anglo tradition, in the Hopi culture, women take the lead in courtship. She also decides to let him know she is ready to marry by bringing him a basket of piki bread. If he agrees to marry her, he shares the piki bread with his male relatives. Weddings are festive occasions. The men of the groom's family typically weave the bride's wedding robe. They also make her a robe that will be used to cover her when she dies. Since corn is a mainstay of the culture, the bride and her mother will bring baskets of corn to the groom and his mother. Like the robe made by the grooms' family, the groom's basket will be buried with him when he dies. The couple will also have a mud fight before the wedding. During this ceremonial fight, the relatives will make jokes about each other. Rather than rice, corn will be used ceremonially dur-ing the wedding as well. Death is a presence not only in the preparation for the wedding but also in the wedding ceremonies.

With the Hopi being a spiritual community, the Hopi men spend a major part of their time on religious activities and ceremonies. Like the Catholic practice of having daily Mass, the Hopi traditionally had their daily ceremo-nies. The Hopi believe that there is both light and dark in the human exis-tence. As there is light and dark, there are also both good helper spirits and the dark or evil witches and demons. Kiva ceremonies are designed to call on the spirits to bring rain to their dry land; to have a good harvest; and to promote good health, peace, and fertility. Every Kiva clan had the duty of performing rituals. Some clans might perform ceremonies to help farmers, other clans to bring rain, still other clans would be expected to perform healing ceremonies, hunting, rain, and health-giving ceremonies. The Kachinas were the link between the Hopi who were on earth and the beings who lived in the spirit world. The living are able to become part of the spirit world when they put on the Kachina mask. The soul journeys to the underworld but the soul does not become a Kachina. When they die, the Hopi hope to become part of this spirit world. Life and death are forever linked in the Hopi culture.

THE HOPI TODAY

Today, the Hopi reservation centers on three mesas where most Hopi live. For many generations, the Dine raided and were the enemies of the Hopi. They moved their villages from the lower lands to the mesas to better be able to defend themselves from the Dine. Since the massacre at Canyon de Chelly and the Dine's forced march to Fort Sumner, New Mexico, where they were imprisoned for five years, the Dine have only battled the Hopi in courts of law over land and water rights among other issues. Like many cultures, the Hopi are divided in what they think is best for their people. The Hopi Tribal Council is to recover the lands that were taken from them by the Dine so that they could profit from the reserves of coal, oil, and uranium that were found on them, but the Tribal Council was opposed by the traditionalist Hopi who argued that the Dine would keep the land as it is, that they had made peace with the Dine, that many had married or were friends with the Dine, that they did not want the Dine to have another "Long Walk," and that the Hopi way was to share (Waldman 1988, 98). Tribal conflict, like political conflict, is to be faced in all cultures.

For many centuries, the Third Mesa was the main population base and the major town of the Hopi, offering protection and proximity to where they grew their crops. It was later also the most western mesa and the most distant from the Indian agency. Perhaps because the Dine were no longer a major threat or because of the protection of the government of the United States, around the turn of the twentieth century, the Third Mesa town of Oraibi as the cultural center and the symbol of unity was divided into several towns and lost its significance as the major town of the Hopi. Historically, the major crop of the Hopi was maize or corn. The Hopi are also known as sheep and goat herders, but those who raided them while taking their crops and animals were far more interested in stealing their more valuable baskets, pottery, blankets, kilts, sashes, and other craft items (Terrell 1973, 69). The Hopi are known as a people who work very hard. While they may not be rich in the White culture's standards, they are rich in their sense of community, knowing who they are, and in their way of life.

CONCLUSIONS

Like many American Indian groups, the Hopi have been able to maintain their traditional and sacred ways. The Hopi may be the most traditional today of all of the North American Indian tribes. Like many other groups, the Hopi do not share their sacred ways with others. As a pueblo people, the Hopi have rich traditions and a long history that has provided an excellent record for analysis. The Hopi along with the Zuni, Pima, and Tohono O'odham are thought to be descendants culturally if not physically to the ancient Mogollon, Anasazi, and Hohokam peoples. The Hopi view themselves as the descendants of the Anasazi or the "ancient ones." The Hopi use of kivas and other practices are viewed as having ties to the ancient practices of their ancestors. The Hopi continue to practice their traditional way of life.

Chapter 20

Lakota and Blackfeet Disposal and Bereavement Practices

The Great Plains were the home to the Utes, Shoshones, Blackfeet, Dakotah, Lakota, Sious, Creeks, Choctaws, Cherokee, Chickasaw, Pawnee, Pottawatomie, Sac and Fox, Kiowa, Comanche, Arrapahoe, Osage, Seminoles, Chippewa, and Ho Chunk. Of all of the Plains tribes, the Lakota are perhaps the most well known among those in the dominant society as they have been widely portrayed in books, movies, and other media.

WHO ARE THE LAKOTA?

As with the Apache and Navajo, the name Sioux is not the name of the tribe. In Teton dialect the Sioux called themselves Lakota or in the Santee dialect Dakota (Terrell 1971, 126). The Lakota speak a Siouan dialect. The word "Sioux" is thought to have come from the Ojibwa word "Nadowe-is-iw" meaning lesser adder or enemy which was later corrupted by the French to "Nadoussioux" and then shortened to "Sioux" (Pritzker 1998, 472). In the Siouan language, the names "Lakota," "Nakota," and "Dakota" all mean allies (Waldman 1988, 223). There are thirteen subdivisions of the Lakota-Dakota-Nakota speakers. The largest branch, the Teton Sioux, would include the Ogala, Brule, Hunkpapa, Miniconjou, Oohenonpa, Itazipco, and the Sihasapa; the Santee Sioux would include the Sisseton, Wahpeton, Wahpekute, and the Mdewkanton; the Yankton Sioux would include only the Yankton; and the fourth branch, the Yanktonai Sioux, would include the Yanktonai, Hunkpatina, and the Assiniboine also know as Assiniboin (Waldman 1988, 223). Of the four branches, the Tetons use the Lakota name for who they are, the Santees use Dakota, and the Yanktons and Yanktonais use Nakota (Waldman 1988, 223).

At one point, the Siouan group of tribes once occupied more territory than any other groups of Indians in what is now the United States ranging from Florida to Virginia to the Carolinas (Marquis 1974, 148). While the Lakota are known as Plains Indians, they were originally Woodlawn Indians, but they were driven out of the region by the Chippewa who had guns given to them by the French causing the Tetons to go the furthest to the Black Hills of South Dakota, Montana, and Wyoming; the Yankton Sioux went to areas along the Missouri River in Minnesota and South Dakota; the Yantonai Sioux occupied the northern areas along the Missouri in what is now North and South Dakota; the Santee stayed along the Minnesota River in what is now Minnesota (Waldman 1988, 223).

There is probably more generalized knowledge of Plains tribes, and particularly the Lakota, than any other Indian culture since they are most often portrayed in movies and television. Unlike the more sedentary tribes of the Southwest, the Plains tribes were mobile on a large scale. With the great temperature variations of the Great Plains, those living on the plains needed to adapt to all kinds of climatic changes. The many tribes living on the plains were primarily dependent upon the bison as a source of food, clothing, and shelter. Elk, pronghorn, and other animals and plant life were also major sources of food, but the bison provided the most dramatic picture of the life of the Plains tribes. The bison not only fed the Lakota and other Siouan groups, but it also provided many useful objects. The hump of the bison could be used for making shields, toys and tools were made from the bones, spoons and cups were made from the horns, the stomach was used to make pots and for carrying food and water, the tongue was used for ceremonies, bison droppings were used for making camp fires, bison hair was used for making ropes and belts, ribs were used to make sleds, and the hides were used to make clothing, tipis, moccasins, rattles, bags, drums, and rawhide for many uses, from ropes to even making splints for broken bones (McGovern 1974, 40–41). There were sedentary tribes on the plains, but the thirteen groups that spoke the Siouan language were the hunters and nomads of film and television.

The arrival of the horse following the coming of the Europeans with their guns added greatly to the legend of their prowess as warriors and hunters. Already a war-like people, they made their name in history by fighting against the European Americans in such famous battles such as "Little Big Horn" and massacres such as "Wounded Knee." The Lakota lifeways associated with these events are portrayed in Kevin Costner's film *Dances with Wolves*, and in the older film, *Little Big Man*, which starred Dustin Hoffman. Many other books, movies, television shows, and documentaries have provided both excellent information and much misinformation about the Lakota historically and culturally.

FACING DYING

The eight (seven main tribes and one, the Assiniboin, were outside of the loose confederation) Siouan-speaking tribes were relatively similar in their burial and mortuary practices. Like many other Western tribes, the Plains tribes believed that everything in the world around them was filled with spirits and powers that affected their lives whether from the sun, the mountains, the buffalo, or the eagle (Stirling 1955, 89).

For the Lakota, both men and women were healers who were typically senior men or women who had a calling to be healers in their dreams or visions that were beyond their control. A person's vision comes from the spirit world. The person may take years to complete his or her vision quest. At one level, the vision quest is a lifelong activity. To determine one's role in life might require only a few weeks or months. The vision quest ceremony is much shorter, but it is an equally powerful event. Stoltzman (1996) gives an excellent description of the ceremony. If one has a calling to be a healer as an herbalist, medicine person, or shaman, one would be obligated to begin healing work. DeMallie and Park (1987) indicate that once a person assumes the obligation to pursue the career, it may take years to acquire the power and reputation to move from an assistant or singer to become a healer (DeMallie and Parks 1987, 174).

Like the Inde and Dine, the Lakota have to request the services of the shaman. Like the Apache and the Navajo, the Lakota shaman may refuse to provide those services. The curing rituals for the Lakota are based upon family and friends being present. Unlike the Inde, the Lakota will want the children to be present. Social support of close friends and family is expected. Friends and family surround a person who is seriously ill to provide social support and share and perform rituals. Even if one uses White medicine, the family and friends might also have Lakota curing rituals performed. The concept of social support is encouraged as a way to help the patient to achieve balance and harmony. A Lakota does not have friends stay in a waiting room. Strangers should not administer treatment to a patient. The sense of wholeness and harmony that is given by the social support of many friends and family members being present will help the patient to have better self-understanding. The presence of friends and family will also provide an awareness of balance and harmony that will also lessen the fears of the illness or injury and to also lower the feelings of depression and loneliness. This is what is known as holistic medicine. The main motif of the Lakota healing rituals is purification. All rituals are based upon their concept of spirituality.

Like most other tribes, the spiritual concepts of the Lakota are dependent upon their knowledge of the laws of nature. Since the borderline of the natural and supernatural is more blurred than that of modern science, they are no less valid to the people that believe them than science. The sense of community that supports the individual and the social group forms the basis of the spirituality of American Indian groups. The belief in spirits, deities, sacred objects, and sacred places is supported by the social structure, clan, and oral histories. Music, sings, and dance are a fundamental part of American Indian culture and spirituality.

The world is full of awe and wonders, and people are given the privilege to live in a world that is so wonderful. The longer that a Lakota lives, the more praise that he or she is to give to others. The healing ceremonies of the Lakota not only seek to heal the sick, but the healing ceremonies also provide a calmness and confidence for the tribal community. Drums, singing, dancing, and prayer are basic elements of the Lakota culture. The traditional ceremonies have been passed down through oral traditions of the Lakota. Since many of them now have been written, there have been changes. The Lakota way of producing a singing voice is somewhat unique. Lakota music produces sounds that range from an ear-piercing sound to a very mellow sound. When the melody descends, the voice gets more rhythmic. When women sing, they often develop a trilling sound to indicate happiness or appreciation. The voices of singers are judged on range, volume, and quality. The Lakota sing about sacred ways, sacred things, and to help others.

LAKOTA SPIRITUALITY AND DEATH

The Lakota are a spiritual people who believe that the spirit world is part of everything around them. The Lakota believe that all things from mountains, to the eagle, the buffalo, the wolf, and the fox all have spiritual powers and medicines that affect the lives and even cause the deaths of people. People are no better nor worse than any other living thing. Whatever will be will be. The earth protects us, feeds us, clothes us, and is there for us to use and to preserve. We are just passing through. We do not own the world. The Great Spirit or Great Mystery is the essence that permeates all life (Steiger 1984, 209). You should know who you are to be able to feel the Great Spirit in nature. It is only through nature that we can gain communion with the Holy Mystery (Steiger 1984, 193). The sacred pipe or calumet is the most sacred of all religious objects for the Lakota. The pipe, like the buffalo, corn, and all other things, is a gift from the holy powers that run the world. By smoking, one expresses the desire to have everything in one's life expressed as prayer that rises to the Great Spirit or Great Mystery (Carmody and Carmody 1993, 70). The world itself is sacramental and full of gifts of God that should cause one to return one's self to that God or spirit (Carmody and Carmody 1993, 73). The Black Hills are sacred hills because everything that the Lakota might need or desire can be found there. The Black Hills are the heartbeat of Earth Mother.

As humans, we are to treat all other humans as brothers and sisters in order to elevate our own inner spirits (Steiger 1984, 151). How we treat others determines what we become as humans (Steiger 1984, 151). For the Lakota, the essence of humans is contemplative in that humans should appreciate the splendors of creations and give a proper return to the Great Spirit who was responsible for providing such creations (Carmody and Carmody 1993, 74). While the Siousan tribes were known as ruthless, overwhelming adversaries, courageous almost to the point of folly, they were also deeply religious and had a rigid moral code (Marquis 1974, 147). There are five great values for the Lakota:

1. Be generous and sharing
2. Live a life of freedom and courage
3. Honor nature
4. Show respect for the old ones
5. Live with nature in a natural lifestyle

Praying, respect, caring and compassion, honesty and truth, generosity and sharing, humility, and wisdom are other important values.

Like the Inde, the Lakota did not develop a strong attachment to material goods. As a nomadic people, the Lakota did not have a permanent place that would allow them to amass a lot of worldly goods. Like the Inde, the Lakota practiced equality. According to Steiger (1984), women served on councils, played a vital role in the affairs of the tribe, and helped make tribal decision in spite of the fact that White leaders refused to meet with them to discuss tribal issues (Steiger 1984, 148). For the Lakota, it was their sacred duty to uphold the dignity of every person. As with the Inde, there are four seasons, four directions, four winds, and four ages of humans. Everything must return to the circle. The circle includes the sun rising each day and setting each night, and if left incomplete in our lives, the lack of a circle affects one's physical, mental, and spiritual self (Steiger 1984, 197).

The Lakota believe that non-Indians should listen to the earth. One should try to hear what the ground has to say. What is the essence of the spirit of the earth? What is the essence of the spirit of the water? Of the mountains? Of the air? What is the message that each of them is saying to us? The Lakota typically carry a medicine bag that contains something of meaning from each of the four elements of the world. This may include ash or burned rock representing fire, a dried plant representing water, a piece of bone or feather representing the air, and a stone or rock from the earth. Each item has something to say to the person. Each person must listen and then learn. The six powers, the Father Sky, the Earth Mother, and the four directions, are all part of the mystery of the Wakan Tanka or the Great Holy. Everything is sacred and is provided to help those who are willing to listen. The Lakota, like many other tribes, accept the concept of a guardian spirit who will also help those who will listen (Opler 1941).

For the Lakota, health, illness, and dying are a part of life. We are to accept our fate. How we live determines our fate. Like the tribes previously discussed, the Lakota feared the dead and would burn the dwelling of the deceased, forbid the use of his or her name, and bury their personal goods with the corpse to keep the ghost of the deceased from coming along to live with friends and relatives, yet they had little fear of death because they believed in an afterlife (Hassrick 1964, 225). Facing death as a Lakota was accepted as the natural end of the life cycle.

DEATH AND BURIAL PRACTICES

When a person died, it was taught that they were "walking on." It was taught that one's journey did not end with death but continued after death. Spirits were a part of the Lakota world. Many Lakota still offer spiritual foods to help the spirit of the deceased on its travels. Traditionally, the Lakota would place gifts such as weapons, tools, pipe, knives, and other possessions in the animal skin that held the body, but today, the gifts are placed in the casket with the body. The Lakota believe that it takes about four days after the burial for the spirit of the dead to make their journey to the next station in life. As with living people, some spirits were good and others not so good. Yet, death in old age was not feared nor was the ghost who was thought to remain among the living for a time after their death (Spencer and Jennings 1965, 376). Like the Hopi, the Lakota seem to accept the dead and their spirits.

The Lakota believe that death will happen to everyone regardless of their achievements, fame, wisdom, bravery, or whatever and that the mortuary practices allowed the living a way of showing their reverent respect for the dead (Hassrick 1965, 293). If the deceased was a young person, and particularly a young child, the mourners would gash their arms and legs and engage in ritual crying (Underhill 1953, 159). If the death happened in the home, the burial would be delayed for a day and a half in the hope that the deceased might revive (Hassrick 1964, 293). They would dress the body in the finest clothes available that would be provided by a relative if the deceased did not have proper clothes. The body would be wrapped tightly in robes with the weapons, tools, medicines, and pipe; and then, the bundle would be placed on a scaffold for air burial with food and drink placed beneath the scaffold for the deceased (Spencer and Jennings 1965, 376). While there is evidence that the Lakota groups used earth burial and mound burial in earlier times, during the winter when scaffolds could not be built, trees were often used for burial (Cox 2010, 87). While tree or platform burial was traditional rather than earth burial, after a year, they would bury the body. They did not bury the body immediately because they thought that the spirit would not be able to escape if the body was buried too soon, but over time, many have adopted the White man's way of immediate burial rather than using trees or scaffolds for a year before burying (Hamilton and Hamilton 1971, 231). After the body was dressed and properly wrapped, the adult members of the family would begin wacekiyapi or the worship ritual for the deceased in which men might drive pegs through their arms or legs, women might slash their limbs or cut off their little fingers at the first joint. Both men and women might express their grief by singing, wailing, or weeping (Hassrick 1964, 296–297). The favorite horse of the deceased would be killed under the scaffold of its deceased and its tail would be tied to the scaffold. The mourning would continue for as long as a year (Grinnell 1972, 160).

The practice of placing the body on a scaffold or in a tree, was believed by the Lakota and other Siouan tribes, would free the soul to be able to rise into the sky if the person died of natural causes. If the person died in battle, the Dakotas would often leave the person on the plains where the warrior died to allow his spirit to rise into the sky (Grinnell 1972, 161). For the Lakota or other Siouan groups, the spirits of the dead are not gone or lost to humankind, but rather continue to exist here and can be reached by the living for support and aid (Grinnell 1972, 163). While some have argued that the Lakota fear the dead and their ghosts, there is little evidence to support that belief.

The following is a transcription of a member of the Lower Brule Sioux:

My name is _____, and I am a member of the Lower Brule Sioux. I've been with the Lakota since 1964, I'm 53 years old. The reason why we relocated from Port George, SD to Pine Ridge is because the place where we live is right along the Missouri River and we were told that there was going to be a flood that will take place. So that was the reason why my mother, I mean my paternal grandmother, she's from the Black Bonnet Clan, a descendant of Sitting Bull. She was out praying, and she got, she received a vision. That's the reason why we came to the Pine Ridge Indian Reservation. Is, the spirit of Crazy Horse gave her instructions to come and live with the Lakota because they have a rich culture and they will preserve their native language. That's the reason why I'm still living in this community. And I left my reservation at the age of 13.

When I first came into this village, I was a young woman and I'm very thankful that very day, I give thanks to my paternal grandmother, she's the one that taught my native language. And as a young girl, the first thing I learned was about astrology. And my paternal grandfather, he's an _____, and he was converted by the _____ of _____, _____ reservation. And what happened there was he had more understanding of the Holy Bible. Because he had a brother, his name was _____. He went to school at _____ and he was the interpreter. Well the teachings that I received at an early age was something that was very, very important to us, was the Big Dipper. That's how I learned how to count 1 to 7 at a very young age. Because the Big Dipper has 7 stars and at this time my grandmother did tell me about, the beliefs, to understand the seven rituals. And the first ritual that was done for me was piercing my ears. And she used a real sharp bone to sharpen my ears. And I was told to listen to Mother Nature. Listen even to the various kinds of trees. The cottonwood trees, listen, they have a message. The pine tree, the cedar tree. Then listen to the animals. Such as the crickets that give us messages for us like warnings that have to do with the weather. The coyotes, if there is going to be sickness, they come close to our home. And also, if there is a bad weather coming, there is a way of learning the difference of the how long. And also, the eagles. The eagles are very sacred. If we see one flying above us, that is one of our ancestors.

Going back to the astrology. The seven stars after what she told me was if they're all fulfilled, that is a life pass to the happy hunting grounds. So, when we die, our spirit will go through the big dipper, go on south, the ghost road. And she really does believe in reincarnation. But the first ritual that was done for me, it was a beautiful. I still remember that event. I still have my horse hairs today. It's in my home. And that's something very sacred to me. And that's to develop my listening skills. And listen to people when they talk, especially the elders. And at this time, I learned the difference between an orphan.

In our little community of Port George, there was about 8 families that all lived about a mile apart. Every Sunday was the day they would come and visit. And orphans are really treated with respect. You give them food, you feed them, if you have anything to spare, like clothing, that's what I always shared, was my clothes with there were two girls that were orphans. And it was really a blessing to me when I was told I earned the first star. The second ritual that was done for me was receiving my name. My grandmother used to watch me at all times especially when I was around the animals. You know such as the puppies, the dogs, the horses, even the chickens. And the name I received was _____. _____ means to have the love for animals, for people, even love my enemies. And at that time, I didn't know what it meant. So that was my second ritual, getting my _____ name. The third one was to get my eagle ____. And this is really a blessing. The _____ represents every month that's when I begin to understand the phases of the moon. When the first new moon appears, this _____ was given to me, it was blessed. And it's got a marking of the _____, _____ is Indian painted scarlet red. And then she put it on my left side close to my brain and she told me to be strong at all times. And so, after that, I was instructed to remember my _____ every month. To pray for my family, my relatives and the nation. And also remember the loved ones that passed on such as our leaders Sitting Bull, _____, _____, and _____ know him as Crazy Horse but we know him as _____. And then that was the third ritual, that was really wonderful.

As a young girl, I never have the opportunity to go out and really play with girls my age because my grandmother was my teacher and I really enjoyed being around her and the other grandmas. The fourth ritual that was done for me was receiving the seven shells and you could find those around the Missouri River. And then I had to take my foot coverings off and try to walk on these shells and it was too prickly and that's when my grandmother told me that's how life is going to be especially if we have to move to a village with a lot of people is to stay home, don't go from house to house because you hear people talking bad about each other, when you do, do not repeat anything that is negative. This is really something, it took my 5th time to walk across and then is how I really learned about the teaching of the white buffalo, ____. And according to the legend, it was really a blessing when we went to the location, it's out in the Black Hills area. And this is a reminder. The pipe is used for your health. It's for the people. If we are given seven rituals and if people fulfill these seven rituals our race will continue to prosper. So that was my fourth ritual that was done, walking through the seven shells. And these shells are not along the river anymore. When I mention about the flood, after we relocated to _____, we went back a few months later and we were heartbroken. It really broke my grandmother's heart because the things that grew along the Missouri river were sacred such as the herbs that were used, like she knows a lot of the herbs especially when us children are sick. I have an older brother, he had scarlet fever. And she gathered the herbs and he got healed. And along the Missouri River a lot of the timber was really thick. And every time we go out for water we were supposed to stick together because it will, they call it _____, and they're very sacred.

They watch over, for instance if a man goes out for vision quests, they give him messages. But after we did see our home, my grandparents' home was underwater, my grandmother starts to sing her death song. And that was bad news. Because to her, everything was taken away from her from this flood. And the rituals that were, the shells that we left, they were gone. So now when I go back to that place, I pray wherever they are at. I was really thankful that I had the opportunity to utilize them.

And after we came into this community the ritual that was done was receiving a weapon. Which was a knife, a hunting knife. And this I had to use it of learning how to skin a deer, small game such as rabbits, ____, and I learned a lot from my grandmother of how to make jerk. You know, meat. You know you cut, you thin out the pieces of meat. And then what you do, you dry them. And it was a lot of work, but it was worth it. She was telling me that pre-reservation life, her grandmother, the weapon she got was to protect herself. But this one here I was instructed to use it for my family. And the next one was getting a chastity belt. A chastity belt, she told me, that it was a blessing. At nights, she would wrap both of my legs before I got to sleep. In the mornings, I detached a rawhide, it's probably about 4 feet long and she told me the day when I became a young woman, she told me that if we lived pre-reservation life, I would have had my own teepee. And when you put your poles, three poles together, this chastity belt would be used to fasten it. But she told me that the next thing she said, I won't see you, I won't be there when you start your own family. The third thing they use it for is to put it, for instance for childbirth, whenever you are going into labor, you put the belt a certain way. And the fourth thing, the fourth thing you will be using for this belt, when you die, you earned, whenever you go through courtship, pre-reservation life you will be given a rope this will come from your husband to be and that's a precious gift.

When you die, you will be buried, you'll be wrapped up in a bunch of rope and your chastity belt that will go with you. So, when I came here as a young woman, to me at first, I was scared. But our home was open to elders, children. And I'm really thankful that I gained a lot of respect from the grandpas because they come over, and my father was a WWII veteran, and the men folks they come and talk about the treaties and I'm really thankful we had the opportunity to meet the late Mr. Matthew King. And at this time, I had an uncle, his name was _____, he's always with us. So, I learned more because I understand their language. It's their ____, I had a hard time at first talking to people because some of the words I learned were way different from the _____. So anyways, the 6th ritual done, that should have been done.

My grandmother since we lived in a village and had a lot of elders come over, one of the rituals that was very, very important and was supposed to be done for me when I reach menopause. But as a young girl, she says, I've been watching you, she said, this ritual I will do for you. And it was the grandpas that witnessed this ritual. And I was really thankful. What happened was this was the blessing of the hands. And what happened there was she put this Indian paint, this ___, and she told me to learn more about the white man's education and first time she ever did see the typewriter, oh she was really excited! And she said I should learn how to use this typewriter, so I could help the people with their business and writing letters and so forth. And then also was to help people, what she meant was make food, cook, and make ___.

And she said, when you help people out, your hands, since you're blessed, you could make spiritual foods, such as you know there are four different kinds of ___, one of them is for the spirits, to feed them, one is for the sick, and one is for going out for vision quests and one is for your family that you bless. If you have a family member that is going astray, like one that is going towards material things or _____ water, that is like a holy communion, that's how I see it now. So anyways, that was done for me, so as of today, I still practice that. I make _____ for people. I don't charge because what I learned there was that when you do something like this, the Great Spirit will give you blessings. I might gain friends, or someone might help me out with whatever, you know. So, the last ritual, I'm still looking for a grandma, I have to, their grandma will give me, I'll be presented an eagle feather, and I'll be marked on my forehead, we call it _____, it's a special marking on the forehead, like a cross.

And I'm 53 years old and the next area that I'd like to get into, with my experience, about like as of today, both of my parents are deceased. And my two older, I have an older brother, a younger brother. My older brother died at the age of 35. My youngest brother died at the age of ten. And my four sisters, I had two older sisters that died before me and I have two younger sisters that died.

And I have something I would really like to share, especially, my mother, her paternal grandmother is from Oklahoma, she's a southern Cheyenne. And there's something we found out on my mother's side, her grandfather, her paternal grandfather is a full-blooded French man. And he's the one, he's the carrier of our H negative. And that's the reason why I'm really thankful that if it wasn't for my grandmother, I wouldn't be sitting here today, I wouldn't be alive. But because of my mother's blood, her blood factor, that's the reason why my sisters didn't live to be a year old. And, at an early age, how I was told about death was, this is a true story, I really believe it because I even share it with my children. And I live in a cluster housing, so if I have young people coming into my home, I share this with them. And this is a legend told to me by my paternal grandmother. Up in the sky, there was life up there. And there was no worries.

A great grandfather chose, he was looking around because he wanted to send someone on a mission to Turtle Island, and he chose a man and a woman. And he told them, I'm sending you on a mission. When you go on a mission, help each other out. Especially your families and you will prosper and have respect, love one and other and help each other out, you know. And he said, one of these days I will send you back and you are going to tell me about your mission. And this is what I really believe in. And I know I miss my mom and dad, my grandparents on both sides, you know, and my family, but they are in a good place. And the thing that we have to do, this is what I was taught, by building these rituals, is I'm preparing myself for the last ritual.

And I have a granddaughter she's three years old. I'm teaching her the _____ language. And at nights, the thing that I learned as a young child, the first four years of a _____ child's life is very, very sacred. They can see spirits, sometimes they talk to people. And my granddaughter that's 3 ½ years old tells me who is in my home. And I listen to her. And she was born with 2 bottom teeth and she's a fluent speaker and I really love my granddaughter. And I prayed about 5 years ago whenever I had a life, it's really an experience that I'll never forget back in 1994. I was really a traditional person. I go to Standing Rock Reservation. The reason I go to these places is because I have my grandmother, the one that was my teacher, her sacred pipe, and to tell you the truth it is really wonderful to walk with a pipe because you are going to shed many, many tears and what I tell people is please respect each other, don't hate one another, don't have jealousy. That's what's really hurting our people. And I did see a lot of miracles happen with my grandmother's pipe. And I really do believe in animals. And when I was doing these as a young child, I really learned how to, I really do understand that we are not living according to what was taught at one time and we lost that. We come from the animal clans and that's what we're forgetting. But four years ago, my oldest daughter gave birth, and she was a preemie. She came in, let's see, she came three months early and I was there to deliver her. And I pray to the bear spirit, and even up to this day, she growls like a bear. And I know they are around us. The bears and the animals that are very sacred. And the vision that I had back in 1994, like I said I was going to the sweat lodge to pray with people and I ended up having a wood tick on the left side of my neck. And I kept going into the sweat lodge to pray for people because there are a lot of people that need prayers and a lot of them are being a _____. For instance, you pray with white people, I pray with all walks of life. We all pray to the same Supreme Being but we all address him in a different way. And then for instance, a thing I would like to mention is my experience with death. When I got sicker, I had this rash around where I pulled off the wood tick. And at this time, my mother was with me. My dad passed away back in 1987. And I always prayed you know go out to a certain tree that was very sacred and communicate with my dad, you know I really believe in that way. And I continued on praying, and I noticed I had a rash and I kept going to our health center and being referred to Pine Ridge. My third week going up there they were doing a lot of blood work. The day that the doctor from Pine Ridge told me I had acute leukemia. My ten-year-old brother, my youngest brother died from leukemia. And first thing I prayed, and I told the Great Spirit that whatever was instructed, whatever was taught, I help my people. Every day, four times a day I remember the elders. I pray for the orphans. I pray for the handicaps that cannot walk, cannot talk, cannot hear. Then I pray for those ones that lost a spouse.

So, when I, my condition got worse, when I was May 14, 1994, I went to Pine Ridge, I couldn't walk. So, from there, I was transferred to East Regional and got put, they took me up to the 9th floor. And twice they took me through the MRI, they didn't know what was wrong. Finally, they did a, oh what's it's called, spinal tap. And then my condition got worse, and I prayed. I couldn't sit up, I couldn't eat. And I was slowly losing my vision. And I prayed to _____, great grandfather, and I told them because I was having this horrible pain and I was praying, I said I did whatever I can, please remember my good deeds from my people. And my condition got worse, I had to be in a private room and I always remember all I could do was listen to people but when I tried to talk my tongue would swell. Then finally I heard this voice saying I'm Dr. Keegan from disease control. Mayo Clinic called, your diagnosis is Lyme Disease. So were gonna start you off with _____ treatment, that's antibiotics and were going to do plasmapheresis (plazma exchange). Okay there's an Evangelist that came and prayed for me and he prayed the Christianity way, but I listened, you know. So, I prayed the way I was taught was asking for whatever I've done, I'm sorry and it's up to you _____ if you want me to live but it's up to you. And that was before I went on my spiritual journey.

I went, I was approached by this grandma, she's really a beautiful woman. She was very, very old. And I happened to look at her feet and she had moccasins on and I could tell she had crow's feet, that's what my grandmother had. And she told me her name was _____, beautiful woman. And she said, we are going on a journey and I was holding onto her and we went to, we came, like it's a downhill, it's out in the Black Hills, and there was a river and two camps that separated this river. And she said we are going to visit the camp on the left side and when we got there, there was lots of mangy dogs. They looked so pitiful. I started to pet them. And I had these dogs, and I looked around to see if I could find any kind of food but there was none. Then I met many of my relatives, they were still intoxicated, they were still drunk. And they were cussing. And I happened to look at the dwellings I did see these teepees. They were not well kept. I went to a teepee and I touched it and it wasn't made out of canvas, it was pieces of remnants of buffalo hides and I looked around. My relatives would not look at me. They were trying to argue, they were arguing, they were trying to fight. I looked to the grandma, I said grandma, I can't take this. She said don't worry, you know, your great grandfather is coming.

And sure, enough there was a man walking with four men behind him. When he got closer, his face was blurry. He had a head dress on, ohh he looked so nice. And there was a teepee, large. It's pretty large. And he went in there with his four followers. I begged some of my relatives to go in there and they refused. They didn't want to go in there. I was curious, so I went in there and sat down at the entrance. And great grandfather talked to the ones that went in and said they had a second chance because when they came to Turtle Island they were too selfish and instead into material things. So, what he wanted for them to do was to ask for forgiveness, so we could go across the river. And it was just a handful that asked for forgiveness. As we came out, I thought he was going to lead us, he looked at me and said, what do you see in that river? So, I looked, and I could see some boulders of rocks, so I told him I could see some eons, some rocks. You lead us. And I thought to myself, okay. I start praying and we went across.

On that side that village was so beautiful. The only thing I did see was dogs. They were black, they looked powerful, they looked strong, they looked healthy. And I did see these women, working together quietly, I did see some of these hides being stretched out and they used these stretchers to scrape off, you know, they're all working very hard and I happen to look at their hands and their hands look pretty rough. So, I see these groups of women working together. When I got to the men folks, I did see my father there. And I looked at him and he smiled at me and he showed me a pipe. And it was my grandma's pipe. He smiled. So, we went around, and I was really happy to see many of my relatives, but they were all older. The ones that I did see on the other side were a lot younger and then when I went inside, into this lodge in the middle of the teepees, and I was, I got my scolding. The grandfather from the west, _____, what he said was, women are not supposed to sun dance. We already have a sacred gift. We're sacred, four days of each month, I guess that's how I can interpret. But what we're doing is overpowering the men. So, I asked for forgiveness, I said thank you for telling me this cause I did sun dance right after my father died because I wanted to see the family tree and I did. And I said I'm very sorry and I was instructed to pray for the men folks because the men are the providers, but they are weak because of _____, you know. And then the thunder beings, their message is there is lot of imitations of Crazy Horse.

And that's the reason why they are very upset, and they are going to spend more time towards East because that's where the civilization of the white men. And now there are bad things coming, it's up in the air so they are going to protect us. And then I was told about the fires that were going to happen, especially at _____ because there are too many offerings being placed there and it's not for anybody's health, it's for material things so they are going to start a fire. And it did happen. We had that fire. And then the grandfather from the north, the buffalo nation. The buffalo that is protecting our nation is on his hind leg. He is ready to collapse. When this happens, Turtle Island will crack in half. And there's going to be seven buffalo calves that are going to be born around us. And we have four today and we have to start reaching out to these younger generations to let them know that they have to take life seriously.

First of all, to learn their language and understand the customs. And the generations we are going to see in a couple hundred years is not going to be very good because there is a lot of . . . the next few generations that's coming is not going to be very good because we have children that are hurt from fire water, I guess today you could call them FAS. And there are a lot of relatives marrying each other, a lot of inbreeds. So, my message was to work with the younger generation to let them know to respect you do not marry your fourth cousin. And the sacred pipe, the original pipe, it is well hidden. And in the descriptions this place is out in the _____mountains in Wyoming. And there is a replica at Greengrass, and that is very sacred too.

And then the grandfather from the east and the elk nation. The elks are getting very weak because we are not using parts of their bodies. One of them is their canine teeth. We don't use them. Our ancestors, the women, they use them, carry them around their neck to protect their bosoms and their wombs. That's the reason why today women are having problems, they have like cervical cancer, breast cancer. And then they have a very powerful medicine but nobody's, not there to pray to them. And this is really something. And there are more bad things coming from that direction, so we are supposed to pray. And then the grandfather from the south. This is the entrance to the happy hunting grounds. At one time the opening was narrow, but it has widened because of our people. What they are doing today is they are selling their religion. They go among the white people and use them for their money. And this is our punishment so after I talk to the grandpa, this grandma took me back and it was to a sweat lodge. And I heard the grandpas pray in there and so her and I we went inside and there was an old bone dish in there with water. And after I came out, I heard a voice saying I was going to meet your four brothers, your big brothers. So, I was really happy, thought I might see some ____. And whatever it was, it was coming, it was making loud noises, it was growling. And I was praying, I had my arms up in the air. When it came, it was ____, a bear. I looked at him, and he said, your ancestors used to come to me, they used to ask for my help, but not anymore. I help people to get well, especially if their body is swollen. With my finger, look at my nails. I see his claws, they were sharp. He said I will puncture a hole and I will suck up sickness. I am looking for a friend. He said do not be afraid of me. He started to dig the ground. As of today, here in my office, I have the bear medicine. He said this will help you to get strong again. Your people, you loved your people, you got yourself real weak. You did real good things in your life and he said I will protect you. So, I touched him, and I prayed for being my big brother. He said always remember me in your prayers and he went over the hill then those two things that came over the hill. It was a wolf and a coyote. And they said both of us are related. I stood there and looked at them. They said, three generations ago, your ancestors were able to talk to us. Nobody talks to us. The wolves are heading towards the north, there are very few that's left. And he said, this is my cousin. He needs help too. And the coyote told me, I come to where you're at. You never come outside, you never feed us. Remember us, we will help you. Later on, in life we want you to live out in the country, we've got messages to give you. So, I touched both of them and I prayed, and they both left. The third visit was from an elk. The elk really smiled and told me about the _____ that he's got, and this elk dwelled around us and where I'm from. And the _____ he's got will help people from sores on their skin because great grandfather is very upset with our people and what they're doing. He's going to come closer to mother earth. And the message that I got was it happened three years, ago, the harvest moon. After that, seven years that's going to happen. So, I thanked the elk for being my brother and I will always remember you. And the fourth one was the buffalo. And the buffalo told me our generation, we're getting weaker, we're losing our native language and we're not eating four kinds of meat every month like we should. An animal that walks swiftly, which is the deer. An animal that flies upwards real fast, which is the grouse. An animal that lives in the water, which is the fish, the catfish provides us brain food. And the fourth animal that crawls on mother earth, which is the turtle, we are forgetting about the turtle. That is the reason why our children are not strong in their minds. So, whatever they see right away, they hang onto that, they cling to it. And then the buffalo also told about the parts of his body not being used like it was at one time. And then he said he's was going to take me on a journey. So, he got on the ground, so I hopped on his back. And he said we have relatives, clear down to Mexico. He took me to a temple. There was a feathered serpent and these people that came, they were dressed in white. White robes and had arm bands. And they came, and they had me touch the serpent and I got more strength and there was a pyramid, a temple that we had to climb. I got ¾ of the way and I turned around and the buffalo said it was time to go home. And after I got on the buffalos back, we came back to the place that we started. And when I woke up, there was nurses around me so all together I went on this journey for 38 days. And I was really thankful that the great grandfather gave me a change and the grandfather is the four directions. And this is what we are losing today, especially with our younger generations.

And as for the burial practices I would like to share. My paternal grandmother, she's got _____ buried among the Missouri River. But that's all, it's from the river, its three miles, on a hillside. This is a true story. Her grandmother is from the _____ man from grandpa from _____ sitting bull. And they drifted long after, they drifted it along the Missouri River and she lost her oldest child, a newborn son. So the women are the ones that did the burying of the baby on the scaffold. So she got her sharp object which was a bone and cut her arms. That's how they create. And I still have my scars on my arms from when my dad died. We shed the blood and I prayed that, you know, what I learned from my dad I'll keep on going and will pass it on to my grandchildren. And the story goes where when she lost her loved one, she went to the burial where her baby was buried, and she prayed. She cried and cried and cried. She got real weak, she got, she just let herself go on the ground and she just laid there cause she did cut herself and she was singing a death song, and someone was licking her cheeks. Her cheek. And I guess she heard a voice saying woman, _____, don't cry. So, she opened her eyes and she looked, it was a coyote. It was a female coyote. She said, you will have more sons. Great grandfather sends you your oldest son for a short mission, he has some other things that he has to do. So, she stopped her crying and she said this is where you will be coming and bring food to us. Sure enough, she got pregnant and she had another son. And then after that, she had three sons that become lawyers.

And so, where my great grandmother, the one that it happened to, this is where she is buried, her and her sons. And this is a very special place. I go back over there every fall. I go to the scaffolds and I did see my grandmother do this, so that's why I do that. I take spiritual food, _____, like tobacco reeds, and I go back to that place and after now all there is, there is eight of them, buffalo skulls. And they are on top of this, just line them up. Sometimes, the wind will, if its real windy and we see any of the remains, the bones, we pray and put it back in there inside the buffalo skull. And I know I love going there because I always hear singing, especially when I take food and it makes me realize that to come back over here I've been here at Oglala Lakota College for 27 years, I've been working as an adult education tutor and I have the opportunity to share my especially you know, to let the young people know that we're here on a special mission and we have to learn more about our customs and then for instance with grieving, one of the rituals is keeping of the spirit, keeping of the soul. We're doing this for my mother, she left us back in 1998 and I told the elders that we'll do this for, mourn for her for 7 years and I really love my mom. I know every meal at home we share a plate for her and with a grieving period, like when my mother passed away, what we do after the burial, after four days, it is our habit. For instance, I keep my children at home, don't let them go out to socialize with their friends. They clean their room so that way I don't have to be reminding them to clean their rooms. And then, cooking, feeding the people. And after four days, for instance, her room, what we used was sage. We have sage and we boil the water and we put the bundle, we put that sage and we wipe her walls. We do that. The reason why we do that is her, if we don't, sometimes we're going to hear her coughing, or you know, somehow, we know. But what we do is we watch ourselves, we don't go to pow wows. We don't go to community gatherings. Instead we put our hands to work. Like we do with our daughters, we do a lot of sewing. So, in seven years we are going to have a dinner and I have a lock of her hair. Pre-reservation life when this ritual was done, they actually put a teepee close to the family's home and you keep the lock of hair inside the teepee.

But since here we can't do that because we live in, we're too modern, but I keep her lock of hair in her closet, you know. And once a month, we pray. She's buried her at the _____ cemetery. And this is what I was truly against when I came into this community was since we are Christian, I mean a lot of us became Christian, we have _____, Catholics, other denominations. And my grandmother didn't want to be buried in the ground, her belief is such as my great grandpa here, Sitting Bull. He was buried the old way, but the government gave the Indian Scouts instructions to bury him in the ground. When that happened, they cut his head, and they sent it to Washington D.C. to analyze his brain. Why is he so powerful?

So, my grandmother didn't believe in burying their loved ones in the ground. When you do, your spirits will be here, it will not go straight up, so that is one of her beliefs. But with my mother, we have to watch what we say, we are not to hurt anybody. I am trying to keep my children from gossiping, or not to be fighting, not to argue. So, the things that I learned was from my paternal grandmother and I know what I'm trying to do is develop a curriculum on this, so I can share with other colleges.

And then I share the story you know, after I came out of this coma, I was told by the doctors, I have five doctors at East Regional. I have to go see a psychiatrist because of the plasmapheresis I was told I might lose, I might have a memory loss. I might not be able to, I am going to have an identity crisis, but I didn't, no. And I was told that I will never, never walk again. So, I came home and met with my uncle _____, we lost him January 9th at the age of 92. And I really do believe in praying with the elders, I really do. And he came into my home, and there was a medicine man that wanted to doctor me, but he wanted $500 so I disagree with that. So, I looked around, I have a lot of people that I prayed with in the sweat lodge, they are all scared of me, scared to come to me. So, it took me five years, I know I talked to two of my grandfather's medicine men and they said because of jealousy they put a curse on me. But I, maybe they did, but I don't believe in that. Because I understand the pipe. When you pray with the pipe, you're not supposed to have bad thoughts of your people. But what I did was I prayed all this time, these five years and I started to retract about all the teachings I got from my grandmother and I know even up to this day I do this early in the morning, I pray to the morning star. _____, but people now, I went to a church school, _____, it's at Methodist, I learned more about the Bible, the Old Testament, the New Testament.

Whatever my grandmother told me was all in there. You know, and the legend she told me about _____, when Jesus, his own people, they killed him, they crucified him. On the third day when he rose he came to Turtle Island and he came to different tribes gave them talkings to use. And I really believe when we pray to the morning star we ask for guidance and strength throughout the day to help our people and also remember our loved ones, you know. So this is what I've been practicing. And it took me five years to really understand life after death. And what I found out is various spirits around us, they can see us, they are hungry and need prayers. What I meant is when they are hungry, tobacco is considered sacred. So, I offer tobacco and if I don't have peppermint tea, I usually substitute with coffee. I share that in the morning and evening. And the morning star represents, for instance, we have to get up at, and even pray at midday. I still do this ritual, I pray to the great grandfather, the sun. And when the sun goes down, I thank the grandfather for giving us energy through the day. And then the spirits, I'll tell you, this is a true story, whatever I am going to say is coming from the heart. I pray and pray, depending on my earthly friends and relatives, and it seems like they just can't get along.

So, what's happening now is my ancestors, my loved ones are helping me to walk. A month after I was able to walk, I went to Deadwood, I should have known better. But I like to go to Deadwood because there's a museum there and now they have casinos. And we went into this casino and I lost my strength. And I looked around and when my loved ones were around me, I could smell like, for instance, sage or sweet grass and I know they are around me. And they left me. I sat there, and I told my daughter, I should have brought my wheelchair. So, I said, well my children can help me. So, after that, I don't go to casinos. But the reason they are helping me walk is to help my people. Like right now its education. You know, it's your future. But the Oglala Lakota College they have a culture studies department. Back in 1996 I just wanted to be a role model, and I was a full-time student. When I first came back to work, I was still paralyzed waist down. But I was able to use my hands and my brain and, you know, I pray every day to ask for strength. But gradually, I got my strength back and I really believe in the spirits, the spirits do come, I don't consider myself a medicine woman, no. But I really thank my paternal grandmother for being with me and always pray to him, like every morning I meditate and the thing I learned from him, for instance, is two years ago I got myself involved with a parent group and our motto is let's put our mind together and see what kind of life we can make for our children, and that is coming from my great grandfather, Sitting Bull. So, I'm really happy I was given a chance to come back and be with them _____, and I'm in _____, I've been gone since 1964 so I never have an opportunity to vote at their chart election because according to their bylaws if you live off the reservation. So, I never got any kind of financial assistance from my tribe. But I really do love the Lakota because they speak their native language. With the college, it took me, they have this program, it's called the _____ language proficiency. And the first time I took it, I tried to use some of the words, and they don't understand me. So, I didn't make it. My second time, I didn't make it. My third time, I had to think like an _____ and here I passed. So, I'm real thankful and the degree I am pursuing now is a Bachelor of Arts, in _____ studies. And I should be done this spring, that way, like what I'm telling you today, I'd like to develop my own curriculum like for instance the sacred numbers, the elements, you know. And like with, this works with what I'm telling you, but you know, some of the words that I really don't understand what was brought to me. But, I'm working on myself every day. I remind myself I'm here for a reason. I always ask for strength and I have young people come to me, you know and, today is a harder time for our younger generation. They are lost. They are lost. And me you know, I'm 53 years old and I'm willing to be a teacher to them. So, thank you for your time. (Cox 2015, 347–375)

THE BLACKFEET

The Blackfeet people are thought to have originated in the Great Lakes region but migrated to the Bow and North Saskatchewan Rivers well before the seventeenth century and by the eighteenth century had moved to the south and displaced the Shoshones in Montana (Pritzker 1998, 430). While little is known for sure about where the Blackfeet originated, the general consensus is that they were an Eastern Woodland tribe that migrated westward several hundred years ago. Before being known as the Blackfeet, they were called Pikuni or Piegan, the Kainah or Blood, and Siksika or Blackfoot who are also known as the Northern Blackfoot to distinguish them from the other two tribes (Ewers 1958, 5). While the three tribes were independent, they spoke the same Algonquian language, generally shared the same customs, intermarried, and made war together against common enemies (Ewers 1958, 5). The three Blackfeet tribes remained in the same areas as each other for centuries.

The name Blackfeet is thought to have originated from the black moccasins that they wore. Whether they painted them or if they were blackened by fires on the prairie is not known. Since the Blackfeet language is part of the Algonquian family linguistically, that bolsters the argument that they were a Woodland tribe. Today, the Blackfeet lived primarily in Alberta and Saskatchewan, Canada, and in Montana.

BLACKFEET LIFEWAYS

They quickly adapted to the plains lifestyle. Like the Lakota, they hunted buffalo or bison, elk, deer, mountain sheep, and pronghorn; lived in tipis;

and used dogs for transport until they were able to get horses after the Spanish brought them into the plains. As the fur trade expanded to the West, the Blackfeet were able to trade hides for medal tools, utensils, and weapons. The coming of the horse, the gun, and expanded trade changed the lifestyle of the Blackfeet. At the same time, the coming of epidemics and disease, the decline of the bison, and, later, whiskey hurt the Blackfeet more than anything (Pritzker 1998, 430). The Blackfeet were also victims of the Baker Massacre which happened in 1870 when the 2nd Cavalry killed 173 mostly women and children from a peaceful band. Major Baker was looking for another band who he had been ordered to capture for a crime, but even though he knew that this was not the bad that he was searching for, he ordered the attack anyway. None of the soldiers were punished or reprimanded in any way.

Because the Blackfeet lived so far north where the winters were long and summers were short, they did not farm, but rather they were nomadic hunters in the region that they shared with the Cree and Assiniboins (Ewers 1958, 9). The Blackfeet were known as a powerful confederacy that controlled a huge area of the northeastern plains from what is now Alberta to the upper Missouri River in Montana to the Rocky Mountains to the west (Waldman 1988, 30). They had to endure long, hard winters which led them to stay in one place during the winters, but in milder weather, they did move to follow the animals that they hunted staying in one place only long enough to grow tobacco, the only crop that they planted (Waldman 1988, 32). As warriors, they had a great reputation. The Blackfeet were generally hostile toward the Whites and struck fear in the mountaineers, miners, and settlers because they were so warlike and that led to the opening of the Canadian and American West to be slowed (Waldman 1988, 33).

As with other Plains tribes, ceremonies, family, and tribe were important to the Blackfeet. Like other Plains tribes, the Blackfeet would gather in the midsummer for the sun dance or the Medicine Lodge Ceremony which was viewed as the most sacred ceremony of not only the Blackfeet, but of all Plains tribes. It was also to be the time that thanks would be given by warriors for surviving danger; when vows would be made; and the time for ceremonies for the Medicine Pipe, bundles, and health would be celebrated. Like other Plains tribes, the Blackfeet used sacred sites, including medicine wheels made from aligning rocks, to form a circle where they had vision quests, prayers, and other spiritual purposes (Josephy 1994, 23).

Like many other tribes, in the Blackfeet culture, children were taught manners and to respect their elders, women were in charge of educating their daughters while men were expected to educate their sons, and while men were the lords of the house, women got the property when the husband died or left her (Ewers 1958, 192–193).

A Kutenai is said to have brought the first horse to the Piegan camp in a desperate attempt to save them from starvation. Horses were called "sky dogs," but the horse did not come from the sky and brought with it disease as did the cattle and the Europeans who came to the plains. Many Plains communities became known as "villages of the dead," because disease not only killed the people, but it also killed the bison as well as their way of life. Seeds, excrement from horses and cows, and Europeans themselves with their germs decimated entire villages and even entire tribes. Death was always a part of the Plains Indians daily life, but the coming of the Europeans with their animals made death an even greater intrusion on their lives. Like other Plains groups, the Blackfeet believed in the immortality of the soul, that the dead became ghosts, that ghosts could return to be among the living and could do good or bad deeds to the living, and that ceremonies must be performed to aid the dead on their journey and to keep them from harming the living (Mails 1995, 177). Traditionally, the Blackfeet women would prepare the body, dressing it in their finest clothes, sew the body into buffalo robes, and typically would place the body in the forks of trees or upon scaffolds, but on occasion would place the body in a ravine or hill top and then covering it with dirt and stones (Ewers 1958, 107). Like other Plains groups, the Blackfeet had "giveaways" to those in attendance of the funerary rites after the burial, and they also mourned after the death with women lamenting for a month or more, cutting off fingers, gashing legs and/or their faces, cutting their hair short, and calling to the deceased, but the men would not mourn for wives or daughters, but rather would mourn for sons and fathers by cutting their hair, gashing, and going without their leggings (Mails 1995, 184). Like the Lakota, some Blackfeet have been able to maintain their traditional practices, while others hire funeral directors, particularly those who incorporate traditional ways with modern practices.

The following is a transcription of Blackfeet practices:

Hello, my name is _____, I own the Funeral Home, _____ Funeral home in St. Ignatius, Montana. Uhh . . . purpose of this video is just to give you kind of an oral history or tribal beliefs about death and dying. My qualifications, I've been in the business 20 years. I've ran Indian funeral homes for 10 years, approximately 80% of our business is Indian, and I am a quarter native but not from this tribe. Uh some very basics here, a lot of this is related to me by my wife, and from practice and literature they have out. So hopefully you can get the basics, uhh, kind of a brief idea. The Salish, which comprises the Flathead portion of Salish Pondrach comprises the Flathead portion of this reservation, that is the bulk of our business. And to give you a very brief history, they moved from the Bitterroot Valley, and in the 1840's they had a vision to accept Catholicism, or the Black Robes. So, they sent three delegations back to Saint Louis to get the Black Robes and they were the tribe that was instrumental to get Father DeSmit to come to this area and at that time they gave up most of their cultural practices and became practicing Catholics.

So, from that point, they had a few trials and tribulations and eventually the last of the tribal members were moved in I believe in 1889 with Chief Charles March from the Bitterroot to here. Their original reservation was to be comprised of the flathead reservation here, a large portion of land which was lost due to a surveying error that they were reimbursed for I believe in the 1930s, and the Bitterroot valley. The Bitterroot valley they lost roughly in the 1880s because it was never, well, basically a lot of fancy paperwork made it where they didn't have it and they were forced to move here. Where we are talking to you from is Saint Agnes, this is the cultural center anymore for what they considered the flathead portion of the Confederate state of the Acutane tribes. The flatheads are the name that the traders gave them because of the sign that the Salish made for their, sign language for who they were. The flatheads truly comprise several tribes, Kalispel, Bitterroot, Salish, Ponderay, there are a few Spokane, so on and so forth, but for the most part, most of them speak a Salish dialect with slight variations so even though their burial practices vary little from family to family to family there are quite a few things which are basically the same.

Currently you are talking to primarily a tribe that is probably on the forefront of most things that are tribal. They are one of the few tribes that is self-governing. They have one of the best Head Start systems in the nation, not just the tribal, but the nations. They are ranked as one of the top three tribes as it comes to the law enforcement systems and the judicial system. This tribe is also one of your more wealthy tribes, and they did it all primarily without gambling. Basically, uh let's see, other things about this tribe, roughly 6000–8000 members in this tribe of which about ¼ are comprised of Kootenais and the other ¾ is primarily, I guess the best way of saying it is a mix of the flathead group which is the Salish, Ponderay, Calasage, etc. Other important things to realize, this tribe has two main languages, Salish, Ponderay, and Kootenai. And Kootenai is actually a separate tribe but on the same reservation. And between the, for the membership of the confederate state of the Kootenai tribe, you're looking at probably less than 1000 that are ½ blood or more, the bulk of the tribe is under half, and they have had a lot of white interaction for the last 8 generations. So, a lot of the things are there, that is kind of just a thumbnail sketch of the history, um there is some very active movements to return to a lot of their roots a lot of their language, so on and so forth. Um, let's see. Beliefs about dying. Most of the Salish beliefs, and this is just what I have been able to sketch about it, is that primarily that of the Catholics because of the conversion to Catholic. So, if you were to take Catholicism how it used to be pre-Vatican around 1900. 1860, 1880 to 1900s, you have most of the beliefs about dying. Um, here, uh, the one I'd say exception to it is the Salish traditional people still believe quite a bit in the fact that the spirits roam the earth and can speak to you in dreams and things like this. But other than this, it is pretty much Catholic. Um, currently though there is a large movement where the catholic church has no longer has the schooling, the education and the programs for the tribal members, there is actually a very large and vital movement here of Pentecostal faith coming in so there beginning to be quite a split, but the irony is even those that are starting to follow the Pentecostal still are adapting those traditional catholic ways and beliefs into their burial practices.

For burial practices, this tribe has some very simple but kind of, I guess, I call them simple, but most morticians wouldn't because it's not the norm, uh when someone is dead or about to die, most of the family will try to be with that person and when the person passes away they a lot of time will smudge the body, they will wait for the mortician and someone will stay with that body until that body is buried. The process itself consists of a 3–5-day wake if you are Salish but only a three day wake if you are Kootenai. Um, they have practices where they wash the body down in rose water, and this is taken from wild roses, they boil the water, the body is in rose, uh the body is washed so it can be prepared. And the family tries to help out as much as possible, they dress the body, they do the hair, they do the makeup, they literally do just about everything but the actual embalming. In this area, if possible, most of the tribal members try to have things that are related to cedars, and _____ blanket culture, things like this.

The actual wake practice is a situation where the moment that the body is passed away, everybody gets a chance to come view and everything before the preparation happens, and everything. Then the preparation happens, the body is placed in the casket, from that point on the wake has begun. And it will go like I say, usually 3, 4 or 5 days for the Salish depending on when they can get the family in. Ideally, they like to have it 3 days and burial on the 4th, when its Salish sometimes they will do 2 days and go burial on the 3rd. The Kootenai never exceed 3 days, their rule is absolute the body is to be buried on the third day prior to noon.

Then how it happens with the wake is after the body is placed out they go either to the home or the longhouse primarily, some stay at the funeral home, but when I say that people need to realize that the funeral home has the facilities for people to sleep, a kitchen for them to cook their meals, and is basically like a big home. Um, but they usually try to go home the first day, and that is a family day. They will have prayers when the body comes in, they will have prayers at six in the morning, noon, six in the evening and midnight *and that is customary throughout the entire period. After that first day they usually go from the house of the person or the funeral home and then will go to usually the longhouse, so they can have the rosary on that second or third day. A rosary is usually done at 8:00 in the evening if you're Salish but I believe it is 7:00 or 7:30 if you are Kootenai, they have distinct time that they almost always do things. And it is a rosary; it is not a vigil service. They always used to be led by priests, it is now beginning to be, because of the lack of priests and some of the separation of those that are becoming Pentecostal background, it is led by the prayer leaders. At that rosary you will have songs sung in Indian, these are all catholic hymns that were translated into Salish or into Kootenai, and that will go in between the decades and they usually do the joyous mysteries, and things like this. Now, then that night that they have the rosary whether it is on the second or third night usually the midnight meal is a meal that comprises of the persons favorite food is what they try to do. Then in the morning they will have the morning prayers and the morning prayer are regarded as probably the most important prayers for the family to accept and receive and they have specified prayers that they use.*

Then the day of the service, they have what they call a wake closing. And they sing a farewell song, and people will get up, they will file past the casket to pay their last respects. Then they greet the family and they return to their seats. Then the family has their last chance to view. Then the prayer leaders will do their last chant and the casket is closed and we usually proceed to the church. Now there are a couple variations. Some of the Salish, primarily those with more of a ponderal background and from the Camus prairie area, they always lead the casket. Those in this area, the casket always went first, so there is a slight variation from place to place. And when they go to church, it should be probably emphasized that if at all possible, it is walked from here to the church. So, you are walking 2–3 blocks from one to the other in a procession. Then you have basically a standard catholic mass. And that catholic mass will comprise of a lot of eulogies, the average mass will usually take over 2 hours, by the time people speak and they have traditional Salish singing, they have standard British singing, things like this, then from there you will go to the cemetery and when you are at the cemetery the priest does his, the Salish prayer leaders will do their blessings and things, the casket is lowered into the grave usually after a prayer is said and a Salish song while they lower. Some families will have an honor drum and a drum at the cemetery and then after that the children are passed over the grave which is a custom that this tribe has done. I'm not sure if it came from here originally, but this is so that, um, well I guess at one time the belief used to be that the person would come back and try to take someone close to them and because of this, the children were at risk. So, they needed to be passed over the grave to leave things in the grave that needed to be and then be taken away from the grave for their own safety. That's how I've had it relayed to me, there are variations, and each family has their own small special twist with that and some families don't do it at all, that's not an absolute, but most of the traditional families do that. And then after that time, everyone places a handful of dirt into the grave. Usually it starts with the priest, followed by the family and then from that, everyone else.

And then at that time, after that is done, the grave is hand-filled with shovel, by shovel, and it is not supposed to be done by anyone who is family, so it is supposed to be exclusively friends. Um, there are times that gets a little difficult because families are quite large here. To give you an idea, a small service here for a tribal member is a rosary of 150–200 people, an average one is usually 3–400 people, it is not unusually to see services with over 500 people. The rosary is usually better attended than the actual mass because most people can make it here in the evening. Other important facts, uh let's see. They have cooks. Cooks are chosen by the family, they have a head cook. The head cook will designate the other. And basically, they take care of the cooking for the next 3–4 days.

After the burial, everyone comes back to a feast. And the feast is a great big meal and at that meal the food is, umm, a prayer is said in Salish, a prayer is said by the priest or whoever the clergy might be and at that meal you will have the out of town people go first and the children will serve the elders and then everyone else and family and then they just sit. And at the end of the meal, all the food is to be gone. It's all given away. So, all the cooked food is gone, all the uncooked food is given away, so on and so forth. And basically then, the family is responsible for helping cleaning up. A couple variations, in the Kootenai culture. They have certain people that are designated to do certain things . . . . (telephone rings) . . . sorry about the phone ringing. Umm. Let's see, in the Kootenai culture, they have certain people and certain families that do things. For example, one family is responsible for maintaining the cemetery and hand digging all the graves there. Um, they have certain ones that are primary in charge of the kitchen. Certain ones to take care of the flowers. Certain ones to take care of the registers, the register books and things like that.

Um, there are some very, very distinct differences between Kootenai and Salish besides the language. Uh, at one time I think a lot of them used to be the same practices but over time they have been evolved to have different things. If you've ever heard the concept of Indian time, the Salish live with Indian time. The Kootenai, they will start a service even if the family is not there because this is the time, this is when you start. The Kootenai have one designated leader per se who makes sure that things run exactly how things go. The Salish will put gifts and things into the casket to be buried and so long as it is not a picture of someone living, they will leave it in. Kootenai prefer *to have things more plain, and simple, and nothing is to go into the casket because it is believing that you might be taking part of yourself into that. The Kootenai's when they go to the cemetery will have a great big white cross placed at the head of the grave and it is placed right in with the cross bearer who leads things. The Salish do not do this hardly anymore, some of them do now, but not all by a long shot. Um, other concepts that I found were kind of ironic. The Kootenai acknowledge that they are not Christian as a rule and they use the catholic service primarily just as closure in the same way that they use the cross. They did not technically convert in the same manner that the flathead portion of the tribe did. Um, and then there is just a lot of little simple things that vary from family to family to family. Most families will have an elder or two within their families that basically says this is what we need to do, this is what we don't do. A few families will bury eagle feathers. But as a rule, that is not something you do on this side of the mountain. That is more something that you do on the western, uhh or eastern side of the mountain, the plains culture. A few of them will have the drums and the honor songs, and once again that is a family thing. It's kind of a variation. We are starting to see more and more of the things you would see at pow wows being brought into them because a lot of the cultural identity is, is identified as native, they are picking up. But the one thing, that um, what I guess the best thing is probably is that there are some very distinct differences. Even, for example, with the Kootenais. You sit down, and you are served the meal, where with the Salish you serve yourself. There are some very distinct differences. It is very obvious that they probably started at the same point, but they have managed to develop their own separate practices that are close but are not quite the same. And if you do one rather than the other, you will get in trouble, because they like the distinction. But that's kind of what they do with their burial practices. And that. And then, um, sometime within the next year, if possible, they will usually try to have a memorial dinner and a giveaway and have prayer said when they place the headstone on the grave.*

Things people don't realize is after a person passes away if they are a traditional family, usually the family will have someone go in and clean the house and everything is packaged up for that year and the house is washed down with rose water. Some families will burn anything that if a person passed away in certain clothing that clothing will be burned to go with them. It is important, for example, that when you comb their hair and things like that if you get any hair that comes out, that stays with them. Things like this. Everything is for the most part is either supposed to be burned with them or stays with them so that everything is kept intact is their mind of belief. But a lot of the practices are very truthfully what you would see with the catholic. We use candles, candles and more candles. We use veils over the caskets. We use rosaries. We use kneelers. We use a lot of the trappings that the Catholic

Church gave up with Vatican one. And I believe Vatican two they've given up more even. But that is their tradition here, that is their culture, and that is what they want to keep.

Um, there is actually a really good book written by Johnny Arleaf, one of the tribal elders and I will give that to you for your references, uh I will turn it over to the culture committee and get you one, okay? Thanks. There is a little sheet here saying the things we need to find out, one way or another. Grief is a personal thing; they go through all the different processes. Most of the tribal members, very few of them live past the age of 55–60 so there are a lot of tragic deaths, and a lot of very emotional times. Um. After life beliefs are pretty much heaven, hell, state sort of concepts but a lot of them still traditionally believe that spirits may roam the earth. And so, they can come back to you. And I think that's the bulk of it. I'm sure I've forgotten something; I'm just so used to doing it that I don't think about it. So, thanks!

Gerry (to them): *So, thank you for your time.* (Cox 2015, 388–397)

Chapter 21

Cheyenne, Shawnee, and the Potawatomi Disposal and Bereavement Practices

The name Cheyenne was a Sioux name for them that meant "red talkers" or "people of a different speech" while the Cheyenne called themselves "Tsistsistas" which means "beautiful people" (Waldman 1988, 48). The Cheyenne are of the Algonquian language grouping that includes the Blackfeet, Arapaho, Atsina, Cree, Fox, Kickapoo, Shawnee, Potawatomi, and Ojibwa (Moore 1996, 2). While generally described as a Great Plains cultural groups, their history is that of a Woodland tribe who lived in the Great Lakes area until driven out by the Chippewa and then farther west by the Lakota (Waldman 1988, 49). Their move westward required a change to their way of life.

THE CHEYENNE ORIGINS

Between the Woodland forests and the mountains of the West are the Great Plains. The plains lacked the trees that gave so much to the Woodland tribes. The plains did not have the maple sap that came from trees, nor the berries, nuts, herbs, and the many items such as their homes that the Woodland made from the wood provided by the trees. They did not have enough water to grow rice, nor the cane that the Southern tribes grew. What they did have was the bison or buffalo. The bison was able to provide all that they needed as the forest did for them in the Woodland areas. The bison not only provided food, but it also allowed them to make clothing from the skins, tools and utensils from its bones, lodge coverings, glue, yarn for weaving from its hair, and weapon points from the bones. The bison became the very source of their existence.

The Cheyenne lived in permanent villages, farmed, hunted, and gathered when they lived in the Woodlands (Waldman 1988, 48). While being known as nomads, the Cheyenne continued to have settlements after they moved to the plains, but they were earth lodge villages where the elders, women, and children stayed while the men hunted (Moore 1996, 19). After the hunt, the men returned to the earthen villages. While the men were gone for most of the year, the earth lodge dwellers maintained the gardens and gathered from the land. When the men were away hunting, they lived in tipis which allowed them to follow the animals that they hunted rather than waiting for them to wander into the areas where there were permanent villages.

As with all tribes, when the Spanish came to the plains with their horses, iron, and guns, life permanently changed for the Plains tribes. The iron and other metals that were in the form of guns, knives, needles, and other items were traded for skins (Grinnell 2008, 9). The iron that the Spanish brought with them allowed them to make much better arrowpoints than they could with stonepoints (Grinnell 2008, 9). Not only did this make it easier to kill their prey, the horse allowed them to move much faster in their pursuit of their prey. After the horse made its way to the plains, the Plains tribes were able to tame them and were able to learn to use them for their needs. Before, a hunter had to chase the bison and maybe chase them over a cliff or kill them at great peril since the bison were not only bigger, but they were also faster than the hunters. With the horse, the hunter could run with the bison and use his weapons from the back of the horse to kill the bison. With the coming of the horse, the Plains tribes became truly nomadic. They gave up their earth lodge villages. Because the horse was able to carry heavy loads unlike the dogs that they previously used, the Plains tribes were able to carry their lodgings and other goods and travel thousands of miles across the plains. Tipis became the lodgings for the Plains tribes. Being nomadic, they did not want heavy items or large items that would be difficult to carry. Because pottery often broke on the trail, they stopped making pottery or baskets like many other groups, but rather they made storage items from light, but stiff rawhide which allowed them to carry what they needed (Waldman 1988, 49). They were even able to make boats from the bison. Leaving their settlements changed their diet. For the most part, after they abandoned their villages, the vegetables that they ate were wild berries, wild potatoes, and other growing roots. They generally did not fish the streams that were abundant with fish even though they had historically lived on the banks of a great body of water (Grinnell 2008, 2). Not all Plains groups were nomadic. The Pawnee, for example, were known as "the People of the Earth Lodges."

The Cheyenne lived among the Blackfeet, Kiowa, Crow, Dakota, and Comanche among others. The Cheyenne were known as great warriors. They had soldier societies with perhaps the most noted being the "Dog Men." When a Cheyenne warrior went into battle, he said good-bye to his relatives, dressed himself for his own funeral, sang their death songs, and then charged the enemy as hard as he can with the attitude that he will not survive (Moore 1996, 112). The Cheyenne had been victims of the "Sand Creek Massacre" and the "Washita River Massacre." At Sand Creek in 1864, after thinking that they had made peace, Colorado soldiers two months later attacked a sleeping Cheyenne camp killing around 230 people (Josephy 1994, 365). In 1868, George Armstrong Custer led his soldiers to attack a peaceful village filled with mostly women, children, and elders murdering more than hundred people even though the Cheyenne displayed a white flag to show that they were peaceful (Josephy 1994, 171). The Cheyenne joined the Sioux and Arapahos to defeat George Armstrong Custer in 1876 at Little Bighorn (Mooney 1964, 395–397). Had both massacres not occurred, the Little Big Horn battle might not have included the Cheyenne.

CHEYENNE BELIEF SYSTEMS

Like other Plains tribes, the Cheyenne believed that a supernatural power permeates every phase of being, including peace, war, hunting, courtship, art, and music (Dorsey 1905, 57). Like the other Plains tribes, the Cheyenne came to depend upon the bison which led to much difficulty in maintaining their lifeways when the bison were taken to near extinction. Like other groups, the Cheyenne have great individual diversity of religious practice and faith. Some believe firmly in spirits, birds, and animals while others are quite skeptical of such beliefs. Perhaps because they lived near a great body of water in earlier times, their creation story begins with the earth being covered by water. The story begins with a man in the water that covered the whole earth asking the water birds to find land for him, but none were able to find land, but a blue duck brought him mud which he rubbed with his fingers until he made it dry and then he piled it on the water until it became land (Grinnell 2008, 1). After the earth was made, a man and woman were created and placed on it with the man being formed by a rib from his own side and then the woman being made from a rib taken from the man (Grinnell 2008, 1).

As with all religions, to explain them is difficult. If you ask three members of the same family to explain their religion, you will get three different explanations. Some generalities do exist that will yield some understanding of the Cheyenne approach to religion. Like most Plains groups, the Cheyenne personified the elements, birds, animals, and natural objects who had mysterious powers that could be transferred to humans (Grinnell 2008, 197). Prayer was essential to the Cheyenne, yet, like all religions, there are those of deep faith and those who are skeptical (Grinnell 2008, 197). The Cheyenne taught that Heammawihio who first made people and made them to live and be dead for only four nights and then be made again found that this made them too brace and led to too much killing which is why people now die forever (Grinnell 1972, 90). The Heammawihio taught the people how to make bows and stone arrows, how to start fires, how to plant and grow corn, that people were living on the other side of the big water, that wars would come to them with many people being killed, and that when they died they would all go up into the sky to live with him (Grinnell 1972, 90–91). For the Cheyenne, the afterlife was above, not below.

Unlike many Southwestern groups who believe that the dead live below, the Cheyenne believe that the place of the dead is above (Grinnell 2008, 198). The place of the dead is above where Heammawihio lives where all who die will go except for those who kill themselves who do not go above (Grinnell 1972, 91). All who die are thought to be equal, and none will be given a reward for good behavior nor is there punishment for evil behavior (Grinnell 1972, 91). Like many other groups, the Cheyenne believe that the dead live as they used to live on earth hunting, having wars, and spending time with other loved ones (Grinnell 1972, 91). They also tell stories of the very sick visiting above, but never actually getting there (Grinnell 1972, 91–92). The stories parallel those of near-death experiences.

The spirit of a person or shade is what others would call a soul, mind, or spiritual part; not the body, but the immortal part (Grinnell 2008, 199). Those who die will become shadows or spirits, and if the living as a sick person sees his or her shadow, he or she will tell others that they are about to die (Grinnell 2008, 199). Some still reject picture taking because it might cause them to see their shadow (Grinnell 1972, 94). Spirits are in many forms including thunder, rainbows, water spirits, mountain spirits, snakes, buffalo, and many others (Grinnell 1972, 94). Like the Blackfeet, the Cheyenne believe in underwater monsters who lived like the people on the prairie with bison and other similar lifeways, but they also lived as people who could change forms and while not feared, were viewed as alarming (Grinnell 1972, 97). Ghosts are generally greatly feared, causing many to sing loudly or to make noises to frighten away ghosts while walking at night (Grinnell 2008, 201). The Mistai ghosts, are usually not the ghost of a person, are seldom seen, but are often heard or felt, the Mistai ghosts also enjoy frightening but not harming people, and the Mistai ghosts can take many forms and be of different types and can even be dead people (Grinnell 2008, 202). The Cheyenne generally exhibit less fear of ghosts and the dead than many other tribes.

CHEYENNE BURIAL PRACTICES

The burial practices of the Cheyenne were like those of the Arapaho, Comanche, Kiowa, Kiowa Apache, and Sioux or Dakota and Lakota Tribes

(Mooney 1905, 397). When the Cheyenne buried their dead in the ground, they would cover the grave with rocks, and those who passed by would place a rock or other symbolic artifact on the grave to give honor to the deceased (Sandoz 1953, 251). Another slight difference in mortuary practices that separates the Cheyenne from the other Plains tribes would be that the Cheyenne would not have presents to make a giveaway for the deceased good friends (Sandoz 1953, 73). Instead, the Cheyenne would give the property not buried with the warrior who died to his widow or to the daughters. To the sons, they would give nothing with the idea that the sons could steal their own goods from their enemies (Llewelyn and Hoebel 1941, 219). Like other Plains groups, the Cheyenne would mourn by having wives and daughters slash their arms and legs and allowing their hair to stream loose with earth and grass in it (Sandoz 1953, 73).

THE SHAWNEE

The Shawnee, like many other tribes, were of the Algonquian dialect group who lived in what is now New York, Georgia, Alabama, South Carolina, Pennsylvania, Ohio, and Tennessee. The Shawnee lived in so many areas because they were largely a migratory group. Since they were largely away from the coastal areas, little was written about them or their relationships with the arriving Europeans. The Delaware Indians claim that they were one tribe with the Shawnee and the Nanticoke. The Shawnee were viewed as "southerners" among the Woodlands tribes and were at least culturally related to the Sauk, Fox, and Kickapoo (Pritzker 1998, 670).

The Shawnee are noted for spreading cultural traits of the northern tribes to the southern tribes and the southern tribes' cultural traits to the northern tribes due to their patterns of movement and allegiances (Waldman 1988, 216). The Shawnee were heavily involved in the fur trade and had mixed allegiances with the French and the British that ultimately led them into debt and whiskey (Pritzker 1998, 671).

SHAWNEE LIFEWAYS

Like most other groups, the Shawnee believed in a supreme deity, but unlike most, the Shawnee saw the deity as a female (Pritzker 1998, 672). Like the Hopi, different groups were expected to be in charge of religious ceremonies, but the major difference is that among the Shawnee, women organized and planned the events, led the ceremonies, and cured diseases with their knowledge of medicinal plants (Pritzker 1998, 673). Politically, women could be chiefs and took part in peace and war organizations and held the right to ask for the cancellation of a war party, to spare prisoners, and to direct feasts and planting crops (Pritzker 1998, 673).

BURIAL PRACTICES OF THE SHAWNEE

The Shawnee burial practices have changed very little over time. Some groups had different practices and some changes did happen, but most kept the same practices over time (Clark 1993, 50). Perhaps because women direct them, the Shawnee are noted for their ceremonialism. They seem to have little Southwestern influence in their burial practices (Howard 1981, 100). They kept the body covered in the dwelling where the person died for one and a half days and then have relatives prepare the body for burial, choose a person to direct the funeral, pick two or three corpse handlers who are not related to the deceased who also serve as grave diggers, have funeral rituals that last four days, feast, and have burial addresses, vigils, condolences, and purification rituals (Clark 1993, 50). Only men buried men, but both men and women could bury a woman (Pritzker 1998, 673). The dead person's possessions were divided among relatives except for some that went to reward friends who played a prominent role in the funeral process (Pritzker 1998, 673).

The grave diggers will typically dig a grave that is about 4 feet deep with an east-west orientation that will be lined with stones or wood and bark. The body is buried after being wrapped in skins or covered with bark. Tobacco will be distributed over the body (Pritzker 1998, 673). Poles are laid across the grave and the dirt that was taken by digging the hole is used to cover the bark with a grave house made of logs often being erected over the grave (Clark 1993, 57). Generally, the mourning period is relatively short except for the widow who is expected to mourn for a year after the death of her husband and to have a replacement ceremony around a year after her husband's death to announce her new husband (Pritzker 1998, 673).

THE POTAWATOMI

The Potawatomi are known as the Fire Nation because their name in Algonquin means "people of the place of fire" (Waldman 1988, 197). Historically, they are thought to have lived between Lake Huron and Lake Michigan, and as well, they are thought to originally been one people with the Chippewas and Ottawas (Waldman 1988, 197). After being driven out of their territory in southern Michigan by the Iroquois, Huron, and other tribes, the Potawatomi took refuge in northern Michigan and in the Green Bay area where they built alliances with the French and as well with other tribes (Pritzker 1988, 657).

The Potawatomi have been scattered across the country since the arrival of Anglo-Europeans. The Potawatomi are closely related to the Ottawas and Ojibwas and were Algonquian-speaking people who lived in the Great Lakes area (Hoxie 1996, 506). The Potawatomi were granted the land that is now Chicago and much of southwestern Michigan, but over time their land was taken over by the Whites (Winger 1939, 147). The Potawatomi over time acculturated with many groups joining the Catholic Church which unlike the Protestant churches did not require the ability to read (Winger 1939, 144). The Catholic influence on the Potawatomi has been strong. The first American Indian Bishop and Archbishop, Charles Chaput, is a Potawatomi. While many no longer practice traditional burial and rituals, strong traditions still exist. Like the Shawnee, the Potawatomi built grave houses at the time of burial with the idea that by building and leaving items behind to give light and feed the soul of the deceased (Landes 1970, 122).

The following is a transcript of a discussion of Potawatomi burial practices and how the influence of Anglo-Europeans has caused significant changes over time:

My name is _____and I am a Pokagon Band Potawatomi. I have lived here in South Bend most of my life. About our tribe, you know, there is quite a few of us Potawatomi and we are all over the country, all over this United States. Even into Canada. We have a fair amount of our people that are in Canada. Within the last few years, they have become more of, more alert about the other peoples and with our businesses with the United States government and all, we always tried to keep track of one another. And throughout the years, it's been more of a task trying to keep up with the better part of our people. And so, we have traditionally, we have already, kept up somewhat paperwork on our descendants.

And I go back, my people go back, to what we call the 1895–1897 according to the census role. And that's how we keep up with each other and all the descendants on those roles. All the other people that are born, Anishinabe people that are born after then, that is who they claim descendants with. And so, my grandfather, my mother's father, is on that role. And of course, my grandparents on my father's side is on that roll. So that's how we trace our heritage and our blood line. According to the United States government, we go by lineage and not a quantum, some of our people have a quantum, most generally, it's usually ¼ blood. But with our dealings with the United States government, they want lineage. And that kind of encompasses all of our descendants that are going to come after us. You know. So, I know there has been a little bit of controversy as to how this all terminates you know because I know that our other tribes, some of the western tribes you know, they go up by a blood quantum and you need to be a certain percent of blood quantum to be able to access some of their fundamental parts of their tribes and if you need any financial, you have to be able to prove that. So, ours just goes back to a lineal decent and usually I think you have an affidavit that indicates who you are, where you come from and of your grandparents or your parents.

So yeah, that's how a better part of our Pokagon people heritage here. And the reason we have our name as Pokagon is because Pokagon was one of the people that our people looked up to. He was a man of, I would say in his late 30s, early 30s, and he was quite a learned person. And he, he had some, I think he had some college education. So, he, they look for a person that has that kind of interest in their people, you know. And that's how we become Pokagon, because his name was Pokagon. So, we have our name now as Pokagon Potawatomi. The band here. And what he'd done is that he had gained enough influence with the government and when they had the removal of our people out west, he went to the government and secured enough of an indulgence with them so that we could stay here. And he gathered up a group here in Indiana. And then after a few years he bought a small tract of land, in fact I think he bought two parcels. That was in and around Dowagiac, Michigan. And I forget what the acreage he had bought there. Anyways, he had boughten that piece of property and I think he also bought a little bit of the land further up in Hartford, Michigan. So those were the only two pieces of property that I would say the Pokagon's actually owned when they receded all their lands to the government and so he did secure enough of us here. And according to my explanation about what my grandparents was telling me, my mother's mother, was saying that when the Pottawatomi's heard about the removal, a lot of them run away, they just run out in the woods, and that's how we got away from that part of it. But anyways, probably when they heard about Pokagon, so he kinda drew them all back. So, generally, we stayed in this area.

And I know that there has been some talk about how you retain some of your Potawatomi language. When I was a boy, it was spoken in around the table and different conversations with our people and my relations and that's how I become somewhat acquainted with our language. Like I said, I'm not really a fluent speaking person, but I do know quite a few of our terms especially around the table and different animals and birds and all that kind of thing. But that's how, that's how, I retain a better part of our language. And I, I believe I'm just about like all the rest, I've just never thought about how I was to pass this on until just a few prior years. I've become more acquainted with that. And then too, with our tribe, since we've had our federal recognition, we got it in 1994 I believe it was, or was it 1992, I forget exactly what year it is. But anyways, we've become more aware of trying to increase our government and trying to increase our tribal people to learn the language and it's been kind of a task because it's like anything else you know, a lot of our people figure we're already gone, you know, so they don't see the process of trying to learn their language, it didn't seem that important to them I would have guessed, these are my own thoughts. But it is, I think it's, the language is one of the potential parts of your culture. Learning about our songs, and there is the whole gamete of cultural, you know. So, I think language is one of the key situations that kind of help that.

And over the years I've taken part in a lot of our, in a lot of our pow wows we have had in around the neighborhood. And I travel with quite a few of our people, and I've been to a some of the surrounding states. I've been to Minnesota; I've been to pow wows in Minnesota, Wisconsin, and Michigan. A few in Ohio. Not so much, there have been a few in Indiana, mostly in the upper part here, not so much in the southern part. And I think that over the few years that I've been on this earth, I've had that opportunity and tried to see that things stays abreast of me, stays afloat. And I've had some success in trying to transport that to my cousins and my nephew. I've had one nephew that still participates in quite a bit of our culture. And like I say, I've been here since I was born, in January of 1934, right now I'm 70 years old, just turned 70. I'll be 71 in January of this coming year. But I believe I'm just one of the middle stream people in this area.

But like I said they are beginning to learn more about our culture, and we have a fair amount that really take part in it. But again, since our tribe is really got down into the politics of our business and so now they are try-ing to go ahead with this with the language and just the whole aspect of our culture. We have our offices set up in Dowagiac, Michigan and, so we have a fair amount of land that we have secured up there and that's where we've got most of our businesses there. A few years ago, they were all in around the city of Dowagiac, so we had just acquired some property out at Rodger's Lake, and this is where we are going to set up our whole administrational complex out there. Hopefully in a year's time we want to try to build our business there and put up our buildings. We have so far secured most of them that were in around the Dowagiac area and have all pulled them into one central location out there, Rodgers Lake. I really like that Rodger's Lake complex, its, a few years back, it was some old campgrounds and for many years it was used as such. And so, it is pretty well plotted out for a campground. It has two, I would say there's a small lake on the south end of it, and there is a small lagoon right in where most of our activities are going to take place.

But we're trying to, like I said, we're trying to secure enough financial ability to build, or erect, a nice building there, so that we can house every-thing all in one building. As it is now, we just have, we have our, oh what do you call them, just our, oh they are temporary housing right now. And we had suffered some loss last year, or was it early part of this year, we had a fire, someone set a fire to the place, they burned down our maintenance building which we had just erected a few years ago, I don't think it was over a couple years old, and when we first moved out there, they had a lot of these trailers, that were small trailers and we had put them together and used them as office space and that's what we were using until the fire came. But anyways, they set fire to the maintenance building and to our administration building, all the trailers we were using. And we were in the process of putting all of these, all these businesses into one complex. So, our latest project right now is the head start of our children and they've got a nice building there. And it's not a big building, but its far better than what we had in town, cause here we were renting spaces. So, we've come along pretty good within the last 10 years. And hopefully if we can keep our head afloat, we will probably be doing far much more better. So, I think that's about what our tribal operation has been doing. Like I said, we just celebrated I think it was our 10th year in the gathering out in Oklahoma, Shawnee, Oklahoma. And I thought it was pretty good. It was a success. It was kind of cumbersome at first, and I think most of them, most of our gatherings, and what I mean by gathering, is that most all of the Potawatomi people from Michigan, Wisconsin, from surrounding areas they all kind of gather, and so each tribe, each portion of them, they're the ones that more or less pull these all together and each year a different band will host this. And so, this year it was hosted in Shawnee Oklahoma. In prior years it was hosted in Wisconsin. Some of our people have, you know, casinos. And casinos, per se, I think, is a major help for our people. Not so much the money part of the casino, the gambling part of it, but it's what the funds can really do for our people, it will help us to maintain our function ability to try to establish our governmental goals and secure some of our finance ability for our languages and for our culture cause I don't think that for us to try and gain, you know that finance ability to help us do that with, I don't think the government would be all that gracious because if they did it would be a long time coming. Cause you can see that in years to come because, well this year it is going to be somewhat of, and then uh, I think politics plays a big game in that, you know. And this is where we are having a process of trying to gain, get our people in that process. A lot of them are not too eager to get into that, and I think it takes a special person to get into the governmental part of it, especially when it has to do with a lot of politics.

A lot of our people, I don't think they're not really, the ones we do have, I know our people are very intelligent. In the years past when I was a boy coming up, you never read a whole lot about our people, you know, about our Pokagon people, even here in the city of south bend, I've lived here most of my life and I've been, I was brought up Catholic, I was brought up

Roman Catholic, and I'd gone through a fair amount of schools. And also, my, I'm sorry to say, that alcohol was very prevalent in most of our tribes. And, my dad, he was involved with that, with that alcohol. And of course, consequently, we kinda moved around the city. And back then, during the Depression, the tail end of the Depression, when I came up, trying to sustain a place to live, and trying to get the funds that your family needs. And I think the whole aspect of living was a little bit different than it is now today, you know. I think young people today have a little bit more of an advantage in some ways and that process. But then everyone, more or less, had to do what they can with what they had. And I know, I'm not saying a whole lot about my father, but I think my father was a good man, but just, when they use that alcohol, it just turns them into Jekyll and Hyde.

But anyways, I had a pretty good life, to some degree. My mother had six, there was six of us in our family, we had three boys and three girls. And so, it was quite a chore to try to keep us all afloat. There was a time in our lives when we were coming up that you never got whatever you needed, you know. And like I always said, I was raised by my parents and I was raised by my grandparents and to be a quiet child is sometimes kind of hair raising to some degree, you know. And when I was a boy, I was always taught that you are to be seen and not heard and speak when you are spoken to, you know. But anyways, I thought I had a fairly good life.

And, like I said, we did have to move from time to time because the finance ability wasn't there and so I had gone to, I had gone to St. Patrick's school here. And I forget how far I was gone in those grades then, I'd say it was probably, might have been in around the 3rd grade, but I think before then I thought we were at St. Joseph high school here in South Bend. So, the last school I'd gone was at a public school here in South Bend and I think that was closer to either 3rd or 4th grade but then I, my mother says that well, she got her help from her mother, my grandmother to put us in, some of us, what we call an Indian boarding school. And this Indian boarding school was up in Michigan, it was up in Petoskey. Just the other side of Petoskey, Michigan, a little town of Harbor Springs. So, I had gone there until 8th grade and I graduated. So, it was kind of a touch and go trying to learn your way up that way, you know. And being that far away from home, it was well over 300 and some odd miles, we never got home that much except when school was out. So, but it was kind of a task, but once I learned my way around and got over my homesickness, course at that time I was probably 11 or 12 or somewhere there about. But I was there 5 years and I got to learn a little bit more about our religion because we, when we were down there we attended school, we attended church. And I made my Holy Communion down here. And when I went to boarding school, then I was confirmed up there. And so, it was, we had, the brothers of the Franciscan and the priest of the, Franciscan priest *and the sisters of Notre Dame were our teachers. So, we had to deal with them every day on a daily basis because we lived right there. So, everyone had their jobs to do, so we did that. And we had our little qualms about what we didn't want to do but then we figured out we had to live together so we had to work together. It was quite a task and I really enjoyed that. But like I said, I got a little bit more knowledge about our way of life. And of course, there were a fair amount of Indian people there, not so much Potawatomi, but there were a few, but that was more or less Ottawa country. So, I got to know quite a few of the kids that come to school up there. There was quite a bit involved with it. So, then I, after I graduated there, I come down here, I think that was about in 1949 cause it was 1943 when I started up there. But I went to high school here, I went to Central Catholic high school, which at that time they ran in the upper part of St. Matthews Cathedral, the school, and I stayed there until 1954. And most of the guys I went to school with graduated in 1954. Consequently, I didn't, cause I quit. Then I started getting into, getting back into the work field, getting to know what work was all about, and that has been a better part of my comings and goings. And from there on, I just, made my way.*

But anything that you want to know about, burial practices and funeral practices. We've umm, those are things that our people kind of bury their people just like others, you know. We have different cemetery plots that they use. We also have our different burial spots that we put our people in. We have one that we call Rush Lake which is just outside of a little town of Waterbowl, Michigan. And then there is also one, there is one at Sacred Heart and when I was talking about Pokegon, that's where he is, that's where his body is buried, supposedly. He is under, he is right under the door of the church when you come in, right in the vestibule, right supposedly he's buried right underneath that. But anyways, they have a burial cemetery there and it also, I think back then the church had a lot to do with that. So, the diesis out of Kalamazoo, I think they secured most of that property. But at that time, they had one of our people that kind of foreseen that to carry the . . . course back then, there were some that they put in the ground there, so this is the persons that did that was his job, but he was also Pottawattamie decent.

Then the other cemetery place there at, what'd they call it, they're just the other side of Owatonna _____, Rush Lake. We have an old cemetery there and the church was also involved with that portion of that. And I think that, I think way back then that their church was involved with quite a bit of our properties that we've had. I think, well I said church had finance ability to secure the property and so now it doesn't, some of our people would like to be buried at Rush Lake and then some of them buried at Silver Creek. Sacred Heart is the name of the church there. That is an old church and there is a lot of history that goes along with that. And there is a lot of history that goes along up at Rush Lake too. At one time there was an old church there that over the years, and I don't remember what happened to it but anyways, all that's left there is the foundation. We do have a committee that of our people that kind of foresees that property. There's quite a few of them that have been buried there recently and according to the state government, I think that you can be buried there in a traditional way. And when I say a traditional way, it means that they can, some of our people, way back when they buried them, they were either in a pine coffin and some were just laid in the ground. And course way back when they sometimes never used no markings, and so, but I'm pretty sure they probably had some kind of way of keeping it up. And over the years, I think some of that has gotten lost, and so we do have a certain amount of people that's been in the process of trying to relocate where those people are put into the ground. And I know that, the process that they go through, today they have to be embalmed, and I think most all of our people are embalmed. I know that some of our people are, this kind of a, more or less a family, it's up to them how they are going to go about with the funeral aspects of it. Most of them today they have a view just as everyone else has.

But there are certain members of the families that lately within the last few years I've noticed there have been more of our traditional way of having our people put away into the ground. They do what we call a regular pipe ceremony and they'll lay them out, maybe in a process that they are very familiar with. So, this is how, it's not a little bit different than normally, they still have their processions to some degree. I've had been involved in different aspects of that and some of them like to have them viewed in the same amount, in 2–3 days, or whatever. And I know that this is kind of, oh how to say, is more of a personal aspect of how they want to do that, you know. And I think that most of your undertaker people today are just about willing to accept whatever way that you feel you want to do this. I know way back when they used to embalm the body and they'd bring it to your house. And it would stay there until they get ready for internment, but you don't see that too much anymore. But I think if it was requested, I think you could do that. But today its, today there's a lot more involved and I can imagine the expense of it is still the same way because I know that people can come and view the person and the way they clothe them whether they want to do it with their _____, they call it, and some of their, they may have them dressed in there, maybe in a ribbon shirt if it's a man or if it's a woman they may have her dressed in some of her traditional clothing. So, that's about, about how it is when we bury our people, but I know that there are different ways. Today most people kind of use their different mortuaries or funeral setups just as everyone else does today. But that's up to the individual and I think it's pretty close to what we have today. (Cox 2015, 399–410)

Chapter 22

Ojibwe/Anishinabe/Chippewa, Shoshone, and Stockbridge-Munsee Disposal and Bereavement Practices

The Chippewa or Ojibwe, Ojibwa, Ojibway, or Anishinabe were part Algonkian linguistic family of the Iroquoian speakers which is thought to have been among the largest north of what is now Mexico. This language group also included the Potawatomis, Foxes, Wyandots, Ottawas, Miamis, Illinois, and others (Richter 2001, 167). In their early years, after being forced from the northeast by the Iroquois, they moved with the Ottawas and Potowatomis to Mackinaw. The three tribes were known as the confederacy of the Three Fires. As a former Eastern tribe who were driven out of their homeland by the Iroquois, they were able to drive the Sioux from their home-land changing them from a woodlands tribe to one who was able to dominate as a Plains tribe. Much of their early history with the Europeans was with the French. As the English took over their regions, they tried to maintain relationships with both the English and the French. They were able to trade with both the French and the English. Perhaps because of their acceptance of both the French and English, the Chippewa today are a mixed population with much intermingling of the French and English with few full-blooded Chippewa remaining.

The Chippewa or Ojibwe lived along the shores of Lake Superior and the banks of the Upper Mississippi (Dodge 1959, xix). Their territory stretched from the shoes of Lake Huron and Lake Superior westward through Minnesota to the Turtle Mountain in North Dakota. Despite their long history in North America mostly along the St. Lawrence River, by 1854, the Chippewa bands of Lac du Flambeau, Bad River, Lac Court Oreilles, and Red Cliff as well as the Menominee and the Stockbridge were all able to make treaties that placed them in their current reservations in the Great Lakes region (Laurie 1987, 20). The Chippewa who are also known as the Ojibwe and as the Anishinabe see themselves as the people of the Great Lakes though their earlier history was in the Northeast. Today, their reservations are located in Canada, Michigan, Wisconsin, North Dakota, Montana, and Minnesota.

The Chippewa were called Nadowe-is-iw or "snake" by the Dakota (Taylor 1994, 24). Interestingly, the name Sioux is taken from a Chippewa word meaning "snake." Generally, the Chippewa are thought to have forced the Sioux to move further westward. The tribes that were armed by the French and English were able to drive out their competitors. The arrival of the horse also changed the lifestyle of the Plains tribes as the weapons did for the Chippewa. For the Chippewa, their lifestyle historically was dependent upon the woodlands for everything.

While exact dates are not known, by at least 500 BCE, the Woodlands tribes had been able to develop horticulture, pottery-making, and had more sedentary lifestyles marked by small settlements (Fagan 2000, 472). Everything that they made from weapons, medicine, clothing, houses, and so forth came for woodland items ranging from wood, bark, plants, animals, and birds from the forests. While tipis were used as temporary shelter, they generally lived in wigwams or dome-shaped houses made from poles and covered with long strips of tree bark. Since the Chippewa survived by hunting and fishing and were timber people, they lived in wigwams and traveled in strongly constructed canoes. Today with hunting and fishing, they also are very much into selling timber as a source of income.

They were considered to be a peaceful people, and perhaps because of their willingness to make treaties and to maintain the peace with the governments, they have experienced far less dislocation from their traditional lands than most other tribes. The reservations and reserved where they live today in both the United States and Canada are still on their traditional homelands. Perhaps because of their being able to remain in their traditional areas, they have been able to continue many of their traditional ways of life.

CHIPPEWA CULTURE

The Chippewa are known as the "wild rice people." In a tradition that continues to today, wild rice has been a Chippewa staple. Because they historically lived north of the climate line that marked the limit of where corn could grow, rice became their major crop (Billard 1979, 121). Like many other tribes, the Chippewa were taught to share. To share with others was a basic tenant of their way of life. To share with others was considered to be a joy rather than a hardship. The Chippewa elders taught that even a grain of corn could be divided among several people. Brothers were taught to protect and care for their sisters, and sisters were taught to care for their brothers. As they grew older, siblings were taught to cease talking to each other. Since they did not speak to each other, there were no chances of cross words being spoken to each other, and since they did not speak to each other they would not have bad feelings between brother and sister. Like other tribes, the Chippewa focused upon being in harmony with nature.

Each spring the Chippewa were able to gather sap from their maple trees. In the fall of each year, they would harvest their wild rice. Spring was said to arrive as the oak trees shed their last leaves to signal that winter was over. Since their main staples were rice and seasonal foods like berries, maple syrup, fishing, and hunting, they were forced to move from their hunting areas to rice lake areas to areas to plant their rice and other plants and to harvest wild berries. The French established a trading post on Madeline Island which became the center of the Chippewa nation. The French traders learned to fish from the Chippewa. The French named the lake on which they fished Lac du Flambeau which means Lake of Flames. The name probably came from the Chippewa using torches to fish at night.

The Iroquoian nations developed a confederacy long before the arrival of the Europeans that reduced feuds and warfare between neighbors, settle disputes, set reparations if needed, and to gather for feasts and ceremonies (Fagan 2000, 483). While not noted for their material poor technological culture, they were highly respected for their effective governing, diplomacy, respect for individual dignity and self-reliance, and for being polite and hospitable to one another (Fagan 2000, 486). The Chippewa women had more freedom and influence than their European counterparts since women owned houses and fields, were able to name their children and raise them, have their husbands move into their family's homes, and had the line of descent on the mother's side (Billar 1979, 124).

Like other Iroquoian groups, the Chippewa prayed many times during each day. Like the Plains and Eastern tribes, tobacco was used as a sacred plant. Because of their relationship and alliance with the French, when the British conquered their areas, they were poorly treated by the British. Over the years, they have been exploited by corporations and have had many of their sacred places defiled and have had ancestors removed from their burial sites. See Gedicks (1993, 2001) for a history and analysis of their struggles.

The Chippewa historically and currently see themselves as hunters, gatherers, fishers, and farmers. Like other tribal groups, elders assumed many roles acting as doctors, healers, teachers, psychiatrists, and most of all human beings. It is not why you do something, but how that is done is important. They view themselves as a medicine society which uses herbal rather than scientific ways. Unfortunately, the Europeans brought with them many diseases that defied their herbs that ultimately decimated their numbers. They also had a very different culture than the Europeans.

CHIPPEWA RELATIONSHIPS

As suggested, the Chippewa generally welcomed the Anglo-Europeans. They are described as loving the French at the same time being willing to sell their furs to New Yorkers (Richter 2001, 168). As keepers of the land, the Chippewa believed that others would care for the land and nature as they did. This belief led them to welcome the Europeans who left their Eden, who did not see the land as holy, and seemed to want to destroy the Eden of the Chippewa. They believed that when you are born, you begin to die. The Chippewa are a gentle people who follow the "sweetgrass way." While they had a rather loose social organization, their Grand Medicine Society had a lot of control of their daily lives. Like many other Algonkian people, they had a creation story that was far different than the Christian story. They also believed that there was a mysterious power in all living and nonliving things. Like the Lakota and others, they believed that dreams offered revelations about life. For the Chippewa, the most important religious object was the calumet which was an elaborately carved stem or a stem with a pipe attached that they would decorate with beads and feathers. The calumet was used like a seal of approval to give the person carrying it safe travel, to appease gods, to ratify treaties, to end wars, to greet strangers, and for many other purposes.

BEREAVEMENT AND BURIAL PRACTICES

The Chippewa historically believed that the spirit would not leave the body until after burial rather than immediately after death. This belief led to a practice of immediate burials or other disposal means to allow the spirit to leave the body. They also taught that it takes four days after the body is buried for the spirit of the dead to reach happiness. These beliefs are central to their disposal and bereavement practices.

As with most tribes and other cultures, when a member of the clan died, his or her body would be prepared for disposal by clan members. The body would be washed and dressed in his or her best clothing. Traditionally, the body would be placed on a platform with the feet to the west for four days to allow the soul spirit to leave (Johnston 1976, 143). A number of forms of burial were used over time. The most common method that was used until around 1910 was the house type with a burial pit with a 4-foot-deep hole, placing the body in a sitting position with a shelf to place food and water for four days (Howard 1977, 227). Like the Shoshone, the Chippewa painted the face with red and brown as being the most commonly used colors to paint the faces. They taught that when the northern lights are moving in the skies, that it is their dead dancing with their torches that light up the sky. Their painted faces allow the deceased to join the other dancers.

After the body is prepared, it is placed in a blanket and covered with birch bark. The body is then carried from wigwam and buried with the feet pointing to the west. The west is where the sun sets and is the direction toward the land of the spirits. A member of the clan will dance around the grave before it is closed. As the rituals continue, the grave will be filled. Like Shawnee and Potawatomie, the Chippewa often built a burial house over the grave. Like many groups, the Chippewa believe that the soul travels for four days, so they would leave food and goods with the body for the spirit's journey. If the death occurred during the winter when the ground was too hard to dig, they would use scaffold or air burial. A third way to dispose of the body would be to simply bury the person in a shallow grave in an extended position and cover it with layers of poles, rocks, and dirt (Howard 1977, 227).

Like many other tribes, for the Chippewa grief lasts for one year, requiring mourning clothes and carrying a spirit bundle that includes a lock of the hair of the person who died. A widow might keep the bundle next to her, feed the bundle, and sleep next to it. During intense grief, mourners will remain unkept, wear less attractive clothes, and not comb their hair. If a baby dies, the mother will often carry the baby's clothing in a cradleboard for the year of mourning. At the end of the year, another ritual will comfort the mourners and offer gifts, and the mourners will then end their grief and resume their normal activities (Johnston 1976, 143–144).

The Chippewa have many rituals designed to protect the living from the dead as well as many for the dead. Spirits could kill the living, haunt their enemies, kill a spouse who takes a lover, so rituals were required to prevent misfortune (Landes 1968, 190–193). Traditionally, the Chippewa believed that the soul exists before, during, and after the human form of existence, and that the spirit continues to live after death as it makes its long journey on the "Path of the Souls to the Land of the Soul" (Dennis and Washington 2018, 108). The conversion to Christianity was made easier by the Chippewa traditions of praying for the dead to ask his or her spirit to intercede for them and to ask that the spirit quietly leave (Jones 1861, 99). Like the Lakota and many other groups, the Chippewa feasted after the funeral and held a giveaway of the possessions of the dead person. Because the person was buried almost immediately, the rituals were typically performed around the grave of the dead person. Their traditional use of torches for many acts including night fishing meant that torches were used in many rituals. The Chippewa would light their torches for four days after the burial at the head of the grave to help guide the spirit on its journey as it guided them in their night fishing and other activities.

Typically, for the feast after the funeral, they would make the favorite food of the dead person, and a member of the family would carry the dish for a year to every meal to honor the dead person. As with the Lakota and others, the Chippewa would say prayers, play drums, have songs, and perform ceremonies to honor the dead person. Like most other groups, the Chippewa often perform Christian ceremonies and then perform their more traditional ceremonies. Some groups combine both Christian and traditional ceremonies.

While there are many Chippewa of note, three would include Leopold Pokagon who became a leader of the Potawatomi. He was captured by the Potawatomi as a child. He was perhaps best known for selling the site that became Chicago to the United States in 1832. He tried to live in peace, but was forced to move his village to Dowagiac, Michigan, as related in the transcription of the oral history from the member of the Potawatomi tribe. A second famous Chippewa would be Rocky Boy or Stone Child for whom the reservation in Montana is named. A third famous Chippewa would be Jane Schoolcraft who married Henry. She aided her husband in his many books and other publications and wrote about the Chippewa culture as well as poems and other contributions that greatly added to our knowledge of the Chippewa people.

The following is a transcription from a Chippewa:

Wife speaks: *Alright we're gonna get started. Today is August the 24th 2004 and it's something like, what time is it? Its 9:52 a.m. Hello, my name is _____, I'm with Chippewa Cree tribe, I'm a member of the tribe. Also, an employee of the tribe, I'm a tribal officer. Today we have Gerry Cox here, professor of sociology from University of Wisconsin—La Crosse, Wisconsin. And I guess just a brief history about the Chippewa and the Cree. There are two tribes here in Rocky Boy, Montana, the Chippewa's and the Crees. The Cree's migrated from Canada back in the days of Louis __ Rebellion and, hold on for a while. . . . . Okay, so I started to tell you that the Cree's migrated from Canada and Chippewa from the Great Lakes area. And they roamed Montana back in the days and then they were given this reservation here, which is now called Rocky Boy. It's named after the Chippewa chief, Rocky Boy. And that's where the name Rocky Boy was derived from, from him. So today it is called the Rocky Boy Reservation of Montana. We are an executive order reservation.*

And today I'm here to talk about the beliefs about dying. We do have beliefs about . . . there is life after death. I guess more people say that life is forever over there when you're called to this kingdom. Anyway, we do have that belief that when you leave here, if you live right, there are some stipulations that you have to lead a good life. You can't be, I guess, a sinful person, you have to lead a good life, work for God. One of them is raising children, your families. That is one of the ways that is a key to the heaven. So, we do have beliefs about dying and then the next thing, I guess burial practices. Yes, we do have . . . back in the early days I guess we used to bury our dead up in the trees. But nowadays, I guess the government changed all that and you have to have proper burials now. You know, where you put them in a coffin and then they bury them in the ground. That's one of the laws now that we have to go through.

But we had our own practices back then. And then uh, we're one of the tribes that really respect our people that dies. We sit up with them, whether it be two nights we have wake, and nobody leaves, that body is not left alone, someone always has to be awake at that wake. And, we sit up all night, they bring food there, they eat, and pay their last respects that way. So, we're one of the tribes that really think a lot about our people that's gone beyond. We sit up with them like I said. And then we have feasts too. Journey feasts we call them. I think it's four nights after death, we count the nights. Like if you were to die today, the 24th, you'd count Tuesday, Wednesday, Thursday, and Friday night. After the fourth night, we have a journey feast. That's when we offer food to them, we have a ceremony. But I can't go into details on that part. But we do have a journey feast we call it, and we eat with them over there. So that's one of our ways also, is our feast that we have.

Then we have one a year after death. A one-year memorial feast that we conduct. It's just a one-year memorial for that person that died. Then we go say, through the same thing we do, it's a pipe feast, we use a pipe, we go through a pipe ceremony. Then we have a giveaway also in memory of that person. We give things away, materialistic things. That's an offering too that goes with that one-year memorial.

And then grief, yes, we do, you know, I guess, with death you have to go through grief. And the grieving process I guess we go through. You know one of the tribes, one of the few tribes that our elders told us that when you're grieving to go to a, you know, don't stay home that one year. We go whether there's a pow wow or whatever is going on. Continue going to those things, those ceremonies that we have. Because I guess when we grieve too much, we have a belief that the way we feel, that's how the person feels, the one that died. The way you feel is like maybe you're feeling bad, well that's the way they feel up there too, they feel bad. So, they tell us not to do that, to try to feel good about yourself. Because the way you feel, that's the way they feel, like I just said, up there, where they're at. So that's how we deal with grief.

And then we have some ways that one specific, I guess it was a ceremony back then, they call it Hand Game, or some people they call it Stick Game. I guess there was a mourner up in the hills grieving, and while this person was up there, he was shown a ceremony; it's called that Stick Game. Anyway, that Stick Game is for this person that was mourning, to try to have him come out of that grief he was going through. So, he was given that ceremony, and when they play that they have a good time, laugh, and I guess try and come out of that grief you're going through. So that's one of our ways that was given us to address grief too.

And not only that, we have ceremonies that we have. We go to these ceremonies, like we are one of the tribes here that still practice our ways, we have our sun dance. We have one ceremony, it's called, the non-Indians call it Ghost Dance, but it's not really a Ghost Dance, it's a Jump Dance they call it. That's one of our ceremonies. Then we have some of our other ceremonies too, like Horse Dance, we have the one Giveaway Dance that's only held in the winter months. Then we have name giving ceremonies.

We have our other ceremonies like sweat lodges. Other ceremonies we still have. We're one of the tribes that still practice our ways here, in Rocky Boy here. To address grief, I guess. You know, you go to these ceremonies, people they pray for you, and you feel good about yourself. I guess there's one ceremony too, the sweat lodge, it's good for the mind, your mind, the physical body, and your self-esteem. That one, you go through these sweats. It's a real nice ceremony, you feel good when you come out of there, you feel like refreshed. Those are the ceremonies I'm talking about, they help with the grieving process. And I think its real good that we still have these ways to rely on.

And then afterlife beliefs, I guess, yeah, like I said, there is life after death up there, where you go. And what our old people told us that it's over there, life is forever, when you die. When you die here. Over there in heaven is, it's forever. Everything is nice over there. They don't have death there, they don't have sickness, and everything is nice over there, the land. Because, you know, we had some people that died, some of our elders and they went up there to where God's Kingdom is, and they were sent back to tell us that there is life after death. And I truly believe that, that there is a place up there for everybody. But like I said earlier, it's how you live your life down here. If you live a good clean life, drug free, and abide by God's rules, that you are going to make it up there, to wherever land is. I'm glad I was asked to give a presentation here today and then I feel good about this. Maybe in the future you know, my people they might use this tape for whatever educational purposes. And I was glad I was able to share this with you today and I know this is going to be used in a good way, not a negative way. So, I'm glad to talk to you and if ever asked to do this again, I will be truly glad to do it then. Thank you for your time today. (Cox 2015, 414–418)

This is a transcription from two Ojibwe/Chippewa/Anishinabe members:

Hello, my name is . . . my Christian name is _____ my spirit name is _____. I am the woman from the four directions. I am a member of the Mole Lake Indian Reservation, also known as the Ojibwe and Chippewa and Anishinabe community. I don't know where to start except for, um, Mole Lake band, our ancestors come from Madeline Island was born on Madeline Island in 1747 and um, in the book that's referred to here, these two books here, insists that he's the chief of the tribe that signed the 1795 Greenville treat and then he also signed the treaty of, uh 1826, 27 and 28 and we have an 1837 treaty, and 1842 treaty, an 1855 treaty.

So, this chief, Kijiwabesheshi, he lived a long time, he was a very old man when he died, and he was born on Madeline Island and he was born to the daughter of Anton Buffalo, the Buffalo that was born on Madeline Island. And, um, his daughter Madeline had two boys, twin boys and, um, the Marten is Kijiwabesheshi, the Great Marten came here to Mole Lake and he was told to go and look for food for his grandma and his mother and his grandpa the chief. So, he left the island and when he came on the mainland and he traveled, and he traveled, and he traveled until he got to the place where food grows on the water. And what I mean by that is that here in Mole Lake we have our rice beds that are over here, and those are ancient rice beds.

Um, my aunt and uncle, Mr. And Mrs. _____ took that wild rice, a grain of wild rice and sent it town to the State of Wisconsin, down to the lab, and they had it aged at 2000 years old, that our wild rice here . . . our wild rice beds are very ancient rice beds. And we believe that our time goes all the way back to that beginning. Cause we believe that we came from the creator, that the creator created us at the same time he made everything else.

And, um, these are the stories that were handed on to me by my mother and my grandmother and my grandpa and my great grandmother, her name was um _____ and she was what we call in our language the head woman, or the first woman, the lead woman and, um, she was my dad's grandma, my grandma's mother and she lived to be 116 years old. So, when she was a young girl, she was born back in the days when (Garbled) was the reigning chief and when she, when she would tell grandma and dad and mom and everybody back in the days about how things were, it was to me, I took pride in that because it wasn't something that you read out of books. It something that you can't explain to somebody unless they understand the way we are as (Garbled) people. And one of the things that grandma shared with us was that she said that her mother was one of the maidens that (Garbled) sent down to the, down to the, down to our neighbor's, the Sioux, because she was one of the maidens that was, uh, that went down by Sitting Bull at a very, very young age. And, she didn't like it over there, and she said, I want to go back home and when she came back home, it's what we call, it's called domestic abuse, I guess, because the chief was very mean to my grandmother. She said, "I don't want to stay there, I want to go home." So, she came home, and that caused hard feelings amongst our people here, because they believe that as Indians that we're all brothers and sisters, and that they shouldn't have been mean to her cause he told them that he would take care of her and be good to her and love her, but that didn't happen. So, she came home and, uh, grandma says, uh, grandma and my aunt and everybody used to say that, uh, "Well, if grandma would have stayed there we probably fought." And I think to myself, and I say to myself, that you know that she made a wise choice when she came home because she didn't want to get hurt, or abused, or battered or whatever you want to call it nowadays. So, she came come, and when she got home, the chief was very upset cause he seen one of his own come home in that kind of shape and that kind of way, and that really hurt him and that caused a lot of friction amongst our tribes and one another.

So, that started a lot of fighting and arguing and, um, our tribe, um, he was known here in Indian Country as the. . . the head chief or the general of the Ojibwe Nation and, um, and he was referred to as the head war chief of the Ojibwe Nation, cause Mole Lake was kind of like the center of the area because we were considered the interior band because we stayed on the mainland, and Chief Buffalo told his grandchildren, his grandson, he said that "you're down there, so what I want you to do is I want you to watch the border," because we were always in conflict with other tribes, you know, the Menomonie's, and the Sac and Fox and the Dakotas, Lakota's and the Sioux and all of those other tribes and I always wondered how come, you know, we were always that way, you know, why are we always fighting, why are we always scrapping, and then my father told me, he said, that ????? was referred to as the scrapper, he was the fighter, and that's what the martin is in the forest, the little pine martin, he's the fiercest of the forest, and he's the one that goes out and checks everybody our and makes sure that everybody does what they're supposed to. If you didn't do you're supposed to do, you got in trouble and he's the one to give you your punishment or correct you and had that right to go over there to tell you what you were supposed to do, you know, and as people we looked up to our chiefs at that time and they were the ones, and, you know, if we did something wrong, they were the ones to correction it, or to discipline us or to choose our punishment or whatever it is that you want to call it. And, um, and he's the one that would discipline the people. Well, anyway, there, we had these other tribes that kept coming in and trying to take over our rice beds and try to take over our hunting grounds, taking over . . . try to come in and invade our, um, our um . . . our homeland.

Cause here, right here in Mole Lake where we're sitting right now in this building, this is my birthplace. Cause, over here in the pine trees, over here to my left is where I was born. I was born in the living room, or the bedroom of my grandmother's home. And that's where I was born here on the reserva-tion, right here, this is my back yard. Cause over here across the road, the blacktop over here, this is Spirit Hill, and over here is Spirit Hill, cause what I feel about my own life and the way I was brought up was, every morning my grandpa would wake up and he'd take his drum, and he'd take his pipe and he'd go over here to that Spirit Hill and he'd go over there and he'd pound on his drum, smoke his pipe to bring in the day so that there would no more fighting and that there wouldn't be no more arguing. Cause we got tired of that, cause we lived in that kind of a life for so long. That it took so long for us to heal ourselves, to get rid of that feeling and that hate.

Today, we still . . . it's still hard for our people to turn the cheek and try to do what we're supposed to do. Cause in our lodges and our teachings that we get from the elders is that we're not supposed to be mean and not supposed to hate one another. What they teach us; we're supposed to love one another and care about one another. And, um, one of the things that my grandma and my aunt, what those people told me was to care about our burials and where our ancestors and where our relatives are buried and where they're at today, and because we lived in such a big area, we have a scattered, sort of say a scattered cemetery, because we have different chiefs and different people buried throughout the territory. (Garbled) our first chief, he was born on Madeline Island, he came here to Wisconsin, to the mainland, and his area was over here in Post Lake, by the dam. He's buried over there a hundred feet from the shore of the dam there. When you came down today, when you called me, I told Fred, that we need to go over there, and we need to offer some tobacco to grandfather. Cause, once again I'll be saying his name and the other ancestors, and when I talk about that I get all choked up [breaking in voice] because when we bury somebody we put them in the ground and we don't like nobody to dig them up, and I don't think anybody else would like that either.

And, um, [long pause] that's what the mining company did to our graves over here on Oak Lake. Excuse me [pause], over here on Oak Lake, in between Oak Lake and Sand Lake, and on the back hill of Spirit Hill is Oak Lake and over there in the Oak Lake is where the old people and the women and the children would go over there to the other side of Spirit Hill and they'd go over there and they'd hide over there cause over here on this area by the rice beds and over here where we sit was the side of the reservation where they fought, you see, cause where we're sitting now is considered the battle ground. Cause no matter where you go you're going to find pottery, different things on the ground and we tell people here at home to go there and when you see that, come and let us know, put your (Garbled) out so they don't bother you. Cause they say when you disturb that that they can come back at you. I don't know what the non-Indians call that, but I don't want them people to come back and haunt me and come back and do stuff to me. That's why I put that ???? out cause I don't want them to bother us. I told them that I'm not going to bring them any harm, that these are good people, and that they're not going to hurt us, because I've learned, I learned through my grandma and my aunties and uncles and the people before us that, uh, people don't know what it means to rest in peace.

And that was one of the things that bothered me about the Exxon Mining Company, back in the early 80s here on the reservation. Um, back in 75, 1975, 1976 around in there Exxon came over here and discovered copper over here and, uh, from 75 to around 76 it started. 1976 to about 1980, 1, 2, and 3 around in that area there, the mining company came over here and I don't know how they did it, maybe somebody can explain that, as far as I know they never got permission from the tribe to go over there to dig in those graves, you see. Under the NAGPRA Act, the Native Americans Repatriation and, uh, graves Act it says that you're supposed to notify the tribe that lives next door or that's around there or in the area to notify them that's, that we've uncovered some Indian remains, or artifacts or whatever you have or whatever it was. Well, they didn't tell us that. What they did was they just dug them up. In the pits are ten pits, and they're about the size of this table here. And what they did was dug them up and put them in plastic bags, but them in boxes and took them down to the Logan Museum in Beloit Wisconsin, and that's all I ever knew about it, all I ever heard about it. Um, um, my father's name is Robert Bandsaw Sr. and when we younger daddy would take us over there, and Dad would go fishing and mom and I and my brothers and sisters would go over there and us girls would pick berries because there's lots of blueberries growing over there, and lots of raspberries and stuff and we'd go over there and pick berries at Oak Lake where the burial grounds that they disturbed used to be.

One of the places where we used to go and have what we used to call our vacation bible school, cause when we were younger grandma and grandpa made us go to church and Sunday school and I just loved it. But anyway, um, um, at Oak Lake where these burials are, like I said, the burial pit's about the size of this table and they took them and dug them all up, and I don't know who did it or when it was, but I know it was the early 80s and somebody told me that there was ten boxes downstairs in the basement of the Logan museum in Beloit, Wisconsin, and they were marked Exxon Mineral Company or Exxon Mineral and Coal and Mining Company or whatever, property of. And I've been talking to a lot of people and I've been trying to find out how that became so. Because how can Indian remains belong to a mining company when we all know that they never had them, those are ours and they're mine and we want them back.

Because those are my relatives, those are our ancestors. They belong here, and what I wanted to do was, if it was all possible, that we could go over there and claim those family members and bring them home and bury them back. And what I'd like to do is put them back over there where they took them out. It might not be the same, the, the, the same way, because they already had their funeral, sort of say, they already had their ceremony, they was already put in the ground, they was already there, and they should have never bothered them. And, the reason it's so close to me is because my Aunt Naiome told me before she died . . . she says, "I want you to do something about getting those bones," she says, "and bringing them back home." And my aunt passed away 1995 and, uh, I had a car accident in 1995 and I got hurt, my aunt came over, and she says, "Oh my God," she says, "I was so scared that you had gotten hurt." And she says, um, she says "I just wanted to find out," she says, "how you were doing." And, um, I got in an accident in April and one of the last things that me and my aunt and us talked about was the burials and how, you know, she'd go and her and my uncle would take care of that, because my Uncle _____, is our last hereditary chief of the tribe, and my Aunt _____ is my dad's last sister, this is my last auntie on my daddy's side.

And, um, and uh, they take care of the cemetery, the cemetery we have now today where we bury our people, but we also still bury our people over here on Spirit Hill, it's still a, uh, it's not a cemetery like somebody else would look at a cemetery, it doesn't have markers and it's that kind of thing, but we know they're there, you know what I mean? Cause, I'd like to say just that much about it. And, um, I'd still like to be able to go over there and mark the graves and find some way to put some kind of a marker or something there to signify that these are graves and say please don't bother them no more. That's what I'd like to do, or I'd like to see.

Uh, I went into the lodge and they told me, they said that in order for us people to go on, that we have to bury our past, and my past is still sitting in Logan Museum down in Beloit, Wisconsin. And until they go back in the ground, my people here are still going to have that same ami, ani, animosity that's been going on because there's some people I know that I've heard that might have had something to do with it, and then I've got people over here that are mad at them, that said, "You guys should have done that." So, we're fighting here, internally, everyday amongst ourselves about those kinds of things. I'm tired of fighting [voice choked up] there's got to be an end to this, there's got to be a solution to our problem. We have to begin there, cause that's where the fighting and the arguing started back then, because when we found out that people were coming in and robbing our graves and nobody was telling us about it [voice cracks] that tore us all apart [quick strong words] all of us.

And to this very day I have a hard time because I still hear the words of our elders reminding us to [pause] to take care of them, go and get them, bring them home, put them back in the ground where they belong. That's what they told us to do. But for me as a person that don't know too much about that, I've never did anything like that, I don't even know where to start [voice cracks]. I went to Madeline Island yesterday, I put my heart out and I asked grandfather to guide me in what I have to do, you called me this morning, and you told me you liked to talk to me about my burials [long pause] you renewed my faith, because I was there on the island, and I was so heartbroken because I didn't know what to do anymore and nowhere to go and didn't know who to talk to. But that ate away at me and inside of me, "What are we going to do, where can I go, who do I talk to, is there somebody here, someway please tell me?" And then you called me, told me you were going to come here. I put my heart out this morning after I talked to you and told the Great Spirit, I says, thank you for sending someone who might know, I didn't know it was going to be this quick [cracking voice—sniffing] I didn't know it was going to be this quick.

So, my husband told me, he says, "well, we're going to have to get over there," he says, "and talk to these people." He says, "because these people have been on the shelf long enough." To me in my heart, they've been there long enough. Twenty years. Um, our people went out to Washington DC last week to celebrate the opening of the new museum, um, museums have their place, but they shouldn't hold our, um, it shouldn't be a place for our, um, our uh, for human remains. And our things to be there and on display so other people can see. Cause I think that all of that stuff, once it's put in the ground is supposed to stay there and nobody has the right to go there to dig it up and take it out and put it on a shelf. I don't care where you are, who you are, where you come from, or what faith or religion you are, we don't do that, and we shouldn't do that to anybody else. In the name of progress or not.

OK, what I had to do, was I had to go over there fight a mighty company for 27 years. 27 years it's taken me to fight these people. It wasn't until last year, that my tribe and the Forest County Potawatomi's got together and went and bought that mining company and the land that it was on and um now today, today, we stand here as a tribe having to pay back that share of that loan and we stand at, uh 8.5 million that's owed to the bank, that I don't know where I'm going to get that kind of money from. And we still got holes in the ground that mining company dug up. Who's going to build up us.

What's the mining company going to do about the burials and our remains that they stole up, stole from us. How am I going to get them back? See, once again, in other people's eyes they can't see this viciousness going on, but we have to endure what these people have done to us. And the only way this is going to stop is if we stop is if we go over there and go down there and give them whatever it needs or whatever it takes, go there, get them, put them back in the ground. And when and how and who, I don't know how it's going to happen, but the creator told me when I was up there on the island that something will happen, and I don't know yet, and I told my husband, I said, "Well, they want to get started and they want to get started right now," I said. He said, "Well, let's get going." Cause we've been at this so long and I'm not getting any younger, I started out back in the . . . when we were all younger and everything else and now we're gotten older. This is my husband _____. I was explaining to them about the burials over there on Oak Lake. My husband was one of the people who walked over there, who went over there, and we seen these people, he's seen these people digging in the ground, digging up those graves, and he went over there, and he asked them what they were doing. They told him to get out of there! Told him to get away and it ain't none of your business. But that's what they told him. That's how we knew about them guys going over there and doing that, see? But we couldn't do nothing about it, and they told us, they said that we couldn't get them back and we couldn't do nothing about it, because it was [emphasized] private land, belongs to the mining company. It still don't mean that they can take our remains and our stuff out of them graves and claim it for themselves. It's not their stuff, that's ours, belongs to the Moe Lake people. But that's what I'm talking about, and that's what I mean. And that's, uh, that's how our people are, like I said about the contract about that loan that we took out to buy this land. We've got that outstanding loan. 8.5 million dollars. It's got to be paid by the year 2006. I don't know where I'm going to get that kind of money, and I don't even know how I'm going to do it.

But I'm not going to lose this land, and I'm not going to lose this fight. 27 years is too long to go over there and lose a battle, cause I'm not going to let my people down. I don't want them to think that they did all of this in vain. Cause it's not . . . it's my home, this is where I live, this is where I was born.

Husband speaks: *Like a lot of stuff that she said [some laughing], Oh . . . I was just going to tell you that, um, some of what she was talking about, it's true that at the time Exxon was getting ready for exploration they had to go through different things through committee, for mining. And one of the things was to go through the area and look for sites and stuff. So, what they were doing, and it's probably within the EIS there's probably different areas where they've been looking for things. I don't know who exactly who the people were, I didn't contact them. I just heard that uh, I don't know if was in the Forest Republican, the local newspaper here, that they might be, um, have some students in the summer go over the area and look for . . .*

Gerry: *archaeological?*

Husband: *yeah, but they were looking for like German or lumber camps, you know, different things, you know, during that time. Uh, it's a situation where somebody buys land and they want to develop it and you need federal permits to discharge or different things where federal law might prohibit you know without getting permits for it. And that's what I believe they were doing. They have to have all these things to get a mining permit, and right now, our tribe we work on archaeological stuff for people. I don't work for the tribe for that. Even though I'm from the tribe, I'm a tribal judge here, and whatever, they want titles and governments want to give people.*

I'm a Anishinabe, an original person here on this land, and every time we come to these burials, ancient or modern Indian, Anishinabe burials those are all my relatives, and, um, [long pause] It's like [heavy sigh] you gotta be a mortician somewhat and modern days somebody puts in a water pipe or looks to put in foundations and if they're doing this on lakes or rivers and areas where we knew our people habitated for a lot of years, thousands of years, they're going to find those things and my job is to go and put their bodies back into mother earth. It's my religion, it's the way I feel about it. Um, we're talking about sites where they dug things out of the ground.

I understand that law somewhat. At the time, my people didn't look into it as much as I do, in my heart. It's with everybody. Some people look at the dollar bill, they forget about their past and their history, not realizing when they take that dollar bill they're making their own history, you know what I mean? So, the way I look at it, they took the things out of the site, there was numerous recordings about it, and news reports about Exxon finding sites, you know, and excavating a lot of Oak Lake area and the whole mine site area really. But they had to do, uh, to get these permits they had to do a lot of them, and they found all kinds of sites all around this area, Some of them four, six to eight thousand years old, mounds. And, um, our people still bury our people the same way. Some are a little bit different, because we have to go through the modern-day mortician kind of regulations, ok, but we bury our people the same way. We have the same thought when I see these mounds and sites and that. The religion hasn't changed in thousands of years, from what I know today in my own Anishinabe religion. When they took them out, see, there was different discussions, though. I don't know how many, or if there was any bones there, or artifacts, I just know they dug in those squares. When you do that, you know what you're doing? You're excavating to see what was there prior to . . . and there's high probability that the site is going to give up some answers to the past. Well, it did to me too. It told me, and reaffirmed me in my own beliefs today, handed down to me. That it still goes on.

Now, when you come to artifacts that we all talk with modern day thoughts about them, there was some discussions going on between I think a newspaper person in Crandon and one of the officials from Exxon at the time when they discovered it and they got a report back and wherever they took them I don't know. But the guy told her it was like finding things from a lost civilization. Now, where do you get. . . . I don't know where his mind frame is. But if you go back and you find these civilizations, those are my people, those are my relatives. And maybe those people we intelligent at the time on earth, like a lot of people were at the time, we don't know. But, today, but I have what's left in my mind on the spirit world is because is because I have to go there my own self.

Now, what people don't realize, and what the importance is, how we feel about this land, our people have been buried here for thousands and thousands of years. Since God put man on earth, that's how I believe. If we've been doing this for thousands and thousands of years and we can see by digging in the mounds and the graves and everything else of the other sites, that there was time frames when our people weren't so intelligent, and there was times when we think they, by looking at their temples, and the mound building, that they were really intelligent. But maybe they were in a way to make the stones and everything, the pyramids, and the temples and the mounds, you know the snake mound and all that turn into something that they use for the resources themselves, and they got greedy and eventually that civilization or whatever you want to call it, would pass out of time in my people's history and we go into another phase of it. People have got to realize that when Columbus he found our people still on these temples and still building highways and mounds and doing habitation for thousands of years. All the time we're burying our dead.

Now our religion says that this is how God put it for me. I'm born here on earth as an Anishinabe person I'm a hunter gatherer. All my life as I go on this earth, walk on this earth, I respect the earth as my mother, OK? The reason why is that is the nourishment that my mother got when she had me. Not my father, my mother, she came from the earth, the earth is the mother because they both give life. There's no chauvinistic thing in my mind about that, I know that is true. Once you get over that chauvinistic thing, that man is first, and man gave the rib up, and all this . . . OK?

When them stories were going on, my people building gigantic highways and making signs across the desert for hundreds of miles, straight lines. Understanding things in the universe that we're just finding out today. So, I go on this path on earth like my ancestors, and I eat all this food, and I drink this water, I enjoy the sunlight and I enjoy the coldness and the dampness sometimes in life I enjoy everything on earth. When I die, my obligation is to put my body back into my mother to repay her for my life here as a human being walking on the earth. When I put my body in the ground, I don't want nobody disturbing it, because that is my payback for my food and my life on earth. So, when you start digging into old ancient mounds, I know those people from a long time ago, men and women, they all lived here, and they died here, and they paid their mother earth back the same way. Ok?

So, that's why there's a confusion, like with _____, she has this heart
. . . I have it too. Um, we were recently at a treaty negotiations ceremony, it
was 150 years ago that our people signed the final agreement with the US
government to give us the reservations here in the territories around the
Great Lakes. And my grandfather, ___'s grandfather, we happen to be rela-
tives with the people who did that. Um, but a lot of people don't talk about
is during the treaty negotiations itself, [cough] there was a stress from not
only for hunting and fishing on reservation, rights of life, as I told you I live
as a hunter gatherer, but also we asked for to leave our cemeteries and our
graves of our fathers alone, not to cut the trees there, not to destroy the land
there, and the simple reason is so the water will go down, soak into the earth
and quench the lips and the thirst of my ancestors. Cause I'm going to go
there too. [big sigh] and I know you guys are going there too. And that's what
it's all about, the feelings we have. Now, they get these things back, they go
through a big rigmarole, but it's just part of the plan to me that they wanted
to down grade the Indian sites and the Indian feelings on this project knowing
that we're right next door,

OK? But there's a thing in the world, through my studying they call 'em,
that the population of that people is so small, and the economic boom is great
for the bigger population it's OK to mess up the little population to get that
stuff out, the economics of the world I guess, or [little laugh] or it's destruc-
tion, the self-destruction of the world. That's what happens. See a long time
ago we built these temples in a good way. But different times, thousand years,
five hundred years, six hundred years, whatever, maybe somebody got evil or
greedy. One of our head men, or if you want to call them a king or chief or
whatever, but they were the people that we respected under our leaderships.
Maybe they got bad and they did things. I recently seen an article, and I
wonder myself, why this happened.

Why would a people who built so good, building these temples and getting
all this stuff, agriculture water irrigation and all that. Why would something,
all the sudden all these people disappear? So, I thought about it, thought
about it. So, then the guy was down here in South America looking at these
pyramids, and I guess they had this one chief, or king there, he had a thing
for paying, or getting all his temples all over the land plastered with white
plaster, or, um, lime, make that lime. Then he said you got to burn a lot of
wood in them days to process lime, so they could plaster, and this one king
wanted it all. So, what happens is if you want to start plastering all these
temples down there, you're going to cut all the rain forests down and the
trees that was naturally growing around them places. You cut your parks
down, you start burning everything to get this plaster. You start getting runoff
with earthquakes and hurricanes like we know, and then disease follows and
destruction, flooding, earth, you know, the whole thing.

Then, all of the sudden, in our history the people pass away except for their burials, and some sites. Now same way with my people. We're talking about here, these people might have been here eight thousand, ten thousand years ago. When the glacier melted, my grandmother told me, my people came back up here home, because we have our traditions, and memories before the glacier came down.

You can add that up all you guys want to but that's a tradition of our burials and that's why Fran has that hard time, because, um, those are our relatives. I smoked a cigarette before I came in here, and I knew I was going to talk about them. They do come around when I talk about them. I'm not crazy, I'm just an Anishinabe person who believes in my way. I don't have to see em or hear em or nothing I just know they're watching me. So, I've always got to be constantly giving them, and humbling myself to them, due to the fact of when my turn comes, I want them to welcome me home, because I'm going home. I know where I come from and I know where I'm going. I'm going home. I came from home as an Indian person, I came to earth, I stayed on earth and my plan is, and the master's plan is of every man and woman the limitations man has, is that I'm going to die and go home. And I want my body left in the earth like my grandfathers asked the government.

But you don't hear too much about that, our chiefs asking to leave our cemeteries and our sites alone. Before anybody could do anything about it, the expansion came over my land, the invasion came over my land and the farmers and everybody else who cut it up, the lumbermen and all that, destroyed a lot in this development of America. Not for me, developing today, but for the new people coming here. And we understood that in our prophecies, and they still go on today. And that's why we're trying to tell you people, and Fran knows it and I know it, there's an urgency in all Indian country to return all our bodies back to mother earth, because the time of the purification of the earth is coming and it's very important for our bodies to be put back into mother earth. We're letting them sit on boxes and shelves for examination and historical societies and museums all over the place, and little farm ranches in Wyoming who might have an artifact in their little museum for tourists or whatever. Those people have to be back in mother earth because those times are coming, that's what our prophecy says and that's why the urgency is getting pushed out to the Indian people today.

Anything we can do to help this along is a good thing for my people who died years and years and years ago. Because my DNA goes back that far. I even know where I come from on my Anglo side. I come from an area way way back in your history called Stonehenge, OK? I know my family there, it goes back in the genealogy in the Mormon church. I know when they sailed out of England, out of Liverpool, when he landed in the harbor in New York, they homesteaded in upper New York, and then one of their sons was an adventurer and he came out west and settled in and I have _____(name). It's not spelled the British way, it's spelled because he married an Indian woman, he put an e on there. It's supposed to be in England ____, and it's_____ from my grandfather spelled it. I met my relative, he looks like you, from New York, he's an undertaker there, and my family he has no blood in him from the Ojibwa nation, but we're relatives. If I went to England, this is how I would look as an British person. If you've ever seen Sherlock Holmes in the British people, they have my features, not just my Indian side, but also from England. So, I realize that, you see, my grandmother left me a coat of arms, the _____ coat of arms from England. What's really part about it is that we go so far back into that tradition in England that it goes back to the time before Stonehenge and what was going on around the world, OK?

So, I connect with both sides of the ocean here, and I can tell you, this is what we're talking about the Indian bones and the Indian cemeteries and the sites is our orders, our commandments from God when he placed us here on turtle island. And it's very important that we put these bones back. We wouldn't like to see any more disturbances, but it's going to happen anyway. My own people dug a water tower here because of the mining issues and wells going bad, we had to put in a central well. When we did the central well, the excavator went eight feet down and found six, seven people, a family probably, seven to eight feet tall, buried right here on my reservation. They had shell-bead work from Madeline Island, they had deer from the woods, they had wild rice, they had pottery from over here, all in them graves. It was prehistoric, or I don't know, but it was older and those are the people who are my relatives.

There's no, um, you have to get this misconception that us Ojibwe people, we originated somewhere out of the east coast. It's not true. We were refugees from the great civil wars and anarchy and murder going on in the south as people were fleeing, what I just told you about, their own self destruction, we ran, we ran up that way. There was wars going on here, eight to four thousand years ago, thousands of people died at a time, and that's our story. We were forced out, and then we came to a time it happened to coincide with the Europeans comings to this continent, that our people got a vision from the ocean. A shell came up and the Great Spirit told us it was time for us to make our migration back home. We started down the St. Lawrence River, came all the way to the Great Lakes, and got to a place where the food grows on the water. The reason why we knew in that prophecy where the food grew on the water, was because it was the original story of the original homeland before we were exoduses out of it, other people and . . . it must have been terrible for my people in those years, think about it.

They have world trade and world peace going on, people coming here, and trading with my people all over this continent back and forth, on big boats, we paddled it or whatever, you know it must have been really kind of devastating because how do you think that our people thought when we went over to the people who maybe played with _____, the copper, they played and they worked that copper, they dug it out, they mined it, they traded it worldwide, and all of the sudden they all start dying out. Where'd they go? Toxic poisoning. The rest of us, even, who were maybe the bowl makers or other kind of gatherers, canoe makers, we all watched them, because they had a good thing going. All I can tell you is that if you get shot with a copper arrow, copper tipped arrow, instead of a stone arrow, you might get it out and operate on it and everything in those days and still live with a stone arrow, but if you had a copper arrow in your body, that poison got in there, and you died anyway, later on, a terrible death of poison, the copper. People would cut themselves if they were making blades, or trinkets for the rich, south wanted more and more. These are all buried in the sites we're talking about and that's why it's all connected.

So, that's why I can tell you I know where I'm coming from, and I know where I'm going. All that we're asking for is the help to start putting these things in the proper place, back to where there can be peace and comfort in my people. It's, um, subconscious . . . I hear it from my wife every now and then. She gets really angry, real angry, when somebody starts talking about them sites. And I'm saying, "Man I just wish I could get them boxes and put them back, so she wouldn't be that way." Cause I love her, but I can feel some people are stronger a little bit in thinking and some people are more or less, like me I think I'm less. Yeah, I can get angry and that, but I can live with a little bit, I'm not so . . . like her, you know, when it comes to her mind those are her ancestors telling her, "Hey, we're telling you to do this, don't stop." I've watched her for twenty some years of my life trying to get them people to bring the things back to us. It made part of her fight to get them back against the company because they had them and they wouldn't get them back. Now we own the company, I don't know how the law works or anything, I don't know what happened to it exactly, who the reports and that . . . but there was a lot of students who was talking up the profession of looking in archaeology and they went around here all summer long, two summers probably, looking at sites, marking them down, working with the federal department of interior, the USGS, and Army Corps of Engineers. They all made lists of all the sites around the area because they were all into the permitting process. They all had people who were highly educated in their profession to know what had to go into this EIS report, um, and then for everybody later on in this project, to find . . . "we don't know where it's at, we don't know what's going on, blah blah blah," "we don't know what it is you're talking about, we don't know about Oak Lake site." You know a lot of the people know about it, there's a . . . you know in my mortician job I had to go over and check out some people on some private land who had sites, eight thousand, ten-thousand-year-old sites, it just back a history, more of the story of my people. And I wasn't in wonder, I was saying "Wow, man, we do the same thing today." When we're allowed to. I make a lodge, or I go do the big drum, we do the seasons, we do all that stuff. If, uh, somebody understood the snake mound in Ohio, it's a well-known, worldwide, a lot of people know about that snake mound in Ohio

Uh, when I was a young boy, they taught us all the traditional dances, and one of them is called snake dance, _____. The dance . . . and that's for the springtime. We do that in the springtime and rejuvenate the earth and the things on it, so we always survived another year, another season, another time. So, we planned out a circle at first and then it turned into a square and then more squares and then more circles and more squares, and they enlarged that serpent mound with the dance. Today when I dance, I do the snake dance, they call it powwows for exhibition or something, we start out, we come out in a thing and we start weaving like a snake all around weaving and we make a circle like this coil and the leader comes up and looks down, people come up, look down and then we go the opposite way and we dance all around like a snake again until we get to the circle and we all get out in a circle, and that's the end of the dance. They call it . . . they bring out the stump, the last part is the stump dance and you've got to jump over that into the new life for a new season. When I see that, I said, Oh, what they were doing was just making that a permanent snake dance area. And the people who were there at the time thought it was so important to have this new crop coming for the year that they made that mound. So, maybe you should end it there. No, but, uh, I just wanted to get you so.

Gerry: *I do have a name for you now that should be able to get them back for you. I hope it works.*

Husband: *See, I could go out tomorrow, but this is what I'm going to tell you, and it's really important if you're going to do this, not just for the boxes we're talking about, but how do you get your own people to understand the in depth feeling we have as human beings. See, it's not in your people, I've studied your people too, because I'm part your people. There was a time the king said, "I want more." So, the poor people who were in these squares in the kingdom, they had to give more crops out for the king, more stuff they had to make, more and more and more. So, the king says, first I want this chunk of land, and I want this chunk of land to be put off and put it into crop and this chunk . . . and then he gives the farmer a little cemetery for the family plots, and a little bitty farm area. "That's yours, and you do all the work for me, and bring that stuff in." He keeps on demanding more. Before you know it, then, the religion and people from the king, and he says "Nope, you can dig your cemeteries up, take all your bodies, you can plant your cemeteries now, because if you're starving that's where you're going to get your crop to live for a year." So, your people start digging them people up, breaking your own traditions of not doing that, and putting them into catacombs and different sites, OK? Did you know there was a time over here in America did the same thing? They call that "Hill of the Dead" here at Crandon. So, at the time frame we did the same things, we just didn't forget about it and understanding . . . see, you know what, see your people turned this town into this kingdom thing and all of the sudden you lose this feeling for the cemeteries.*

Husband: *OK, we're all done here, but I gotta key to get out of here to lock up, but I just wanted to tell you that, so you understand that I understand both sides of this thing. Because if you ask me right now, "Fred, what do you think about your family here in Stonehenge?"* (Cox 2015, 418–445).

The following is a transcription from a Chippewa Cree:

And most of these things, they are not, everything I'm going to be telling you is sacred. It's not a matter of just a . . . , or John Wayne or a Boy Scout story. It's not . . . things like this . . . am I on right now?

My name is _____ I am from Rocky Boy, Montana, Chippewa Cree Tribe. My Indian name means Good Feathered Man. And my color is blue. My family, my father _____, is uhh . . . his dad, my grandfather, his name was _____, means Chief. No, that's my mother's dad _____, means Chief _____. My grandpa, my dad's dad is _____. And he is named after the center pole from the sun dance lodge. And, we derive from Canada. A small band in Canada that came down this way and subsequently, the boarder cut some of our tribe's folks and moved into different areas. One of the main ones that was established was Rocky Way. Stone Child after _____. _____ means stone, _____ means child. So right from the get go, the government had translated _____ wrong, instead they called it Rocky Boy. Rock is something else and boy means _____ so that Rocky Way on a map is not Rocky Way. It was supposed to be the main one, I got it here, Stone child _____.

So, we just now, in the past 15 years, we started getting the truth of America. Especially when the tribes on a national level are starting to really get into their origin, their belief system, customs, culture. And like myself, I grew up speaking Cree and everything was, every day on a daily basis in our household was spoken in Cree. I hardly knew any British when I first started school. Everything now talked to us was always talked in Cree or sacrum, sacrilegious way on a daily basis. We'd light the sweet grass or the smudge in the morning when the sun come up, I could hear my dad praying, hear my mother prayer, and we say our blessing with our food, we'd lift up our food and ask the ones who have gone to eat with us and give us good health, wellbeing, good luck and for the betterment of our people. And that's just like the Blackfoot Indian saying grace, same meaning. At noontime, they say the same time every time you see a Cree or a Rocky Boy or other natives too, other tribes, they lift up their plates and say grace. That's what that means, that's what they're doing, they are saying a prayer and blessing the food.

And then in the evening, help them set up rocks, set up a sweat, go on and sweat, our sweat lodge is, the hole for the rocks is in the middle, and our lodge faces the south, and everything that we've been taught from my father within our family and grandfather and so forth, they've learned on a daily basis. Especially in a traditional, a cultural way. Today I really strongly believe that my father, my mother and other people in existence that are elders now, they have existed because of that, because of that belief system. Our Cree belief system is a whole, it's our, the nucleus of our whole existence of why we still practice, why we still exercise our Cree way, have our language, interpretations. And everything now has, everything has been handed down, since the beginning of time. Created by_____. I'm a fairly young person, I've got a long, I don't know, I'm not a, not a really knowledgeable person but I would like to be. Especially when I look at my father. When I look at my father I see this man with an abundance of knowledge, wisdom, songs, prayerful ways, how to use a pipe, how to direct people of our ways, especially in the sun dance or sweat lodge, all these ways that how I would like to be like him, like my father. And he cried when he lost his father, my grandpa. When he died in his sleep he was 107 years old. And, my father expresses tears cause he felt that he didn't know, he didn't really quite know as much, that little bit that his father taught him, as much as his father knew, in a Cree way. So, in time, my father took his time and very patiently taught us and told us and tried to, in his best to teach us in a Cree way. From since I was a child. And, I love my father dearly, and I love my childhood.

Because, today, this present day, I could say that our tribe is fluently speaks their language, exercises our practices and our ceremonies, we have the ghost dance, the horse dance, we have the sweats, we have the pow wow, we have the ghost dance, and we have the, we have an abundance amount of songs. It's like the top charts, like you see on the radio, top hits in America, we have top hits like that. We have song for a birthday song, name songs, we have so many sets of songs. But life and since you come, from the day you come out of the womb when you are being called to the creator, it's all one learning process. It's all one life-long learning process. And everything that you do down here gets you up there. And that's what my father used to tell us all the time. So, he tried his best to try to have respect for ourselves and for our families, especially the female. Mother Earth. One who provides nourishment, strength, healing. Where the female comes into the picture. My mother, my grandma, my sisters, my aunties, my daughters, my granddaughters, and *so forth. Men and female, they walk hand in hand. And that's the whole belief system is based on the Cree way. Father, son, Mother Earth. All of these. And the colors signifies all that strength that carries that shield and watches us over. That name carries us throughout our lifetime. _____ doesn't mean a thing to me. That's what the government calls me. _____, they interpreted _____, mystic.*

Most of these Indian names that we have in the past are interpreted wrong. And since the beginning of time ever since I've known, they've taught us. I come from a generation where it was okay to do these things, it was okay to like the sweet grass, to talk in your language, smoke the pipe, go in the sweat lodge, sun dance. But then prior to my father's generation, before that, they were tortured. They were punished. Some of them was even hung. The woman folk were raped. My goodness, they . . . just because we practiced our ways. Now today, I still look at the . . . it doesn't make me bitter, it doesn't get me so upset when I hear these kinds of things now how they are cutting off funds, especially for school, now they're starting to bring culture and traditions into the school, they got language in the school, and right here . . . . right across the street here they show these little kids how to tan hides, make moccasins, bead. Language is important. It's our life.

To this day, when you look way back in the past, still the non-Indian, B.C., and all this, blind. They can't see that, what has happened in the past. But today, we still have those. We still practice and exercise those. In a good way, we pray for who doesn't understand. We share, try to educate them in the classroom. Today these gentlemen are here to ask about how the spirit that sent them in some way out of reserve, this sacred traditional way, and time and time again, this is the importance, how we carry this message through. And I would love for the globe to look at this tape and say "hey, we're all together on this one globe, this short life that the creator gave us to share." Respect our ways, our language, our traditions, our culture. Japanese, Chinese, all four corners of the earth. Sacred four seasons, sacred number four, all of these things have meaning. Everything that we talk about in the sacred sacrilegious ways are very, very sacred. It's not a toy, it's not something that you can go cuss around, get mad over for, fight over for. Who's number one. Who's doing it the right way. This lesson learned from our mistakes and go from there. Smoke that pipe. Give somebody tobacco from another tribe. Here grandpa, teach me, say some good words for me. One of these days, I know you are getting old, you're going to pass on. I want you to, I want you to tell me what I could use here, when the creator calls you. That's what my father said to me all the time.

And I went through the alcohol, drug bit. Today, I'm alive because I believed. I was pronounced dead twice. Got stabbed and got shot. Still got bullet wounds here, got a bullet here. Got a bullet through my knee. Through

*my throat. Got in a car accident and broke my back. Couldn't play basket-
ball like I used to. Now I got a wife, beautiful kids. My son _____,
_____, _____, _____. I got grandsons, _____. I got beautiful
family. All just because my family gave tobacco to give me another chance.
And, my friends all at once went to Vietnam. There's only three of us now that
used to run around together. There used to be 17 of us. Buried 'em. Gone.
Some of them got murdered.*

*When I was out there on the coast and come back, that's when I started
waking up on my life. Come on _____, had to go to Portland to bury my
sister. She called me a couple days before that said she wanted to come
home with me and stay with me. But the creator has plans for each person.
When I come back, instead of taking her home with me, the creator took her.
At that time, my family gave tobacco. I was gonna, ____ wanted to speak,
_____ wanted to cook. It was up to the cook to give tobacco. To ask for help.
Pallbearers. Pallbearers give each pallbearer tobacco. Each time, everything
that is done from the course, the whole duration since that person is called
on. How they go, when they go take their clothes, their Indian color. Try to,
their names. Put them in their grave, make sure they have that color, when
they wear that when they go on their journey. Make sure they have a pipe
in there. There's a woman's pipe, too. Women have a smaller pipe that goes
in there. And then during the course of the, wakes, we fix them a little, like
a doggy bag, like a lunch or a snack. We put little berries and stuff in there,
soups, or whatever. A little plate to put inside that casket for that journey.
And when we, when we start to call certain people, if it's a woman, we call
certain women that we know were very close that they knew this person and
say here, say something about this person, say something about my sister.
Call my auntie and _____ speaks on her behalf. But she can't say to the
creator, my auntie wouldn't be able to say, I'm trying to think of what a young
one has to say. Or vice versa. Some of them that pass away, they couldn't
talk British. Now we have an interpreter there. My brother _____ can
write a word _____, means standing rock, _____. We have people
there. Designated people from the tribe. They say here, interpret for me. Go
ahead. So, they, these gentlemen, they express, for the family. Each time you
do things, tobacco comes first, pipe comes first.*

*When they dress the person in the casket, they try and have their mocca-
sins, or some of them, no jewelry, you're not supposed to put eagle feathers
in their casket or something that's not really, that they can't take with them.
Put a cane in there or something warm too, a coat. Sometimes they bury them
in the winter, and they got a long journey. So that morning before we bury
our ones who been called, when the sun comes up we sing a morning song,
or a song, a journey song. Face the casket, not supposed to look back. Sing
them songs. Pray for that person. Them songs, take that person home. Going*

home. Then go talk for us. Then go speak for us, on our behalf down here. We take that, we go bury this person. Come back. Everything, that feast has to be, everything has to be served at noon. Right at noon. Everything, that pipe has to be, that pipe has to be passed around, that food has to be passed out and you're eating because the south . . . when that feast is going on when we bury this person, gotta open that pipe, is a key to the gates of heaven to open that door for this person to get in. And that door opens at midday when the sun is right in the middle, that person has that pipe, come home, I come home. And the pipe smoke. And we eat with those people that feast, we eat with our loved ones, our relatives, our friends who we come in contact with, the doctor, eat with them, feast. And it's very important, everything is important, sacred. So, when everybody eats, they don't, people in the feast, they don't touch until that person says so. Whoever the family designated to call on to smoke that pipe, I think there is a pipe. And then everyone else too. And the servers, the cooks and the servers, the helpers. Who's going to dig that grave? Who's going to be up there to stay? Who's going to take care of that fire? We have to have a fire burning, all the time. Day and night stay out there. Some tribes, they don't sweat. They don't want to sweat. Say no, can't sweat. Our Cree tribe, the people that I belong to, Cree's. Right away, when somebody passes on up there, we go in right away and pray for that person. Their spirit. And we pray for that family and their relatives or maybe the wife, or the husband or the kids or whatever. We pray for them. Maybe sometimes they will have a morning sweat and sometimes everyday they'll have a sweat. I know there is always sweats involved when there's a passing on, when there's a death in the tribe. Or they'll hear someone from a different tribe. Say "hey, your relative passed away over here, or somebody passed away." They'll, right away, they'll set them up, go pray for the people or the tribe. So, after that, after that, the feast, they put the pipes away, then they go, they eat, clean up, everybody helps clean up, and then they go sweat. And then, there's a mourning period for different families.

Each family has a different way of mourning. Sometimes, some people cut their hair. Some people take skin out, an offering. Some people don't dance. Some people can't. It just depends on their medicines, their families, and maybe the tribe as a whole. But then afterwards, a year after, sometime they'll start dancing again. Or they'll have a feast, a giveaway. And then in remembrance they'll have dedications. They'll have a lot of, everything we do nowadays, the teachings, the chiefs a long time ago, our sacred people, our medicine people, everything that I'm saying today is in translation of what they said, how it was going to be for today, what my father had taught us how to say in a good way, without bringing harm. Or for somebody not to exploit this kind of stuff, and not to even change it in a classroom or a book.

Those John Wayne boy scout stories, they brainwashed our kids, even society today. Taught the white man how, white man, we did a lot of damage for our history, the way that we are. Sacred people. We bleed the same blood, learn from the same mistakes. Our belief system teaches us; therefore, we walk through life together, on the sacred path in a sacred manner. And we all pray to one god, one supreme being. And that's the way it was in the beginning of time. Who are we, are the other people, to change that? You can't. Everything that we do, not only from our sacred burials, but there's different ways like our ceremonies, marriage ceremonies, our celebrations, our horse dances.

Everything's done really detailed or intricate. You think the constitution is hard. You go over there and go to one of our ceremonies, there are certain ways that you spin that pipe a certain way, a certain way where the woman has to sit, a certain time of the day, a certain color you have to use, certain direction that, what spirit to pray to, certain color, certain number, certain number of songs you have to sing because of that. See a lot of people don't know that. Think I'm a long-haired savage. I have a reason for my long hair. I have a reason for my, to wear an earring. I have a reason to talk about the way, I need to talk about things because of the betterment of myself and my family and other people. And all of it to be enjoyed. Not to be, I wasn't brought up to make fun of people. Laugh at people just because they're white. We go work them over, we kill them because _____ made a mistake. That's not of our way. We pray for people rather than make fun. Try to help them out the best way we can. So, in some ways, that's the best way how we can preserve our ways is to respect when they leave this world, use their knowledge, what they've gained here to leave it that with us, so we can add on our knowledge that we've got already to their kids and to their family and other people that want to know.

When they change worlds, they can watch over us from up there. Still show us and direct us how we can do things on mother earth. We still have that belief system. It's still here, it's still in existence. And we still practice that all of the time. So, I hope my father sees this tape and I know that he'll, he always appreciates, even when I make a mistake he always appreciates. And other tribes too. Other tribes have different ways. I kinda scratched the surface of what . . . Here. Come to Rocky Boy, go to a different reservation, take a pipe of tobacco and a gift and go up to an elder, man or woman. And say, "here, grandpa, grandma. Teach me something. Tell me something." Begin your life. It's not hard. They'll cry, they'll cry because you want to ask them.

Because the government is trying to work with us to teach that in our classroom. But for the younger generation of Native Americans today I'd slap them in the face because their grandma is sitting right there in front of them.

They don't have no reason to listen to rap music, to turn to gangs, to shoot somebody, cause they're "cool." Being cool is knowing how to talk your language. Being cool is going into the sweat and using that pipe and praying to the creator singing those songs. Being cool is going to the pow wow sober. Go to the wakes and respect without using drugs. Just go and help out at these wakes, go help that family.

These people here, I'm a Cree. Blackfeet, they're good. When I lost somebody up there, boy they helped me out get up there, come home, smoked, prayed for me, prayed for my family. Other places where I went that's the way the Native Americans, even non-agency, they understand. Some of them even grieve even more than I did. They hurt more than I did, because they knew my father, they know my family, they know the friends that I know. So on, it's a tight-linked chain, it's a sacred link, from this life to that life up there. That's the antidote. And I mean, some people know they are going to pass on, some people don't. But then they know. Each person knows that they have to do some good in their lifetime to have sacred eternal life. And that's what they try to teach through this pipe. In all tribes. And I know I'm alive because of this. And my brother, which is a Vietnam veteran, went to work and came back. A few scars, but he's alive. He's alive because of that. All these crazy, my crazy buddies, crazy Native Americans, they're alive because of that. Even people who ____, belief system. And, our grieving period teaches us a lot. That's when they say that the spirits that have gone on teach us the most. How to pick ourselves up. Teach us how, what they have had . . . for instance if they dance, they sang, teach us those songs through spirit through grieving, that morning time. Do best how to respect that and do those kinds of things that they people do. To use those in a good way. And some people, they can't take it. Subsequently they die of loneliness. Commit suicide, or they just give up. Or they just seem like they make a joke out of life. But others, when they turn around, that grieving period, that mourning period, is the best teacher when a person passes on. That's when you really find out that you really loved somebody, someone. It hurts that you loved them so much. But one day, you are going to see that persons again. One time. So, when I start talking about these things, these sacred traditional ways, and these, our sacred way, our Cree culture, there is no ending. There is always tomorrow. And every second of the hour of the day of the week of the month of the year of our lifetime through our whole existence, that's just like the sacred ____ is still going since the beginning of time, still going to carry on forever. And that's what the way, Cree way of life is all about. That's how sacred it is. To be respected. To be respected by other people. Especially by the U.S. government. (Cox 2015, 446–458)

Transcription of a member of the Shoshone tribe:

*I had to stop at Casper, one of the little Indian girls from up off the reserva-
tion there, she had a baby that died of suffocation and a friend of hers asked
me to come down and put on a, do a ceremony and everything, paint the baby
and everything else. So, I just got through doing that yesterday. My name
is _____ and I'm an enrolled member of an Eastern Shoshone
tribe of the Wind River Indian Reservation. And some of the beliefs about
our people when they pass on and go to the other side that it is probably one
of the final stages of what I consider the four stages of life. Our life here on
Mother Earth is just a very short period of time. From the time we're first
born, we go through that stage of being a very young child, a baby. And we
go through our childhood to our adoles=cents and then into middle age and
then of course into our time when we come to be senior citizens or elders.
Some of our things of life is, some of our _____, how we do things, how we
live, what kind of person we are here on the face of Mother Earth, a lot of it
depends on what our life is going to be when the creator calls our time, when
it comes to be our time when we get ready to pass over to go to what they
might say the happy hunting grounds, or heaven, whatever the concept may
be that different people believe in. Some of our things that we do are a little
bit different among the Shoshone people are very secretive, very secretive.
Not a lot of the things are really exploited. We also are a firm believer that the
importance of facial paint when a person passes away. That should be done
by a member of the tribe so that it is done in a very respectful way that they
can go ahead and pass on without having any problems. Also, that during one
of the procedures that we try to do too when a person passes on is we usually, they're remembered, or an individual will sun dance for them. We'll also
make prayers during some of our ceremonies that I don't really want to get
into in depth. But them are some of the very, very spiritual things that make
it, make that journey, make that life journey when its complete, when its time.*

*When that spirit is sent to the other side. And grieving, it's a part of life.
Life will continue to go on, but also the grieving is a time that, for the ones
that are left here on the face of Mother Earth, we like to share that time in
a way that we do this in memory of them loved ones that went before us,
passed on, whether it be a mother, father, sister, brother, grandpa, grandma,
aunties, uncles, even our children, grandchildren, great grandchildren. You
know we grieve in a way that we want to go and show respect to their life,
show respect to the way that . . . grandfather would be happy with the way
we show respect to him, _____. We like to also do it in a way that we can
go ahead and have our own self-healing. So that during the grieving process
we know that, the way I've been taught with our elders and those that, when
we pass on we know that they don't want us to grieve for a long time. They
want us to go ahead and go in that sacred way. That's the reason a lot of*

times some of our elders will tell us to do certain things and go on with our lives when somebody passes away, you go about your life and make it work. They don't want you to continue to grieve, they don't want you to continue to cry, let your heart be sad.

When that times comes for the burial ceremony, there are different ways, different things as I've mentioned earlier that the body of the person, the remains, is usually painted. We have a long, usually a very, very long time between where everybody gets to stop by and say their goodbyes and send him or her in a very good way. Also, some of the things that we utilize that, I want to go ahead and share with you off camera for your studies, some of the things that, I don't want to have recorded, I'll just share this with you personally. And then, you know, there's the ways of our people have changed a lot from the old historical way. One of the things of our Shoshone people, a lot of them were buried in caves, crevices. I used to know, and I still know of a couple places that are sacred burial grounds up here on the reservation up here, in several of the canyons. Also, I knew where one of our tribal members had been buried. But when people find out about it, they get curious, look around. It's alright, look, but leave them alone, get away from them. But then sometimes peoples picking up things and that's not good, that's not a good way because we wouldn't go to a white man's cemetery and start taking flowers off the graves, we wouldn't come in there and take a picture of the headstone or something like that.

The respect of death is probably one of the greatest honors that you can give to a person. Many times, some of these funerals, wakes, it's done in different ways. We can also combine them with the ways of Christianity, Shoshone traditional ways. Sometimes we can run them parallel. We may have our local clergy priests come in, pastors whatever may be come in and want to do it their way. And we still do our traditional ways.

A lot of times, in the body preparation, during the wake, we will have them in a tee pee and a lot of time people will come and make visitations, say goodbye. We always have a big feast during the wake, we'll have a big feast after the funeral. And usually we'll have elders speak at the wake or when they put them in the ground. And it's for the spirit of a person, as I said earlier on the tape, when a person passes over, we like to send them on a good, straight, fast, straight journey to get there as fast as possible with no detours, no wandering around. We like to have them go that direction, on the straightaway, straight over to the other side. And also, that these ways are, like I mentioned, some of them are done during our ceremonies, that you and I can discuss. Some of the ways of the Shoshone people, taking on a lot of different traditional ways. Taking on a lot of different ways that we have accepted.

We have brought into our culture a lot of the European culture, like I said. On our reservation up there, the missionaries, they came in early, the

Catholic missionaries, the Episcopalian missionaries, and also all the other different denominations of churches that came in, come in to help us with these ceremonies you know because our Shoshone traditions. So that's the reason that our beliefs of life here after goes to wherever. Maybe that spirit will go over real quick. We don't want them to have to wander in order to go. Also, too, we also have beliefs in everything else that many of those spirits will come back and visit us periodically, which is not a bad thing, it's a good thing. Coming back to check on us, to check on our people, check on our ways. See that we're doing the right thing. Cause elders, the older people, they were our real teachers, mentors. And so, what I see in present day that a lot of these always coming back, getting stronger, getting stronger. Getting involved with some of the ceremonies, make it work, help out with the people. These ways of even having a major giveaway after the ceremonies was to honor their people, that person, honor that life. Along with the services that we have.

I've been very fortunate that I'd been asked to, in my short lifetime, that I've done several services. Some of the toughest ones is the little ones. Some of the toughest ones are lifetime friends that you grew up with that pass on before you. But also, I'm a firm believer that the Creator he is the one that helps us through these ceremonies, helps us through these times. Cause he helps us make these decisions, helps us make these words, so that that ceremony is done. The ceremonies done for the people that's left here, cause that spirits already taken off, its already passed away. (Cox 2015, 458–464)

THE STOCKBRIDGE-MUNSEE TRIBE

The Mahican were known as the "People of the Waters That Are Never Still" and are often confused with the Mohegans, a Connecticut tribe immortalized in the book, *Last of the Mohicans,* by James Fenimore Cooper (Pritzker 1998, 613). The Mahican, Mohegan, and Mohican are probably the three most confused Indian names with all three meaning "wolf" in Algonquian (Waldman 1988, 119). The Mahican and Munsee tribes are of the Algonquin language grouping. The Mahicans and Munsee tribes were Woodland Indians with lifeways typical of other Algonquin peoples (Waldman 1988, 120). They were drawn into the fur trade after meeting Henry Hudson in 1609 (Pritzker 1998, 613).

Like the Anishinabe, before the arrival of the Europeans, the Mahican and Munsee tribes lived in what is now known as the New England. The Mahican were located primarily along the Hudson River to Lake Champlain but also lived in other areas. The Munsee lived originally west of the Hudson River and along the Delaware River in what later became New Jersey as well as in the Mahican areas of New York. The Delaware tribes including the Munsees, Lenapes, and Mahican were forced out of their traditional homelands (Richter 2001, 168). As they were pushed further and further west, the Delaware burned homes, murdered people, and were themselves murdered by the Europeans (Richter 2001, 185). Today the Mahican and Munsee tribes have merged into one group, the Stockbridge-Munsee tribe. They have historically been known as Mahican, Housatonic Indians, River Indians, or Muh-he-con-neok. The Munsee were part of a larger group known as the Delaware Indians (Waldman 1988, 120). The Mahicans warred with the Five Nations, but peace brokered by the English that became part of the English-Indian alliances (Richter 2001, 147). They were enemies of the Iroquois tribes, especially the Mohawks who often raided their villages (Waldman 1988, 120).

The Mahican and Munsee Indians lived similar lifestyles and in areas near each other and over time merged together. After merging and the arrival of the Anglo-Europeans, the Mahican and Munsee tribes formed a community in Massachusetts known as Stockbridge. The name was taken to Wisconsin with them. They were masters of spears and clubs, bows and arrows, nets and traps, and used their skills for hunting and fishing as well as gathering wild plants, especially maple syrup, and growing corn, beans, and squash (Waldman 1988, 120).

As the bison provided for the Plains Indians, the forests that ranged from the Atlantic coast to the Great Lakes with pines, cedars, maples, ash, elm, hickory, oak, and other trees provided not only cover from attack, but also for housing, arrows, bows, maple sap, and a way of life for the "People of the Leaves." The Woodland tribes were many including not only the Stockbridge-Munsee, but also the Delaware, Iroquois, Ho Chunk, Onieda, Sauk and Fox, Ojibwe, Miami, Kickapoos, Potawatomie, Shawnee, and many others who shared similar lifestyles. The forest was not just a friend, but was also a brother.

To the Woodland Indian, trees were a sacred and living thing. Like the bison, every part of the tree was useful. Leaves could help make a bed or start a fire. The trunks of trees could be used for poles to build the lodge, the bark could be used to keep out the rain, and the branches and limbs could be used to make many items. Many tools and hunting items were made of wood. Trees were used for weaving materials. Because trees are also seen as being living things, Woodland Indians never cleared forests, but rather they only destroyed the life of the trees that they needed. Over time, they developed snow shoes and canoes that made traveling easier and allowed them to cover more areas. Like all early civilizations, fire was very important for their survival in cold winters. The living trees were also used for heat and cooking. Trees and other growing, living forms of nature also gave them needed herbs, medicines, and items used for curing, ceremonies, and decorations. For the most part, the Woodland Indians used tools made from wood rather than stone or metals. The Woodland also provided fruits, berries, and nuts which also added to their diet over time. The Stockbridge-Munsee tribe continues to share this heritage.

The Stockbridge-Munsee are known for living in Longhouses; having forest lifestyles; and for hunting, fishing, and gardening. To make their Longhouses warmer in the cold winters, they often had three fireplaces and hung animal skins on the walls for insulation to keep them warm (Pritzker 1998, 615). They typically lived near rivers and in forests. They moved every eight to ten years (Pritzker 1998, 615). As many as two hundred people lived in a typical village. Women did the gardening and men hunted. Most of their technology was wood based, with wood being used to make bowls, utensils, woven wood baskets, bag, and mats (Pritzker 1998, 615). Like the Anishinabe/Chippewa, they were also known for sharing. No one ever went hungry.

The Munsee are also known for their rock piling. Many return to Stockbridge, Massachusetts, to Monument Mountain and bring a rock with them to add to the pile as a way to say thank you for the safe journey.

The following is a transcription from a member of the Stockbridge-Munsee tribe:

I'm _____ from Boulder, WI, Stockbridge Munsee Reservation. And we arrived in Wisconsin in 1822 up at _____ on the Fox River. And we were there about 10 years and they decided it was too good for us. Menomonee's was getting influence from the French, and we had to move. But we went in there with a lot of white men's ideas and they didn't trust us too good. _____ just the French people just wanted it that bad. But we moved, and we got over to east side of Lake Winnebago where they told us we could go and then they were kinda crowded over there because they had been migrating there from the East, the Brotherton, and the _____ and the _____. And it was too crowded we thought, we didn't have enough room like the rest of them. So back to Washington they had to go to find a place for us. And it came back, we were first to go to White River, Indiana was supposed to be our next place after we left out East, but we got there, and the governor had forced the Delaware Indians to sell the land that they were saving for us and there was no place to go but they allowed us to stay until we found a place. So, after Washington _____, and take a long time in those days because to get some place was slow and then to get on the agenda and then get back. So, I think it was about 5 years he was gone. How he survived in all that time I don't know. I wonder often about that. Because we were orally taught, we didn't have no money ideas, we didn't have no police ideas, everybody was brought up to behave themselves and mind and we were very close-knit families. Until each one would get a little bigger, then they'd move on. First thing you know you got a lot of clans, different clans. But they run under their own government each time. And well, when he did get back, they said well we got two townships in _____ County and we'll take your _____.

What happened after the Revolutionary War, the women had a hard time getting along and so they got mixed with whites. Because whatever was handy, it was wilderness in those days, and you got to realize that. So, when they arrived here, we had a few little white breeds, half-breeds rather. And they wanted to live like white folks, they didn't want to follow the Indian system, so they stayed in this county, I mean this township, which is _____, and the other one was Red Springs. So, the Indians went to Red Springs. Well, it's strange how things go, and I don't know how fast information traveled about, they knew that this was all stone and swamp and we were supposed to be farmers. They always wanted us to be farmers, they always stressed that. I don't know if it was, they didn't believe we'd make it if we couldn't be farmers, or what. But we didn't believe that way. We believed that the country was wide open, you could move when you wanted, we weren't used to all this organization stuff. Still going on, but we got used to it I guess. But we came here, and it was rough getting started again, getting settled in, feeling like home. And Red Springs was a little better farming than up in _____ here, along the river is stone, swamp. So, they got settled in all pretty quick. They had _____ settled with white people and then they branched out and wanted land.

Course the hard times came, which they always seemed to be happy when we were troubled with poverty. So that was an opportunity for them because they were looking for land. They liked to have it after it's cleared so the Indians would clear it and then they'd want it. Well that kept up till the First World War, we always went to war, we was in every war that was here. We believed this was our country. But we were pushed down because we know how to survive, they didn't worry about that. We knew what was good eating in the woods. We knew what was medicine, and we did survive. Which they never believed we'd survived this long. I can't believe it myself. But it's thinning out pretty much. I don't know.

Well anyway, burial practices. We do, we do the burials that we get from the museums and that we put them in little boxes and have a little ceremony over them and we put food and water and everything in the grave with the person because of our belief that that was how we would take care of them if they were here. That's the only burial practices I know. But they go through a lot of, the tribes that can talk their own language, __, ____, _____, I left one out, Chippewa's, they all got more formal patterns than we have, we just have to copy what we see around or hear and read. Of course, but it was rough.

And every war we lost people until we were 25,000 at one time. And after Revolutionary War, it was only 250. So, when they went back to Massachusetts, where Massachusetts had given them a 10-mile square and said they wouldn't bother us, when we got back from the Revolutionary War, it was all taken up. Cause the women couldn't control it, and they couldn't fight it, they didn't have time, survival you know. So, the men were very, very discouraged, didn't know which way to turn. Well the _____ people invited them to New York because they thought they had a space of land and they thought might as well put the Indians in there, as to have the white people come and force their way in there. So, we settled there until this governor decided there were too many, everywhere we went, these other _____ speaking people came where we were. So, it multiplied real fast. And then they get scared, they afraid that the Indian people are going to attack them. Well we were very peaceful tribe because we took care of them when they landed here in the first place. Columbus got here with his crew and we put them up, give them land, help them survive through the winter, show them how to cook the vegetables and stuff that we had, and they survived and turned on us. So, it's very, very irritating situation. I mean it's a story that you hate to tell. But at the same time now we gotta live with them. We can't, we can't take them away or can't do nothing about it. So, we just survive the best we know how. Although now, if they would have given us what they had in the treaties that they were gonna do for us in the first place, we would have been even with them by the time they got so powerful, but they put us back. Well now that we're getting a little money of our own and the promises are being fought, they are having to educate us. So, there's quite a few that are getting educated.

And I hope someday for one to get big enough to go to Washington himself. But those are all hopes. I can't say too much about grief. They tell me I'm strong, but I don't believe in crying forever and ever. I've lived through two husbands, and so I know how to get along, so I just go on. As far as afterlife, I believe in god and I think he's got a place for us, so that's about all I can say. (Cox 2015, 465–469)

Part IV

UNDERSTANDING THE SOCIOLOGY OF DYING, DEATH, AND THE AMERICAN INDIAN

All can gain an understanding of dying and death as the natural end of the life cycle. By focusing upon the social processes and interactions involved in the dying and death process, one can develop an understanding of the social nature of dying and death and can develop his or her own personal views of dying and death. Our views impact the ways in which we are able to manage or not manage our losses.

The diversity within the various sociological approaches facilitates critical thinking, develops the sociological imagination, and assists the process of reality construction, both personal and societal. An understanding of dying and death in its personal, social, institution, and comparative dimensions facilitates the integration of complex emotional and intellectual phenomena in one's life. This will allow individuals to give life more meaning, to clarify its purposes, and to engage in social exchanges with more assurance and self-confidence. The sociology of death and dying is rewarding, intellectually stimulating, and definitely sociological.

Chapter 23, "Dying: What We Can Learn from American Indians" and Chapter 24, "Conclusions" summarize the central ideas presented in the previous chapters.

Chapter 23

Dying

What We Can Learn from American Indians

Sociology as a discipline offers a framework for analysis. American Indians provide a model for facing dying and death, living until one dies, disposal of our dead, and responses to grief and bereavement. While everyone we know will die, we must learn how to respond to our losses and yet at the same time to learn to live with our losses and continue with our lives. Our dead loved ones would prefer that we live well and be as happy and productive as we can be without having them in our lives. We, too, must face the prospect of our own dying and death. None of us are promised tomorrow, so the trick is to learn to live fully each day. American Indians traditionally live each day fully with little thought to the future or to the past. Their focus is upon people and proper behavior, balance, and sharing. The dominant culture is more concerned with what will happen tomorrow even though it is not guaranteed, on obtaining things, social status, wealth, and privilege. Many fear getting old, facing death, and what others think of them. American Indians anticipate aging or becoming an elder with joy rather than fear. Death is viewed as a change rather than the end. The focus is upon living until one is dead rather than focusing upon dying or pain. Hospice and palliative care have generally adopted the attitudes of the American Indians by trying to help their clients live until they die.

THE ROLE OF AGING AND AMERICAN INDIAN SPIRITUALITY

Part of living until one dies for the American Indian is the concept that all is one. Every animal, rock, star, person, and plant is connected to one another. While American Indians grieve, miss their loved ones, and ache for their

losses of all sorts, they also recognize that they have obligations and responsibilities to others. In traditional times, if a hunter was successful in the hunt,
he shared his prey with other families in his clan. He knew that when he was
not successful that hunters from other families in his clan would share their
capture with his family. Rather than filling personal store houses with grain
and other items, the Maya, Inca, and other ancient Indian societies developed
communal warehouses. While there were rich individuals particularly with
the royal and clergy, the poor, orphans, and widows were generally provided
for by the larger society. The spiritual covered all behavior.

Spirituality for American Indians is a way of life rather than what is
learned from reading a sacred book. As the Dine face the East to greet the sun
as it brings forth a new day, all human acts are a prayer or spiritual response.
Weavers view their rugs as sacred. The weaver may deliberately make a mistake to demonstrate that she or he is not perfect. Strangers are given gifts and
greeted with joy. Even conflict with enemies is thought to be a spiritual act. If
one is about to die at the hands of his enemies, the person will pray. Animals
and plants that are taken for food are offered prayers for giving their life so
we may survive. Chiefs are not dictators, but rather are leaders who with their
wisdom can advise and direct, but at the same time can be overruled. Many
tribes view being a chief as a burden that must be endured for the good of
his or her people. Rather than focus upon my rights, the chief and others are
expected to focus upon their duties, obligations, and responsibilities to others
and not upon personal power, financial gain, or fame.

The sacred is found in everything that one observes, does, and uses.
Building a Hogan or wickiup is a sacred act. All labor is sacred. One who is a
doctor or chief is not better than one who is farmer or homeless or whatever.
While some have not found their balance or where they fit in life, they are
viewed as searching rather than as lesser people. What makes one a good
person is how one relates to others rather than how much fame or how much
money that one has. To be spiritual means to be involved with the realm of
the sacred in thought, action, and social forms. It constitutes a totals system of
symbols with deep meaning that leads to a personal transformation. What is
good and the ultimate good of human life has to do with relating to the sacred.
American Indians' encounters with the sacred often evoke tremendous emotions and responses in the form of music, dance, drama, art, and sculpture.

The sacred can be intellectual, practical, or social with the intellectual
ranging from theology, scholarship, stories, myths, and so forth; the practical
including doing and saying spiritual things and acts; and the social involves
acts of community and fellowship that evoke feelings and responses. The
spiritual is not an individual act. It involves others. For those who are caregivers, hospice workers, nurses, and so forth, the spiritual community through
the clan or other kinship group needs to be included in the process.

American Indian spiritual groups have sacred stories, historical context, a sense of meaning for humans, ritual, art, symbols, and so forth. The stories provide explanations of why things occur in the world, including birth, death, and even existence itself. The spiritual offers a way to manage loss as well as to transform those who have experienced great loss. For an American Indian the journey is paramount. Dying and death are part of this process. It may be very important for hospice to aid the dying in their journey toward transformation. Change, repentance, seeking help from sacred powers, and following a new path to transform from a fractured existence are all part of the journey. Then one can begin to live real life. While hospice often work with people who focus upon the impending death, American Indians live for today and the dying are still living. The focus is not upon the dying, but rather to continue to journey until death. One can then be healed spiritually even while dying.

For the American Indian, the power for life comes from ritual, sharing with family and community, and living according to the model of spirituality of the group. While some are motivated to become spiritual and develop a relationship with the sacred, others seem to either not need or no longer need centers of meaning and purpose to their lives. Dying, suffering, and pain may lead to a return to the sacred. Rituals, ceremonies, and sacred events may at least temporarily replace parties, sports, entertainment, vacations, holidays, and so forth. Those you work with may call for ceremonies to allow them to return to the sacred way. Let them determine your role in these ceremonies, but definitely encourage their traditional rituals. As a non-Indian, as you age, you also need to find meaning and purpose in your life. Everyone needs a reason to get up in the morning. Everyone needs a reason to look forward to each day. Aging is not dreaded when one has a sense of purpose. For some people spirituality is something that you do, but for the American Indian, it is not an act or attitude, but something that permeates everything that they do.

DEATH AND THE AMERICAN INDIAN

Death may be viewed differently by American Indians. Stories of children dying symbolic deaths, battling mythic monsters, battling with spirits, and so forth abound. In funeral rites, the newly dead are often thought to be in an in-between state. The dead may be welcomed back as an ancestor. The dead may be feared as a potential source of death for the living. Rituals to manage dead spirits are developed to cope with grief and loss. Artistic expression may be used to aid with loss. The Hopi teach that life is cyclical and that on one's journey one goes from birth to dying to rebirth. The Hopi, Lakota, and others use the symbol of the butterfly as a symbol with the person transforming from a caterpillar to a butterfly. The person transforms when he or she dies suggesting that their spirit lives on after death.

American Indian beliefs and traditions include reverence and respect for life. Death is not all that different than life. Everything is sacred. Every part of the dirt, rocks, trees, of all things, is sacred. The ashes of the dead are resting in sacred ground. Rather than disconnecting with the dead, American Indians continue to have a relationship with the dead. Rather than fearing death, it is rather part of life and to be accepted. One continues to love after someone has died. The dead do not cease to love us, to care for us, and to protect us. Of course, some of the dead did not do those things when they were alive. Chances are they will not do so from the afterlife.

It is important to understand that all life is important, and the death of the person is not more important than any other death. An American Indian takes more time to eat a meal because whatever one does in life is sacred including the animals and plants who are being eaten who must be thanked for giving their lives to nourish humans.

AMERICAN INDIAN CULTURE

It is also important to know that American Indians living in an urban environment view the world quite differently than those who live on or near the reservation. While the unemployment rate on reservations is 49 percent and limited resources, poor economics, inadequate health care, and so forth are a part of life, the American Indian has the support of the clan or tribe and culture that is missing in urban environments (Robertson 2008, 609–610). In the urban environment, one's occupation is far more important than in a tribal community. Being homeless, unemployed, underemployed, lacking health insurance, and so forth are far bigger handicaps in an urban environment. American Indians have patterns of sharing along kinship lines as well. This may include money, childcare, housing, rides, help with work, or whatever is needed. Generosity and sharing are strong cultural values. These practices are often missing in an urban environment. The amassing of money and possessions is not a traditional practice. Goods are to be shared and savings are to be used. The giveaway ceremonies are still practiced among many groups. Family, clan, tribe, and even the BIA can help on the reservation. Indigenous knowledge and practices are being used to design and deliver services otherwise unavailable or culturally inappropriate (Robertson 2008, 610).

The advantage of the tribal community is its simplicity. The child learns a more consistent normative pattern, has security of knowing people around him or her, and has fewer roles to identify and develop. The extended family has more influence on the person. People know what you do or don't do. Sharing is a major value. Whether one works or not, food, clothing, and a place to live will be given on the reservation that would not be so freely given in an urban environment.

American Indians often communicate differently using more nonverbal behaviors and silence. How close does one stand when talking to another? How long does one take before responding to the words of another? How necessary is it to fill the air with words, or is it proper to continue to remain silent? Does one look the other in the eye when speaking to them or avert one's eyes? Some groups do not look another in the eye until a bond has been established.

American Indians generally value silence more than those in the dominant white culture. Personal space is not prized as in the white culture. Imagine giving a speech with the persons in the audience being within 1½ feet of you or talking to a baby from a distance of 12 or more feet rather than holding them. Words are treasurers that must be sparingly used. Space is generally further away in the white culture.

Unlike the dominant culture, American Indians are likely to use folk medicine, traditional healers, ceremonials, rituals, and treatment at home or at least in the community which leads many American Indians to be intimidated by the environment of hospitals, nurses, physicians, bureaucrats, and pharmacies. People carrying clipboards, use of strange machines, the hospital garb, the sterile environment, and strange smells may frighten those working with hospice workers. Such fears do not lead to healing or resolution of grief.

The dominant White culture in both Canada and the United States tends to focus on the future with an eye on the past. It is not unusual to begin to make college plans for children who are not yet even in high school. American Indians tend to live in the present. One cannot change the past. The future has not yet happened. Why worry? The healing, illnesses, and even death are present issues, not future or past issues. If one drank or smoked or whatever in the past that led to his or her illness and ultimate death, one does not blame the victim and focus upon his or her failings. People are accepted for where they are now rather than for past accomplishments or even past mistakes. Grief is for today. The dying are still living. White culture focuses upon the fact that they are dying.

The White culture tends to focus on the future without the deceased. The traditional American Indian will focus on missing them today. Various actions will be taken to make tomorrow better than today. American Indians are generally accepting of death. "We live, and then we live again."

WORKING WITH DYING OR GRIEVING
AMERICAN INDIANS

First of all, it is impossible to say precisely what to do with any individual or group. American Indians do not fit stereotypes and can be found in all walks of life from being cowboys to shaman. They come in all colors, sizes, and value systems. Many are Christian. Many are not. The policies since the seventeenth century have forced many to adopt the dominant European culture, but immense diversity remains. There are ways to better meet the needs of those you serve in hospice who come from culturally diverse backgrounds. It is important to respect the dignity of the American Indians with whom you work. Respect their rituals, ceremonies, and culture, but do not attempt to appropriate the activities. Allow them the respect of conducting their activities, and if invited take part, but remember, the activities are theirs, not yours. Imagine dressing up as a Catholic priest and offering Mass and claiming to be the real thing (Pritzer 1999, 102).

For the American Indian, death is as natural as birth. It is not one's choice to be born or to die. For those who take their own life may be condemned to wander as spirits in the next life. There is no single American Indian religion. American Indians dwell in a world filled with spirits. Birds carry messages, animals tell tales, rocks speak to us, and spirits roam the earth with us. Communication with mysterious beings is available to all. Dreams and visions provide messages or instructions that all may receive as a gift from the spirits. All life has a purpose. All are here for a reason. It may take a lifetime to determine that reason. Visions, dreams, rivers, rocks, animals, birds, and spirits can give messages if one listens. Cultures with oral traditions can travel back as far as the chain of memory will allow. In a world filled with spirits, the past provides a guide to the present. Storyteller's tales of animals that talk, of spirits that roam the earth, and of rocks that have messages both instruct and entertain those who listen. American Indian storytellers do not just talk. They may drum, sing, and even dance as they weave their tales. Masks, costumes, regalia, and performance mark the stories. Storytelling can be part of the hospice experience. Knowledge of the spirit world is essential to practices relating to dying, death, and grief.

Generally, the stories suggest that rocks, plants, animals, and all living things are tied together and have souls. The stories teach how people are judged and why they are admired. Each person is responsible for the other and must protect the other. This includes following correct ritual, forgiveness, patience, sharing, and living a spiritual life. The dying and their survivors will want to do these things.

The dying are not judged by their status as in the White world. One does not need to be a warrior, chief, or major leader to be admired. Having wealth is not a major criterion for status. Living in a world of spirituality, the spiritual nature of everything in life becomes second nature. One also has ceremonies that reinforce the spiritual nature of the world. Life is to be lived even when dying. One engages in rituals, ceremonies, and community. Death is not feared. It is natural and to be accepted. Even spirits meet death in stories. These sacred stories and myths teach one how and why to live. While many view myths as not real or not true, myths represent that which is the truth. The myths, sacred stories, songs, epics, and so forth are models or paradigms around which to live one's life. These oral traditions come from ancestors and sacred beings. They permeate everything. Engaging in traditional rituals should be a part of the hospice approach.

The Navajo or Dine story teaches that the Sun must be placated by human death. Each day someone must die, or the sun would not move. A part of the story or myth is that those who die and go to the Fifth World must return to live in the Fourth World after death. Death is not the end of life but rather a change. The coyote, the interpreter of signs, told the people (Dine) that someone had to die every night, though it did not necessarily have to be one of the people (Dine). The coyote also said that death would come quickly to those who gazed upon the face of the dead. The Dine therefore cover the faces of the dead and bury quickly to avoid death themselves. For examples of American Indian stories, see Benton-Benai (1979); Lavitt and McDowell (1990); Edmonds and Clark (2003); Marriott and Rachlin (1975); Gridley (1939); Waters (1950); Babcock, Monthan, and Monthan (1986); and Burton (1974).

It is also important to remember that American Indians may not completely trust non-Indians who are caregivers. Oppression and exploitation of American Indians has not stopped and many believe that hospice workers and others are pressuring American Indians to give up their culture and traditions (Pritzker 1999, xx).

IMPORTANCE OF ELDERS

Elders are very important and treated in a special way. Elders are the living legacy of the tribe. Children are taught as soon as they are able to understand to respect and to listen to the elders. Elders may or may not be tribal leaders, but they help make decisions in all things that are important to the group, including education, jobs, health and health care, housing, hunting, fishing, and general living. Elders teach songs, tell stories, and teach children to respect themselves. One of the main tasks of elders is to teach the young. American Indian religion teaches the three R's. The three R's include respect, reciprocity, and relationships. A fourth R might be responsibility. All children are taught the R's.

When groups gather for events of all sorts, the elders are always asked to begin ceremonies, are served first at meals, and are acknowledged before others speak. Hospice workers would do well to have elders begin the hospice process, to bless them and their work, and to pray for the people involved. Elders try to live in a way that allows them to earn the respect of others and to be a model so that others can learn to respect themselves. Elders enjoy being active and learning and teaching others. Hospice workers need to include them in the process. Elders have a lot to offer. When an elder is the person who is dying, they can serve as a great example to teach others how to live until they die. Death is not feared, but a natural part of life. It is important to live each day fully until death does occur. For hospice workers, this means that the process should focus on living well until death rather than focusing upon the impending death.

The respect that elders have earned means that there are protocols or proper ways of behaving with them. This would include allowing those who are older to talk first. Doing what you are told by elders. Listen carefully to the elders so that you can learn from them. Appreciate what you have. Help take care of those who are too old or unable to take care of themselves. Do not interrupt when someone is talking. Smile and say hello to elders. Let them know you care. Adhering to these norms will allow hospice to be more effective. American Indians are taught to help those who need help, to listen and learn from others, to observe and learn, and to be friendly and smile.

Other important values would include personal sovereignty/autonomy. Elders do not make choices for others. One is free to make his or her own choices. One does not interfere with the decisions of others or judge them. An elder may offer thoughts on decisions, but the decision is not made by the elder. A chief or leader may say that a course of action should be taken, but the decision to go to war or whatever is not made by the leader, but by the group or individual. One does not tell others how to live. Hospice workers should not dictate to those they are working with, but rather offer suggestions, guidelines, or advice. One is expected to show respect, compassion, and to help the sick, poor, and the needy. Money is not an issue. It is not worthy to seek wealth for its own sake. People are not valued for their wealth or occupation. It is important to have enough to care for families and less fortunate.

Elder epistemology suggests that elders are the window to roots of identity, vision of Mother Earth, and life. Elders are the teachers who have knowledge to help those who are dying and grieving. Hospice workers need to tap this knowledge.

Hospice teams might consider developing a list of elders in their area along with listings of healers, shaman, singers, medicine practitioners, and others who have earned respect in their clans.

While most object, the use of alternative medicines and healing ceremonies should not only be tolerated but accepted. Not all healing comes from hospitals and drugs, nor is healing only physical. While it creates problems, ceremonies including the burning of sage, using tobacco or sweet grass are vital to healing. It may be necessary to have an outbuilding or somewhere without smoke detectors and automatic sprinklers, but such ceremonies are of immense importance to many groups. Many healing rituals, death rituals, and cleansing rituals exist and may make the hospice workers' job a great deal easier if they not only tolerate such activities, but if they give them the same respect and support that they give to physicians and prescribed medicines. Preparation for death can take many forms. Those developed and supported by white caregivers are not the only effective ones available. The respect that the elder teaches needs to be given to the ways of the American Indians. Aging is a lot less difficult if one feels that one's life has had meaning, purpose, and respect from others.

GRIEVING CEREMONIES

While accepting that death is natural, normal, and inevitable, American Indians still experience a deep sense of loss. Grieving ceremonies are very important to all clans because generally it is believed that what the living do can impact the dead and what the dead do can impact the living. All deaths take away from the clan. Life has a purpose, a reason for being. If the coyote becomes extinct, the message of the coyote is lost forever. The world will all be the less for not learning their message. Each death must be mourned. Some do not like to use the word death. Rather they leave the world and go on a spirit trail. When death occurs, one sees all of his or her relatives and waits for one's descendants to join them.

Most clans exhibit a people-centered, group-centered approach to life with values that include less attachment to material things. Of course, casinos and other sources of revenue and exposure to White lifestyle can certainly be changing this. Each is doing what they were meant to do. All life is important not just those of the rich or the powerful. It is impossible to become rich if one helps his or her relatives. The social status of the person and family that you work with is not based upon job or money. Most clans face death without concern for one's acts or failures. If one lived a life of integrity and giving dignity to others, one has no reason to fear death. Death is the natural end of life. Death is merely a changing of worlds (Steiger 1974, 25).

American Indians face grief with the beliefs that death does impact survivors, but with the hope that others who care that one are no longer among the living. All are still alive as long as the living remember their dead. Death is meant to occur. Life cannot occur without death. "We live and then we live again." Death is a painful separation for the living, but when one dies, the dead can wait for their descendants to join them.

AMERICAN INDIAN CARE OF THE
DYING AND GRIEVING

Culturally, the focus on people rather than things has led to many cultural practices that distinguish American Indian culture. American Indians are generally quite aware of their kinship system and how they are related to others. Relatives are a part of their social circle and friendship grouping. One's clan or lineage is part of one's life. Each clan has duties and obligations that go with such membership. One may be called upon to be a storyteller, dancer, singer, or whatever because of one's clan or lineage. Families care for the elderly at home. People die among their clan or family groupings. Golden (1996) suggests that the rituals of Potlatch Ceremony of the Athabaskan tribes of the Northwest North America allow the entire community and not just the grieving family to move from grief into a more joyous ceremony (Golden 1996). He laments that the dominant U.S. culture does not have grief rituals like the Potlatch which causes our grief to be private and makes it more difficult to make the connection to the grief within (Golden 1996).

Nursing homes have emerged on some reservations and many now die in hospitals, but traditionally, American Indians educate, respect, and work together, but they also care for the living, the dying, and the dead as family groups. Public ceremonies are also organized along kinship lines. Even dying has a ceremony.

Maintaining health is of primary concern for people in all cultures. Caring for the terminally ill can raise questions of the meaning of life, cause us to experience tragedy and tears, relief from pent-up emotions, and at the same time can offer those giving care immense gratification.

The care of the dying by American Indians differs from that offer by White society.

The influence of the White culture has modified American Indian practices. The current American Indian practices are somewhat fragmented and confused, yet there are still basic principles that are the foundation of their care of the dying and deceased.

American Indians also have a strong sense of humor. For American Indian peoples, all aspects of life, including death, are subjects of humor and laughter. The naturalistic philosophy of tribes generally means that when it is one's time to die, then one should die. They would not use medically futile interventions for the dying. One should die naturally without tubes and machines.

One does not show love by trying to keep a person alive as long as possible. One does not allow a loved one to die with strangers.

IMPLICATIONS FOR END-OF-LIFE CARE

Those providing end-of-life care to American Indians need to be aware that American Indians are not past but present and to have a genuine interest in American Indian values, culture, and practices. As hospice personnel, it is also important to be nonjudgmental and to try to develop an understanding and empathy for American Indian ways. It is also useful to acknowledge the role of elders in the dying and grieving process; to respect diversity and tolerate differences; to allow ceremonies, rituals, and practices that seem contrary to own experience; and to recognize that American Indian spirituality is all inclusive and permeates all that one does. Culturally, one also needs to understand that those who live on or near reservations are typically more traditional than those from urban areas and thus have needs that are not typical of hospice experience and to be aware that for American Indians social status is not based upon wealth or position but person.

DEATH, DYING, AND HOSPICE IN
NATIVE AMERICAN COMMUNITIES

Perhaps you know these people. A very old woman will never leave the bed where she has been confined for several months. A not so old man has been bedridden from an accident that has left him dependent upon others for life. Parents keep vigil with their child who is dying from cancer. All are ordinary people with extraordinary situations. The difference is that these people are American Indians who have different values and cultures. As a hospice worker, you visit the sick, the grieving, the aged, and the dying. You offer support, comfort from person to person, and aid families in their time of need. Unfortunately, many of the patterns and techniques of care that you have developed over time seem to offend or not be effective with this new clientele. Knowledge of American Indian culture, values, rituals, and ceremonies will help you to better serve this population and will allow you to develop processes and techniques that will help you administer care and design programs.

While hospice had not neglected American Indians, less than 1 percent of those served by hospice are American Indians. Hospice continues to serve a predominantly white population (Connor 1998, 175). While the values and practices of American Indians are often quite different, they have much to teach to hospice. Hospice has much to offer to them as well. Hospice is a special gift that is shared with others—a gift that brings compassion and care to those in extraordinary circumstances.

CONCLUSIONS

The beauty of ministering to the American Indians is the growth that care-givers and the dying and grieving can share. In the cultural diversity is the opportunity to grow. Understanding American Indian spirituality; respecting elders; encouraging traditional ways including ceremonies, rituals, sings, and burning sage; allowing alternative medicines and healing; and using American Indian resources to support the hospice approach will make working with American Indians enriching for all concerned.

Conclusion

While many view American Indians as a relic of the past, hundreds of tribes and clans are still struggling to maintain their way of life in the face of almost constant treats to their way of life. Seemingly, all cultures vigorously defend their own way of life. For most ancient cultures, the threats were from other tribes or clans, environmental and climate change, famine, disease, or other natural threats. Many ancient societies were able to survive and maintain their cultures and way of life for centuries. For the American Indians, the arrival of the Europeans, technology, science, the horse, guns, the "Indian Wars," and later boarding schools, reservations, the BIA have caused profound change. Historically, as in most ancient cultures little changed from one generation to the next. Generally, if technology, birth and death rates, knowledge production, and relations with other cultures remained stable, cultures did not experience dramatic changes. Parents, elders, friends, and relatives are the main agents of socialization who teach the new members of their culture the proper ways of the Dine, Inde, or whoever. The young are taught the cultural rules or norms as well as the acceptable patterns of relationships. People are given a path to follow on their life's journey by those who socialize them. They can choose to follow the path chosen for them by others; to follow their own path; or be forced to change their path by wars, natural disasters, dictators, economic disasters, famines, disease, and many other threats to their way of life. Most view their journey through life as predictable, orderly, and socially approved, but seldom is one's journey what was expected.

SOCIOLOGICAL THEORY AND CULTURE

Clearly, there is a need for order and stability not only for the individual, but also for the culture. With the advent of science came the understanding that if we can understand it, we can control it. The goal for cultures and individuals would seem to be that we need to build human societies that meet the needs for order and stability for the collectivity and also meet the needs for freedom and growth of the individual. From the very beginnings of sociology, theorists have tried to explain the question of balance between individual and societal needs. Several theoretical approaches emerged in sociology. Auguste Comte, Herbert Spencer, William Graham Sumner, and Carl Zimmerman among others have tried to explain historical change as a giant pendulum that swung back and forth over time. These theorists were known as "rise and fall" theorists. For them history is a chain of events that is beyond human control. They applied their ideas to the rise and fall of the Romans, Greeks, and many other civilizations. Herbert Spencer and others who developed this approach were influenced by the work of Charles Darwin and his evolutionary concepts (Ritzer 2000, 39). As nature evolves without human control, societies also evolve without human control. Pitirim Sorokin modified this approach somewhat by developing a cyclical theory. Sorokin, who was hired the year that the sociology department was created at Harvard and became its first chair, saw social change as being the result of three different mentalities: Ideational, sensate, and idealistic (Ritzer 2000, 58–59). His thought was that rather than a rise and fall approach of a civilization that would eventually doom that society, it could instead it could swing like a pendulum from being dominated by the sensate to the idealist to the Ideational and manage to survive. The general concept would suggest that societies could survive social change by changing its focus.

Others have argued that human civilizations, cultures, societies, and groups are not predetermined and that there is not inevitable or necessary direction in human development. These theorists would generally argue that human rationality is basic in the creation of human arrangements. They would focus upon the development of human potential. Human history is filled with examples of failure to bring reality in line with ideal versions of what it should be. While it may seem that there is no way to understand what guides us, the answer is culture. Culture is one of the most precious possessions that humans have. When social disasters like the arrival of the Europeans, the forced relocations, reservations, boarding schools, and so forth happen, the cultural trauma is answered by traditional cultural means. Those in concentration camps, prisoners of war, in battles, or whatever are able to turn to what they have been taught to manage seemingly impossible situations. In the modern era, the basic needs for food and shelter must be met, but on some reservations because of poverty and lack of resources, accepting the ways of a different culture may be the only way for some to survive. Other theoretical perspectives have a different explanation and have reached different conclusions.

W. E. B. Du Bois argued that the richness of cultures and their contributions to civilization meant that minorities should not assimilate but rather cultural pluralism should be the proper way to respond to social change (Du Bois 2008, 143). His concept of being Black in White America led to what he coined as "double consciousness" or the division of a person's identity into two or more social realities (Schaefer 2013, 13). Du Bois's concept of double consciousness applies equally to American Indians. Harriet Martineau focused upon the impact of the economy, laws, trade, health, and population control could have upon social problems and social change (Schaefer 2013, 10). For her social change was the result of activism and campaigned for the rights of women, emancipation of slaves, and religious tolerance (Schaefer 2013, 10). Like Du Bois, Martineau called for social change that was the result of activism and not simply social forces. Similarly, Jane Addams, Ida Wells-Barnett, and other early feminist sociologists argued for social reform of what they viewed as a corrupt society, mistreatment of immigrants, and urban poverty. For these theorists, social change was not cyclical, evolutionary, or inevitable, but the result of social action.

By contrast, functionalist theorist would focus upon what maintains the system and generally view social change as an alteration of the system that is not explainable by the past acts of the society nor by the environment (Martindale 1960, 492). Marion Levy, Robert K. Merton, and Talcott Parsons would argue that a society is able to adjust to social change by adjusting to changes in other parts (Schaefer 2013, 468). Culture is thus viewed as a system of action of society that is apart from the operation of the society (Martindale 1960, 492). This would suggest that American Indian societies would resist social change and would adjust within their tribe or clans when technology, invasion, relocation, or other traumatic changes were forced upon them. The focus for the functionalist is to maintain order or "equilibrium" over time rather than trying to change with the times. The tribe or clan would try to adjust to the change to be able to maintain their "normal" lives.

The conflict theory takes a radically different approach. Rather than resisting social change, the conflict theorist view change as the way to maintain societies' balance or equilibrium (Schaefer 2013, 468). Perhaps the most well-known conflict theorist is Karl Marx. While perhaps a polarizing figure politically, his sociology is far more acceptable. Marx viewed people as inherently social and endowed with creative impulses that combined with their social nature allowed them to work together to do what was needed to survive, but that the "mean" conditions of the "primitive society" and later the structural arrangements made by society in the course of history corrupted their natural impulses to work together (Ritzer 2000, 26). Marx saw capitalistic societies as causing the most acute breakdown of the natural impulses of working together, and that the breakdown of the natural impulses led to alienation with the emergence of the two class system which differentiated people (Ritzer 2000, 26). Applied to the American Indian, Marx would argue that the invasion of the Europeans and their various cultures were a major source of conflict and ultimate social change. Conflict theorist Ralf Dahrendorf saw the contrast between the functional approach with its emphasis upon stability and the conflict approach with its emphasis upon change as reflecting the contradictory nature of society in that societies are stable and long lasting, but at the same time, societies experience major conflict (Schaefer 2013, 459). From Dahrendorf's perspective, the invasion of Europeancultures and their ways to the Americas was not only inevitable, but it was as natural as was the American Indian response of trying to continue their way of life in the face of severe threats to that way of life.

For the American Indian, the perpetuation of their way of life has remained a common goal for centuries. The struggle to maintain their way of life is seemingly a never ending struggle. From a sociological perspective, the discussion of culture is often viewed as belonging to someone else or what others do, but each person needs to understand that the parts of their culture that are the most accessible to them belong to each of them. We are the culture. While the outside culture influences us and our culture, as humans, each of us is free to shape our own destiny. That is what freedom really is about. Our culture will continue or be lost based upon what decisions we make as individuals.

AMERICAN INDIAN BELIEFS AND TRADITIONS

American Indian beliefs and traditions concerning dying and death have emerged over the centuries. Their historical development was contrasted with contemporary issues that have been challenged by modernity and Christianity that the European immigrants brought with them. Specific practices including burial and cremation were examined.

American Indian beliefs and traditions include reverence and respect for life. Death is viewed as being not all that different than life. Everything is sacred. Everything around us is sacred. The American Indians used many forms of disposal with the focus upon maintaining rather than disconnecting with the dead; American Indians continue to have a relationship with the dead. Rather than fearing death, death is viewed as a part of life and to be accepted. While not a practice shared by all tribes, most tribes would continue to have a relationship with their deceased loved one. The dead are thought to continue to love us even though they are no longer with us. They will continue to love us, to care for us, and to protect us. Of course, some of the dead did not love and protect us when they were alive, and it is generally thought that they will not do so from the afterlife. As one remembers one's ancestors and asks for their help, one must also thank the animals, plants, and so forth that give their lives to allow us to eat and to live. Mother Earth should also be thanked for providing all that we need to live. We must also thank the least among us who also contributed to our ability to survive. All ways of life have honor, not just those who have wealth, status, or privilege. American Indians have faced centuries of attempts to destroy their way of life, their culture, their religion, their language, and their very existence.

HISTORICAL DEVELOPMENT AND DECLINE OF TRADITION

As the way of life, religion, culture, and even where they are allowed to live have forced social change over the centuries, American Indians have been able to maintain many traditions. American Indian burial and bereavement practices have changed, been modified, and forgotten over the centuries. The often forced acceptance of European religions, the lack of a written history of religious and spiritual practices, and the decline of language may mean that many practices and ceremonies have been lost forever. While some tribal groups have ceased traditional ways because they felt that they were too sophisticated, cultured, religious, or educated to follow the traditional ways, for all cultural groups, death remains a community affair. People wash and prepare the body. Family and friends mourn the loss; some wear mourning clothes. All engage in mourning practices. Some cremate, some bury the deceased. The deceased is aided on his or her journey by song, laments, eulogies, gossip, laughter, joking, with appeals to spirits, appeal to God, dancing, prayer, and ritual.

Those who commit suicide may be viewed differently than those who die of other causes. The American Indian culture places great value on children. Prayers and rituals are performed to give health and life to children (Voget 1995, 22). My own study of suicide among fourteen tribes suggests that ethnic renewal will lower suicide rates among American Indians. Consistently, those who responded to questions about suicide reported that loneliness, isolation, peer pressure, difficulty, depression, and bad spirits were the causes of suicide. They also consistently indicated that those who suicide will wander the earth as lost, lonely spirits who will never rest in peace. They also generally suggested that suicide could be avoided by following traditional ways, prayer, rituals, and remaining spiritual. Every life has a purpose. A vision quest may be undertaken to find that purpose. Death by suicide prevents one from living the life that was intended. Similarly, euthanasia may prevent one from following his or her vision quest. It is generally taught that when it is one's time to die, then one will die. One should not prevent death if it is one's time, nor should one cause another person or oneself to die before his or her time. When death does occur, specific rituals and practices should be followed to dispose of the dead.

There is evidence that U.S. tribes used all known methods of disposal of the dead, ranging from burial both in the ground and in the air, cremation, and mummification. It is also probable that the cause of death, where the death occurred, the age of the deceased, the sex of the deceased, and the social status of the deceased would change the mortuary and burial practices of the tribe. There is a lack of sufficient information about how such factors influence burial practices. Evidence tends to show a general pattern that many tribes exhibit a fear of the dead. It is also likely that climate, weather, availability of materials to dispose of the body, and religious beliefs were major determinants as to how the dead were disposed. Burial practices also seemed to remain stable for a remarkably long period of time in most tribes. Almost universally, tribes provide provisions for a spirit journey whether for a single burial or for a group burial (Atkinson 1963, 159–160).

If nothing else is known, it is clear that tribal groups did not abandon their dead. They provided them with ceremonies and gave them a dignified disposal. American Indians provide social support through the tribe or clan of the individual in the dying, death, and burial process. That same social support system sustains the bereaved after the disposal of the dead. The grief process generally includes the ceremony of the funeral, burial rituals, and may also include a giveaway ceremony. As with other cultures, emotional responses to the death are usually managed or at least eased by these ceremonies. The spiritual presence of the living and the dead permeates the entire process. While the oldest skeletons to have been found in North America are thought to be around thirteen thousand years old, but that date often changes with new discoveries. All of the early burials found in North America demonstrate that the dead were disposed of with ritual and care.

IMPACT OF CHRISTIANITY

Like many clans, the Flathead have combined Christian and quite often Catholic traditions with their own traditions. Some Christian clergy go to great lengths to respect and preserve traditional ways. Many funeral directors also make great efforts to respect and preserve traditional ways. Others have attempted to destroy the traditional practices and beliefs. In the name of religion, many sought to end the religion of the American Indians. Others who seemingly respected the traditional religion attempted to incorporate traditional American Indian religion into Christianity. Many funeral directors are able to incorporate traditional songs, prayers, rituals, and other practices into funerals in a respectful manner. Prayers will be spoken while the grave is opened and closed, during the procession to the church for the funeral, during the funeral, during the procession to the cemetery, and during memorial and feast days. Years ago, feasts and memorial giveaways were planned for a year after the death, but today, most plan their memorial dinner and giveaways for immediately after the burial. The problem with this practice is that everything is over, and nothing helps with the future. This gives the family little time to finish everything due to their state of sorrow. Those who receive the keepsakes of the deceased help take away the sorrow of the bereaved. The things are not important, but the love that the items represent is important. The sorrow and sadness continue for a long time after the funeral. By waiting for the feast day and for the memorial dinner, the family can then release their sorrow rather than feeling abandoned and alone. Christianity and modern practices such as funeral directors have eroded traditional ways and beliefs.

BURIAL AND BEREAVEMENT PRACTICES

Burial and bereavement practices vary from clan to clan and from region to region. The Ojibwe, for example, believe that it is important to feel good about themselves and to live a life that cares about all living things and avoid harming or destroying life. Ceremonies begin with a tobacco prayer offering. The pipe's smoke carries the prayer to the Creator. The Ojibwe bury their dead dressed in their best clothes with tools or other items and leave tobacco and food with them for their journey to the land of the souls. Many burial mounds that housed the dead have been sold with houses, roads, or other intrusions build on them. Although many burial sites have been looted, excavated by archaeologists, and bulldozed by builders, the Wisconsin Ojibway have purchased many of these mounds. The Altern Mounds site, for example, contains fifty-two burial sites.

The Iroquois also bury objects with their dead. They fast for ten days and surviving spouses do not remarry for a year. Some groups would blacken the face of the mourners and the dead person. After tattooing the body, the corpse is decorated with feathers and wrapped in furs and then buried either in the air on a scaffold or below ground. The Iroquois believe that the soul does not leave until the Tenth Day Feast. At this feast, all of the possessions of the deceased are given away and the favorite foods of the deceased are served to guests.

The Assiniboine of the Great Plains place the bodies of the deceased on scaffolds with the feet pointed to the west. After the scaffolds rot and fall, the Assiniboine collect the bones and, except for the skull, bury them. The skulls are then used in a sacred village of the dead ceremony in which friends and relatives speak to the dead and leave gifts.

The Hopi are noted for having simple ceremonies to honor the dead. While covering the face of the deceased with a mask symbolizing a rain cloud, a woman would be buried in her marriage gown while a man would be dressed in clothing representing his status in his clan. After carrying the body to its burial place, the Hopi silently lowered it into the ground with prayer sticks. Upon covering the grave, food was left for the journey to the spirit world.

The Dine or Navajo believe disease and death result from evil doing, or witchcraft, spells, and dreams. One counters evil by ceremonies against evil and blessing ceremonies. Death does not represent the end of life, but a journey to the next life. The Dine or Navajo are taught to respect and listen to elders. Because respect is carefully taught, grandparents receive respect from the children. The child listens intently to elders who speak of life and death and grief.

Throughout the life span, the Navajo passively accept death and the other traumas of life. Withdrawal into oneself is a common response to grief and loss. Women are more likely to cry openly. Men also cry, but more often not publicly. Both are likely to have engaged in long periods of non-productivity while experiencing a loss of interest in life and its pleasures. Although mothers and sisters may continue to work during loss and grief, it may be months before the grandfather returns to his craft or sheep herding. Children, on the other hand, return to their curious ways more quickly than adults.

The Inde use strong communications, humor, music, art, and social support to cure and deal with illness, injury, and grief. The Apache believe that when a person dies his or her spirit does not go immediately to the underworld, but rather, the spirit stays for a while. Relatives who touch the body are likely to get ghost sickness and may themselves need healing ceremonies conducted for them.

Inde dead are dressed in the best clothes, wrapped in a blanket, carried to the hills, placed into a crevice, or buried in a shallow grave. For the Western Apache, ashes and pollen are sprinkled in a circle around the grave beginning at the southwest corner to offer the soul a safe journey to heaven. The Inde pride themselves in caring for those in need, often leaving a jug of water for the deceased to drink.

The Inde hold a wake and cry and wail for the deceased. The Apache sometimes leave the body in the wickiup and push it down on top of the body. The Chiricahua Apache wives and children would cut their hair short, cover their faces with mud and ashes, and dance to keep the ghosts from capturing them after the death of a warrior. The Yuma Apache are the only Apache group that cremated their dead. They would also burn all of the possessions including the deceased's wickiup. In recent years, however, funerals and wakes have become common practice.

For most deaths, the Apache mourn and wail for a few days. They often cut their hair short, continuing to mourn until the hair length is reestablished. Many Apache or Inde have incorporated nontraditional ways such as memorial dinners, Christian hymns and rituals, and the use of funeral directors.

The Plains tribes attitudes and beliefs pertaining to dying and death are not static. Rather ideas about dying and death vary from individual to individual. Most plains tribes separate the soul. The Lakota, like many other Plains tribes, view the soul as having at least four distinct attributes. Like the air that leaves with the breath from the body on a winter day, Ni un (life) leaves the body at the moment of death. But it is this aspect of the soul or spirit that is most feared because of the uncertainty of when the body is free of the spirit.

Sicun (spirit helper) is the second aspect. Like the Kachinas of the Hopi, the dead can help the living. Like the Catholic concept of guardian angel or guardian spirit, the Plains tribes look to the dead to help the living. As Catholics look to saints and deceased relatives to intercede for them, the Plains tribes look to the Sicun.

The third aspect, wann'gi (spirit shadow), is able to help others, or it can be upset or angry with the living. The shadow world and shadow spirits are discussed by many tribes. Non-tribal members have also described visits from the dead. Christianity has many such stories as do other religions. Stories and tales of wandering ghosts or displaced spirits are found in all cultures. These spirit shadows dare not be offended. Much of the secrecy surrounding burial and grieving practices is based upon this concept. The final aspect is Ton (power that makes something). One should listen to the earth to hear what she has to say. Rocks, earth, plants, feathers, and tobacco, for example, are used to make medicine in other ways with ritual, sacred songs to help the living because they have power and can teach the living.

Grieving ceremonies are very important to the Plains tribes because generally it is believed that what the living do can impact the dead and what the dead do can impact the living. Each death takes away from the tribe. Each life has a purpose, a reason for being. As the fox, coyote, squirrel, or rabbit has a purpose, so do each of us. Violent death, suicide, or accidents may cause one to die before their time. If the coyote becomes extinct, we will lose their message. We will all be the less for not learning their message. Each death must be mourned. Lakota do not like to use the word death. Rather they leave the world and go on a spirit trail. When death occurs, one sees all of his or her relatives and waits for one's descendants to join them.

CREMATION

Cremation was the dominate form of body disposal for Yuman-speaking tribes including the Walapai, Yavapai, Havasupai, Mohave, Cocopa, and Maricopa, the Diegueno, and other California groups. The Yuma of the Lower Colorado River and the Shoshone tribes of the Great Basin also employed cremation as did some Northwestern Central and South American tribes. But mission life generally destroyed traditional aspects of cultural life for most tribes. Crowded into small towns the culture of these tribes was dramatically transformed to include new crafts and methods of farming, new foods, new forms of housing, and different religion.

Catholic missionaries encouraged tribes to practice earth burial. With great difficulty, the missionaries convinced the Northwest Coast Indians to adopt the white man's cemetery even though they viewed earth burial with horror. The non-Mission Indians, who had less contact with the Spanish and their missionaries, were able to keep more of their traditions and way of life intact.

The Mohave were able to resist the mission movement. When death occurs among the Mohave, the dead person is quickly laid on a funeral pyre that will be prepared before death if the dying is anticipated and cremated as soon as possible. The funeral pyre is dug in sand, logs placed above it with other burnable items piled on top of the logs and body by the mourners. After the fire is lit, mourners wail, throw goods, and even their own clothes onto the fire. After the fire is complete, the mourners push the ashes and remaining debris into the trench or pit and covered it with sand. Generally, all of the dead person's property, clothes, goods, and even food, is burned, and all evidence of them ever having lived is gone. Ceremonies continue for four days, including abstinence from eating meat, fish, salt, or drinking even water. Purification rituals are part of the activities of the mourners. The Mohave believe that the soul remains for four days before departing. Those who prepare the body or touch the dead person or give speeches typically are part of these purification activities. This would involve cutting hair, bathing, smoke ceremonies, and other more secret rituals. While most of the old ways, foods, housing, dress, plants, and ways of making a living, have disappeared, clan and cremation have remained among those who live in the old way. While their religion is mostly gone, the Mohave have not become Christian like most tribes.

Less affected by the Catholic mission system the Quechan or Yuma are also known for using cremation. The Yuma also were less impacted by the mission system. Near neighbors of the Mohave, their cremation practices are similar. The Yuma built funeral pyres that were a house-high mass of logs upon which they placed the dead person and put mesquite beans on the pile. Mourners wail, cry, dance, sing, tear their clothes and throw them into the flames, scratch their faces, throw offerings or even money into the fire, request spirits to take this dead person and those who have died before, burn images of the dead person, and burn their personal items. They mourn for four days.

The Shoshone habitat varied ranging from the Death Valley to the Yellowstone Park area. The West Coast Shoshonean include Mono, Serrano, Gabrieleno, Luiseno, and Cahuilla. The Southern California Cahuilla also practiced cremation. Some Cahuillas were Mission Indians and others were not. Originally called Kawia, Cahuilla is a Hispanic name given to the tribe. The mission system had less impact on the Cahuilla than on other tribes. The Cahuilla also cremated their dead, burned their houses, mourned, and held mourning ceremonies.

Ancient tribes also practiced cremation. The Hopewell of the Middle Woodlands have been studied perhaps more than most Woodland cultures. Their burial customs are well known because of the hundreds of burials that have been excavated demonstrating that both burial and cremation were used.

CHANGES IN PRACTICES

There are so many cultures, tribes, societies, and civilizations that could have been included in this book. The key point is that all cultures seem to have developed mortuary customs to dispose of their dead. While there are many beliefs about what happens after death, it is what a group believes happens that impacts their decisions about what to do with the dead body. Whatever the relationship was between the dead person and the living will have a decided impact upon what happens after the person is dead. If the person was a slave, an enemy in war, a person from a hated group, or a potential victim of one's crime, the concern for their body and perhaps even the importance or value of their life will play an important role in the methods of preparation of the body if any, and the rituals used if any for the person who dies or is killed. By contrast, a beloved member of the group, a king, president, great hunter, treasured child, beloved shaman, or other valued member of the group will have socially approved methods of preparation of the body, appropriate rituals, proper disposal of the body, and socially appropriate mourning. Prejudice, discrimination, and socially taught devaluation of other groups have caused different responses to dying, death, disposal practices, and mourning rituals between the subjugated group and the dominant group throughout history. As slaves and others were not given the same treatment as those in the dominant group among the Aztecs, Egyptians, and so many other societies, in the modern era, the homeless, the indigenous groups, and those of despised groups such as immigrants from despised countries or despised political groups are also not given the same level of concern and ritual as those from the dominant group.

While modern society has made great gains technologically and economically, the social gains do not appear to be as dramatic. The lack of concern for those who are less fortunate or from groups that are considered to be inferior or otherwise not viewed as equals, whether the gay community, political rivals, immigrants, those living on reservations, or other stigmatized groups, will not receive the same benefits upon their deaths. The choice to give all of the proscribed procedures with the dead person or to simply abandon them is socially determined. The choice to socially acclaim or to publicly ignore the death is also socially determined. How often is there an extensive obituary or even a written obituary for a homeless person? How often is the life of an actor or actress or sports star covered in the media for an extended time after their death? The difference is social acceptance and norms that value certain people over others.

Ancient societies were characterized by collective cultures. Collective cultures are typically more concerned with the well-being of the group than with their own well-being. By contrast, modern societies are characterized by individual concerns. The differences account for many of the changes over time in funeral, disposal, and mourning practices. The value of rituals, community support, caring for the dying, and caring for the dead have been demonstrated rather dramatically during the COVID pandemic of the 2019–2021 years. The ancient cultures were aware of the value of social support, community support, rituals, spending time with the dying, and caring for the dead. While many today have tried to do away with traditional rituals and practices, the pandemic has forced many to reconsider whether or not to reinstitute traditional practices for caring for the dying and dead. Rituals and being around others who are also grieving were established by the ancients and still offers a lesson to today's cultures. The funerary rituals are a way to honor the dead that has been practiced for thousands of years. Rituals are a way to celebrate our love and memories of the dead. The ancients had ways to remember their dead. Today, with modern calendars, people celebrate the anniversaries of birthdays, weddings, death, or other memorable days of the year by lighting candles, offering incense, or other ways to remember their dead.

The impact of social systems upon practices is present in all cultural groups. Beliefs about after life or the lack of such beliefs greatly impacts the choices made upon a death. Social pressure compels the living to meet certain social obligations with the preparation, funeral, rituals, disposal, and mourning practices to be socially acceptable in the community in which he or she lives. Different roles and obligations exist for men than for women, for the elderly than for children, and for the social elites than for the socially disenfranchised. Spiritual and religious beliefs of the cultural group will also impact the decisions made when a death occurs. What is appropriate to say to the grieving is also socially determined.

For all societies, there is an economic impact when someone dies. For those with simple disposition practices, the economic loss will be less, but the loss of the person's contribution to the family, clan, or groups will still be lost. For those with elaborate disposition practices, the economic loss could be staggering. The Taj Mahal, the Egyptian pyramids, or the burial of the queen or king of a society could cause economic disaster for the group. For clans, families, and even communities, some deaths have more impact than others. Many rural counties in the United States, many have well over half of their population that are over age sixty-five. As the elderly die, the populations continue to decline. Schools close, small towns die without schools, and young to replace the elderly. Hospitals close. Businesses close. More people move out. The impact of having people die is felt far more severely than in an urban area that has crowded schools, labor shortages, and a bustling economy where a single death has far less economic impact. As in the ancient cultures, those with small clans, villages, or nomadic tribes, a single death has far more impact than in ancient groups that developed empires. The comparisons between the ancients and the modern societies and the impact of death have changed little over time. People still grieve, have to make social and economic adjustments, and must find socially acceptable ways to dispose of their dead. By studying the ancients and their ways, those living in the modern era can learn a lot! The pandemic of the 2020s has forced modern cultures to reexamine their need for rituals, mourning practices, and ways to say good-bye to their loved ones. As modern societies have become far more secular and having fewer rituals in disposing of their dead, the pandemic has brought home the great emptiness that resulted from not being able to say good-bye to their loved ones. Regardless of the historical era, people need rituals and social support to manage loss of all sorts.

Seemingly, all societies have developed rituals to dispose of their dead. At the same time, all societies also seem to revere the dead person, but still have fear or negative feelings for the dead body. Tending to the dead body is a task that has often been handed over to others who are less connected to the person who died. In ancient Egypt, a profession grew to mummify and prepare the dead for their graves whether in pyramids or caverns. In the modern era, funeral directors, embalmers, grave diggers, beauticians, and others prepare the body for the family. The concern for the body seems to have a historical precedent in concern for the loved on who inhabited the body. Again, seemingly all societies have developed rituals to demonstrate their love and concern for the person who died. While some seem to want to dispose of the body quickly and completely by cremation, sea burial, and so forth, others seem to want to preserve it by mummification, cryonics, embalming, and so forth. Both practices are apparently motivated by the desire to keep the dead as close and long as possible and at the same time the desire to somehow move on knowing that the person is no longer present in their body. By caring for the body, choosing the method of disposal, the funerary rituals, and the commemorative ceremonies, the grieving can honor both attitudes by removing the body and yet still keeping the presence of the dead person.

Some develop tombs, pyramids, headstones, and other ways to offer the living a place to continue their relationship with the dead. Those who bury at sea, spread as the ashes in special places, and so forth also have a place to commune with the dead, but the attitudes are intended to maintain the love and relationship with the dead. The attitudes toward the dead are also part of the attitudes toward life and death. For some societies and cultures, the concept that the afterlife is more peaceful and preferable to life lived on earth. Others view the afterlife as a transition to something similar to what is experienced in this life, thus the need for items from this life to be taken to the next life. Many societies invoke a spiritual or supernatural element to life and death. This allows for imagining life beyond the grave which is often of great comfort to the grieving. It allows them to anticipate joining their lost loved ones in the afterlife. The beliefs in immortality are present in most cultures. Whether the dead are immortal or simply dead does not change the outcome. Everyone dies. It is only the outcome that is in question. While an individual dies, the response to the death of a person is decidedly social and involves the community.

While some societies view life, events in one's life, and death as divine will, others suggest that individual's ideas of self, those of the community about the individual, social institutions, occupation, social class, and so forth determine how one lives and dies. For those who adopt a spiritual or religious conception of life, their individual conceptions of who they are become intertwined with their spiritual and religious conceptions and with societal expectations, norms, and values which all shape who they become. While some societies focus upon the goodness of god(s), others focus upon the goodness of people. The question becomes are people good to each other because they are basically good, or are people good to each other because each society has norms that they enforce to insure that most of the time people are good to each other.

Death occurs to all people. While all societies have rituals to dispose of their dead, the attitudes toward what happens after death are not as consistent from one group to another. Some believe that life continues after death while others think that it ends at the moment of death while still others think that they will be reincarnated after leaving this life. How a society views death has an impact on what the culture becomes, people's attitudes toward the disposal of the dead body, what type of rituals may be used for the dead, and whether mourning is focused upon joining the deceased in the next life or saying good-bye forever.

HOW SOCIOLOGY HELPS UNDERSTANDING
THE AMERICAN INDIAN

Sociology helps to paint a picture of cultures, societies, social groups, and other forms of human social interaction. As C. Wright Mills (1959) argued that sociologists should use their sociological imagination to study the activities of humans, so, too, should we use our creative vision of our own making and apart from the popular or dominant view prevalent in society. Perhaps the best way to truly understand the American Indian is to develop the creative vision of an artist. Western societies tend to view artists as either working in obscurity and without recognition as with Vincent van Gogh or with great acclaim and honor during their life like Pablo Picasso. Both are viewed as great artists who had creative visions that they were able to translate to canvas or other mediums. Artists are thought to be deep thinkers who are able to reach into our spirits to challenge our basic views, to aid us in our search for hidden truths, and to enlighten us as to the nature of things in the world. For the American Indian, the ability to be artistic is a gift from the Creator that should be used for the good of the community. Each of us is born with talents. Some are able to be accomplished storytellers, to weave blankets, to make quilts, to sew bead dresses, to paint teepees, to build wickiups, to care for children, or to be artists. Each of us must search for what talents we have been given, and then we must use them to honor our Creator and to help our people on their journey in life. We must help people to learn to love beauty and belief to teach about values, ethics, and ways of thinking for present and future generations. As the artist uses a canvas to present creative visions, so, too, should the sociologist use the lens of the artist to present a vision of the cultures, societies, communities, groups, and other forms of human relations that are presented in their work. As the kaleidoscope changes what one sees, so, too, should your attempts to analyze the world around you be shaped by using different lens than those around you.

Human society is the result of social groups who over time develop and transmit to future generations sets of rules or norms that have emerged out of their particular environments. This is essentially the work of sociologists, to study cultures and their ways. Culture is the basis of society. The culture of any group is generally thought to be the best way to live. It is common for groups of people whether as cultures, communities, nations, or ethnic groups to see themselves as having the best country, religion, or whatever. This is called ethnocentrism. Those who write history write it from the point of view of their particular cultural group. The history of the Americas is typically written as beginning in 1492 when Columbus arrived, yet, the American Indians did have a history long before the arrival of Columbus or even the Vikings arrived. While the history of American Indians was not written for the most part, it has been carefully documented, preserved, defended, and passed down through generations for centuries even before the arrival of Columbus using storytelling, art, chants, ceremonies, rituals, and teachings of elders.

FINAL THOUGHTS

In conclusion it is clear that tribal groups provided the dead with ceremonies and dignified disposal. There is much evidence that North American tribes employed all known methods of disposal of the dead, including burial (both ground and air), cremation, and mummification. It is also probable that the cause of death, where the death occurred, the age of the deceased, the sex of the deceased, and the social status of the deceased impacted the mortuary and burial practices of the tribe. However, sufficient information about how such factors influenced burial practices is not conclusive. It is likely that climate, availability of materials to dispose of the body, and religious beliefs were major determinants in how bodies of the dead were disposed. American Indians provide social support through the tribe or clan of the individual in the dying and burial process. That same social support system sustains the bereaved after the disposal of the dead. The grief process includes the ceremony of the funeral, the cremation, and the bereavement ceremonies. Extreme emotions are usually managed by these ceremonies. The spiritual nature of the living and the dead permeates the entire process.

References

Aguirre, Aldaberto and Jonathan H. Turner. 2004. *American Ethnicity: The Dynamics and Consequences of Discrimination*. New York: McGraw-Hill.

Allen, T. D. 1963. *Navahos Have Five Fingers*. Norman, OK: University of Oklahoma Press.

Altman, Linda Jacobs. 1995. *Genocide: The Systematic Killing of a People*. Springfield, NJ: Enslow Publishers.

Alvarez, Alex. 2016. *Native America and the Question of Genocide*. Lanham, MD: Rowman & Littlefield.

Alvord, Lori Arviso, and Elizabeth Cohen Van Pelt. 1999. *The Scalpel and the Silver Bear*. New York: Bantam.

Anderson, Douglas and Barbara Anderson. 1981. *Chaco Canyon: Center of a Culture*. Southwest Parks and Monuments Association.

Anderson, Owanah. 1997. *400 Years: Anglican/Episcopal Mission Among American Indians*. Cincinnati, OH: Forward Movement Publications.

Andrist, Ralph K. 1964. *The Long Death: The Last Days of the Plains Indian*. New York: Collier Books.

Archuleta, Margaret and Rennard Strickland. 1991. *Shared Visions: Native American Painters and Sculptors in the Twentieth Century*. Phoenix, AZ: Heard Museum.

Arnold, Caroline. 1992. *The Ancient Cliff Dwellers of Mesa Verde*. New York: Clarion Book.

Atkinson, M. Jourdan. 1935. *Indians of the Southwest*. San Antonio, TX: Naylor.

Attig, Thomas. 2001. "Relearning the World: Making and Finding Meanings." In Robert A. Neimeyer (ed.), *Meaning Reconstruction & the Experience of Loss*. Washington, DC: American Psychological Association, pp. 33–53.

Babcock, Barbara A., Guy Monthan, and Doris Monthan. *The Pueblo Storytell*. 1986. Tucson, AZ: University of Arizona Press.

Bahti, Tom and Mark Bahti. 1999. *Southwestern Indian Tribes*. Las Vegas, NV: KC Publications.

Bail, Raymond. 2000. *The Ojibwe*. New York: Benchmark Books.

Baldwin, Gordon C. 1969. *Games of the American Indian*. New York: Norton.

Barrett, Carole A. and Harvey J. Markowitz, eds. 2004. *American Indian Culture*. Vol. 1. Pasadena, CA: Salem Press.

Basso, Keith H. 1970. *The Cibecue Apache*. New York: Holt, Rinehart and Winston.

Basso, Keith H. 1970. "To Give Up On Words: Silence in Western Apache Culture." *Southwestern Journal of Anthropology* 26 (3), pp. 213–230.

Beaglehole, Ernest and Pearl Beaglehole. 1935. *Hopi of the Second Mesa. Memoirs of the American Anthropological Association*. New York: Kraus Reprint.

Becker, Ernest. 1968. *The Structure of Evil: An Essay on the Unification of the Science of Man*. New York: Free Press.

Benton-Banai, Edward. 1979. *The Mishomis Book: The Voice of the Ojibway*. St. Paul, MN: Indian Country Press.

Billard, Jules B. 1974. *The World of the American Indian*. Washington, DC: National Geographic Society.

Boadt, Lawrence. 1984. *Reading the Old Testament: An Introduction*. New York: Paulist Press.

Brasser, Ted J. 1974. *Riding on the Frontier's Crest: Mahican Indian Culture and Culture Change*. Chicago: University of Chicago Press.

Browman, David L. 1980. *Early Native Americans: Prehistoric Demography, Economy, and Technology*. The Hague: Mouton Publishers.

Brown, Dee. 1970. *Wounded Knee: An Indian History of the American West*. New York: Dell.

Brown, Joseph E. 1982. *The Spiritual Legacy of the American Indian*. New York: Crossroads.

Bruchac. Joseph. 1995. *The Boy Who Lived with the Bears and Other Iroquois stories*. New York: HarperCollins.

Brugge, David M. 1985. *Navajos in the Catholic Church Records of New Mexico 1694–1875*. Tsaile, AZ: Navajo Community College Press.

Bsumek, Erika Marie. 2008. *Indian-Made: Navajo Culture in the Marketplace, 1868–1940*. Lawrence, KS: University of Kansas Press.

Burland, Cottie. 1968. *North American Indian Mythology*. Feltham: Hamlyn.

Burland, Cottie. 1985. *North American Indian Mythology*. New York: Barnes and Noble.

Burton, Jimalee. 1974. *Indian Heritage, Indian Pride: Stories That Touched My Life*. Norman, OK: University of Oklahoma Press.

Carmody, Denise L. and John T. Carmody. 1993. *Native American Religions: An Introduction*. New York: Paulist Press.

Carrasco, D. 1999. *City of Sacrifice: The Aztec Empire and the Role of Violence in Civilization*. Boston, MA: Beacon Press.

Carrasco, D. 2013. "Sacrifice/Human Sacrifice in Religious Traditions." In M. Jerryson (ed.), *The Oxford Handbook of Religion and Violence*. New York: Oxford University Press, pp. 209–235.

Carter, Forrest. 1976. *The Education of Little Tree*. New York: Delacorte Press.

Catlin, George. 1841. *Letters and Notes on the Manners, Customs, and Conditions of the North American Indians*. London: Gall & Inglis.

Catlin, George. 1861. *Life Amongst the Indians: A Book for Youth.* London: Gall and Inglis.

Catlin, George. 1866. *Last Rambles Amongst the Indians of the Rocky Mountains and the Andes.* London: Gall and Inglis.

Catlin, George. 1913. *North American Indians: Being Letters and Notes on Their Manners, Customs, and Conditions, Written During Eight Years Travel Amongst the Wildest Tribes of Indians in North America, 1832–1839.* 2 Vols. Philadelphia, PA: Leary, Stuart and Company.

Cattawich, George S., Jr. 1980. *Long House: Mesa Verde National Park, Colorado.* Washington, DC: National Park Service.

Cheek, Lawrence W. 2004. *Kokopelli.* Tucson, AZ: Rio Nuevo Publishers.

Churchill, Ward. 1995. *Since Predator Came: Notes from the Struggle for American Indian Liberation.* Littleton, CO: Aigis Publications.

Churchill, Ward. 1999. "The Crucible of American Indian Identity: Native Tradition Versus Colonial Imposition in Postconquest North America." In Duane Champagne (ed.), *Contemporary Native American Cultural Issues.* Walnut Creek, CA: Alta Mira Press, pp. 39–67.

Collier, John. 1947. *The Indians of the Americas.* New York: W.W. Norton.

Connor, Stephen R. 1998. *Hospice: Practice, Pitfalls, and Promise.* Bristol, PA: Taylor & Francis.

Coolidge, Dane and Mary Roberts Coolidge. 1930. *The Navajo Indians.* Boston: Houghton Mifflin.

Cordell, Linda S. 1994. *Ancient Pueblo Peoples.* Washington, DC: Smithsonian.

Corr, Charles A. 2018. "Elisabeth Kubler-Ross and the 'Five Stages' Model in a Sampling of Recent American Textbooks." *Omega* 0 (0), pp. 1–29.

Corr, Charles A., Clyde M. Nabe, and Donna M. Corr. 2009. *Death & Dying, Life & Living.* Belmont, CA: Wadsworth.

Courlander, Harold. 1971. *The Fourth World of the Hopis.* New York: Crown.

Cremony, John C. 1868. *Life Among the Apaches.* San Francisco, CA: A. Roman.

Cremony, John C. 1951. *Life Among the Apaches: 1849–1864.* San Francisco, CA: Roman and Company.

Cremony, John C. 1969. *Life Among the Apaches, Glorieta.* Glorieta, NM: Rio Grande.

Cronon, William. 1983. *Changes in Their Land: Indians, Colonists, and the Ecology of New England.* New York: Hill and Wang.

Curtis, Edward S. 1972. *In a Sacred Manner We Live: Photographs of the North American Indian.* Barre, MA: Barre Publishers.

Curtis, Natalie. 1987. *The Indians' Book: An Offering by the American Indians of Indian Lore, Musical and Narrative, to Form a Record of the Songs and Legends of Their Race.* New York: Bonanza Books.

Davies, Wade. 2001. *Healing Ways: Navajo Health Care in the Twentieth Century.* Albuquerque, NM: University of New Mexico Press.

Delanglez, Jean. 1935. *French Jesuits in Lower Louisiana (1700–1763).* New Orleans, LA: Loyola University Press.

Deloria, Jr., Vine. 1969. *Custer Died for Your Sins: An Indian manifesto*. London: Collier-Macmillan Limited.

De Mallie, Raymond J. 1987. "Lakota Belief and Ritual in the Nineteenth Century." In Raymond J. DeMallie and Douglas R. Parks (eds.), *Sioux Indian Religion*. Norman, OK: University of Oklahoma Press, pp. 25–44.

De Mallie, Raymond J. and Douglas R. Parks, eds. 1987. *Sioux Indian Religion: Tradition and Innovation*. Norman, OK: University of Oklahoma Press.

Dennis, Mary Kate and Karla T. Washington. 2018. "Ways of Grieving Among Ojibwe Elders: 'They're All Around Us. They're Always.'" *Omega* 78 (2), pp. 107–119.

Dennis, Wayne. 1940. *The Hopi Child*. New York: Wiley.

DeSpelder, Lynne Ann and Albert Strickland. 2002. *The Last Dance: Encountering Death and Dying*. New York: McGraw-Hill.

Deverell, William. 2004. *A Companion to the American West*. Malden, MA: Blackwell Publishing.

Dobyns. Henry R. 1997. "Diseases." In Frederick E. Hoxie (ed.), *Encyclopedia of North American Indians*. New York: Houghton Mifflin, pp. 162–165.

Dodge, Richard I. 1959. *The Plains of the Great West*. New York: Archer House.

Dorsey, George A. 1971. *The Cheyenne*. Glorieta, NM: Rio Grande Press.

Driver, Harold E., ed. 1964. *The Americas on the Eve of Discovery*. Englewood Cliffs, NJ: Prentice-Hall.

Driver, Harold. 1969. *Indians of North America*. Chicago: University of Chicago Press.

Drucker, Philip. 1954. *Indians of the Plains*. New York: McGraw-Hill.

Drucker, Philip. 1955. *Indians of the Northwest Coast*. New York: McGraw-Hill.

Du Bois, W. E. B. 2008. "The Conservation of Races." In Peter Kivisto (ed.), *Social Theory: Roots and Branches*. New York: Oxford University Press, pp. 143–147.

Duncan, W. N., Balkansky, A. K., Crawford, K., Lapham, H. A., and Meissner, N. J. 2008. "Human Cremation in Mexico 3,000 Years Ago." *PNAS* 105 (14), pp. 5315–5320.

Durkheim, Emile. 1915. *The Elementary Forms of the Religious Life*. New York: Free Press.

Echo-Hawk, Roger C. and Walter R. Echo-Hawk. 1994. *Battlefields and Burial Grounds: The Indian Struggle to Protect Ancestral Graves in the United States*. Minneapolis, MN: Learner Publications.

Edmonds, Margot and Ella E. Clark. 2003. *Voices of the Winds: Native American Legends*. Edison, NJ: Castle Books.

Embree, Edwin R. 1939. *Indians of the Americas: Historical Pageant*. Boston, MA: Houghton Mifflin.

Erdoes, Richard and Alfonso Ortiz. 1984. *American Indian Myths and Legends*. New York: Pantheon Books.

Erlandson, Jon M., Torben C. Rick, and Rene L. Vellanoweth. 2008. *A Canyon through Time: Archaeology, History, and Ecology of the Tecolote Canyon Area, Santa Barbara County California*. Salt Lake City, UT: University of Utah Press.

Evans, Susan Tobey. 2004. *Ancient Mexico & Central America*. London: Thames & Hudson.

Ewers, John C. 1958. *The Blackfeet: Raiders of the Northwestern Plains.* Norman: University of Oklahoma Press.

Fagan, Brian M. 2000. *Ancient North America: Archaeology of a Continent.* London: Thames and Hudson.

Fergusson, Erna. 1931. *Dancing Gods.* Albuquerque, NM: University of New Mexico Press.

Fewkes, Jesse Walter. 1903. *Hopi Katcinas.* Washington, DC: Twenty-First Annual Report of the Bureau of American Ethnology to the Secretary of the Smithsonian Institution, 1899–1900.

Field, Tiffany. 2007. *The Amazing Infant.* Oxford, England: Blackwell.

Firestone, Robert W. and Joyce Catlett. 2009. *Beyond Death Anxiety.* New York: Springer.

Flaharty, Thomsa H. 1992. *Mound Builders & Cliff Dwellers.* Alexandria, VA: Time-Life Books.

Flood, Renee Sansom. 1995. *Lost Bird of Wounded Knee: Spirit of the Lakota.* New York: Scribner.

Forbes, Jack. 1982. *Native Americans of California and Nevada. Happy Camp.* California: Naturegraph Publishers.

Fraser, J. G. 1886. "On Certain Burial Customs as Illustrative of Primitive Theory of the Soul." *Royal Anthropological Institute of Great Britain and Ireland* 15, pp. 64–104.

Frazier, Ian. 2000. *On the Rez.* New York: Farrar, Straus, and Giroux.

Fulton, Robert, David J. Gottesman, and Greg M. Own. 1982. "Loss, Social Change, and the Prospect of Mourning." *Death Education* 6, pp. 137–153.

Gaston, E. Thayer. ed. 1968. *Music in Therapy.* New York: Macmillan.

Gedicks, Al. 1993. *The New Resource Wars: Nature and Environmental Struggles against Multinational Corporations.* Cambridge, MA: South End Press.

Gedicks, Al. 2001. *Resource Rebels: Native Challenge to Mining and Oil Corporations.* Cambridge, MA: South End Press.

Geertz, Armin W. and Michael Lomatuway'ma. 1987. *Children of Cottonwood: Piety and Ceremonialism in Hopi Indian Puppetry.* Lincoln, NE: University of Nebraska Press.

Gidley, Mick. 1977. *The Vanishing Race: Selections from Edward S. Curtis' The North American Indian.* New York: Taplinger Publishing Company.

Gill, Sam D. 1981. *Sacred Words: A Study of Navajo Religion and Prayer.* Westport, CT: Greenwood.

Gill, Sam D. 1982. *Native American Religions: An Introduction.* Belmont, CA: Wadsworth.

Glubok, Shirley. 1971. *The Art of the Southwest Indians.* New York: Macmillan.

Goldman, Thomas R. 1996. *Swallowed by a Snake: The Gift of the Masculine Side of Healing.* Kensington, MD: Golden Healing Publishing.

Goodwin, Grenville. 1942. *The Social Organization of the Western Apache.* Chicago: University of Chicago Press.

Gridley, Marion E. 1939. *Indian Legends of American Scenes.* Northbrook, IL: Hubbard Press.

Grinnell, George Bird. 1972. *The Cheyenne Indians: War, Ceremonies, and Religion.* Lincoln, NE: University of Nebraska.

Grinnell, George Bird. 2008. *The Cheyenne Indians: Their History and Lifeways.* Bloomington, IN: World Wisdom.

Grobsmith, Elizabeth S. 1981. *Lakota of the Rosebud: A Contemporary Ethnography.* New York: Holt, Rinehart and Winston.

Gustafson, F. R. 1997. *Dancing Between Two Worlds: Jung and the Native American Soul.* New York: Paulist Press.

Habenstein, Robert W. and William Lamers. 1963. *Funeral Customs the World Over.* Milwaukee: Bulfin Printers.

Haig-Brown, Celia and David A. Nock. 2006. *With Good Intentions: Euro-Canadian and Aboriginal Relations in Colonial Canada.* Vancouver: UBC Press.

Haley, James L. 1981. *Apaches: A History and Cultural Portrait.* Garden City, NY: Doubleday.

Hamilton, Henry W. and Jean Tyree Hamilton. 1971. *The Sioux of the Rosebud.* Norman, OK: University of Oklahoma.

Hardoy, Jorge E. 1973. *Pre-Columbian Cities.* New York: Walker and Company.

Harmsen, William D. 1977. *Patterns and Sources of Navajo Weaving.* Tewell's Printing and Lithographing Company.

Harner, M. 1977. "The Ecological Basis for Aztec Sacrifice." *American Ethnologist* 4 (1), pp. 117–135.

Hassrick, Royal B. 1964. *The Sioux: Life and Customs of a Warrior Society.* Norman, OK: University of Oklahoma Press.

Hausman, Gerald. 1993. *The Gift of the Gila Monster.* New York: Touchstone.

Hecht, Robert A. 1991. *Oliver La Farge and the American Indian: A Bibliography.* Metuchen, NJ: Scarecrow Press.

Hoebel, E. Adamson. 1960. *The Cheyenne: Indians of the Great Plains.* New York: Holt, Rinehart, and Winston.

Hollister, Uriah S. 1903. *The Navajo and his Blanket.* Glorieta, NM: The Rio Grande Press.

Howard, James H. 1977. *The Plains-Ojibwa or Bungi: Hunters and Warriors of the Northern Prairies with Special Reference to the Turtle Mountain Band.* Lincoln, NE: J and L Reprint Co.

Hoxie, Frederick E., ed. 1996. *Encyclopedia of North American Indians.* New York: Houghton Mifflin.

Hultkrantz, Ake. 1979. *The Religions of the American Indians.* Berkeley, CA: University of California Press.

Hultkranz, Ake. 1982. *Belief and Worship in Native North America.* Syracuse, NY: Syracuse University Press.

Hyde, George E. 1937. *Red Cloud's Folk: A History of the Oglala Sioux Indians.* Norman, OK: University of Oklahoma Press.

Isaac, B. L. 2002. "Cannibalism among Aztecs and their Neighbors: Analysis of the 1577–1586 'Relaciones Geográficas' for Nueva España and Nueva Galicia Provinces." *Journal of Anthropological Research* 58 (2), pp. 203–224.

Jaenen, Cornelius J. 1976. *Friend and Foe: Aspects of French-American Indian Cultural Contact in the Sixteenth and Seventeenth Centuries.* New York: Columbia University Press.

James, George Wharton. 1903. *Indian Basketry, and How to Make Indian and Other Baskets.* Glorieta, NM: Rio Grande Press.

James, Harry C. 1956. *Hopi Indians.* Calwell, ID: Caxton.

Jeanne, LaVerne Masayesva. 1997. "Languages." In Frederick E. Hoxie (ed.), *Encyclopedia of North American Indians.* New York: Houghton Mifflin, pp. 329–334.

Johnston, Basil. 1976. *Ojibway Heritage.* New York: Columbia University Press.

Jones, David M. and Brian L. Molyneaux. 2004. *Mythology of the American Nations: An Illustrated Encyclopedia of the Gods, Heroes, Spirits, Sacred Places, Rituals and Ancient Beliefs of the North American Indian, Inuit, Aztec, Inca and Maya Nations.* London: Hermes House.

Jones, Peter. 1861. *History of the Ojibway Indians.* Freeport, NY: Books for Libraries Press.

Jones, Terry L. and Kathryn A. Klar, eds. 2007. *California Prehistory, Colonialization, Culture, and Complexity.* Plymouth, UK: Alta Mira Press.

Josephy, Alvin M., Jr. 1963. *The Indian Heritage of America.* New York: Alfred A. Knopf.

Josephy, Alvien M., Jr. 1994. *500 Nations: An Illustrated History of North American Indians.* New York: Gramercy Books.

Kapoun, Robert W. 1997. *Language of the Robe: American Indian Trade Blankets.* Layton, UT: Gibbs-Smith.

Kastenbaum, Robert and Beatri Kastenbaum, eds. 1989. *Encyclopedia of Death.* Phoenix, AZ: Oryx Press.

Kehoe, Alice Beck. 2001. *The Ghost Dance: Ethnohistory and Revitalization.* Belmont, CA: Wadsworth; Thompson Learning.

Keyser, James D. and Linea Sundstrom. 1984. *Rock Art of Western South Dakota: The North Cave Hills and the Southern Black Hills.* Sioux Falls, SD: South Dakota Archaeological Society.

Klass, Dennis. 1999. *The Spiritual Lives of Bereaved Parents.* Philadelphia, PA: Taylor and Francis.

Kluckhohn, Clyde and Dorothea Leighton. 1962. *The Navaho.* New York: Doubleday.

Kneale, Albert A. 1950. *Indian Agent.* Caldwell, ID: Caxton Printers.

Kroeber, A. L. 1971. "Elements of Culture in Native California." In Robert F. Heizer and M. A. Whipple (eds.), *The California Indians: A Source Book.* Berkeley, CA: University of California Press, pp. 3–65.

LaDuke, Winona. 1999. *All Our Relations: Native Struggles for Land and Life.* Cambridge, MA: South End Press.

La Farge, Oliver. 1956. *A Pictorial History of the American Indian.* New York: Crown.

Lamphere, Louise. 1977. *To Run After Them: Cultural and Social Bases of Cooperation in a Navajo Community.* Tucson, AZ: University of Arizona Press.

Landes, Ruth. 1968. *Ojibwa Religion and the Midewiwin*. Madison, WI: University of Wisconsin.

Llewellyn, Karl N. and E. Adamson Hoebel. 1941. *The Cheyenne Way: Conflict and Case Law in Primitive Jurisprudence*. Norman, OK: University of Oklahoma Press.

Laski, Vera. 1958. *Seeking Life*. Philadelphia, PA: American Folklore Society.

Lavitt, Edward and Robert E. McDowell, eds. 1990. *Nihancan's Feast of Beaver: Animal Tales of the North American Indians*. Santa Fe, NM: Museum of New Mexico Press.

Leeming, David and Margaret Leeming. 1994. *A Dictionary of Creation Myths*. New York: Oxford University Press.

Leighton, Dorothea and Clyde Kluckhohn. 1969. *Children of the People: The Navaho Individual and His Development*. New York: Octagon Books.

Leeming, David and Margaret Leeming. 1994. *A Dictionary of Creation Myths*. New York: Oxford University Press.

Lindig, Wolfgang. 1991. *Navajo*. New York: Facts on File.

Lindquist, G. E. E. 1973. *The Red Man in the United States*. Clifton, NY: Augustus M. Kelly.

Llewellyn, Karl N. and E. Adamson Hoebel. 1941. *The Cheyenne Way: Conflict and Case Law in Primitive Jurisprudence*. Norman, OK: University of Oklahoma Press.

Lockard, Craig. A. 2015. *Societies, Networks, and Transitions: A Global History*. Stamford, CT: Cengage.

Locke, Raymond Friday. 1972. *The Book of the Navajo*. Los Angeles, CA: Mankind Publishing Company.

Lowis, M. J. and J. Hughes. 1997. "A Comparison of the Effects of Sacred and Secular Music on Elderly People." *Journal of Psychology* 131, pp. 45–55.

Mails, Thomas E. 1970. *Fools Crow*. Garden City, NY: Doubleday.

Mails, Thomas E. 1973. *Dog Soldiers, Bear Men, and Buffalo Women: A Study of the Societies and Cults of the Plains Indians*. Englewood Cliffs, NJ: Prentice-Hall.

Mails, Thomas E. 1974. *The People Called Apache*. Englewood Cliffs, NJ: Prentice-Hall.

Mails, Thomas E. 1978. *Sundancing at Rosebud and Pine Ridge*. Lake Mills, IA: Graphic Publishing Company.

Mails, Thomas. 1993. *The People Called Apache*. New York: BDD Illustrated Books.

Mails, Thomas E. 1995. *The Mystic Warriors of the Plains: The Culture, Arts, and Religion of the Plains Indians*. New York: Barnes and Noble.

Malinowski, Bronislaw. 1925. *Magic, Science, and Religion and Other Essays*. Garden City, NY: Doubleday.

Mann, Charles C. 2006. *1491: New Revelations of the Americas Before Columbus*. New York: Vintage Books.

Marriott, Alice and Carol K. Rachlin. 1875. *Plains Indian Mythology*. New York: Thomas Y. Crowell.

Marrin, Albert. 2000. *Sitting Bull and His World*. New York: Dutton Children's Books.

Marquis, Arnold. 1974. *A Guide to America's Indians: Ceremonials, Reservations, and Museums*. Norman, OK: University of Oklahoma Press.

Martindale, Don. 1960. *The Nature and Types of Sociological Theory.* Cambridge, MA: The Riverside Press.

Mason, Bernard S. 1946. *The Book of Indian-Crafts and Costumes.* New York: Ronald Press.

Mason, Otis Tufton. 1904. "Aboriginal American Basketry." Annual Report, Smithsonian Institution 1902. Washington, DC: Report of the U.S. National Museum.

Matthews, Washington. 1994. *Navaho Legends.* Salt Lake City, UT: University of Utah Press.

Maxwell, James A. 1978. *American's Fascinating Indian Heritage.* Pleasantville, NY: Reader's Digest.

McClosky, Joanne. 2007. *Living through the Generations: Continuity and Change in Navajo Women's Lives.* Tucson, AZ: University of Arizona Press.

McGaa, Ed. 1990. *Mother Earth Spirituality: Native American Paths to Healing Ourselves and Our World.* San Francisco: Harper.

McGovern, Ann. 1974. *If You Lived with the Sioux Indians.* New York: Four Winds Press.

McKenna, Peter J. and Marcia L. Truell. 1986. *Small Site Architecture of Chaco Canyon New Mexico.* Santa Fe, NM: National Park Service.

McKenney, Thomas L. and James Hall. 1933. *The Indian Tribes of North America: With Biographical Sketches and Anecdotes of the Principle Chiefs.* 3 Vols. Edinburgh: John Grant.

McKissock, Dianne. 1998. *The Grief of Our Children.* Sydney, Australia: Australian Broadcasting Company.

McMaster, Gerald and Clifford E. Trafzer, eds. 2004. *Native Universe: Voices of Indian America.* Washington, DC: Smithsonian: National Museum of the American Indian.

Mead, Margaret. 1966. *The Changing Culture of an Indian Tribe.* New York: Capricorn.

Medicine, Beatrice. 1987. "Indian Women and the Renaissance of Traditional Religion." In Raymond J. DeMallie and Douglas R. Parks (ed.), *Sioux Indian Religion.* Norman, OK: University of Oklahoma Press, pp.159–172.

Merton, Thomas. 1963. *Life and Holiness.* New York: Doubleday.

Michno, Gregory R. 2003. *Encyclopedia of Indian Wars: Western battles and Skirmishes, 1850–1890.* Missoula, MT: Mountain Press Publishing Company.

Mills, C. Wright. 1956. *The Sociological Imagination.* New York: Oxford University Press.

Monroe, Jean G. and Ray A. Williamson. 1987. *They Dance in the Sky: Native American Star Myth.* Boston, MA: Houghton Mifflin.

Mooney, J. 1964. *The Cheyenne Indians. Bureau of American Ethnology*: Washington, DC, Kraus Reprint: New York.

Moore, John H. 1996. *The Cheyenne.* Cambridge, MA: Blackwell.

Morgan, John D. "Toward a Definition of Spirituality. The Forum Newletter." *The Association for Death Education and Counseling* 26 (2), pp. 1–2.

Moskowitz, Ira and John Collier. 1949. *Patterns and Ceremonials of the Indians of the Southwest.* New York: Dutton.

Muench, David. 1974. *Anasazi: Ancient People of the Rock*. Palo Alto, CA: American West Publishing Company.

Nabokov, Peter. 1987. *Indian Running: Native American History and Tradition*. Santa Fe, NM: Ancient City Press.

Nabokov, Peter. 2006. *Where Lightning Strikes: The Live of American Indian Sacred Places*. New York: Penguin.

Nabokov, Peter and Robert Easton. 1989. *Native American Architecture*. New York: Oxford University Press.

Nadeau, Janice Winchester. 1998. *Families Making Sense of Death*. Thousand Oaks, CA: Sage.

Naranjo, Tito. 1993. *Native Americans of the Southwest: A Journey of Discovery*. Philadelphia, PA: Running Press.

Nelson, N. C. 1971. "San Francisco Bay Shell Mounds." In Robert Heizer and M. A. Whipple (eds.), *The California Indians: A Source Book*. Berkeley: University of California Press, pp. 144–157.

Noble, David Grant. 1981. *Ancient Ruins of the Southwest: An Archaeological Guide*. Flagstaff, AZ: Northland Press.

Nouwen, Henri J. M. 1981. *The Way of the Heart: Desert Spirituality and Contemporary Ministry*. New York: Seabury Press.

Opler, Morris E. 1941. *An Apache Life-Way: The Economic, Social, and Religious Institutions of the Chiricahua Indians*. Chicago: University of Chicago Press.

Opler, Morris. 1969. *Apache Odyssey: A Journey Between Two Worlds*. New York: Holt, Rinehart, and Winston.

Oswalt, Wendell H. 1973. *This Land Was Theirs*. New York: John Wiley & Sons.

Oxendine, Joseph B. 1988. *American Indian Sports Heritage*. Champaign, IL: Human Kinetics Books.

Paige, Harry W. 1970. *Songs of the Teton Sioux*. Los Angeles: Westernlore Press.

Parkes, Colin M. 2002. "Grief: Lessons from the past, visions for the future." *Bereavement Care* 21 (2, Summer), pp. 19–23.

Parezo, N. J. 1983. *Navajo Sandpainting: From Religions Act to Commercial Art*. Tucson, AZ: University of Arizona.

Parsons, Elsie, ed. 1922. *An Indian Life*. Lincoln, NE: University of Nebraska Press.

Parsons, Elsie. 1964. *Hopi and Zuni Ceremonialism*. Washington, DC: Bureau of American Ethnology, Kraus Reprint: New York.

Peckham, Howard and Charles Gibson, eds. 1969. *Attitudes of Colonial Powers toward the American Indian*. Salt Lake City, UT: University of Utah Press.

Perry, Richard J. 1991. *Western Apache Heritage: People of the Mountain Corridor*. Austin, TX: University of Texas.

Peters, Virginia Bergman. 1995. *Women of the Earth Lodges: Tribal Life on the Plains*. North Haven, CT: Archon Books; Hermes House.

Powell, John W. 1879–1880. "Indian Linguistic Families of American North of Mexico." *Annual Report of the Bureau of American Ethnology* 25, pp. 454–475.

Powers, William K. 1972. *Indians of the Southern Plains*. New York: Capricorn.

Powers, William K. 1982. *Yuwipi, Vision and Experience in Oglala Ritual*. Lincoln, NE: University of Nebraska Press.

Pritzker, Barry M. 1998. *Native Americans: An Encyclopedia of History, Culture, and Peoples.* Santa Barbara, CA: ABC-CLIO.

Pritzker, Barry M. 1999. *Native America Today: A Guide to Community Politics and Culture.* Santa Barbara, CA: ABC-CLIO.

Prucha, Francis Paul. 1979. *Churches and the Indian Schools 1888–1912.* Lincoln, NE: University of Nebraska Press.

Psvlik, Steve. 2014. *The Navajo and the Animal People: Native American Traditional Ecological Knowledge and Ethnozoology.* Golden, CO: Fulcrum Publishing.

Quadagno, Jill 2014. *Aging and the Life Course: An Introduction to Social Gerontology.* New York: McGraw-Hill.

Radin, Paul. 1970. *The Winnebago Tribe.* Lincoln, NE: University of Nebraska Press.

Ramirez, Susan Berry Brill de. 2008. *Native American Life-History Narratives: Colonial and Postcolonial Navajo Ethnography.* Albuquerque, NM: University of New Mexico Press.

Ramirez, Susan Berry Brill de. 2008. *Native American Life-History Narratives: Colonial and Postcolonial Navajo Ethnography.* Albuquerque, NM: University of New Mexico Press.

Rasmussen, R. Kent. 2000. *American Indian Tribes.* Pasadena, CA: Salem Press.

Reed, Paul F. 2000. *Foundations of Anasazi Culture: The Basketmaker-Pueblo Transition.* Salt Lake City, UT: University of Utah Press.

Reno, Philip. 1972. *Taos Pueblo.* Chicago: Swallow Press.

Restall, Matthew and Amara Solari. 2020. *The Maya: A Very Short Introduction.* New York: Oxford University Press.

Richardson, Boyce. 1991. *Strangers Devour the Land.* Post Mills, VT: Chelsea Green Publishing Company.

Richter, Daniel K. 2001. *Facing East from Indian Country: A Native History of Early America.* Cambridge, MA: Harvard University Press.

Ritzer, George. 2000. *Modern Sociological Theory.* New York: McGraw-Hill.

Roberts, Helen H. 1931. "The Basketry of the San Carlos Apache Indians." *American Museum of Natural History Anthropological Papers* XXXI (Part II).

Robertson, Paul. 2008. "Native Americans, Reservation Life." In Vincent N. Parrillo (ed.), *Encyclopedia of Social Problems.* Thousand Oaks, CA: Sage.

Roper, Donna C. and Elizabeth P. Pauls, eds. 2005. *Plains Earthlodges: Ethnographic and Archaeological Perspectives.* Tuscaloosa, AL: University of Alabama Press.

Ross, Allen C. 1989. *Mitakuye Oyasin: We Are All Related.* Denver: Wiconi Waste.

Sandoz, Ma. 1953. *Cheyenne Autumn.* New York: Hastings House.

Sarita, Joe. 1995. *The Dull Knifes of Pine Ridge: A Lakota Odyssey.* New York: Putnam.

Schaefer, Richard T. 2008. *Racial and Ethnic Groups.* Upper Saddle River, NJ: Pearson Prentice Hall.

Schaefer, Richard T. 2013. *Sociology in Modules.* New York: McGraw-Hill.

Schaefer, Richard T. 2015. *Racial and Ethnic Groups.* Upper Saddle, NJ: Pearson.

Schaefer, Richard T. and Robert P. Lamm. 2006. *Sociology: A Brief Introduction.* New York: McGraw-Hill.

Schoolcraft, Henry. 1860. *Information Respecting the History, Conditions and Prospects of the Indian Tribes of the United States*. 6 Vols. Philadelphia, PA: Lippincott, Grambo & Company.

Schwarz, Maureen Trudelie. 2001. *Navajo Lifeways: Contemporary Issues, Ancient Knowledge*. Norman, OK: University of Oklahoma Press.

Sharer, Robert J. and Traxler, Loa P. 2006. *The Ancient Maya*. Stanford, CA: Stanford University Press.

Sheehan, Bernard W. 1973. *Seeds of Extinction: Jeffersonian Philanthropy and the American Indian*. New York: W.W. Norton.

Sheltrone, Henry Clyde. 2004. *The Mound-Builders: A Reconstruction of the Life of a Prehistoric American Race through Exploration of Their Earth Mounds, Their Burials, and Their Cultural Remains*. Tuscaloosa, AL: University of Alabama Press.

Sherman, Josepha. 1996. *Indian Tribes of North America*. New York: Crescent Books.

Shorris, Earl. 1971. *The Death of the Great Spirit: An Elegy for the American Indian*. New York: Crescent Books.

Silko, Leslie Marmon. 1981. *Storyteller*. New York: Little, Brown, and Company.

Silverberg, Robert. 1968. *Mound Builders of Ancient America: The Archaeology of a Myth*. Greenwich, CT: New York Graphic Society.

Simms, Eva A. 2008. *The Child in the World: Embodiment, Time, and Language in Early Childhood*. Detroit, MI: Wayne State University Press.

Simonelli, Jeanne. 2008. *Crossing between Worlds: The Navajo of Canyon de Chelly*. Long Grove, IL: Waveland Press.

Smithsonian Institution. 1979. *The Year of the Hopi: Paintings and Photographs by Joseph Mora, 1904–1906*. Washington, DC: Smithsonian.

Solomon, Julian Harris. 1928. *The Book of Indian Crafts & Indian Lore*. New York: Harper & Brothers.

Spencer, Raymond F. and Jesse D. Jennings, et. al. 1965. *The Native American*. New York: Harper and Row.

Spencer, Robert F. and Jesse D. Jennings, et. al. 1977. *The Native Americans*. New York: Harper & Row.

Starkey, Marion L. 1995. *The Cherokee Nation*. North Dighton, MA: World Publications.

Starkloff, Carl. 1974. *The People of the Center: American Indian Religion and Christianity*. New York: Seabury Press.

Steele, William O. 1978. *Talking Bones: Secrets of Indian Burial Mounds*. New York: Harper and Row.

Steiger, Brad. 1974. *Medicine Power: The American Indian's Revival of His Spiritual Heritage and Its Relevance for Modern Man*. Garden City, NY: Doubleday.

Steiger, Brad. 1984. *Indian Medicine Power*. West Chester, PA: Whitford Press.

Steiner, Stan. 1968. *The New Indians*. New York: Dell.

Steven, Laura. 2004. *The Poor Indians: British Missionaries, Native Americans, and Colonial Sensibilities*. Philadelphia, PA: University of Pennsylvania Press.

Stirling, Matthew W., Herget W. Landon, H. M. Kihn, and John Oliver La Grace. 1955. *National Geographic on Indians of the Americas*. Washington, DC: National Geographic Society.

Stoekel, H. Henrietta. 1993. *Survival of the Spirit*. Reno, NV: University of Nevada Press.

Stolzman, William. 1986. *How to Take Part in Lakota Ceremonies*. Chamberlain, SD: Tipi Press.

Swanton, John R. 1984. *Indian Tribes of North America*. Washington, DC: Smithsonian Institution.

Taylor, Colin F. 1994. *Native American Myths and Legends*. London: Salamander Books.

Terrell, John Upton. 1971. *The American Indian Almanac*. New York: Barnes and Noble.

Terrell, John Upton. 1972. *Apache Chronicles*. New York: World Publishing.

Terrell, John Upton. 1974. *Pueblos, Gods & Spaniards*. New York: Dial Press.

Thomas, David Hurst. 1994. *Exploring Ancient Native America: An Archaeological Guide*. New York: Macmillan.

Thompson, Laura. 1950. *Culture in Crisis: A Study of the Hopi Indians*. New York: Harper and Brothers.

Thompson, Laura and Alice Joseph. 1944. *The Hopi Way*. New York: Russell and Russell.

Thompson, M. Terry and Steven M. Egesdal, eds. 2008. *Salish Myths and Legends: Our People's Stories*. Lincoln, NE: University of Nebraska Press.

Thornton, Russell. 1978. "American Indian Studies as an Academic Discipline." *American Indian Culture and Research Journal* 2, nos. 3–4, pp. 10–19.

Tiller, Veronica E. 1983. *The Jicarilla Apache Tribe: A History, 1846–1970*. Lincoln, NE: University of Nebraska.

Tinker, George E. "Tink." 2008. *American Indian Liberation: A Theology of Sovereignty*. Maryknoll, NY: Orbis Books.

Tooker, Elizabeth. 1997. "John N. B. Hewitt." In Frederick E. Hoxie (ed.), *Encyclopedia of North American Indians*. New York: Houghton Mifflin, pp. 244–245.

Trimble, Stephen. 1993. *Indians of the American Southwest*. Santa Fe, NM: SAR Press.

Underhill, Ruth Murray. 1938. *Singing for Power: The Song Magic of the Papago Indians of Southern Arizona*. Berkley, CA: University of California Press.

Underhill, Ruth Murray. 1945. *Indians of the Pacific Northwest*. Phoenix, AZ: United States Indian Service.

Underhill, Ruth Murray. 1946. *Work-a-Day Life of the Pueblos*. Phoenix, AZ: United States Indian Service.

Underhill, Ruth Murray. 1948. *Ceremonial Patterns in the Greater Southwest*. New York: American Ethnological Society Memoirs.

Underhill, Ruth Murray. 1953. *Red Man's America: A History of Indians in the United States*. Chicago: University of Chicago Press.

Underhill, Ruth Murray. 1956. *The Navajo*. Norman, OK: University of Oklahoma Press.

Underhill, Ruth Murray. 1965. *Red Man's Religion: Beliefs and Practices*. Chicago: University of Chicago Press.

U.S. Census Bureau. 2006. *Statistical Abstract of the United States: 2009*. Washington, DC: U.S. Government Printing Office.

Utter, Jack. 2001. *American Indians: Answers to Today's Questions*. Norman, OK: University of Oklahoma Press.

Voget, Fred W. 1995. *They Call Me Agnes: A Crow Narrative Based on the Life of Agnes Yellowtail Deernose*. Norman, OK: University of Oklahoma Press.

Waldman, Carl. 1988. *Encyclopedia of Native American Tribes*. New York: Facts on File.

Waldman, Carl. 2009. *Atlas of the North American Indian*. New York: Checkmark Books.

Wall, Steve and Harvey Arden. 1990. *Wisdomkeepers: Meetings with Native American Spiritual Elders*. Hillsboro, OR: Beyond Words Publishing.

Walton, D. 2021. "Bloodletting in Ancient Central Mexico: Using Lithic Analyses to Detect Changes in Ritual Practices and Local Ontologies." *Journal of Archaeological Method and Theory* 28, pp. 274–306.

Warren, A. Helen and Frances Joan Mathen. "Prehistoric and Historic Turquoise Mining in the Cerrillos District: Time and Place." In Charles H. Lange (ed.), *Southwestern Culture History: Collected Papers in Honor of Albert H. Schroeder*, pp. 83–128.

Waters, Frank. 1950. *Masked Gods: Navaho and Pueblo Ceremonialism*. Chicago: The Swallow Press.

Watkins, Joe. 2013. "How Ancients Become Ammunition: Politics and Ethics of Human Skeleton." In Sarah Tarlow and Liv Nilsson Stutz (eds.), *The Oxford Handbook of The Archaeology of Death & Burial*. Oxford, UK: Oxford University Press, pp. 695–708.

Watson, Don. 1961a. *Cliff Dwellings of the Mesa Verde: A Story in Pictures*. Mesa Verde, CO: Mesa Verde National Park.

Watson, Don. 1961b. *The Indians of Mesa Verde*. Ann Arbor, Mesa Verde, CO: Mesa Verde Museum Association.

Weiner, Michael A. 1980. *Earth Medicine Earth Food: Plant Remedies, Drugs & Natural Foods of the North American Indians*. New York: Macmillan.

Weiss-Krejci. 2013. "The Unburied Dead." In Sarah Tarlow and Liv Nelsson Stutz (eds.), *The Oxford Handbook of The Archaeology of Death & Burial*. Oxford, UK: Oxford University Press, pp. 281–301.

Whitely, Peter M. 1998. *Rethinking Hopi Ethnography*. Washington, DC: Smithsonian.

Wicks, Robert S. and Roland H. Harrison. 1999. *Buried Cities, Forgotten Gods: William Niven's Life of Discovery and Revolution in Mexico and the American Southwest*. Lubbock, TX: Texas Tech University Press.

Winger, Otho. 1939. *The Potawatomi Indians*. Elgin, IL: Elgin Press.

Young, John V. 1990. *Kokopelli: Casanova of the Cliff Dwellers*. Palmer Lake, CO: Filter Press.

Zolbrod, Paul G. 1984. *Dine Bahane: The Navajo Creation Story*. Albuquerque, NM: University of New Mexico Press.

Index

Aataentsic, 8
Aboriginals. *See* Indians
Abraham, 105
Acoma, 18, 85, 217
Addams, Jane, 25
Adena/Hopewell cultures, 189
Africa, 10, 12, 18
afterworld, 108, 120, 157–58, 183–84, 326
Algonquian, 6, 59, 85, 262, 316; language group, 271, 275, 283, 318; Yurok, 85
alienation, 47
all is one, 323
Altern Mounds. *See* mounds
Alzheimer, 196
American Professional Football Association, 65
Anasazi, 7, 75, 84, 167–74, 199, 202, 238, 241; Kayenta, 169–70
ancestors, 119, 287, 325, 329, 339; worship, 108
ancients, 165, 174, 215, 346–47; civilizations, 165, 324; ones, 118, 171, 215; societies, 21, 23, 165–66, 185, 335, 345, 347
anger, 97
animals, 6, 71–72, 117, 120, 126–27, 135–37, 182, 190, 194, 208, 244, 262–64, 272–74, 323–24, 326, 338–39
animism, 106–7
Anishinabe. *See* Chippewa
Apache. *See* Inde
Appalachia, 80
Arapahoe, 85, 88, 243, 271, 273
archaeology, 11, 14, 87–88, 116, 173, 181, 215
Arikara, 75, 157
arrow points. *See* medicine bundles
art, 194, 274, 325, 350
arts and crafts, 66–69, 119, 160–62, 170–71, 174, 176, 187, 194, 216–17, 235, 244, 324–25
Ashanti, 138
ashes, 116, 247, 326, 342, 348
Asia, 10
assimilation, 143–45
Assiniboine Sioux, 245, 263, 342
Athabascan, 136; language, 193; tribes, 59, 332
Atsina, 271
Attig, Thomas, 150
attitudes, 22–31, 103–4, 107–8, 325, 348
Australia, 18, 108
Aztecs, 7, 12–13, 75, 83–84, 175–81, 183, 188, 345

Bad River. *See* Chippewa

Baker Massacre, 263

balance, 93–95, 200, 238, 245, 323–24

Bear Butte, 85

bears, 5, 84, 130, 135

Becker, Ernest, 25

Begaye, Jay, 85

beliefs, 105, 200, 236–37, 273–74, 287, 326, 331, 338, 340, 343, 346, 350

Beothuk, 10

bereavement. *See* grief

Bering, Virus, 145

Bering Straits, 17, 194

Bernstein, Harry, 132

BIA (Bureau of Indian Affairs), 3, 79, 81, 85, 136, 326, 335

Bible, 4, 9

Biden, Joseph, 97

Big Centipedes, 106

Big Turtle, 8

Big Ye'i, 106

bison, 14, 71, 73, 120, 130, 244, 246, 262, 264, 271–71, 317

Blackfeet, 5, 94, 118, 243, 264–72; Kainah (blood), 262; Kutenai, 264; lifeways, 262–64

Black Fox, 85

Black Hills clan, 244, 246

Black Lives Matter, 71

Black Madonna, 89, 116

Black Muslim Movement, 79

Blackrobes, 89, 114, 116

Blacks, 76

Blessing Way. *See* ceremonies

boarding schools. *See* schools

bonding, 153, 155–57, 327

borrowing, 133

bounties, 19

Boyz from the Rez, 85

brain surgery, 83

Brer Rabbit, 188

Brexit, 52

British, 45, 70–72, 75–76, 83, 117, 143, 275, 285–86, 288

Bronze Age, 12

Buddhist, 124

burial, 115, 143, 149, 157, 172–73, 179, 184, 188–90, 200–203, 248–49, 264, 274–76, 288–90, 329, 339–42, 344, 347, 350; air burial, 278; burial house, 289; burial pit, 288; tree burial, 249, 264

Cahuilla, 345

calendar161, 346

California, 18–19, 58–59, 97; Indians, 18–19, 58–62

calumet, 288

Canyon de Chelly. *See* pueblos

Canyon Records, 85

Cape Cod, 83

caregivers, 41–43, 150, 154–59, 329–32

Carson, Kit, 18

Carter, Forrest, 80

casinos, 81–82, 137, 145, 331

caskets, 143

Catholic, 53, 67, 97, 114, 134–35, 144, 217, 235, 277, 328, 343

Catlin, George, 74

cavalry, 76, 263

Center for Death Education, 2

Centre for Education about Death and Bereavement, 2

ceremonies, 58, 64, 66, 84, 93, 95, 116, 120, 128, 137, 140, 158, 162–63, 194, 199–200, 239–40, 245, 264, 276, 297, 325, 328–29, 332, 341, 344, 350; bear ceremonies, 130; Blessing Way, 104, 106, 109; Coming of Age Ceremony, 5; Ghost Dance, 53, 107, 202; Ghostway, 202; giveaway, 88, 158, 264, 274, 340; healing, 5, 105, 124–25, 208, 325; Holy Way Chant, 202; lifeway ritual, 104, 202; Lone Tipi, 103; Medicine Lodge Ceremony, 263; Moon Lodge Ceremony, 106; Mountaintop Way, 129; Mountainway Chant, 104; Sun Dance, 86, 102, 157; sweat, 116, 120, 156

Chaco Canyon. *See* pueblos
change of life, 139
Changing Bear Maiden, 106
Changing Woman, 89, 105, 107, 118
Chaptut, Archbishop Charles, 277
Chee, Connor, 86
Cherokee, 4, 8, 85, 243
Cheyenne (Tsistsistas), 5, 48, 88, 103, 107, 271–75
Chickasaw, 243
children, 32, 43, 64, 80, 86, 92, 95–96, 116, 127, 129–30, 135–36, 144, 146, 153, 156, 160, 180, 195–97, 236–37, 263, 273, 286–87, 325–27, 329, 333
Chippewa/Ojibwa/Anishinabe, 6, 13, 85, 157, 243–44, 271, 276, 285–318, 341–42, 345; Bad River, 285; Lac Court Oreilles, 285; Lac du Flambeau (Lake of Flames), 285, 287; Red Cliff, 285; wild rice people, 286
Chiricahua Apache. *See* Inde
Choctaws, 243
choice making, 35–38
Chosen People, 236
Christian, 5, 18, 85, 88; Christianity, 53–54, 101–12, 114–15, 124, 128, 130, 134–35, 144, 209, 338, 340–41
Churchill, Winston, 132
Cibecue Apache. *See* Inde
civilizations, 7, 13, 15, 83, 175–76, 180, 182, 185, 336–37, 345; Mixtec civilization, 183
Civil Rights Act, 77–78
Civil Rights Movement, 78
Civil War. *See* War between the States
clan, 21, 55, 64, 118, 137, 158–59, 165, 177, 195–96, 205, 207, 217, 237–40, 324, 331–32, 335–42, 347
clergy, 53, 89, 91, 115, 180, 201, 238, 324, 340
Cloud People, 118
Clovis site. *See* mounds
Cochise, 205; Cochise Culture, 171
Cocopa, 58, 344

codetalkers, 193–94
Cody, Iron Eyes, 117
coercion, 103, 115, 144
Coeur d'Alene, 114
Collier, John, 69
Columbus, Christopher, 6, 10, 14, 59, 73, 75, 349–50
Comanche, 13, 243, 272
Coming of Age Ceremony. *See* ceremonies
communications, 96, 172, 327, 342
community, 21, 67, 128, 132, 136, 141, 237–38, 246, 264, 326, 329, 348–49
compassion, 17–20, 133, 144, 158, 247, 334
Comte, Auguste, 336
conflict, 116; conflicting values, 16–17; conflict theory, 337
contributions, 83, 133, 158, 171–72, 176–77, 181–83
Cooper, Anna Julia, 25
Costner, Kevin, 244
COVID, 21, 69, 86, 346
Coyote, 8, 130, 137–38, 142, 194, 209, 329, 331, 343
Crazy Horse, 146
creation, 157; creation stories, 7–9, 118, 141, 273–74, 288
creator, 107, 236, 349
Cree, 263, 271
Creeks, 85, 243
cremation, 18, 32, 59, 180, 339–40, 343–44
criminal justice system, 76
Critical Race Theory, 71
critical thinking, 22
Crow, 5, 272
Crow Creek Reservation. *See* reservations
culture, 21, 45–54, 194–99, 286–87, 326–28, 333, 335, 337–38, 349; awareness, 42–43; change, 52–54; conflict, 145; denigration, 71–90; differences, 69–70, 73, 115; diversity, 4, 13–14, 22, 155, 273,

328, 341; dominant, 64–65, 78, 80–81, 88, 135, 137, 143, 157, 162, 323, 327–28, 332, 345; genocide, 76–77; groups, 21–22, 158; prescriptions, 33; wars, 52
curses, 94

Dahrendorf, Ralf, 338
Dakota (Dakotah), 243, 272, 285
Dances with Wolves, 244
Darwin, Charles, 336
death, 87–88, 115–16, 121, 126, 145–47, 149–58, 183–84, 195, 200–203, 237, 247–48, 323, 325–26, 328–30, 332, 338, 343–44, 346, 348, 350; death awareness movement, 32; management practices, 32; rituals, 69–70; songs, 272
Death Valley, 14, 80, 125; Death Valley National Park, 80
decision-making, 3
Delaware Indians, 275, 317; Housatonic, 317; Lenapes, 316; Mahican, 316; Muh-he-conneok, 317; Munsee, 316; River, 317
desert culture, 171
Desoto, Hernando, 188
destiny, 338
Dgorib, 13
Diablo, 206
Diegueno, 344
dignity, 130, 143, 147, 159, 237, 247, 328, 331, 340
Dine, 1, 6, 8–9, 48, 51–52, 63, 68–89, 105–12, 129–30, 139, 157–58, 162, 178, 193–203, 235–37, 243–45, 329, 335
discrimination, 18, 345
disease, 14, 73, 77, 79, 86–87, 103, 125, 133, 150, 202, 207–9, 236, 264, 287, 335
disposal, 21, 56, 87–88, 166, 184, 288–90, 340, 345, 347
diversity, 4, 13–14, 22, 77, 155, 273, 328, 341

Dog Men, 272
dreams, 6, 94, 120, 125, 127, 155, 202, 207, 238, 288, 328, 342; dream catchers, 113, 116
Druids, 138
Dual Citizenship Act, 77
Du Bois, W. E. B., 337
Durkheim, Emile, 25, 55, 99–112, 179
Dutch, 75–76
dying and death, 21–43, 237–38, 323, 325, 328, 332–33, 338, 345

Earth Mother, 247–48
education, 92, 143–45, 185, 329
Egypt, 17, 87–88, 116, 166, 179–80, 184, 190, 345, 347
elders, 37–38, 81, 84, 90, 96, 118, 125, 196, 263, 274, 286–87, 323, 328–29, 333–35, 342, 346, 350; elder epistemology, 132; elderly, 130–49, 347
elements of religion, 101–12
Eliot, Thomas, 2
end-of-life-care, 333
entrepreneurship, 90
Europeans, 3–4, 7, 9–18, 52, 59, 63, 76–79, 83, 91, 114–15, 117–18, 127, 141–45, 162, 177, 182–83, 187–88, 198–200, 203, 209, 217, 236, 238, 244, 277, 288, 317, 328, 336, 338–39
evil, 110, 119, 130, 207, 342
exploitation, 329

False Face Societies, 156
family, 31–32, 66–69, 88, 94, 96, 131, 141–42, 159, 177, 180, 194–95, 203, 208, 245, 327, 332–33, 339–41, 347
Father Heaven, 248
fear, 28–39, 52, 78–79, 94, 116, 147, 200–201, 208, 263, 274, 323, 330; of death, 28–29, 237, 248–49, 326, 329, 331, 338; of dying, 28–29
Feifel, Herman, 21
Fetterman's Massacre, 76

Field Museum of Natural History, 78
First Man, 137, 141
First Woman, 137, 141
Flathead, 85, 88, 114, 340
folk music, 85
Folkway Records, 85
folkways, 51
Fools Crow, Frank, 85
Fort Apache. *See* reservations
Four Corners, 167, 169
Freeman, Morgan, 132
French Lick, IN, 132
frontier, 15
Fulton, Robert, 2, 21
functional theory, 338
funeral, 22, 30, 32, 88, 111, 126, 180,
    264, 290, 340–41, 344, 346; funeral
    directors, 55, 115, 143, 201, 264–70,
    340–41; funeral pyre, 344

Gahan, 209
games, 65–66
Garden of Gethsemane, 38
genocide, 18, 77, 81
Geronimo, 206
ghost, 130, 206–7, 209–10, 236, 274,
    342; ghost keeping, 120, 158;
    maleovolent ghosts, 236
Gillman, Charlotte Perkins, 25
Gopher Woman, 106
Goreman, Carl, 162
grandchildren, 9, 133, 139, 146–47,
    196, 207; grandfathers, 198;
    grandmotherese, 139; grandmothers,
    207; grandparents, 64, 139–41, 196,
    207, 226, 239, 342
graves, 56–57, 202, 209, 237, 290, 345;
    grave diggers, 276; grave houses,
    276–77
Great Spirit (Great Mystery), 246–47
Greeks, 87–88, 115, 138, 180, 184,
    336
Greeley, Horace, 15
Green Bay Packers, 37
Green Frog People, 106

Greenland, 10, 13
grief, 22–27, 58–62, 66–69, 137, 143,
    149–63, 196, 249, 288–90, 323–24,
    337, 339, 346, 348
guardian angels, 106, 343
guardian spirits, 93, 106, 343
guilt, 3, 132
guns, 71, 73, 244, 263, 335

Haaland, Deb, 81
Habenstein, Robert, 2
Haida, 84, 130
Haile, Father Bernard, 109
harmony, 93, 119, 127, 200, 217, 236,
    245
hatqali, 199
healers, 95–96, 152, 200, 245, 327
health, 94, 131, 149–53, 200, 245, 248,
    329–32; care, 93–95, 149–53, 329
Heammawihio, 273–74
Hebrew Bible, 12, 105
hieroglyphs, 7, 184
HIV/AIDS, 70
Ho Chunk, 63, 130, 243, 317
Hoffman, Dustin, 244
Hogan, 37, 64–65, 84, 114, 201–3, 209,
    324
Hohokam, 75, 171, 215–16, 241
holistic approach, 21, 152, 245
holocaust Denial, 71
Holy Family, 9, 141
Holy People, 8
Hopi, 1, 51–52, 66, 68–69, 107,
    116, 118, 146, 156, 173, 184, 197,
    235–42, 325; Hopi way, 118–19
horses, 71, 73, 182, 244, 263, 335
hospice, 21, 323, 325, 327–34
hospitals, 94, 149–52, 327, 347
Housatonic Indians, 317
housing, 84
Hudson, Henry, 316
Hudson Bay, 10
Huitzilopochtli, 179
human activity, 25
humor, 93, 162, 209, 332, 342

Illinois Indians, 255
illness, 82, 93–95, 125, 149–53, 199, 202, 207–9, 248, 274, 333
immigration, 70, 218, 338; immigrants, 113, 345
immortality, 274, 348
Inca, 1, 7, 71, 75, 176, 188, 325
Inde (Apache), 1, 5, 13, 48, 63, 74, 84, 103, 134, 137–38, 193, 199, 205–16, 237, 242–45, 324, 342, 343; Chiricahua Apache, 5, 34; Cibecue Apache, 211–12; culture, 206–7; Fort Apache, 74; Jicarilla Apache, 74; Mescalero Apache, 74; San Carlos, 74
Indian Gaming Regulatory Act, 82
Indian House Records, 85
Indians, 1–23
Indian Wars, 11, 15, 79, 97, 205, 215, 335
Inktomi, 120
inter-marriage, 64
International Death, Grief, and Bereavement Conference, 2
intimacy, 139, 142; intimacy impairment, 131–47
Inuit, 10, 13, 75, 206
Iron Age, 12
Iroquois, 68, 156–57, 276, 285; nations, 287, 317, 341
Isaacs, Ida, 85
Isaacs, Tony, 85

jaguars, 7
Japanese, 194
Jefferson, Thomas, 88, 116
Jesus Christ, 83, 102, 105, 141
Jewish, 9, 75, 105, 134
Joseph, Frank, 12
Judeo-Christian ethic, 14

Kachinas, 11, 68, 89, 107, 146, 236–37, 240, 343
Kainah. *See* Blackfeet
Kastenbaum, Robert, 29
Kawia. *See* Cahuilla

Kayenta. *See* Anasazi
Kensington Stone, 10
Kickapoo, 271, 317
kinship, 63–64, 80, 92, 136, 324, 326, 332
Kin Ya's, 172
Kiowa, 68, 88, 243, 272
Kitche Manitou, 155
kivas, 84, 167–73, 184, 238–41; clans, 240
Kokopelli, 169
Koran, 105
Koyukon, 13
Kroc, Ray, 132
Kubler-Ross, Elizabeth, 21
Kutenai. *See* Blackfeet
Kwakiutl, 84, 130

Lac Court Oreilles. *See* Chippewa
Lac du Flambeau. *See* Chippewa
La Farge, Peter, 85
Laguna Pueblo. *See* Pueblos
Lakota, 48, 56, 63, 74–75, 84–85, 118, 120, 150–51, 157, 162, 178, 193, 200, 242–62, 264, 288, 325; Lakota Way, 120, 244–46
Lamers, William, 2
language, 1, 4, 7, 12, 74–75, 86–87, 109, 143–44, 154, 193–94, 215, 235–36, 243–45, 262, 339
Leakey, Louis, 6
Lenapes. *See* Delaware Indians
lesson of death, 36–38
Library of Congress Music Division, 85
Lifeway rituals. *See* ceremonies
listening, 247, 343
Little Big Horn, 76, 97, 244, 273
Little Big Man, 244
Little Turtle, 8
live for today, 17
Lomax, Allen, 85
Lone Tipi. *See* ceremonies
longhouses, 318
Long Walk, 240
loss, 17–20, 123–30, 134, 324–25, 328, 342; loss of tradition, 145

magic, 102–3
Mahican. *See* Delaware Indians
Maiden Who Became a Bear, 106
Malcolm X, 79
malevolent ghosts. *See* ghosts
Mandan, 84
Mangas Colorados, 206
Manifest destiny, 15
Manito, 155
Maricopa, 344
Martineau, Harriet, 25, 337
Marx, Karl, 45, 337–38
Masau'u, 118, 238
massacres, 18, 76
matrilineal, 146, 194
matrilocal, 194
Maya, 1, 7, 13, 75, 176, 179, 181–85, 188, 205, 324
McCourt, Frank, 132
Mead. Margaret, 130
meaning, 126, 321, 331–32
Medicare, 133
medicine, 11; medicine bag, 5, 57; medicine bundle, 5, 121, 156–57, 263; medicine pipe, 263; medicine wheel, 263
Medicine Lodge Ceremony. *See* ceremonies
Menominee, 285
Merton, Robert K., 337
mesas, 239
Mesa Verde. *See* pueblos
Mescalero Apache. *See* Inde
Meskwaki, 85
Meso-American, 58, 175, 177–81
Metacom, 144
Mexico, 18, 138
Miamis, 285, 317
Mills, Billy, 65
Mills, C. Wright, 50, 349
minorities, 45, 130
missions, 18, 144, 235, 344; mission Indians, 60–62; non-mission Indians, 60–62, 344
Mixtec civilization. *See* civilizations

Modoc, 58
Mogollon, 75, 171, 241
Mohammed, 105
Mohave, 58, 60–61, 344
Mohegans, 316
Mohican. *See* Delaware Indians
Montelores, 170
Moon God, 106
Moon Lodge Ceremony. *See* ceremonies
Moqui (Moki), 235
Morgan, John D., 2, 16–17, 67, 123
Moses, Grandma, 132
Mother Earth, 125, 140, 147, 155, 330, 339
Mother Nature, 106
mounds, 56, 116, 166, 187–91, 341; Altern Mounds, 341; Angel Site, 188; Builders, 75, 166, 187–91, 205; Cahokia Site, 75, 188, 190; Clovis Site, 75, 188; Effigy Mounds, 190; Hopewell, 345; mounds burial, 249; Moundsville Site, 75, 188; Natchez mounds, 75
Mountain Spirit. *See* Gahan
Mountaintop Way. *See* ceremonies
Mountainway Chant. *See* ceremonies
mourning, 157, 166, 202, 210, 224, 276, 339, 343–45
mummification, 56
Munsee. *See* Delaware Indians
music, 84–86, 125, 160, 162, 208, 246, 273, 324
Muslims, 5, 113, 135
myths, 107, 128, 137, 329

Nadeau, Janice Winchester, 95
Nakai, R. Carlos, 85
Nakota, 243
Nanticoke, 275
Natchez mounds. *See* mounds
National Football League, 65
National Museum of the American Indian, 81
National Parks, 167, 172, 174
Navajo. *See* Dine

Neanderthals, 70
near-death experiences, 274
New World, 15, 75, 182
New World Records, 85
Ni un (life), 343
Nootka, 130
nursing homes, 64, 133, 332

Oaxaca, 183
obligations, 324, 332, 346
Ojibwa. *See* Chippewa
Oklahoma, 4, 77
Old Man, 118, 120
old old, 131–32
old ways, 92
Old Woman, 120
Old World, 182, 184
Olmecs, 7, 176, 181–82
Oneida, 63, 317
Oneota, 75
Opler, Morris, 5
oppression, 26, 329
Oraibi, 240
oral histories: Blackfeet, 264–70;
    Chippewa, 290–313; Inde, 211–15;
    Lakota, 249–62; Potawatomi, 277–83;
    Shoshone, 313–16; Stockbridge-
    Munsee, 318–20; Tohono O'odham,
    218–33
oral traditions, 106, 329
orphans, 34, 324
Osage, 243
Ottawas, 285

Pachacoma, 7
Paiute, 13, 53
Park, Robert, 143
Parkes, Colin Murray, 41
Parsons, Talcott, 337
patterns of behavior, 46, 49–50, 160,
    333, 335
Pawnee, 84, 118, 243
Penasco Blanco. *See* pueblos
people-centered, 92, 137, 153–54, 331;
    people-oriented, 63–64; people-
    watching, 2

Petroglyphs, 169
Peyote Cults, 53
peyote religion, 53
Picasso, Pablo, 349
pilgrims, 88
Pima, 85, 215–17, 241
pipe, 113, 116, 120, 156, 246, 263,
    288
Plato, 17
pluralism, 145
Pokagon, Leopold, 290
Potawatomi, 82, 243, 271, 276–83, 285,
    317
poverty, 80, 91, 136, 336
Powell, John Wesley, 13
power, 4–6, 94, 147, 150, 207, 236,
    247–48, 273, 288, 324–25
prayer, 94, 114, 117, 119–20, 139, 155,
    238, 247, 273, 287, 324, 339–41
prejudice, 18, 162
problems today, 78, 86–87, 218
Prokosch Kurath, Gertrude, 337
Protestant, 144; Protestant ethic, 114
psychological perspective, 21–23
Pueblos, 75, 79, 84, 119, 167–69, 174,
    194, 217, 235–41; Canyon de Chelly,
    18, 167; Chaco Canyon, 167, 169–
    72, 196; Laguana, 81; Mesa Verde,
    167–72, 174; Penasco Blanco, 172;
    Pueblo Bonito, 170; Rio Grande
    Pueblo, 168; San Juan Pueblo, 85;
    Taos pueblo, 85; Tewan Pueblo, 69;
    Yellow Jacket site, 170; Zuni/Acoma
    Pueb0, 235
purpose in life, 126, 128, 150, 331, 339,
    343
Pyramid of the Sun, 183
pyramids, 7, 182–83, 190, 347–48

Quadagno, Jill, 28
Quechan. *See* Yuma

Redbow, Buddy, 85
Red Cliff. *See* Chippwa
relationships, 3, 116, 145–47, 287, 335,
    338

religion, 4–5, 74, 77, 92, 101–21, 126, 136, 177–79, 194, 247, 273–74, 328, 339
relocation, 336
reservations, 64, 74, 80, 88, 89, 149, 193, 203, 206, 215, 218, 240, 333, 336; Crow Creek reservation, 80; Fort Apache, 74; schools, 3, 81, 177
resilience, 4, 64
respect, 4–5, 37–38, 115–16, 120, 139–40, 145, 159–60, 247, 332, 338, 342
responsibility, 324
retirement, 132
revealed truths, 105–6
revisionist history, 71–76
Rio Grande Pueblo. *See* pueblos
rise and fall theories, 336
rituals, 3, 53, 58–59, 66–69, 86–89, 95, 104–5, 114, 116, 120, 129, 143, 155, 157, 194, 199–200, 239, 245, 277, 288–90, 325, 328–29, 331, 339, 346–47; baptism, 104; rites of passage, 336
rock piling, 318
Rocky Boy (Stone Child), 290
Romans, 180, 184, 336
Rowling, J.K., 132

Sacagawea, 117
Sac and Fox, 243, 317
sacred, 4, 102–3, 116, 128–30, 247, 324, 343; duties, 247; objects, 5, 95, 199, 237, 246, 288, 317, 324; places, 71, 81, 85, 246, 287; powers, 325; stories, 117, 124, 126–28, 329, 338, 343; writings, 4, 324
Saint-Marie, Buffy, 85
Salish Sioux, 114
San Carlos. *See* Inde
Sand Creek, 18, 76, 88, 116, 272
Sanders, Colonel, 132
sand paintings, 113–14, 194, 200, 208–9, 217
San Juan Pueblo. *See* pueblos
Santee Sioux, 243; dialect, 243
Sauk and Fox, 84

Saunders, Cicely, 21
Schaefer, Richard, 26
Schoolcraft, Henry C., 188
Schoolcraft, Jane, 290
schools, 3, 81, 89, 177, 207; boarding schools, 80, 89, 144–45, 236, 336
science, 3, 143, 150, 183, 245
Seminole, 84, 243
Serrano People, 8
Seventh Calvary, 53
shaman, 102, 106, 109, 152, 155, 199–200, 207–9, 245, 328, 330, 345
sharing, 92, 135–36, 139, 158, 240, 247, 286, 318, 325–26
Shawnee, 275–77
Shoshone, 8, 13, 58, 235, 262, 288, 345; Timbisha Shoshone, 80
Shungopovi, 236
Sicun (spirit Helper), 343
significant others, 3
silence, 42, 91, 96, 121, 124, 134, 158–59, 162, 196, 207, 327
Sioux, 74–75, 273–74
Sipapu, 168
Sky, Patrick, 85
slavery, 18
Smith, John, 49
Snohomish, 7
social, 3; norms, 3, 23, 51, 92, 165; social action, 3; social beings, 64; social change, 131–32, 335–37; social class, 338; social contract, 322; social expectations, 158; social groups, 31, 48–49, 147, 349; social institutions, 22, 165; social life, 47–48; social organization, 47, 95, 194; social pressure, 165, 346; social processes, 23; social regulation, 47; social relationships, 47–48, 159; social status, 339; social structure, 21, 165, 246; social support, 33, 147, 342; social systems, 346
socialization, 143, 335
society, 25, 45–54, 324, 336, 345, 347–48

sociological concepts: acculturation, 81, 143, 157–58; definition-of-the-situation, 39; detachment theory, 132; ethnocentrism, 50–51, 91, 105, 114, 154; labeling theory, 114–15, 132; power elite, 180; reciprocity, 16; self-fulfilling prophecy, 39; sociological analysis, 22; sociological imagination, 22, 349; sociological insights, 21; sociological perspective, 21–43, 99, 337; sociological theory, 336; values, 23, 37–38, 51–52, 64, 70, 92–93, 103, 159–60, 194–99, 247, 326, 330, 333

sociology of dying and death, 25–43, 321–22

Sorokin, Pitirim, 336

sorrow, 89, 340–41

soul, 110, 237, 264, 290, 328, 341, 343–44

Spanish, 12, 18, 19, 71, 76, 117, 175–78, 188, 194, 205–6, 215, 217, 235–36, 263, 272

Spencer, Herbert, 336

spirits, 120, 155–57, 201, 209, 246, 274, 290, 328, 339

spiritual, 324, 348, 350

spirituality, 5–6, 16–18, 63, 81, 93–95, 101, 123–30, 134, 162–63, 246–48, 324–25, 334, 343, 345, 348; spiritual acts, 113; spiritual beings, 101; spiritual journey, 5, 201, 237, 340; spiritual life, 127, 236, 328; spiritual paths, 95, 343

spirit world, 245, 328, 342

Sponge Bob Square Pants, 138

St. Augustine, 77–78

stereotypes, 131, 328

Stockbridge-Munsee, 285, 316–20

Stone Age, 12, 185

stories, 118, 128–29, 132, 139, 144, 196–98, 328–29, 343; story teller, 64, 129, 328, 349; story telling, 11, 45, 95, 127, 129, 138, 328, 350

suicide, 162, 339–40, 343

Summer People, 239

Sumner, William Graham, 336

Sun Belt, 133

Sun Dance. *See* ceremonies

supernatural, 245, 274, 348

Supreme Being, 17, 207, 209

sweat. *See* ceremonies

sweet grass, 125, 288

Taos. *See* pueblos

Tatanka Records, 85

Tekakwitha, Kateri, 117, 144

temples, 7, 176, 178, 183

Tenocha, 178

Tenochtitlan, 18, 83, 183

Teotihuacan, 178

Tesuques, 69

Teton Sioux, 243

Tewan Pueblo. *See* pueblos

Thomas, William Isaac, 39

Thorpe, Jim, 65

Thorvaldsson, Erik the Red, 9, 14

Three Fires, 285

three R's, 139, 329

Tiger and Zit, 85

Timbisha Shoshone. *See* Shoshone

time, 93, 96, 153, 160–62, 198

Tirawa, 118

Tlingit, 84, 130

Tohono O'odham, 13, 83, 94, 215–18, 241

Tokahe, 120

Tolowa, 85

Toltecs, 178

tombs, 87, 176, 184, 189, 348

tombstones, 165

totems, 107–8, 166

tradition, 31, 166, 339–40

tree burial. *See* burial

tribes, 21, 145, 335, 338–39, 345, 350

Trickster, 120, 138–39

Trump, Donald, 52

Tsegi Canyon, 169

Tulsa massacre, 76

Turner, Frederick Jackson, 15
Turquoise Woman, 118
"Twilight Series," 7

underworld, 118, 209, 238, 342
unfinished business, 3
Ungava Bay, 10
University of Minnesota, 2
University of Wisconsin-La Crosse, 2
upper world, 120, 237
Utes, 13
Uto-Axtecan language, 236

variables, 91–92
Vernon, Glen, 2
Vikings, 6, 9–10, 14, 71, 186, 349
Villages of the Dead, 342
Viracocha, 7
Virgin Mary, 88, 116
vision quest, 102, 245
visions, 127, 136–37, 155, 245, 328, 339, 349

wail, 210, 343–44
Wakan Tanka, 118, 120, 155, 248
wake, 88, 210, 343–43
Walapai, 344
Walton, Sam, 132
Wann gi (shadow spirit), 343
war, 18, 69, 335
war between the States, 16, 87, 116
Washita, 18, 273
Water Beetle, 8
Way of Life, 74, 339
wealth, 135, 179–80, 323, 328–29, 333, 339
Wells, Ida Barret, 337
Westerman, Floyd, 85

White Buffalo Calf Woman, 120
White Eagle, 8
Wichita, 84
wickiup, 209, 324, 343, 349
widow, 134, 274
Wilder, Laura Ingalls, 132
Wild Rice People. *See* Chippwa
Wilson, Jack. *See* Wovoka
Winds Running Series, 65
Winnebago. *See* Ho Chunk
Winter People, 239
wisdom, 38, 129, 159
witchcraft, 52, 117, 199, 207, 342
Woman Who Fell From the Sky, 8
women, 8–9, 84, 86, 146, 153, 195–97, 207, 210, 212, 226, 236, 239, 249, 263–64, 272–73, 275–77, 287–90, 318, 324, 333, 342
Woodland tribes, 244, 262, 271, 285, 317, 345
work, 92, 160–61, 324, 332
Wounded Knee, 18, 53, 97, 120, 244
Wovoka, 53
writing, 75
Wyandots, 285

Yankton, 243–44
Yanktonai Sioux, 243–44
Yaqui, 13
Yavapai, 344
Yellow Jacket Site. *See* pueblos
Yuma, 58, 216, 344; Quechan Yuma, 344; Yuma Apache, 209, 343

Zapotec, 182–83
Zimmerman, Carl, 336
Zuni, 6, 85, 156, 173, 241
Zuni/Acoma Pueblo. *See* pueblos

About the Author

Gerry R. Cox is professor emeritus of sociology at University of Wisconsin—La Crosse. He served as the director of the Center for Death Education and Bioethics. He has served as host of the International Death, Grief, and Bereavement Conference for more than twenty years. His teaching focused upon theory/theory construction, deviance and criminology, death and dying, social psychology, and minority peoples. He has over 150 publications, including more than 30 books. He has served as editor of *Illness, Crisis, and Loss* and for *The Midwest Sociologist.* He has been active as a member of the International Work Group on Dying, Death, and Bereavement; the Midwest Sociological Society; the American Sociological Association; the International Sociological Association; Phi Kappa Phi; and Great Plains Sociological Society. He served on the board of directors of the National Prison Hospice Association.

www.ingramcontent.com/pod-product-compliance
Lightning Source LLC
Chambersburg PA
CBHW022258280326
41932CB00010B/911